STAGES AND SCREENS

Broomend of Crichie. Photograph by Matthew Davidson, reproduced by his kind permission

STAGES AND SCREENS

An Investigation of Four Henge Monuments in Northern and North-eastern Scotland

RICHARD BRADLEY

with Amanda Clarke, Andrew Fitzpatrick, Hugo Lamdin-Whymark, Roderick McCullagh
and Alison Sheridan

and with contributions by Alex Brown, Anwen Cooper, Rosemary Cowie, Elise Fraser,
Phil Harding, Mary Lewis, Jacqueline McKinley, Wendy Matthews, Amy Poole,
D Rankin, Thomas Rees and Karen Wicks

Edinburgh 2011
SOCIETY OF ANTIQUARIES OF SCOTLAND

FRONT COVER IMAGES
Matthew Davidson and Richard Bradley
BACK COVER IMAGES
Hugo Lamdin-Whymark and NMS

Published in 2011 by Society of Antiquaries of Scotland

Society of Antiquaries of Scotland
National Museum of Scotland
Chambers Street
Edinburgh EH1 1JF
Tel 0131 247 4115
Fax 0131 247 4163
Email administration@socantscot.org
Website www.soctantscot.org

The Society of Antiquaries of Scotland is a registered charity no. SCO 10440.

ISBN 978 0 903903 38 7

British Library Cataloguing-in-Publication Data
A catalogue record for this book is available from the British Library.

The Society gratefully acknowledges grant-aid towards the publication of this volume from
Historic Scotland and National Museums of Scotland

Typeset in Bembo by Waverley Typesetters
Designed by Lawrie Law and Alison Rae
Manufactured in Spain by Graphicems

CONTENTS

PART I

EXCAVATIONS AT BROOMEND OF CRICHIE AND THEIR IMPLICATIONS

PART II

EXCAVATIONS IN SUTHERLAND AND CAITHNESS AND THEIR IMPLICATIONS

PREFACE

In 1997 while I was working at Balnuaran of Clava, I lectured in Aberdeen. On that occasion Ian Shepherd gave me a copy of a book he had published jointly with Moira Grieg. It was only later I realised that on the flyleaf he had written 'To tempt you eastwards'. That was a temptation I was unable to resist, so between 1999 and 2001 I excavated three stone circles in north-east Scotland. Ian played a crucial part in organising that project and even took me on a tour of eighteen sites that seemed especially promising. At the end of a long day, we stopped at a field south of Inverurie and visited the henge at Broomend of Crichie, until then a monument I knew only from published sources. We saw it again on other occasions and it soon became clear that he was keen for new fieldwork to be undertaken at this remarkable site. Eventually that took place over three seasons between 2005 and 2007. As ever, Ian was generous with his time, advice and practical assistance. I am pleased that he saw the work through to completion and very sad that he will never read this book. It is dedicated to his memory.

When I was excavating the stone circle at Tomnaverie, I came to know Paul Humphreys who made an enormous contribution to the work, travelling from Caithness to take part in the excavation. In 2008 I made that journey in reverse, excavating the small henge monument at Pullyhour. That was only possible because of the help and enthusiasm of local archaeologists, and it was Paul who made sure that the project reached a successful conclusion even in appalling weather. He worked on the excavation, he provided equipment and contacts, and he shared his special knowledge of the local archaeology. He is the second dedicatee of this book.

Ronnie Scott has played a pivotal role in all my Scottish projects over the last few years. He has taken part in fieldwalking surveys in Inverness-shire and Aberdeenshire; he has surveyed and recorded important monuments in the north; and he has played a central role in the excavations reported here as well as that at Tomnaverie. His field skills are second to none, and his artist's eye has made me aware of many things I might easily have overlooked. He and Pat have also provided a base from which many of these projects have been planned. Indeed, he has even allowed his studio to be overrun by my samples and records. I want to express my gratitude for their help and hospitality by dedicating the book to Ronnie and Pat.

There are other people who have played a crucial role in this project and its publication. There are my co-directors, Amanda Clarke, who worked at Broomend of Crichie between 2005 and 2007, and Anwen Cooper who took part in the 2006 season. At Pullyhour my co-director was Hugo Lamdin-Whymark. It was a pleasure to work with all three of them, and the project would have been the poorer without their skills, dedication and insight. In Reading, two other people played a crucial role in bringing this project to a conclusion. Margaret Matthews has produced almost all the illustrations in the monograph, maintaining a fantastic rate of production and submitting cheerfully to my many changes of mind. Elise Fraser, who worked in the field at Broomend of Crichie and Pullyhour, has organised the site records, artefacts and samples and has also edited the photographic record. Their contribution has been vital, and this book could not have been completed without them. Marion O'Neill drew the pottery, stone pendant and bone pin from Broomend of Crichie. All the photographs of Pullyhour are by Hugo Lamdin-Whymark. Unless otherwise stated, those of Broomend of Crichie are my own.

I must also thank Andrew Fitzpatrick, Phil Harding and Roderick McCullagh for allowing me to include reports on their projects at Migdale and Lairg respectively. It is because of their help and enthusiasm that the volume considers four excavations rather than two. It is important to record my debt to the many specialists who have contributed to these studies. I would particularly like to thank Alison Sheridan for many discussions of Broomend of Crichie and its implications. If my interpretation of the monument differs from that in interim accounts, it is because Alison's encyclopaedic knowledge and eye for detail have had such a vital influence. Needless to say, she has also contributed to our ideas about later monuments like Pullyhour.

Many people took part in the projects reported here, and I would like to thank them all. It is invidious to name particular people but some worked with us for so long and provided so much practical help that it would be wrong not to mention them here. They are: Chris Ball, Nicola Berry, Chloe Brown, Diana Coles, Sheila Duthie, Charlotte Faiers, Nigel and Janet Healy, Elizabeth Jones, Jamie Jones, Tom Lyons, Hazel MacFarlane, Mick Miles, Dinkar and Heather Sabnis, Emma Sanderson, Catherine Stevenson, Jon Tierney and Sheila Young. Jim Henderson provided vital assistance with the site photography. They made the project enjoyable for everyone. At Pullyhour we also drew on the skills of members of the North of Scotland Archaeological Society and the Caithness Archaeological Trust.

Work at Broomend of Crichie took place by kind permission of the landowner, International Paper. Historic Scotland provided Scheduled Monument Consent for the work to happen. The excavation at Pullyhour was undertaken with the permission of the farmer George McDonald, and we would like to thank him for all his help and support. At different times the work at Broomend of Crichie was carried out in consultation with a number of members of staff of Historic Scotland: Gordon Barclay, Martin Brann, Rosemary Fielden, Ann MacSween and Allan Rutherford. I also benefited from discussions with Strat Halliday of the Royal Commission, David Clarke, Trevor Cowie and Alison Sheridan from the National Museum, Ian Shepherd and Moira Grieg of Aberdeenshire Archaeology, and many other colleagues. Moira Grieg took the fine air photographs of Broomend of Crichie.

The project has received considerable help in kind from Reading University and was funded by the Society of Antiquaries of Scotland, the British Academy and the National Museum, which also provided many of the radiocarbon dates and the illustrations of the artefacts from Broomend of Crichie. The excavation at Lairg was funded by Historic Scotland, including the cost of radiocarbon dates for samples from the site.

Although this preface carries a single name, it expresses the sentiments of a large number of people. Our thanks to everyone who helped us on our way.

RICHARD BRADLEY

LIST OF ILLUSTRATIONS

AN INTRODUCTION TO THE PROJECT

RICHARD BRADLEY

'This rather curious heading'

The monuments described as henges have played many roles in modern archaeology. They were first defined by Thomas Kendrick in a passage that could hardly have been more circumspect, but over the next seventy-five years they became such a central feature of prehistoric studies that whole books were written about them.

Kendrick never intended this to happen, for his original statement was extremely cautious. Chapter VII of his co-authored study *Archaeology in England and Wales 1914–1931* is entitled 'The "henge" monuments'. The use of inverted commas is significant for Kendrick's original account of these structures is tentative, even defensive:

> Under this rather curious heading I am going to group a number of prehistoric 'sacred places' which I cannot, or dare not, sort out into 'period' chapters. I choose the title, of course, because Stonehenge and Woodhenge come first in the list, and I daresay that some readers may not approve of my including as members of the same family certain apparently empty 'rings' and 'stone circles'. I admit, furthermore, we are not agreed that all these monuments are of about the same age and are ceremonial sites, that is to say 'temples' or 'meeting-places'; but on the whole I think myself that the chances are in favour of their having that much in common. So for the sake of simplification I am venturing to segregate them here as being monuments that are presumably not burial-places, and belong, as far as it is possible to tell, either to the late neolithic period or the first half of the Bronze Age … (Kendrick & Hawkes 1932, 83).

Although the name 'henge' was suggested by Stonehenge, Kendrick's choice has proved to be unfortunate. The word actually describes the setting of monoliths and lintels on that site and comes from the Old English 'stan-hen(c)gen', meaning a stone gallows. This may have been intended literally as an early medieval execution burial has been found there (Reynolds 2009, 210–11). Henge monuments, on the other hand, are circular earthwork enclosures. Unfortunately, the term is so well established that it is too late to suggest an alternative.

Kendrick's original definition was modified several times over the course of the twentieth century, but in each case the main emphasis was on the form of the enclosure rather than the structures it contained. These sites might be bounded by a single earthwork or by a pair of concentric rings. They might have either one or two entrances, and occasionally there were even more. The only common features were that they were roughly circular and *had internal ditches* and *external banks* (illus 1; Harding & Lee 1987*)*. Even those criteria were relaxed in individual cases. Stonehenge, for instance, has its ditch on the outside, so that it shares more in common with earlier causewayed enclosures. Although it could have been rebuilt with an external bank (Parker Pearson *et al* 2009; Field *et al* 2010), Kendrick's type site may not belong to the category he defined.

At the same time, some enclosures had recognisable structures inside them whist others apparently did not. It was hard to incorporate these features in a single classification, as the available information was influenced by different kinds of fieldwork (Burl 1969). The earthworks of henges were the most obvious components of those sites investigated by survey and air photography, while internal structures − post circles, stone circles and burials − were more commonly identified by excavation. Most of those investigations were in southern Britain and indicated that some of the wooden structures had been replaced by settings of monoliths (Wainwright 1989). That suggests further connections, for there are many freestanding stone circles in upland areas, and recent excavations in other regions have identified timber circles which were never surrounded by earthworks (Gibson 2005).

Emerging problems

All too often archaeologists treat their *type sites* as the *prototypes* for a tradition of prehistoric architecture. Although Stonehenge has always seemed exceptional, the fact that the first henges to be excavated were in the south gave a misleading impression of their history. So did the assumption that they were the successors of causewayed enclosures (Harding 2003). More recent work suggests another possibility, for some of the oldest earthworks of this kind may have been in the north where an obvious example is provided by the Stones of Stenness (Ritchie 1976). Such structures date from the beginning of the third millennium BC and are several hundred years earlier than the best documented henges in the south. Their distribution is quite distinct from that of causewayed enclosures. Those points were not always appreciated, and as a result Scottish sites have played a limited role in general accounts of these monuments. Such studies are epitomised by Geoffrey Wainwright's 1989 book *The Henge Monuments* which locates the Ring of Brodgar and the Stones of Stenness on a map of Shetland (Wainwright 1989, fig 1). As happened in the case of cursuses (Thomas 2006), a kind of monument that may have developed in northern Britain was first researched in the south. This has biased the ways in which it is understood.

In recent years the definition of henge monuments became increasingly vague as more monuments were admitted to the category. The possible roles of these sites have also extended beyond those described in 1932.

The definition of henge monuments has widened to cover structures which are much smaller than those discussed by Kendrick. It also takes in monuments that were used over a longer period of time than he envisaged. The smallest sites pose particular problems. Those in southern Britain are commonly described as *hengiform enclosures* and are usually compared with large structures defined by a bank and ditch (Wainwright 1969, fig 1). Few of their earthworks survive above ground and often it is impossible to establish whether they are the remains of round barrows, or the sites of monuments with an internal bank like a causewayed enclosure. Indeed, some are not circular but oval and were probably reduced versions of the last long barrows. In most cases they have been attributed to the Late Neolithic – the period of many henge monuments – on the incorrect assumption that this was the date of the pottery with which they were associated (Gibson & Kinnes 1997).

In northern Britain some of the small enclosures still survive above ground, and here it is possible to say more about their earthworks. A significant number of sites do have external banks. They may have one or two entrances which provide access to a surprisingly small interior, which can be less than 10m in diameter. If their form is clearly documented, the same cannot be said for their chronology as no example has been

excavated and published. They survive best on marginal land in the north of Scotland and bear a certain resemblance to monuments of similar form in Ireland (Woodham 1953; Bradley 2007, 200). To add to the confusion, the Irish sites have a history running from the Early Bronze Age to the Iron Age (Waddell 1998, 365–8).

The chronological problem is exacerbated because there is evidence that monuments of several kinds were reused after a period of abandonment. It usually happened during the Late Bronze Age. This kind of punctuated sequence has been identified at a series of stone-built monuments in Scotland, including Clava Cairns and recumbent stone circles, as well as individual sites like those at Croft Moraig (Bradley & Sheridan 2005) and Temple Wood (Scott 1989). That development was unexpected and requires new research.

New interpretations

There are problems of interpretation. Kendrick's account said that

> We are not agreed that all these monuments … are ceremonial sites, that is to say 'temples' or 'meeting-places' … So for the sake of simplification I am venturing to segregate them here as being monuments that are presumably not burial-places (Kendrick & Hawkes 1932, 83).

Even that statement must be qualified. Recent excavations at the Wessex henge of Durrington Walls have identified the remains of a number of Late Neolithic houses buried below the bank. More were recognised within a small enclosure near to one of the entrances. They may have been occupied at specific times of year and it seems likely that some of them accommodated visitors to the site (Parker Pearson 2007). On the other hand, a similar building may once have existed inside the Stones of Stenness (Richards 2004, 222–3). The evidence is not compelling, but it undermines any attempt to distinguish between 'meeting-places' and occupation sites. In the same way, it has long been known that a number of henges contain human burials, and that a few of these monuments were directly associated with barrows. Such mounds are usually interpreted as a secondary development, but that was not always the case. For example, at Catterick in north-east England an older mortuary cairn was incorporated in the bank of one of these enclosures (Moloney *et al* 2003). Kendrick's original argument that henges 'are presumably not burial-places' can no longer be accepted.

One of the problems is that early studies of these sites took little account of sequence. They considered the earthwork perimeters of henges in relation to the structures found inside them but did not discuss the order in which those features were built. It was assumed that the enclosure was primary and that other elements were established within its area, either when the bank and ditch were built or at a later stage. It was tempting to compare the characteristic form of the henge with that of a Roman amphitheatre in which spectators congregated on the bank to watch events taking place in the interior. Because of the special character of the prehistoric monuments the audience was separated from the performers by a ditch.

Alex Gibson (2004a) contrasts this interpretation with the results of excavations at Clava Cairns and related monuments. Here the ring of standing stones was the last element to be built. Those places had already been employed in ritual and the commemoration of the dead and it was as their period of use came to an end that they were surrounded by monoliths. This was the case at recumbent stone circles where the dominant feature of the perimeter resembles a closed door (Bradley 2005).

Gibson argues that a similar sequence can be recognised at some – but probably not all – henge monuments, and his own excavation provides stratigraphic evidence for this development at the Welsh site of Dyffryn Lane (Alex Gibson pers comm). Such a clear-cut structural sequence is bound to be unusual, but he has also drawn attention to monuments where it would have been difficult to erect rings of uprights if their earthworks were already in place. There are other sites at which close attention to the ground plan shows that the internal structures do not conform to the outline of the bank and ditch, suggesting that they were built at different times. The evidence from the Scottish site of North Mains, Strathallan, is especially revealing (Barclay 2005, 86–9). When it was excavated it appeared that at least one timber circle was contemporary with the earthwork. More recently, it has been possible to date a cremation burial sealed beneath the bank. This showed that the enclosure was much later than the timber circles inside it and was not constructed until the site was reused as an Early Bronze Age cemetery.

The implication of these ideas is obvious. It is no longer possible to study henge monuments on the basis of their earthworks alone, for the banks and ditches may have been among the latest elements on those sites. Their building may even have brought the use of such places to an end. Nor is it useful to classify the sites by combining an account of the perimeter with a study of the structures within it, for these different elements may not have been used together. Henge monuments cannot be treated as unitary phenomena unless there are good reasons for doing so.

Illustration 0.1
The henge monument at Broomend of Crichie, Aberdeenshire, during excavation in 2007. Air photograph by Moira Grieg, Aberdeenshire Council

From classification to architecture

So far this account has traced some of the problems that have arisen since Kendrick coined the term 'henge monument' three-quarters of a century ago. There are well known sites that do not fit the accepted classification; there are circular enclosures that acted as settlements and burial places; and the absolute chronology of excavated examples is longer than he could have imagined. More serious is the suggestion that the creation of an earthwork enclosure was only one event – often a very late one – in the history of individual sites. How should such problems be addressed?

It is important to go beyond questions of classification. Such undertakings as the construction of a henge must have been public works which consumed the energies of a large number of people. But why build these earthworks in the first place? They were particularly impressive examples of prehistoric architecture, and it is in architectural terms that they should be interpreted. How would they have been perceived and used by people in the past, and how did these structures contribute to the ceremonies undertaken there?

Several elements are important. They provide the starting point for the project reported here.

The first is the distinctive form of henge monuments with their external banks and internal ditches. It is surprising that it is so rarely discussed. It seems to have been sufficient to diagnose the distinctive character of the sites, but why was this ground plan so important? On one level it separates activities within the monument from those in the surrounding area and might have divided the people participating in activities within the enclosure from a larger audience who were left outside. It is possible that on some sites events were watched from the bank, but this would be less significant if the earthwork was among the last structures to be built.

Another possibility has been suggested by Richard Warner (2000) in a discussion of the royal centres of Iron Age Ireland. He emphasises the contrast between defensive architecture in which an aggressor is faced by an external ditch and an internal bank, and the form taken by enclosures in which that relationship is reversed. Perhaps they were dangerous places where people came into contact with supernatural powers. The internal ditch was meant to contain those forces and to prevent them from escaping. It was a kind

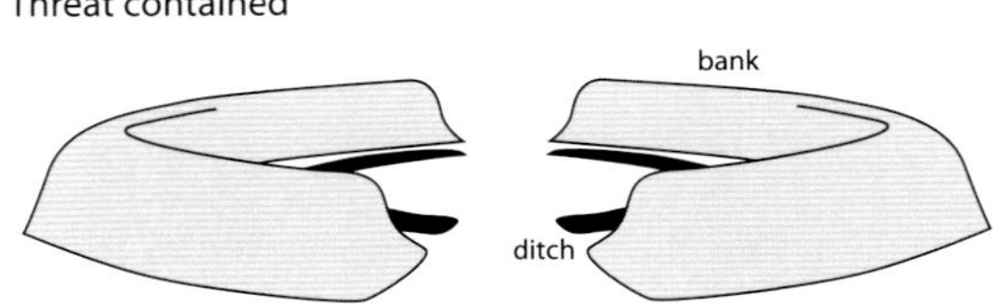

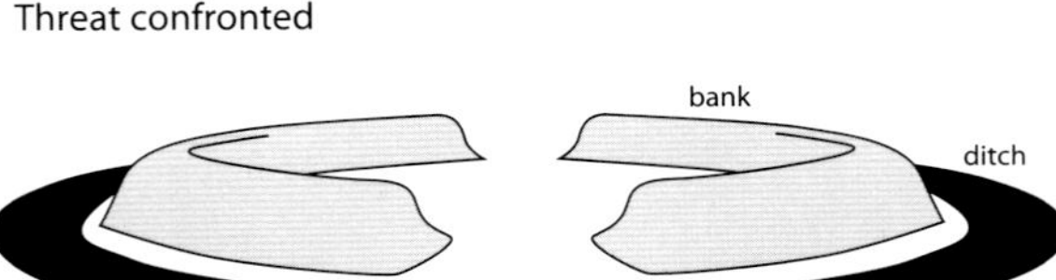

Illustration 0.2
A model summarising the contrast between enclosures with an external ditch and those with an internal ditch. In the first case, the form of the earthwork protects the special character of the monument and contains its power. In the second, it defends the interior from external threats

of defence in reverse that could have been equally appropriate during earlier periods (illus 0.2).

It is an attractive idea, but there is another possibility to consider. Henges reversed the normal configuration of Neolithic monuments, from causewayed enclosures to long barrows and from cursuses to round mounds. They were the only structures to have been built in this manner and they invert a pattern that would have been familiar in daily life. Perhaps this is related to the special character of public ritual.

When Arnold van Gennep wrote his classic account of *The Rites of Passage* a hundred years ago he distinguished between three different elements (van Gennep 1909). The first were *rites of separation*, in which the participants were removed from the everyday world. There followed a *liminal stage* in which the conventions of society were relaxed or even reversed. Then the process ended with *rites of incorporation* when people returned to their normal lives with new identities. The same tripartite structure has been identified in other kinds of public ritual (Turner 1969) and may be particularly relevant to the use of henges. Perhaps these were places in which the familiar order was inverted. If so, that process could have been expressed through the configuration of their earthworks (illus 0.3).

One reason for emphasising this connection is the importance of seclusion. The banks of the largest henge monuments screened the interior space from those outside: a process that can also be recognised at

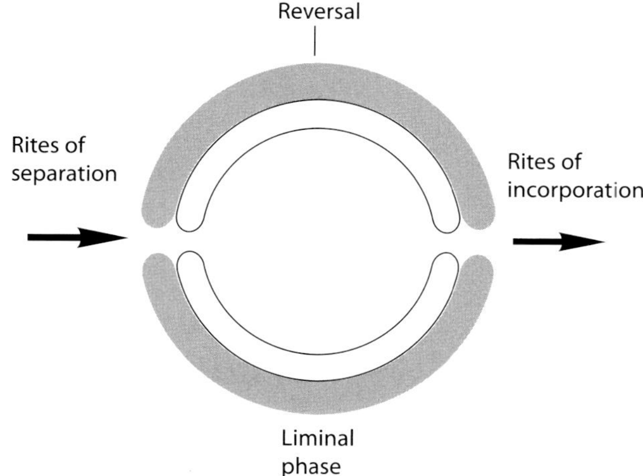

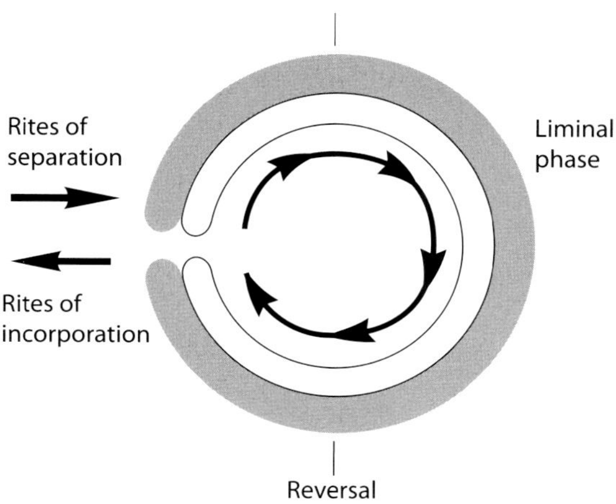

Illustration 0.3
The earthworks of henge monuments in relation to the threefold structure of the rites of passage, as interpreted by Arnold van Gennep (1909) and Victor Turner (1969)

the palisaded enclosures of the Late Neolithic period (Gibson 2004b). In the same way, the characteristic earthworks of a henge concealed the surrounding area from those within it, so that the only connection between the interior and exterior was through the entrance.

Van Gennep himself described the period of transformation as the 'liminal' phase. The term is important as the word *limen* refers to an entrance or a threshold. The entrances of henge monuments have not received enough attention from archaeologists who have been more interested in their alignment than their other characteristics. Otherwise the entrances

are excavated because they produce concentrations of artefacts. There is a fundamental distinction between ditches with a single causeway and those with more than one. In a monument with only one entrance the participants must have entered and left by the same route, whereas an enclosure breached by two causeways would allow people to cross the interior and to leave at another point. At times these entrance(s) were constricted by posts or monoliths. Their positions could also be emphasised by the provision of an avenue. For van Gennep it is the crossing of such thresholds that punctuates the ritual process. In this way the architecture of henges would have orchestrated the movements of the participants.

At the same time it is obvious that individual monuments changed their character over time. A good example is provided by a recent interpretation of Stonehenge. Parker Pearson and Ramilsonina (1998) draw attention to the contrasting associations of that site and the nearby henge of Durrington Walls. The wooden monuments provided evidence of feasting, while the stone structure was associated with human remains. They suggest that the differences between these places are explained by the choice of building material. Wood is an organic substance. It is taken from living trees and after a time it decays, whereas stone is inorganic and virtually indestructible. In this interpretation the living are associated with the finite lifespan of timber, while the remains of the dead, like stone, last for ever. At certain sites one kind of building replaced the other, so that monuments that were originally devoted to the activities of the living were increasingly associated with death. The implication is obvious: the same monument may have played quite different roles during separate stages in its history.

What applies to the development of individual sites may apply to henge monuments as a whole. Their roles could have altered during the period in which they were used and no single interpretation could possibly encapsulate the full range of variation. For that reason it is necessary to treat individual examples in more detail than is sometimes the case. Is there any evidence that particular sites changed their character, and are the developments at specific henges peculiar to those monuments or can they be identified over a wider region?

It is important to characterise particular monuments, paying due attention to both their individuality and diversity: features that are often overlooked in seeking a simple classification of these earthworks. At the same time, it is essential to document the ways in which such apparently stereotyped structures changed their forms and functions in relation to broader changes in society. Both these aims were pursued in the project presented here.

The sites investigated

Such questions apply to many regions and to monuments built during more than one period of prehistory, but work in northern Britain suffers from a particular limitation. Although henges may have originated in the north, there are large gaps in the distribution of excavated and published sites. There have been a number of valuable excavations in Scotland, such as those at Cairnpapple (Piggott 1948), North Mains (Barclay 1983), Balfarg (Mercer 1981; Barclay & Russell-White 1993) and Pict's Knowe (Thomas 2007), but these are in the southern half of the country and no henge monument has been excavated and published between Montcrieffe (Stewart 1985) and the Stones of Stenness (Ritchie 1976): a distance of nearly 300km. Despite this problem, the academic literature places a great emphasis on the form and distribution of sites which are known only from earthwork survey or air photographs.

The area that remained unexplored in recent times is particularly important for two reasons. The first is that the earliest henge in Orkney is so distant in time and space from most of those excavated in other parts of Scotland. If this kind of monument originated there, it would be important to compare its form and chronology with sites in regions that were not too far distant. That was especially significant as Orkney seems to have been where Grooved Ware first developed (Hunter & MacSween 1991). This ceramic tradition is regularly associated with henges.

A second reason for focusing on the gap in the distribution of excavated henges was suggested by earlier work on Clava Cairns and recumbent stone circles. They had also been claimed as Neolithic monuments, but, somewhat unexpectedly, both traditions were of later date (Bradley 2000, 2005). That suggested two hypotheses which need exploring. Either the unexcavated henges were the 'missing' Late Neolithic monuments in this area, or they would date from the Chalcolithic and the Bronze Age. If so, it would suggest that large structures of this kind did not form part of the architectural repertoire in northern and north-eastern Scotland before the adoption of metalwork.

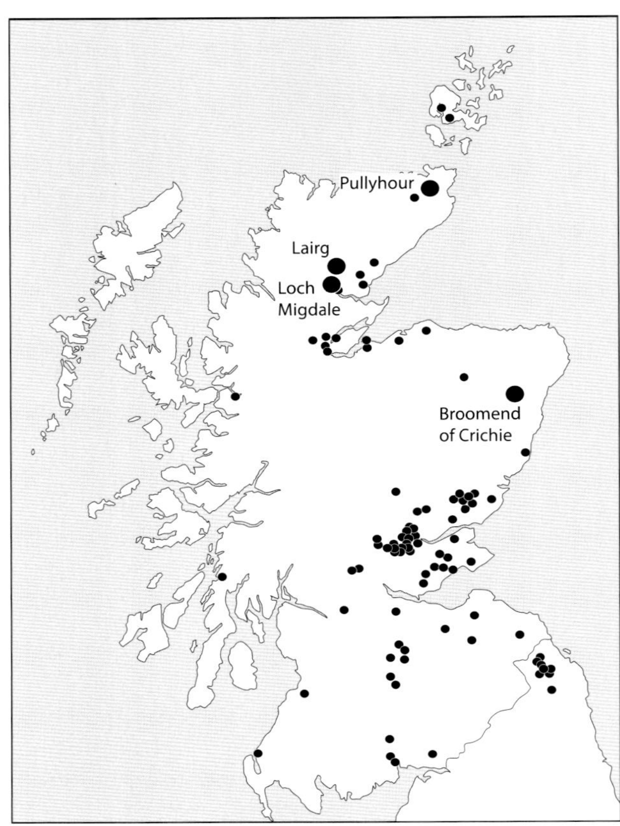

Illustration 0.4
The distribution of Scottish henge monuments according to Barclay (2005), showing the locations of the four excavated sites studied in this volume

In order to explore these ideas it was necessary to investigate enclosures of quite different kinds (illus 0.4). The first site to be examined was the large earthwork at Broomend of Crichie in Aberdeenshire, first excavated in 1855 when traces of a stone setting and a series of burials were identified (Dalrymple 1884). It had the added advantage that the henge formed only part of a more extensive series of prehistoric structures. The second site was a diminutive enclosure at Pullyhour in Caithness. This was surprisingly well preserved, and for that reason it was excavated on a more limited scale. There was the added incentive that the results of this work could be compared directly with two excavated monuments in Sutherland: Lairg and Loch Migdale. The results of those investigations have not been published before.

The work had three main objectives. Firstly, it was designed to establish the absolute chronology of henge monuments in northern and north-eastern Scotland, combining new excavations with a reassessment of those that were already documented. Secondly, it aimed to establish the sequence of activity on those sites and to consider how their roles changed over time. Thirdly, it was intended to offer detailed interpretations of how particular structures had been used and their relationships with other monuments in the vicinity. Thus rather than treating these earthworks as 'types', it was hoped to investigate their distinctive architecture in relation to the audiences who used them and the rituals they might have conducted there.

There is much to be gained from treating the monuments together. It allows the reader to appreciate the changing character and functions of these earthworks in relation to an archaeological sequence that extends across at least a thousand years. It permits broader comparisons to be made not only between these sites, but also between them and prehistoric structures which would normally be considered separately: in particular timber circles, stone circles, avenues, cremation cemeteries, ring barrows and ring cairns. This framework also makes it possible to consider how these places were used in relation to the landscapes of which they formed a part.

The organisation of the volume

The main aim of the volume is to present the results of two research excavations: at Broomend of Crichie, Aberdeenshire, where the work was co-directed by Amanda Clarke and Richard Bradley between 2005 and 2007; and Pullyhour, Caithness, where the work was co-directed by Hugo Lamdin-Whymark and Richard Bradley in 2008. The opportunity is also taken to publish excavations at two monuments in Sutherland: Roderick McCullagh's investigation of a small enclosure at Lairg; and the project undertaken by Time Team at the henge monument overlooking Loch Migdale. The latter is included at the invitation of Wessex Archaeology which has assumed responsibility for its publication.

The remainder of the volume is divided into two sections.

In Part I the emphasis is on a single site. Chapter 1 introduces the monument complex at Broomend of Crichie and summarises previous accounts of its archaeology. It also presents the results of the recent excavation. Chapter 2 draws this information together to offer a new interpretation of the henge and associated structures. Then Chapter 3 examines the same themes in relation to other sites in northern Britain.

Part II discusses the smaller and (in at least two cases) later structures at Pullyhour, Lairg and Migdale. Chapter 4 outlines the results of excavation at each of these sites, while Chapter 5 considers how far they conform to a wider pattern in northern and north-eastern Scotland. Finally, Chapter 6 considers their wider significance in the Bronze Age.

There follows a short conclusion which sums up the main results of the project and outlines a number of ideas that could be developed in future research.

PART I

Excavations at Broomend of Crichie and their implications

Chapter 1

EXCAVATIONS AT BROOMEND OF CRICHIE, 2005–7

RICHARD BRADLEY & AMANDA CLARKE

Introduction: the background to the project

The introduction has explained why the project included the excavation of a large henge monument, but it did not say how Broomend of Crichie was selected. There were three reasons for the choice. The first was that excavation in 1855 had already established that the monument contained a series of Early Bronze Age burials (Dalrymple 1884). In the light of the discussions summarised in the Introduction, it was important to discover whether they represented an episode in a longer sequence or whether the earthwork was originally built at that time. Secondly, a study published by James Ritchie in 1920 had showed that the enclosure formed only one element in a larger monument complex, the separate parts of which had rarely been considered together. The third reason for selecting Broomend of Crichie was entirely pragmatic. Its bank still survived, suggesting that it might be possible to date it using methods that would not be feasible on a site that had been levelled by the plough. At the same time, so much damage had been caused by excavation and quarrying over the last two hundred years that it was justifiable to work on a scale that would be unacceptable at a well preserved monument.

This chapter is divided into four sections. The first summarises the early records of Broomend of Crichie and associated monuments, and the second outlines the result of the 1855 excavation. The third section presents the results of the recent excavation, and the final section contains a series of studies of the material

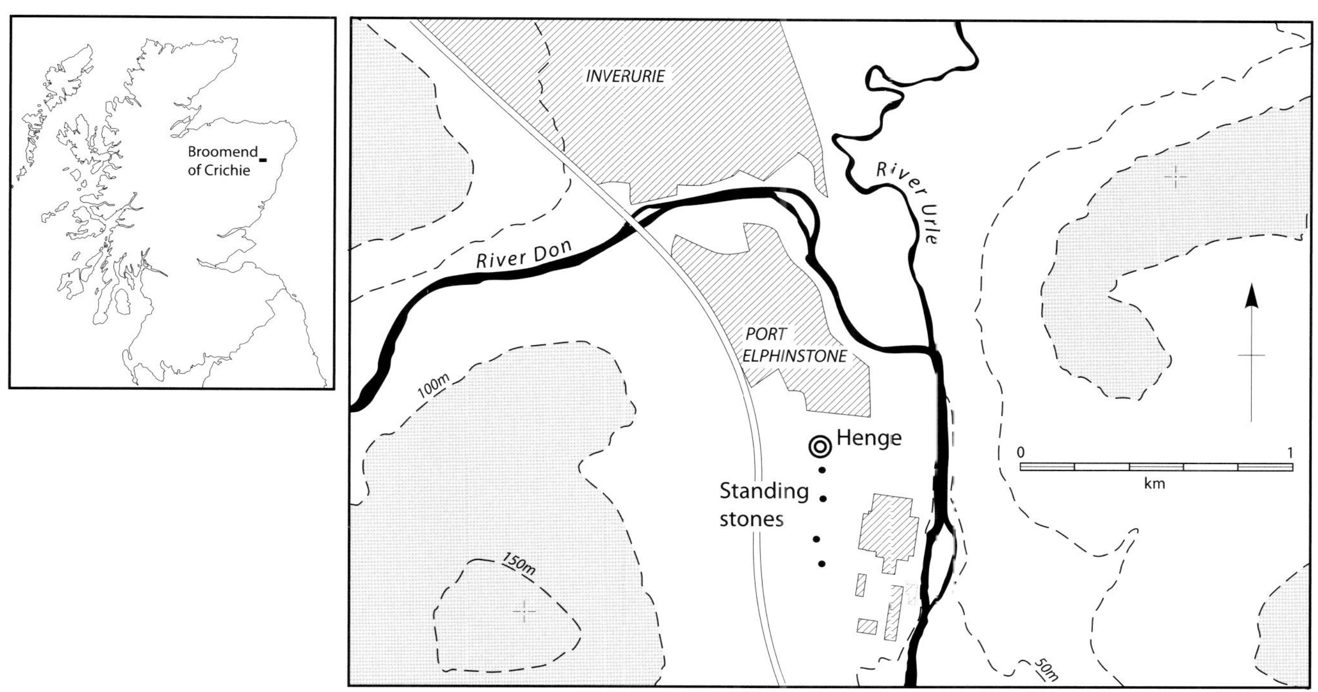

Illustration 1.1

The siting of the henge monument at Broomend of Crichie in relation to the confluence of the Don and the Urie, the local topography and the position of the surviving stones of its avenue. The areas occupied by modern buildings are hatched. Reproduced by kind permission of the Ordnance Survey.
© Crown copyright 2010

found in 2005–7. Since the interpretation of the henge involves a detailed discussion of other parts of the monument complex, all these observations are brought together in Chapter 2 which also discusses a nearby cist cemetery found in 1866.

The components of the monument complex (illus 1.1)

RICHARD BRADLEY & AMANDA CLARKE

The identification of the monuments

Broomend of Crichie has featured in the archaeological literature since John Aubrey visited the site in the seventeenth century when he described two standing monuments. He recognised that they were different from one another, but by the time he wrote his account he could not recall the details:

> I remember to have seen on the highway betwixt Kintor and Inverney nine miles from Aberdeen two small monuments consisting of two circles of stone apiece with a trench or dry ditch, which in the one was without both the circles of stone which it encompassed, and in the other betwixt the two circles, and one of the monuments (I do not remember which) had two entries (or interruptions) in the ditch to the ground enclosed by it, whereof the one was directly opposite to the other (Aubrey 1980 (1665–1693), 208–9).

More information is provided by Maitland's description of the site which dates from 1757:

> [The] … temple consists of two parts, the smallest, lying towards the south, is surrounded with a ditch, and the largest encompassed with three rows of stones erect, with a small cairn or heap in the middle. That this appears to have been a place of worship of great eminence and distinction appears by its long avenue of about 200 yards enclosed with a row of large stones erected on each side; it leads from the south to the lesser circle, and having crossed the same, continues its short course, to the larger enclosed with stones … Near to this there is said to have been an altar of one stone with a cavity in the upper part wherein some of the blood of the sacrifice was put and offered as a further propitiation for the trespass of the offender. This altar, for burnt offering, like those in other temples was an artificial heap, or cairn, with a large flat stone on the upper part whereon to burn the sacrifices (quoted by Ritchie 1920, 168).

Ritchie was able to identify the positions of both these monuments on a map of the Barony of Crichie made in 1780 (illus 1.2). It showed the position of an earthwork enclosure with four monoliths inside it.

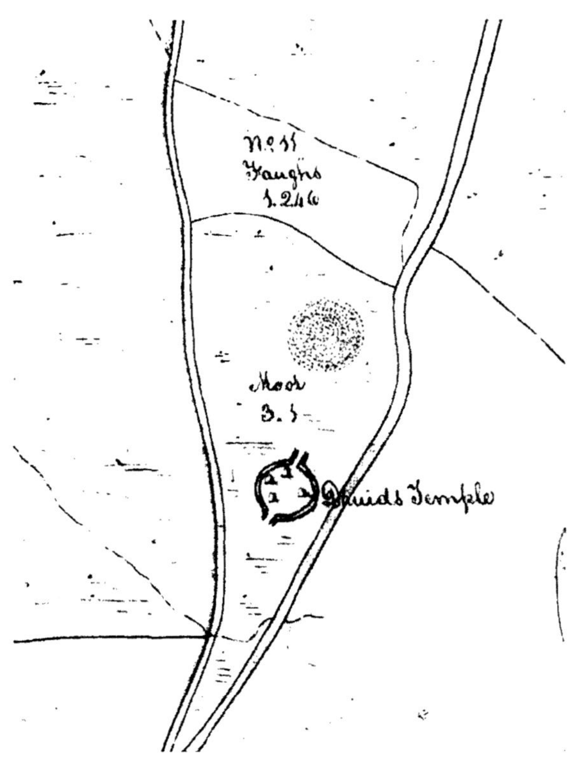

Illustration 1.2
Broomend of Crichie in the eighteenth century. Extract from an estate map of 1780, published by Ritchie (1920)

About 50m to its NNE was the larger circle described by Maitland. The map did not indicate the position of the avenue.

By the middle of the nineteenth century the northernmost monument had been completely removed by quarrying. Part of the avenue was destroyed at about the same time as the land south of the surviving earthwork was trenched to prepare it for cultivation. It is recorded that one of the standing stones was blown up in 1851 (Ritchie 1920). Urned cremations were discovered beside two of the monoliths. Close to the southern end of the avenue were three more, each of them capped by a flat stone.

Further burials came to light in the same area in 1866 when four cists were discovered in 'a natural mound' (Chalmers 1866; Davidson 1866). Two of the cists were especially large, and each contained a pair of inhumation burials. They were associated with Beaker pottery and other artefacts. A third cist seems to have been entirely empty, while the fourth was smaller and included the remains of a child and a further pot. They are discussed in detail in Chapter 2.

There was yet another cist in the garden at Allanshaw where it was next to a standing stone belonging to the avenue. It was discovered and excavated in 1993. Again it was unusually large. The capstone was 1.4m long and had been covered by a small cairn of rounded boulders. Although the corners had been sealed by clay to make it watertight, the cist was entirely empty (Greig & Shepherd 1993). In that respect it compares with the first burial discovered in 1866.

How were these different monuments related to one another? They were distributed over a distance of about 500m, extending along a terrace of fluvioglacial gravel running parallel to the River Don, approximately 360m to their east (illus 1.3). The northernmost monument was the large stone circle, of which no trace survives. Before quarrying commenced it would have occupied a low eminence commanding a view over the confluence of the Don and the Urie (NGR NJ 778197). The line of the avenue seems to have extended down a slight slope from that monument as far as the cist cemetery found in the nineteenth century. This area has also been disturbed but it seems as though it originally marked the opposite end of the terrace where it was cut by a tributary of the river. If so, the avenue ended close to the 'mound' removed in 1866, from which it would have been possible to look down the valley of the Don towards an area where more prehistoric monuments have been found.

As Maitland noted, the avenue crossed the position of the surviving henge, utilising both its entrances. No trace of it survives in the area to the north of this monument, virtually all of which was removed by the sand pit, but in the opposite direction there are four isolated monoliths that appear to mark its course (illus 1.4). One remains in the field to the south of the henge and was associated with an urned cremation. Another

Illustration 1.3

The monument complex at Broomend of Crichie showing the places and monuments referred to in the text. Air photograph by Moira Grieg, Aberdeenshire Council

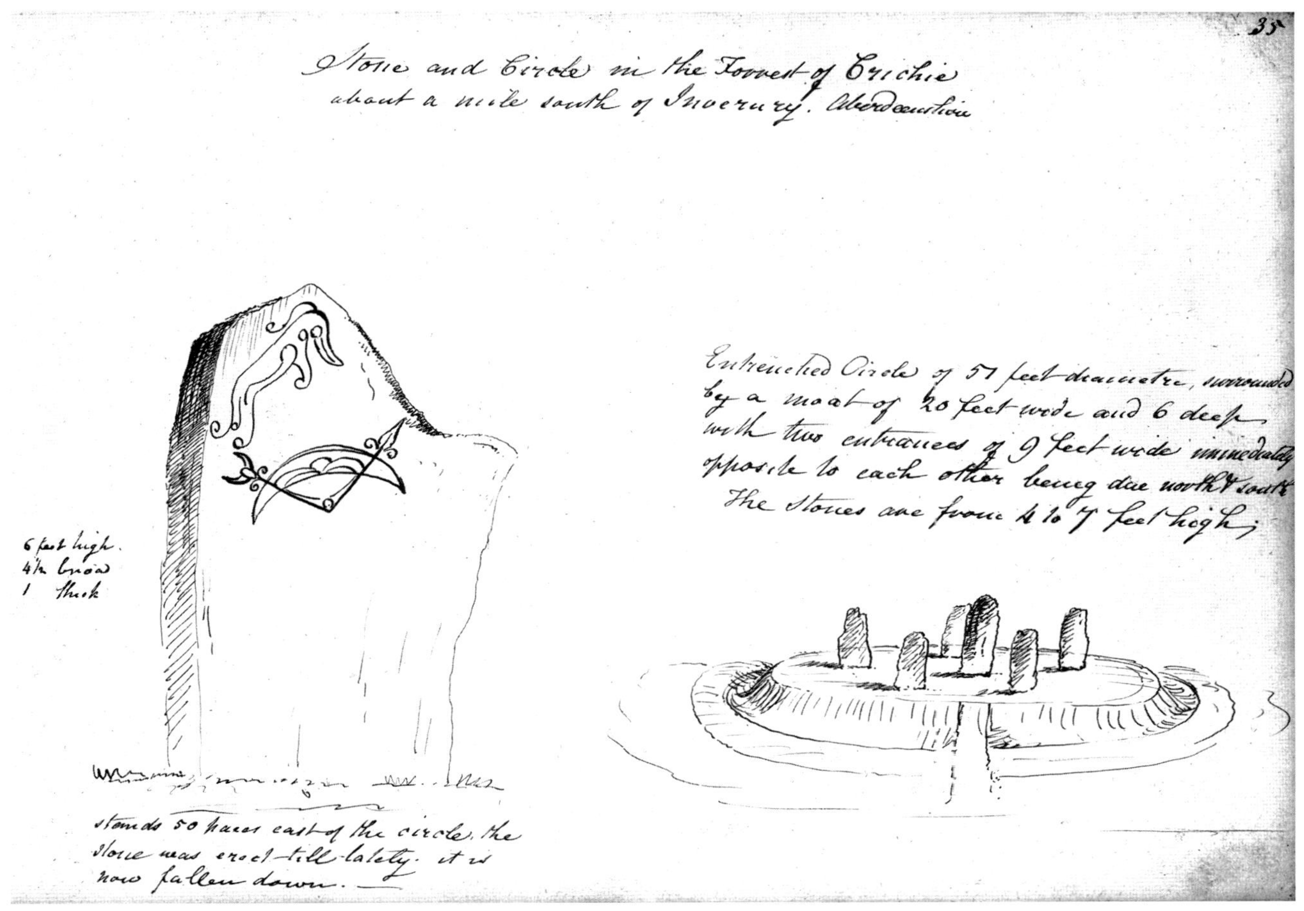

Illustration 1.5
The henge monument and the Pictish sculpture at Broomend of Crichie as drawn by John Skene in 1832. Reproduced by permission of NMRS

is located beside the cist discovered at Allanshaw, and a third monolith is about 50m east of the cemetery discovered in 1866. The fourth, at Crichiebank, is in an area landscaped in the nineteenth century and in this case Ritchie was uncertain whether it was in its original position. On the basis of a verbal description of the avenue when more of its stones remained intact he estimated that it consisted of two parallel rows of monoliths. He was unsure of the interval between the lines, but the individual stones were probably set approximately 11.5m apart. He suggested that this structure contained about 70 uprights (Ritchie 1920, 158–9).

Illustration 1.4
The surviving monoliths of the southern avenue and the reconstructed cist at Allanshaw

The henge

The henge has had a complex history since it was first recorded. The oldest plan is the map of 1780. It depicts four monoliths inside the enclosure, those closest to the northern entrance offset from the long axis of the monument. In that respect they reflect the situation today. A second source is a drawing by John Skene of Rubislaw which dates from 1832 (illus 1.5). This shows a view of the interior of the monument as it appeared through the northern entrance. It represents the earthwork, the entrances and six standing stones. Two of the monoliths are just inside the causeway, while three others are located on the opposite side of the enclosure near to the southern entrance. A notable feature of his drawing is a tall monolith in the centre of the site. Skene notes that these stones were between four and seven feet high. His sketch is especially valuable as he is known to have been a good observer. Graham Ritchie describes his drawings as 'among the most attractive and accurate representations' of Aberdeenshire stone circles (Ritchie 1998, 176). Skene also drew a Pictish symbol stone which still survives at Broomend of Crichie, and this certainly provides a correct record of the design (illus 1.5).

These details are important as the monument was badly damaged between the time of Skene's illustration and Charles Elphinstone Dalrymple's excavation twenty-three years later. By this time, only two of the monoliths – those flanking the northern entrance – still survived. The others had been removed or destroyed. John Stuart says that they 'were used for building purposes' (1856, xx). Dalrymple's friend Alexander Watt who worked with him on the excavation recalled the original form of the stone setting, but it is not clear how accurate his recollection might have been:

> The circle consisted of six stones round the outer circumference, with a seventh in the centre. All but two had been taken away before our digging took place, but I had the benefit of the experience of a friend who remembered them *in situ*, and the marks of where they had stood were still plain (Dalrymple 1884, 319).

Although it has been taken literally, Dalrymple's plan presents an idealised view of the site (illus 1.6). It appears to be precisely symmetrical. The two entrances are exactly opposite one another and the six monoliths are arranged in pairs around the inner edge of the ditch. The central monolith is located in the middle of this setting, its long axis directed towards the northern and southern entrances.

By contrast, Fred Coles's site plan, published in 1901, depicts a more irregular earthwork, with a longer arc of ditch in its eastern half and a slightly shorter length to the west (illus 1.6; Coles 1901, fig 27). It shows the only two monoliths that remained, neither of which was mapped in the correct position by Dalrymple. Coles's survey demonstrated that the space between these stones was not in line with the entrance, and he said as much in his article. The same anomaly is represented in the Royal Commission's recent survey of the monument which also shows that the banks extended *beyond the ditch terminals* at the northern entrance, leaving a gap only a metre wide (RCAHMS 2007, 57–8). To the south the ends of the bank had been spread by cultivation, but in Coles's plan, prepared before much of this damage took place, the break is *exactly the same width* as the causeway in the ditch.

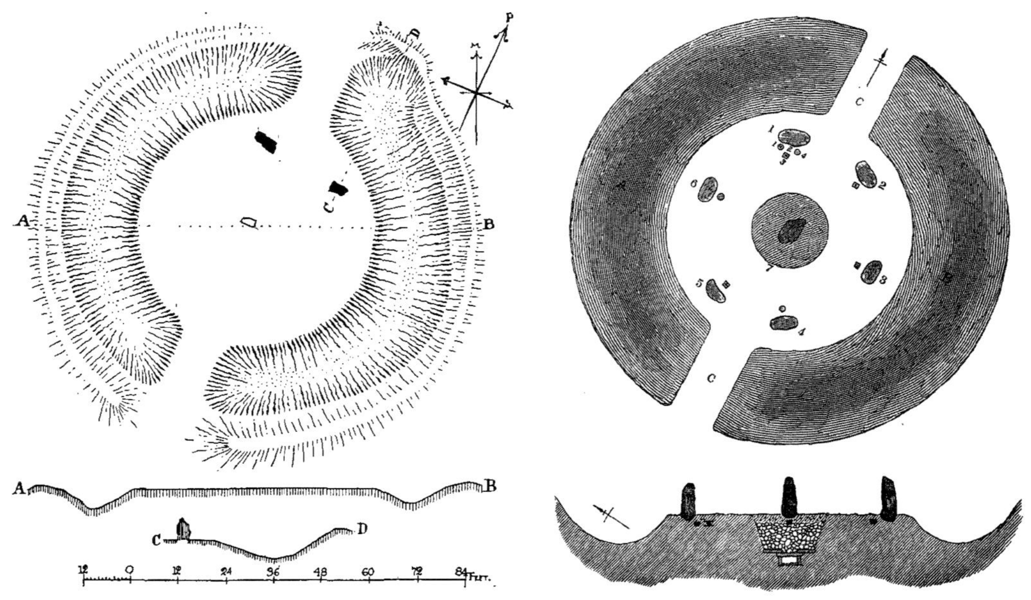

Illustration 1.6
The henge monument at Broomend of Crichie, as recorded by Coles in 1901 (left) and by Dalrymple in 1884 (right)

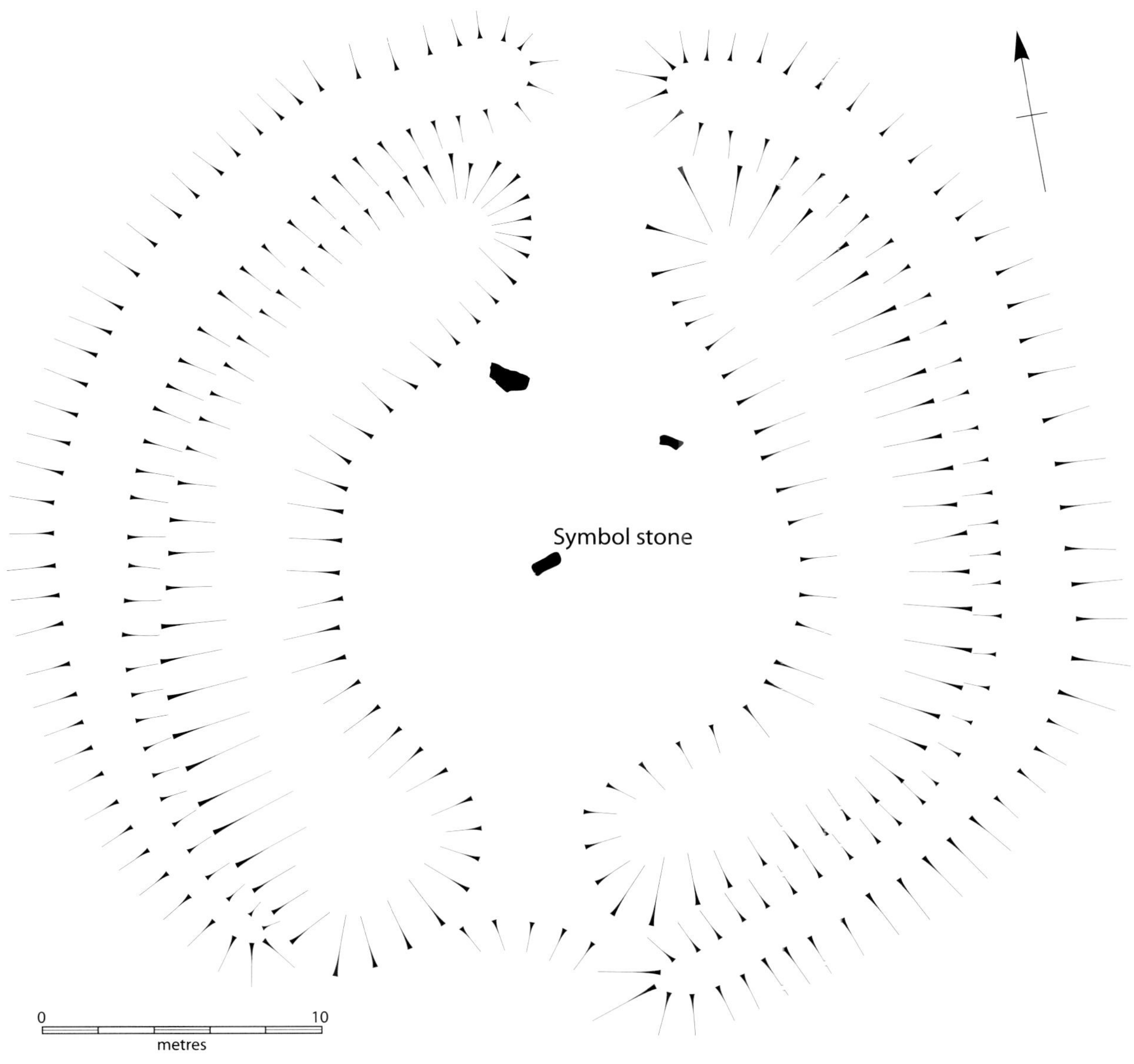

Illustration 1.7
The henge monument at Broomend of Crichie as it survived in 2005, showing the positions of the two surviving monoliths inside the north entrance
and the re-erected symbol stone in the centre

Another feature is the asymmetrical ground plan of the enclosure whose perimeter was rather broader towards the west (illus 1.7).

James Ritchie's unpublished photographs of the site are in the National Monuments Record of Scotland. They include a further detail which could easily be overlooked. Against the edge of the bank on the south side of the monument one shows a bank of rubble. The explanation may be found in his paper:

Round the outer circumference of … [the] 'rampart there lies a ring of stones having the appearance of an enclosure wall now in ruins. This outer ring, however, is of comparatively recent date, and forms no part of the original structure. The stones were collected when the field was trenched and were laid down in their present position for the purpose of supplying material for a stone wall to enclose and protect the circle, but the wall was never completed (Ritchie 1920, 160).

Among the rubble are two large stones which may have been broken monoliths.

The 1855 excavation

RICHARD BRADLEY & AMANDA CLARKE

Two points are particularly important in discussing Dalrymple's excavation of the henge.

The first is that the work formed only part of a larger project organised by John Stuart, the results of which were published in *The Sculptured Stones of Scotland* (Stuart 1856) That is why the earliest account of the excavation appeared in the preface to his book. Dalrymple worked at a number of sites on behalf of Stuart. Some were Pictish symbol stones and others were stone circles, but the basic aim was to investigate their contexts by excavation. In planning the research no distinction was made between prehistoric remains and those of the first millennium AD.

A second observation is that Dalrymple's paper on Broomend of Crichie did not appear until 1884, twenty-nine years after the project had taken place. It is not clear how far he was working from memory, but his report is rather different from the summary in Stuart's book which came out in 1856. Moreover, Stuart's text is almost the same as that that published by Dalrymple's colleague Alexander Watt a decade after the excavation (Stuart 1856, xx; Watt 1865, 153–4). These accounts suggest that more urned burials were discovered than Dalrymple records – it is a warning against taking his findings at face value. Unfortunately, no other documentation of his project has been found, so that the best way of assessing his conclusions was by re-excavating the nineteenth-century trenches. It did not happen for 150 years. During that time archaeologists placed more weight on Dalrymple's account than it could bear.

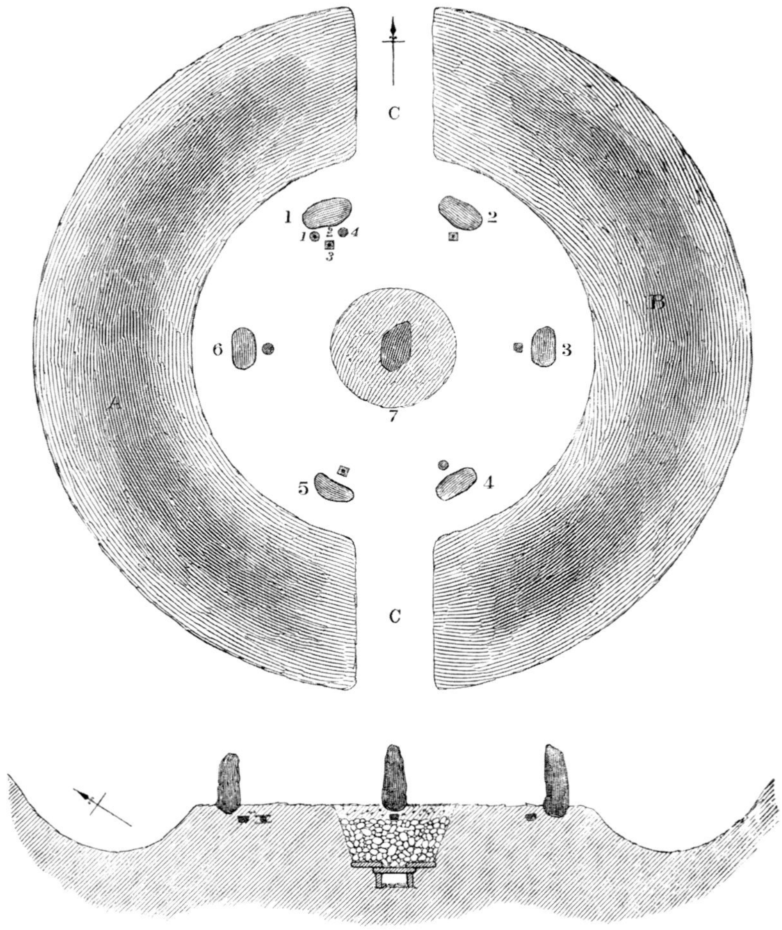

In the interests of clarity this summary begins with Dalrymple's report, before considering additional details mentioned in the other sources. His account provides a brief summary of the excavated features inside the enclosure, together with a schematic site plan and illustrations of two artefacts.

All the excavated deposits are related to the positions of the standing stones (illus 1.8), and this raises another problem. By 1855 only the monoliths by the northern entrance remained. As mentioned earlier, the positions of the others were estimated on the basis of Alexander Watt's recollection and 'the marks of where they had stood'; what form those traces took is never explained. In the circumstances more weight can be placed on features related to the stones that still survived. The other parts of Dalrymple's report may be less reliable.

The westerly 'portal stone' was associated with several different deposits:

A small circular cist (so to call it), 1 foot deep and 9 inches across, formed of slips of stone, evidently broken for the purpose, and arranged so as to taper towards the bottom, and filled with calcined bone. Close to this

Illustration 1.8
Dalrymple's plan of the excavated monument at Broomend of Crichie published in 1884.
The numbers relate to the burials found in 1855

Illustration 1.9
The re-erected symbol stone in the centre of the enclosure at Broomend o′ Crichie

> was ... a stone hammer ... perforated for the handle ...
> A little outwards from this ... was ... an urn ... full of
> calcined bones, placed mouth downwards on a small flat
> stone, a similar stone being placed above it. ... Only
> 18 inches from this was a deposit of calcined bones
> unenclosed in either urn or stones ... (Dalrymple 1884,
> 321–2)

> [Beside the other portal stone] was found an inverted
> urn, full of calcined bones, a flat stone above and below
> (Dalrymple 1884, 322).

Dalrymple illustrated the battle axe. He also drew an urn found beside the western portal stone. Although it is the only illustration of the pottery from his excavation, the other vessel was illustrated by Fred Coles (1901) and is of the same type. They are discussed by Alison Sheridan on p 51 below.

Dalrymple mentions similar deposits associated with four other standing stones on the edge of the ditch. They were very similar to the examples just described:

> [One] was a small square cist, 11 inches by 9, 16 inches
> deep, filled with [calcined] bones ... , a flat stone above
> and below. [A second] was a deposit of burnt matter and
> bone dust in a small round pit, without urn or cist. [A third
> was] an urn, placed like the others mouth downwards,
> and built around with slips of stone to protect it, filled
> with the same sort of bones, and with the usual flat slabs
> above and below (Dalrymple 1884, 322).

The fourth of these deposits raises a problem. Dalrymple claims that it was 'just east' of his Stone 6 and consisted of 'a deposit of burnt matter, enclosed' – that is all he says about it. The difficulty is that no monolith is represented in this position in Skene's drawing, and there was no sign of a stone socket when the same area was excavated in 2006. It seems possible that this burial was an isolated feature.

The central burial pit is described in greater detail. It is worth quoting Dalrymple's account in full:

> Under where the central monolith had stood, was,
> first, a deposit of burnt matter about 18 inches below
> the surface, resting on the top of what may be called
> an underground cairn of small boulder stones extending
> 5½ feet in depth, filling a hole 15 feet in diameter at
> the top, narrowing to 10 feet below, where it rested on
> a pavement of heavy slabs, laid with considerable care.
> Two of these overlapped the ends of another, which was
> found to cover a cist containing the remains of a human
> skeleton; of which the skull and leg bones were tolerably
> entire, and along with which, about the centre of the cist,
> lay a quantity of incinerated human bones, but no urn or
> implement of any kind (Dalrymple 1884, 322–3).

Dalrymple's schematic profile of the site suggests that the floor of the cist was 3.3m below the surface.

He drew two conclusions from the excavation. The first was that this was a cemetery and that 'the great ... [deposit] ... in the centre was the *raison d'être* of the circle ... [T]he small ones round the circumference were subsidiary to it' (Dalrymple 1884, 323). Another observation concerned the earthwork enclosure. He says that 'it must have been impossible for any one standing in the area of the circle to see out of it, except through the openings to the north and south, where the entrance passages are left' (Dalrymple 1884, 319). Both these ideas are discussed in Chapter 3.

Dalrymple restored the site in a way that has caused confusion. Whilst he was working at the henge he investigated the position of a symbol stone in the same field. Here, according to Watt, he found a 'large urn' (1865, 154). Since the stone was in danger of being damaged, he erected it in the middle of the enclosure where it replaced the central monolith which had been destroyed (illus 1.9). This ensured its preservation, but it also meant that the shaft grave underneath it could not be investigated in 2005–7.

Other published sources supplement the information provided by Dalrymple. Stuart noted that one of the excavated cists was circular and 'imbedded in clay ... This cist was shaped like an urn and lined with small stones, evidently broken for the purpose' (1856, xx). He also provides information on the excavated deposit on the western perimeter of the circle where it is not clear whether there had been a standing stone:

> On digging about the spot where a sixth stone had stood,
> it appeared that a deposit had been buried near it also,
> about the usual distance of one and half feet from it.
> *This deposit, however, had been disturbed*, probably by a tree
> which had been planted close to it ... [our emphasis].

Perhaps it was because this part of the site was disturbed that its archaeology poses problems.

Stuart provided more information on the cist burial in the shaft grave:

> The bottom' [of the pit] 'was paved with large slabs of
> stone, of which those at the sides overlapped the edges of
> one large one in the centre, which formed the cover of a
> cist, three feet eleven inches long by two feet ten inches
> wide. The cist contained a skull at the west end. At the
> opposite end were the leg-bones, *lying across the cist* (1856,
> xx; our emphasis).

His description suggests that the burial was a crouched inhumation.

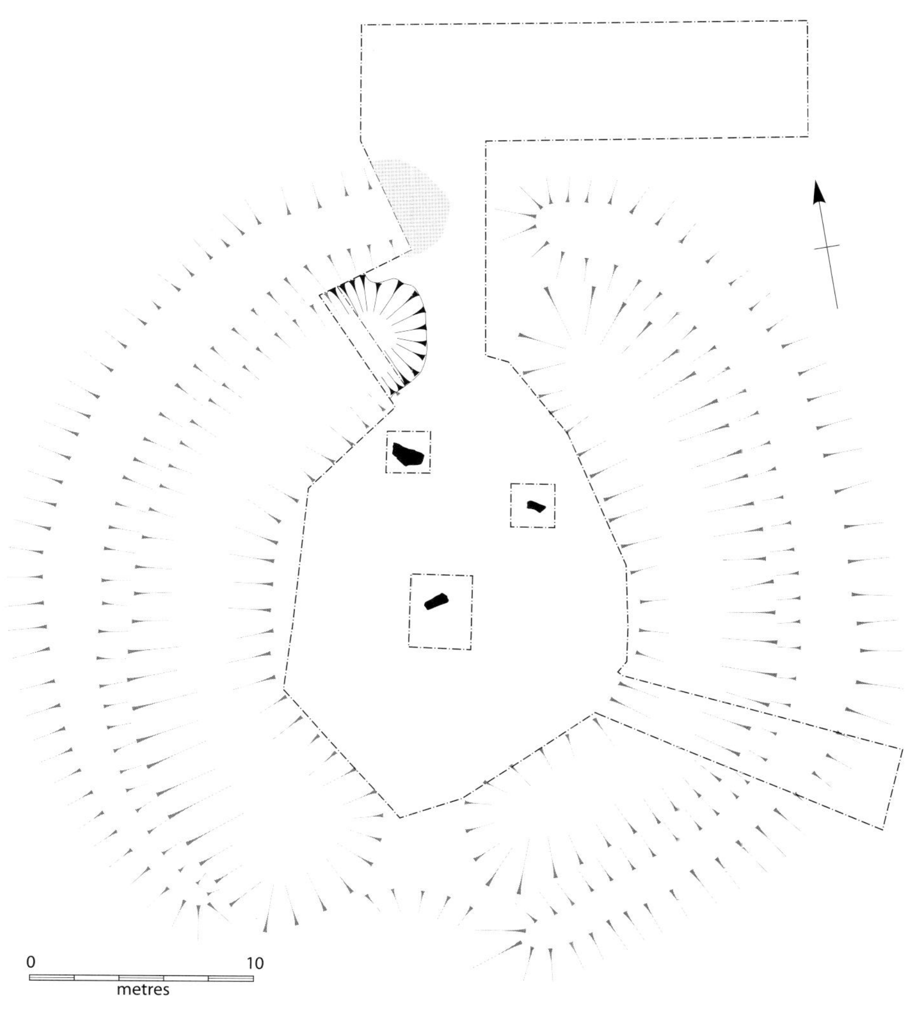

Illustration 1.10
Plan of the earthwork monument at Broomend of Crichie, showing the extent of excavation in 2005–7

Illustration 1.11
General view of the 2005 excavation with the south-eastern section through the bank and ditch in the foreground

Watt's account of 1865 supplies another tantalising detail. He follows his description of the excavation by summarising 'the order in which the discoveries were made'. Two entries are worth quoting here (Watt 1865, 154). The first reads 'Friday, 16th November: 3 men digging all day. Stone celt and four urns found'. The 'celt' was presumably the battle axe discovered close to the western portal stone, but Dalrymple claimed that there was only one vessel here. Similarly, on 22 November, Watt records 'Whole Day with three men – five urns found', whereas Dalrymple's account records just three vessels from the entire project. Since Watt's records predate Dalrymple's by nearly twenty years, he is likely to have been correct. Assuming the 'missing' vessels had held bones, it means that at least nine urned cremations were found in 1855.

Excavations at Broomend of Crichie 2005–7

RICHARD BRADLEY & AMANDA CLARKE,
WITH ANWEN COOPER & ELISE FRASER

Introduction

The surviving earthworks at Broomend of Crichie comprise two arcs of ditch with an external bank, broken by opposed entrances to the north and south (illus 1.10). The earthworks are up to 11m wide, and the monument has an external diameter of 39m. The interior is approximately oval, with a long axis of about 20m and a short axis of 17.5m. Today the ditch is 6m wide and the bank is up to 1.7m high. Only two of the original monoliths survive. Both are incomplete. The central monolith, a reused symbol stone, was erected by Dalrymple after his excavation.

The recent excavations had three distinct foci: the earthwork perimeter of the monument; the interior of the henge; and the areas outside its northern and southern entrances respectively.

Several features influenced the character of the new excavation (illus 1.10, 1.11). There was no information on the nature or chronology of the surrounding earthwork, which had not been investigated before. This work was especially timely as the bank and ditch are disturbed by rabbits. The northern entrance posed a special problem as it did not seem to conform to the same alignment as the portal stones. Here it was essential to leave some deposits intact to allow more work in the future, and for that reason only half was excavated. The south entrance was also left untouched, but the bank and ditch on this side of the enclosure were sectioned at a point 11m from the causeway.

The interior of the henge was cleared entirely by hand and, apart from some of the trenches dug 150 years earlier, the subsoil features were excavated completely. That did not apply to the central shaft grave, since Dalrymple had erected a symbol stone in its position in 1855. The surface of his excavation was carefully cleaned, but none of the redeposited material was removed.

Outside the northern entrance a narrow strip of undisturbed ground remained between the outer edge of the earthwork and the position of the refilled quarry. Since the area has been cultivated in the past, the ploughsoil was removed mechanically. The aim of

this work was to look for any trace of the northern avenue documented by Ritchie (1920).

A similar procedure was followed to the south of the surviving monument, but in this case it was possible to strip a larger area in order to look for traces of the avenue. A gap of 4m separated the excavation from the tail of the bank which had been damaged by cultivation. At the same time four 1m-square test pits, one at each corner of the excavated area, were dug by hand and their contents were sieved. Only one flint flake was found by this method. In the event the main focus of this work proved to be the post-holes of a timber circle whose discovery was entirely unexpected.

Excavation of the earthwork perimeter, 2005–6

Dalrymple did not investigate the bank and ditch, but it is clear that the earthwork has been reduced by ploughing since 1855. This was particularly evident on the south side of the monument. To its north, however, there was only a limited area in between the monument and the edge of a disused quarry, and here cultivation may have been less intensive. That is evident from the size of the surviving bank. Close to the southern entrance where it had been spread by the plough, it was 8m wide, but at the northern edge of the site its width was only 5m.

The earthwork was sectioned at two points: at its terminal against the north entrance; and on the southern perimeter of the enclosure.

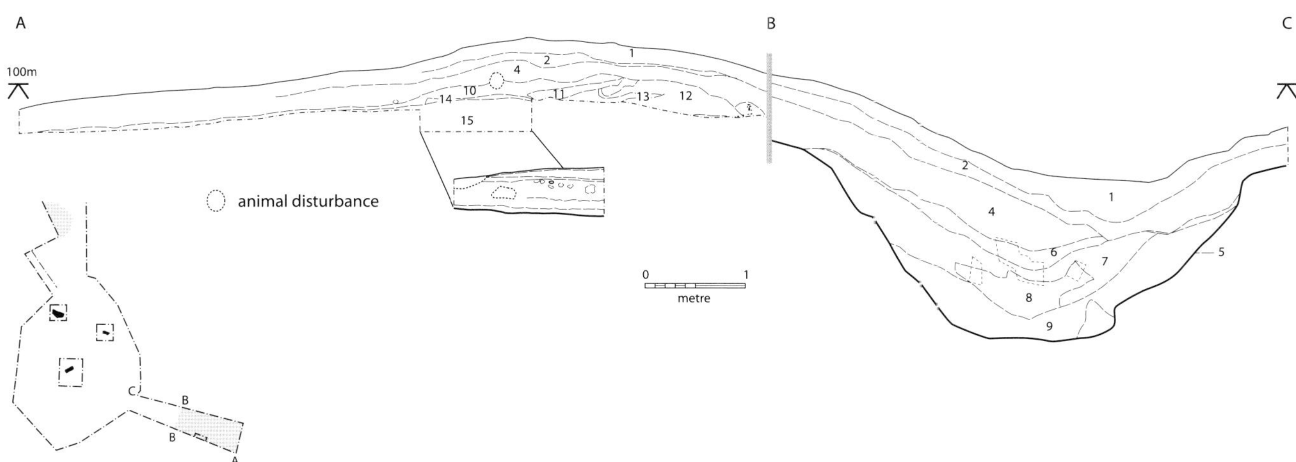

Illustration 1.12
Section of the bank and ditch on the south-east side of the earthwork. Insets show the locations of the sections illustrated and a detail of the buried soil

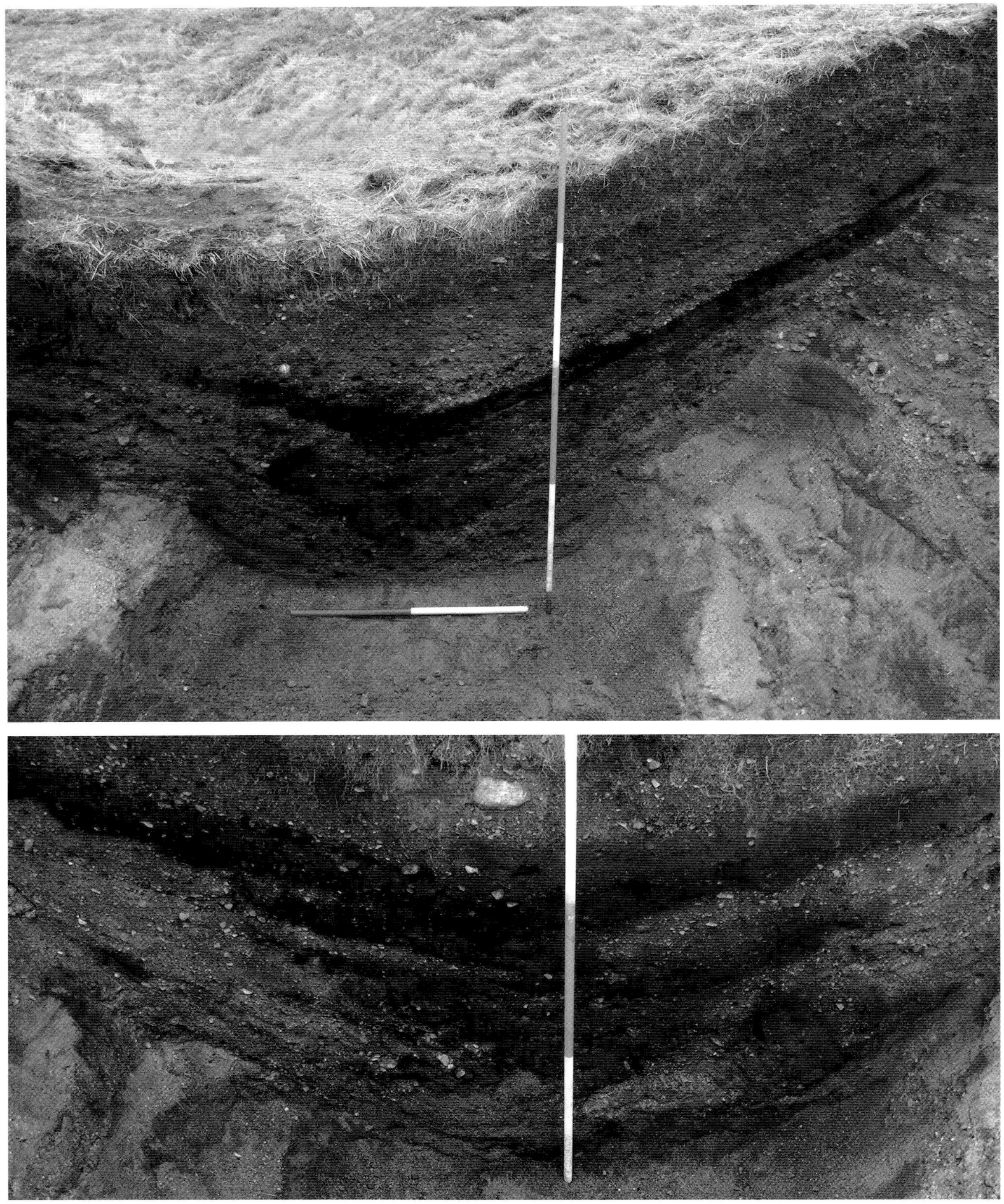

Illustration 1.13
Two sections of the henge ditch on the south-eastern perimeter of the enclosure

Illustration 1.14
Sections of the bank and buried soil on the south–eastern perimeter of the enclosure

15

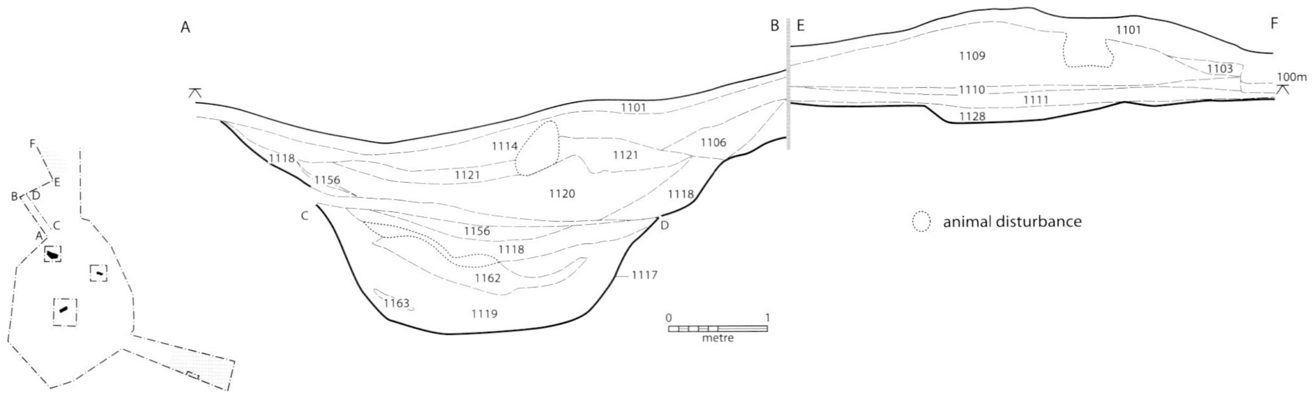

Illustration 1.15
Section of the bank and ditch at the northern entrance to the monument. The inset shows the locations of the sections illustrated

Illustration 1.16
Section of the henge ditch at the northern entrance of the enclosure

The ditch (illus 1.12–1.16)

The scale of the ditch varied considerably between the excavated sections. Close to the south entrance, it was 5m wide and had been dug almost 2m into the natural gravel. Where it terminated against the northern entrance, its width was virtually the same, but here it was almost 3m deep. In each case the profile of the earthwork was the same. The faces of the ditch were steeply cut, and in both sections it had an almost flat bottom. The ditch would have presented a significant obstacle to anyone attempting to cross it.

Both sections through the earthwork showed the same sequence. The sides of the ditch had eroded rapidly and primary silts of loose gravel had accumulated in the bottom (illus 1.12, 7, 8, 9; illus 1.15, 1118, 1119, 1156, 1162, 1163). No attempt had been made to remove this material, nor was there any evidence of recutting. Above this level there was a substantial deposit of fluvioglacial gravel which had accumulated from the exterior – the position of the bank. This included lenses of coarser material and several complete turves. The process seems to have ended when the surface of this deposit was colonised by vegetation (illus 1.12, 6; illus 1.16, 1156). The secondary filling of the ditch consisted of coarser gravel entering this feature from the outside (illus 1.12, 4, 5, 6; illus 1.16, 1114, 1118, 1120, 1121, 1156). Again it seems to have happened as the remaining part of the bank collapsed or – more likely – was demolished. This interpretation is supported by the results of soil micromorphology. The details of this analysis appear on pp 61–70.

There were few contrasts between the excavated sections of the earthwork, but the northern entrance provided the most convincing evidence for the sudden collapse of the bank. It happened as soon as the primary silts had accumulated, and nowhere was there any evidence that they had stabilised before they were covered over. The evidence is particularly clear since the earliest deposit of material from the bank contained turves which had kept their structure intact. The faces of the ditch had been excavated through layers of unstable sand and gravel. In view of the steep profile of this feature it is hard to believe that they could have remained exposed for long. The erosion of the ditch may have precipitated the collapse of the bank, especially as there is no indication that they had been separated by a berm. At all events those two processes followed one another without a break. In each section there was a marked hiatus after the initial collapse of the bank (illus 1.12, 6; illus 1.16, 1156). More of that material entered the ditch during a subsequent phase. This may have been a result of deliberate destruction when the surrounding area was cleared for cultivation.

No artefacts were found in either excavation of the ditch, but the section through the earthwork close to the southern entrance identified a small concentration of burnt twigs at the base of the collapsed material of the bank (illus 1.12, 7). Although they could not be identified to species, they were submitted for radiocarbon dating, but, unfortunately, they consisted of residual material dating from the Early Neolithic period. At 2σ these dates were 4060–3960 BC (Beta-2156 12) and 3790–3650 BC (Beta-2156 13). Samples of broadly similar age came from the buried soil beneath the northern entrance.

Illustration 1.17
Longitudinal section of the henge bank at the northern entrance of the enclosure

The bank (illus 1.12, 1.14, 1.15, 1.17)

The bank was poorly preserved in both the excavated areas. On the southern perimeter of the monument it had been reduced by cultivation, and at the northern entrance the surviving deposits were disturbed by rabbit burrows. Both sealed a well preserved buried soil which provided important material for pollen analysis, soil micromorphology and radiocarbon dating (illus 1.12, 14).

Details of this work appear on pp 61–72, but the dates themselves fall into two groups. The first consist of four samples of short-lived species, either hazel or alder, from the lower part of the buried soil. Three samples came from the base of the old land surface. At 2σ they provided dates of 4230–3960 BC (SUERC-13995), 4230–3980 BC (SUERC-13990) and 3950–3690 BC (SUERC-13994). A fourth sample, which was stratified just above them, has a date of 3770–3640 BC (SUERC-13989) The second group consisted of samples of short lived species, mainly *calluna vulgaris*. They came from the surface of the buried soil and probably derive from episodes of land clearance before

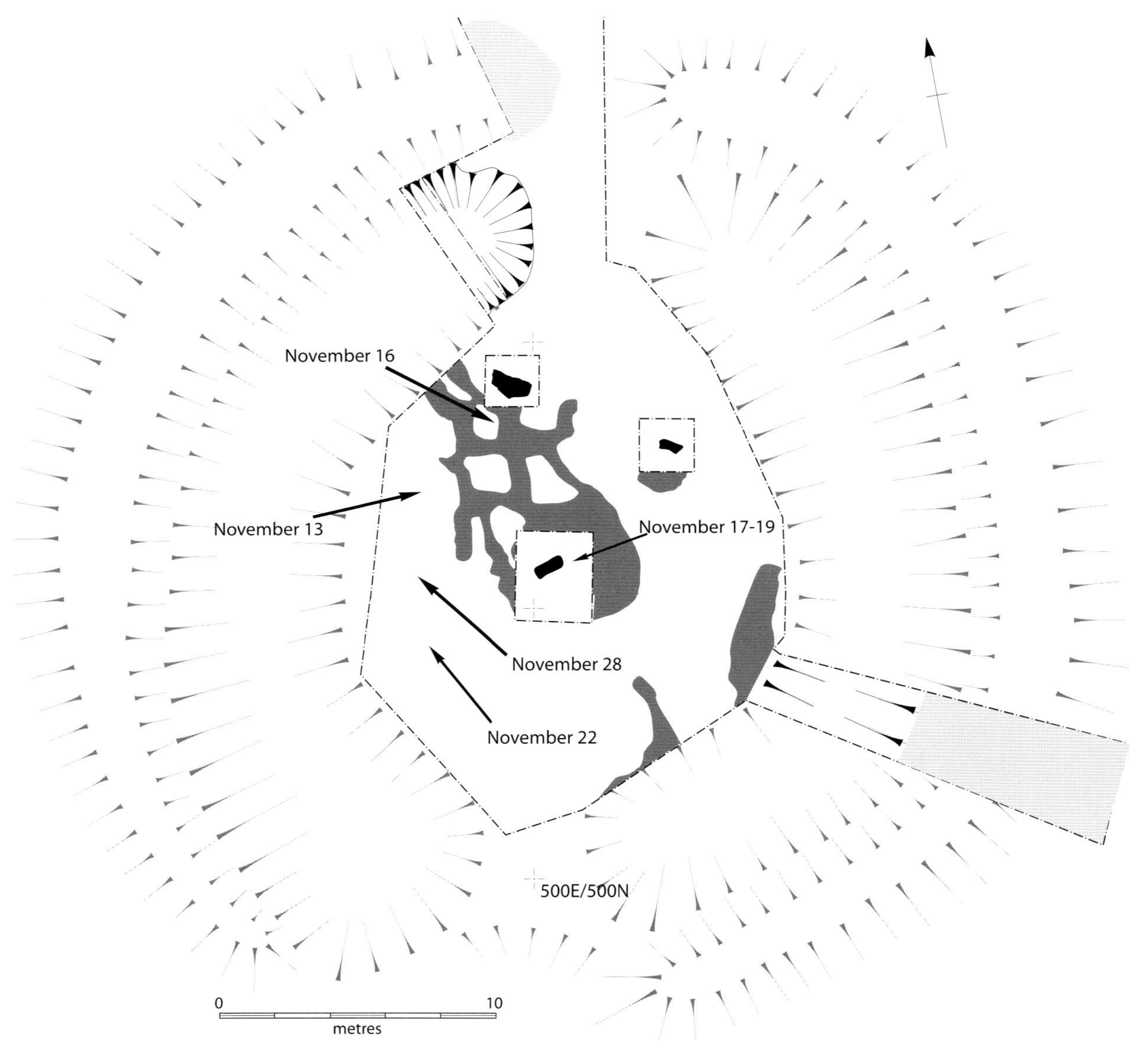

Illustration 1.18
The trenches and pits excavated in 1855, showing the dates on which parts of the work were undertaken

the henge was built. These dates are 2140–1940 BC (SUERC-13986), 2130–1890 BC (SUERC-13987) and 1940–1740 BC (SUERC-13988). They should provide a *terminus post quem* for the construction of the earthwork.

The only evidence that can be associated with the building of the monument is a clearance horizon evidenced in both trenches by a concentration of charcoal on top of the buried soil (illus 1.12, 14; illus 1.15, 1110). It provided the samples for radiocarbon dating. The southern section of the bank did not identify any subsoil features underneath the earthwork. In the northern entrance, however, a shallow hollow was identified beneath the terminal of the bank, but predated its construction by a substantial interval (illus 1.15, 1128). This feature was interpreted as a tree hole

and was probably of the same age as the radiocarbon samples which dated from the late fifth/early fourth millennium BC.

Towards the southern entrance the bank survived as a thin deposit of coarse gravel, within which only one tip line could be distinguished. There was no evidence that it had been built in more than one phase (illus 1.12, 1, 2, 4, 10, 11, 12, 13). The same was true at the northern entrance, where rather more of the earthwork remained intact (illus 1.15, 1101, 1109). Here the terminal was also examined in longitudinal section. On this part of the site the core of the bank consisted of a compact dump of coarse gravel, overlain by a deposit of finer, sandier material. In this case clear tip lines could be recognised against the terminal (illus 1.17). These deposits could have

Illustration 1.19
General view of the 2005 excavation seen from the south, showing the excavated stone sockets and other features

Illustration 1.20
General view of the 2006 excavation showing the network of narrow trenches dug in 1855

derived from the initial weathering of the bank as there was no indication of any revetment. Like the ditch, the bank seems to have been constructed in a single phase and there was no indication that it was maintained after that time.

Excavation inside the enclosure

New light on the 1855 excavation (illus 1.18)

Before presenting the results of excavation in 2005 and 2006, it is necessary to say more about the character of Dalrymple's work. That is because it set limits on what could be achieved in the course of the project. At the same time re-excavation of his trenches has made it easier to understand his published report. It is necessary to consider what he could have observed

– and what would not have been apparent to someone using his methods.

The whole of the interior of the henge had been badly disturbed, and the entire soil profile from the modern surface to that of the natural gravel contained a mixture of modern rubbish, stone flakes from the destruction of the monoliths, prehistoric pottery and pieces of cremated bone. They were spread about the site in no apparent order, although it was clear that the sherds and the human remains were largely confined to the area that had been delimited by standing stones. These finds were entirely unstratified. That is hardly surprising since the site has been used as a rubbish tip in recent years. It seems likely that this covering layer was turned over in its entirety during the course of Dalrymple's project. One reason for taking this view is that at no point did the upcast from his excavation seal an old land surface.

It is clear from Watt's account that Dalrymple and his colleagues employed labourers to carry out the digging, although both men may have been present throughout. Other sponsors of the project attended on at last two occasions as they signed their names on slivers of window glass which were buried in the filling of the excavation. The clearest indication of the methods used in 1855 is provided by an irregular network of narrow trenches dug into the natural gravel. There were as many as ten of these, the majority of them in the area between the central burial pit and the western portal stone where they may have been organised on a very informal grid at intervals of about five feet. The shaft grave appears to have excavated in its entirety.

Dalrymple's trenches were about the width of a spade and extended between the entrance, the position of the central monolith and the assumed position of another standing stone on the western perimeter of the monument (illus 1.19, 1.20, 1.21). Two further trenches were identified in the south-eastern part of the interior where a further monolith may have existed. Their absence from other areas is probably explained by the changing character of the natural geology. Most of his trenches were dug into soft sandy silt, while the areas where he did not dig to such a depth included a dense deposit of gravel which would have been difficult to remove. It seems as if he directed his workmen to dig these trenches between the sites of the standing stones. In addition, he excavated at the foot of both the monoliths that still remained in place. Those pits were only partly

Illustration 1.21
General view of the 2006 excavation showing the network of narrow trenches dug in 1855

reopened in 2005–6 as they were deep enough to threaten the stability of the stones.

The filling of Dalrymple's excavation contained two bottles containing pieces of glass bearing the dates on which the work was undertaken. The first – dated 13 November – was buried three days before any of the finds documented by Watt and comes from the western perimeter of the site (illus 1.22). The second, dated November 22, was in its south-western sector (illus 1.23). The dates of other discoveries are given in Watt's account of the project. They can be related to the descriptions published by Dalrymple (1884) whose report contains a site plan. Taken together, these sources suggest that the workmen started digging towards the western edge of the enclosure. They continued at the west portal stone and then proceeded clockwise around the perimeter until they ended more or less where they had started. The shaft grave was opened at the same time as the other features (illus 1.18).

The work was obviously carried out rapidly and with little attention to detail. It seems likely that six of the urns had been lost by the time of Dalrymple's article. Excavation in 2005 even suggests that one vessel was broken by the workmen and covered up again. The only cremated bones collected in 1855 lack any provenance. The others were left in the filling of the trenches, in the pits where they may have been found, or scattered across the superficial layer that covers the whole site. It seemed possible that the groups of cremated bone left in the original excavation might retain some integrity, but, with one possible exception (Context 1143), detailed analysis has shown that this was not the case. On the other hand, so little attention was paid to them when they were first found that what were probably pyre goods were recovered from these collections.

At two points it was possible to compare Dalrymple's account with specific features in his excavation. That was because he had left deposits for later excavators

Illustration 1.22
The bottle and railway timetable left by Dalrymple in the filling of Context 1057. The slivers of window glass sealed inside the bottle give the date and the names of the excavators. Photograph: NMS

to discover. The first was a whisky bottle containing pieces of window glass with the signatures of those supporting the excavation, and the date – 13 November 1855. It was accompanied by that month's timetable for the Great North of Scotland Railway, in which Dalrymple had shares. It was placed inside an irregular setting of slabs within one of his trenches. No prehistoric material was found there, but it suggests what he might have meant when he referred to small 'cists' (illus 1.22, 1.23).

The second was another bottle, this time for a non-alcoholic drink, set upright in the bottom of a pit beside one of the stone sockets. Again it contained pieces of glass with signatures and a date (November 22), and in this case it included a press report of Dalrymple's address to the total abstainers of the north-east (illus 1.24). There were fragments of cremated bone in the filling of the pit. To judge by Watt's list of dates, it was where five urns were found.

Monoliths and stone sockets (illus 1.25)

Early accounts do not agree on the original number of monoliths inside the henge. Dalrymple, Watt and Stuart opted for six, with a seventh standing stone in the

Illustration 1.23
Stone 'cist' erected by Dalrymple in the filling of the 1855 excavation. This covered a bottle containing slivers of glass with signatures and the date, as well as a railway timetable. These are shown in illus 1.22

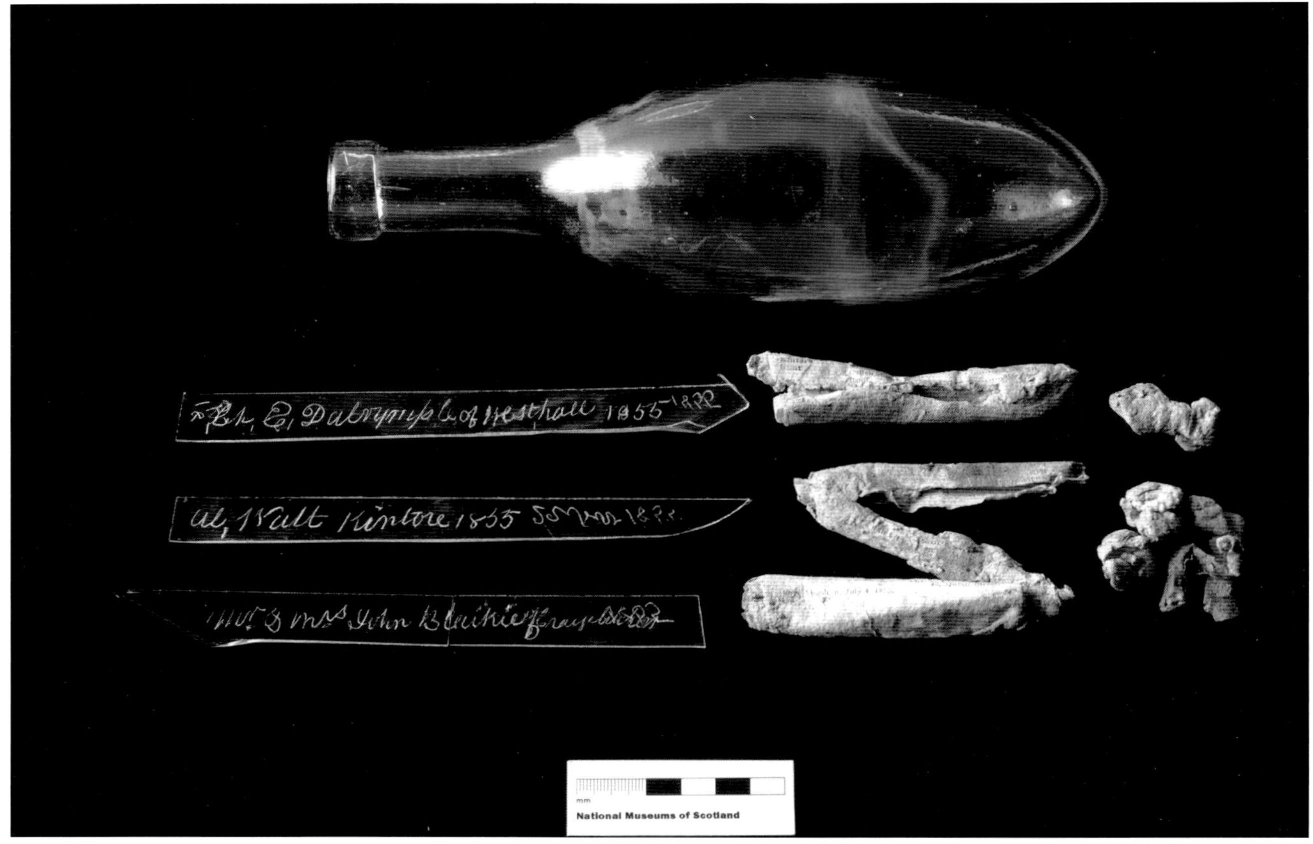

Illustration 1.24
The bottle and newspaper left by Dalrymple in the cist features in illus 1.23. The slivers of window glass sealed inside the bottle give the date and the names of the excavators. Photograph: NMS

middle of the site. Skene's drawing of the monument of 1832 shows only six. His illustration was unknown to James Ritchie, who accepted much of Dalrymple's account of the monument but doubted the existence of a central pillar.

Despite these differences, there is no disagreement that the portal stones by the northern entrance formed part of the original monument. Even though they are poorly aligned with the entrance, neither has been moved since 1855 as there are obvious traces of Dalrymple's excavation at the foot of both the monoliths. On the other hand, they have certainly been damaged, for both of them carry flake scars where pieces had been detached. A small number of pieces from the disturbed overburden could be fitted back onto these two stones. Why had they survived when the others were destroyed? Rosemary Stewart (pers comm) suggests that it was because they were of two kinds of granodiorite which would have been

harder to break than the other materials used on the site.

She has also examined a sample of struck flakes which had been incorporated in the filling of the nineteenth-century excavation. Four more rocks were represented here: a pink granite; a grey quartzy schist; a fine-grained blue grey basalt; and a grey speckled diorite. All these samples must have come from monoliths that have now disappeared. Whilst their arrangement within the monument can no longer be reconstructed, it seems much more than a coincidence that a total of six different lithologies should be represented. That agrees with the number of standing stones in Skene's illustration.

How does this reconstruction fare in the light of the new excavation? An arc of three stone sockets was found in the excavated area (illus 1.26). The largest was a shallow flat-bottomed basin almost 2m in diameter, the bottom of which had been consolidated by a considerable weight (illus 1.26, 1047). The surrounding soil contained a quantity of rounded boulders which could have been employed as packing stones. No trace of a monolith was left, but the filling of this feature contained a number of granite flakes (illus 1.27). The edge of the socket was cut by a pit containing an urn and a cremation burial. It was also cut by a pit opened by Dalrymple (illus 1.28, 1058). The filling of the nineteenth-century excavation contained pieces of cremated bone. This was probably the position of the south-western monolith in the stone setting and may mark the position of a large flat-bottomed stone like those in the entrance.

The second socket was directly opposite the southern entrance of the henge (illus 1.26, 1024). Again this lacked any trace of a standing stone, but there were two large boulders on its base which may originally have been packing. Others were found broken in the filling of this feature. The stone had been removed before the 1855 excavation, but this feature seems to have been disturbed and included a few fragments of cremated bone. The stone socket was 75cm deep and consisted of a steep-sided pit 75cm in diameter with a steep ramp extending towards the east. In contrast to the feature just described, it may have held a rather slender monolith which was probably lifted from the ground in one piece.

The third stone socket was in the south-eastern sector of the monument (illus 1.26, 1035). It was very similar to the feature just described. In this case it was only 32cm deep, but again it consisted of a steep-sided pit with a ramp. No trace of the stone survived, although it must have been between 40 and 50cm in maximum dimension. It had been lowered into this feature from the south or south-west. The monolith had been removed some time before the 1855 excavation. The socket contained two sherds of Beaker pottery, but appears to have been disturbed by Dalrymple. The upper filling of this feature also contained a small amount of cremated bone, and more was found together with parts of a Collared Urn in a pit (1022) just to its north.

The identification of these features as stone sockets depends on three criteria: in one case the base of the feature had been compressed by a heavy weight; in two instances large boulders suitable as packing stones were associated with these features; and two of them possessed ramps suitable for manoeuvring a monolith into position. Despite

Illustration 1.25
General view of the 2006 excavation showing the network of narrow trenches dug in 1855

Stone sockets

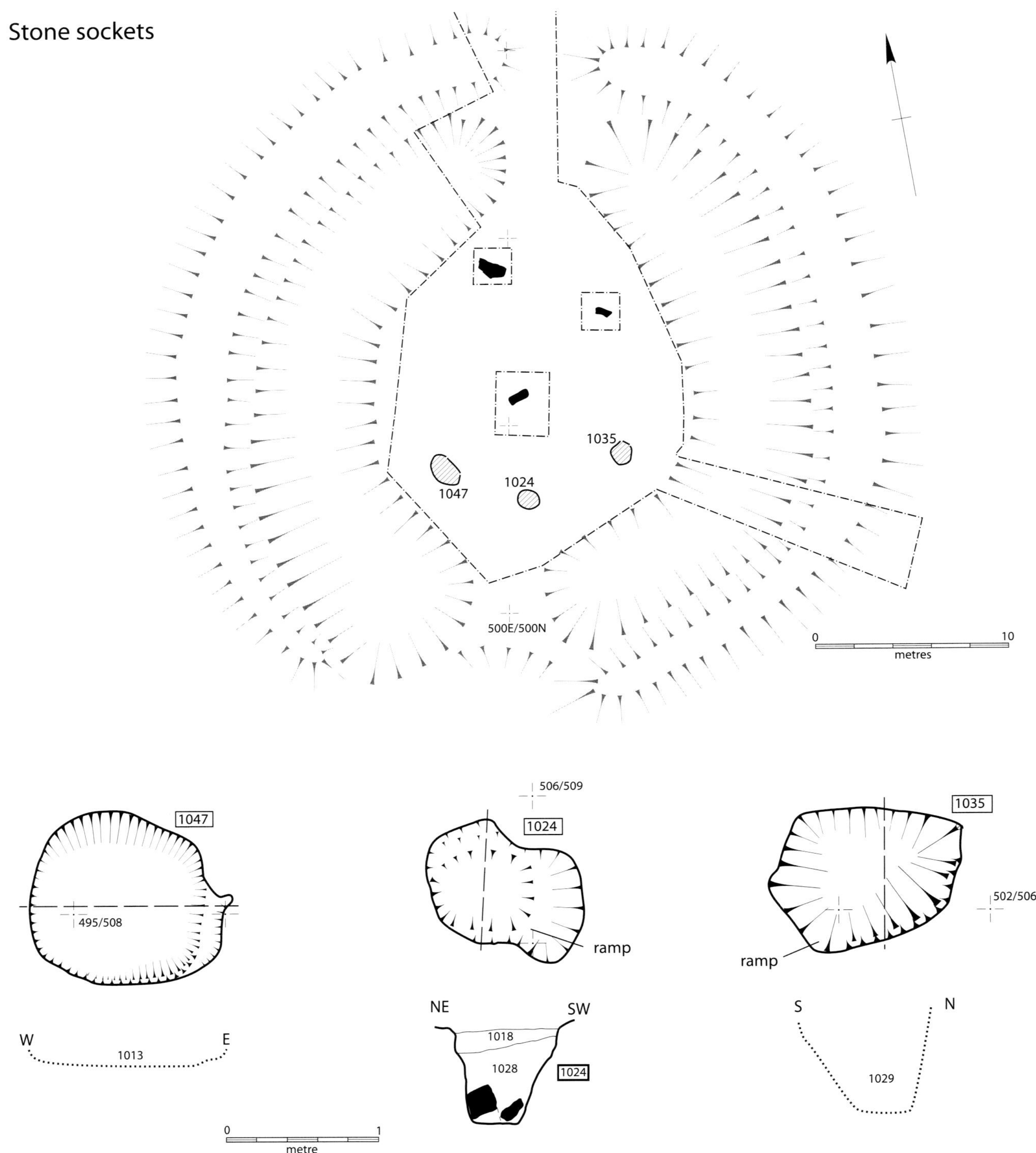

Illustration 1.26

The locations of the excavated stone sockets. 1024 is shown in section; 1047 and 1035 are represented by profiles because they were disturbed in the nineteenth century

Illustration 1.27

The upper part of the picture shows Context 1047, the setting for a monolith which had been broken up. Around the edge of this feature are granite flakes apparently detached with a sledgehammer. In the foreground is Context 1057, which was originally excavated by Dalrymple, who seems to have found a series of urned cremations there. He deposited the bottle shown in illus 1.24 in the bottom of this feature, before refilling the pit with rounded boulders, perhaps the packing stones associated with the adjacent monolith

Pits

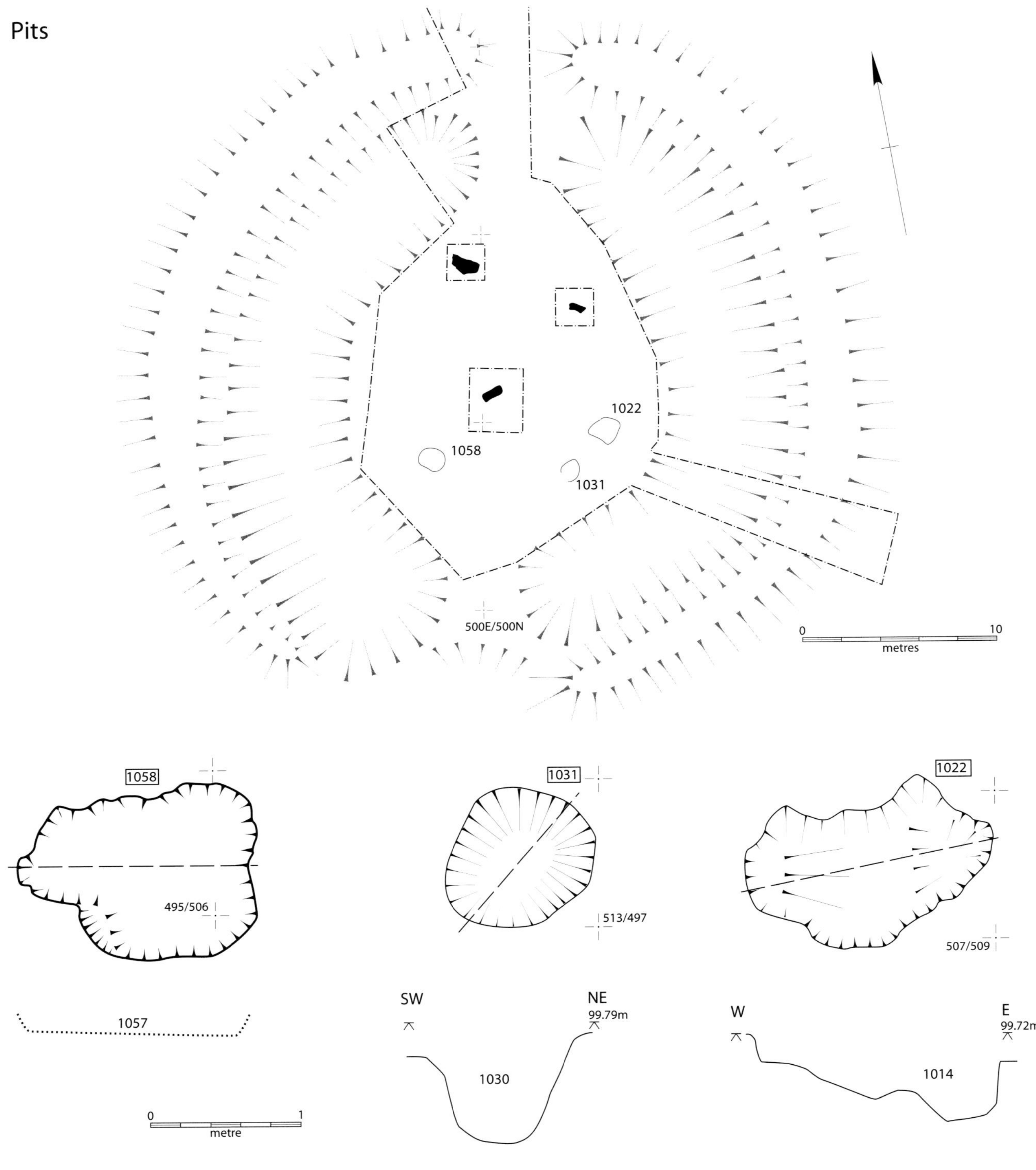

Illustration 1.28
The locations of the excavated pits. They are shown in profile because their fillings were disturbed during the 1855 excavation

what is said in an interim account of the project, no other feature excavated in 2005–6 possessed any of these characteristics. It is worth adding that both the surviving portal stones were associated with cremation burials. The same applied to all three features just described.

Pits (illus 1.28)

There were three pits in the excavated area, all of them located beside standing stones in the southern half of the enclosure.

The first (illus 1.28, 1022) had been badly disturbed in the previous excavation and contained a mixture of cremated bones, fragments of glass, and sherds belonging to a Collared Urn. Examination of the human remains suggests that they included at least

two individuals The presence of so many pieces of a single vessel suggests that there might have been a burial at the foot of the adjacent monolith. It is hard to understand why the pot was not removed in 1855, but Dalrymple's text perhaps supplies a clue (Dalrymple 1884, 322). Although he refers to 'a small square cist' beside the stone, there is no mention of any pottery in his account. Perhaps it was broken by the workmen who reburied it before the damage was observed. No trace of any cist remained and the original edges of the pit may have been removed in the nineteenth-century excavation.

The second feature (illus 1.28, 1057) was located beside the monolith in the south-western part of the enclosure. It was a deep, rounded pit which had been excavated through the edge of the stone

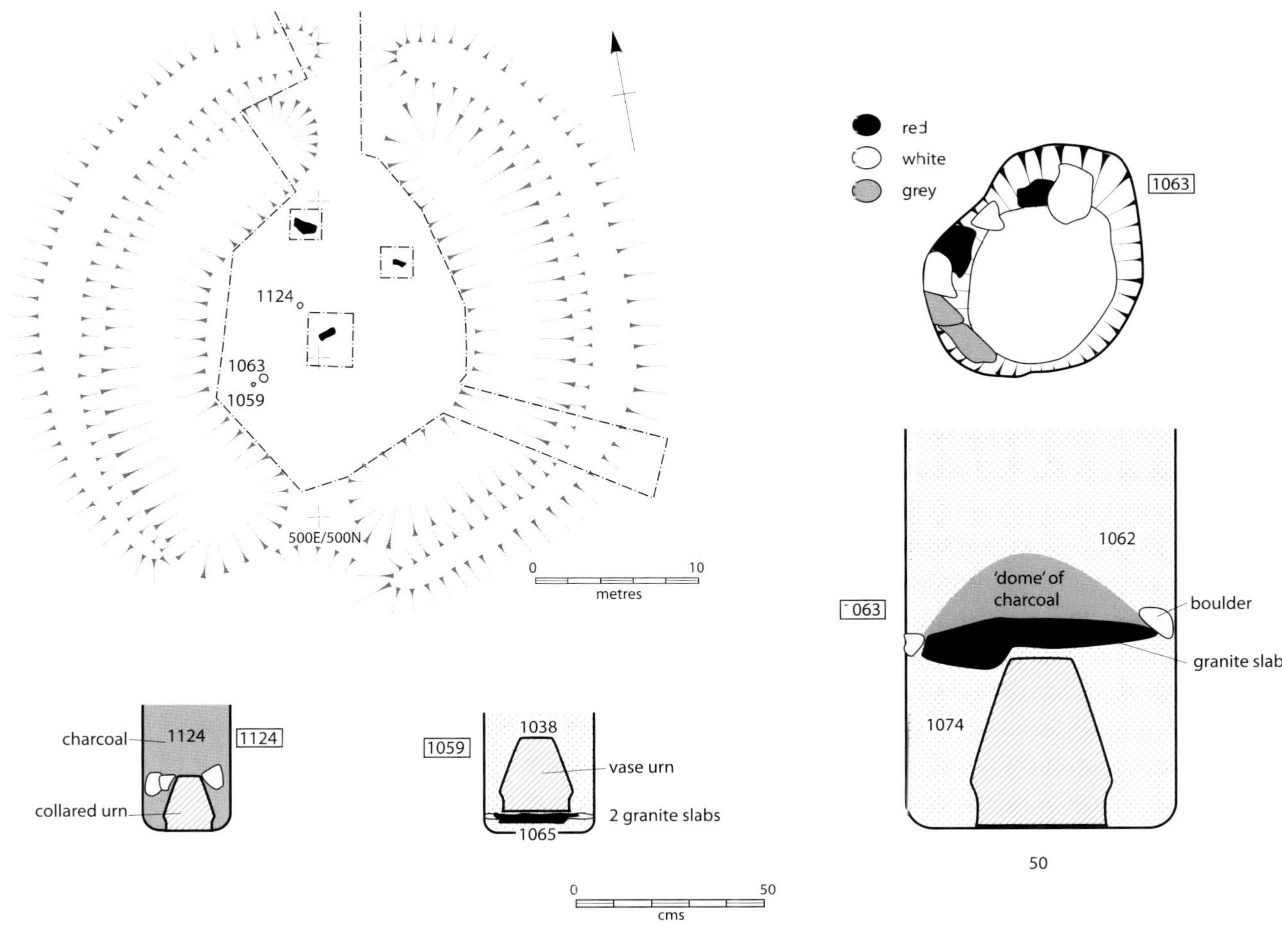

Illustration 1.29
Locations and details of the three urned cremations excavated in 2005–6. The plan of 1063 shows the arc of coloured stones arranged around a large boulder which covered an inverted urn

Illustration 1.30
The inverted urn from Context 1123 in the course of excavation

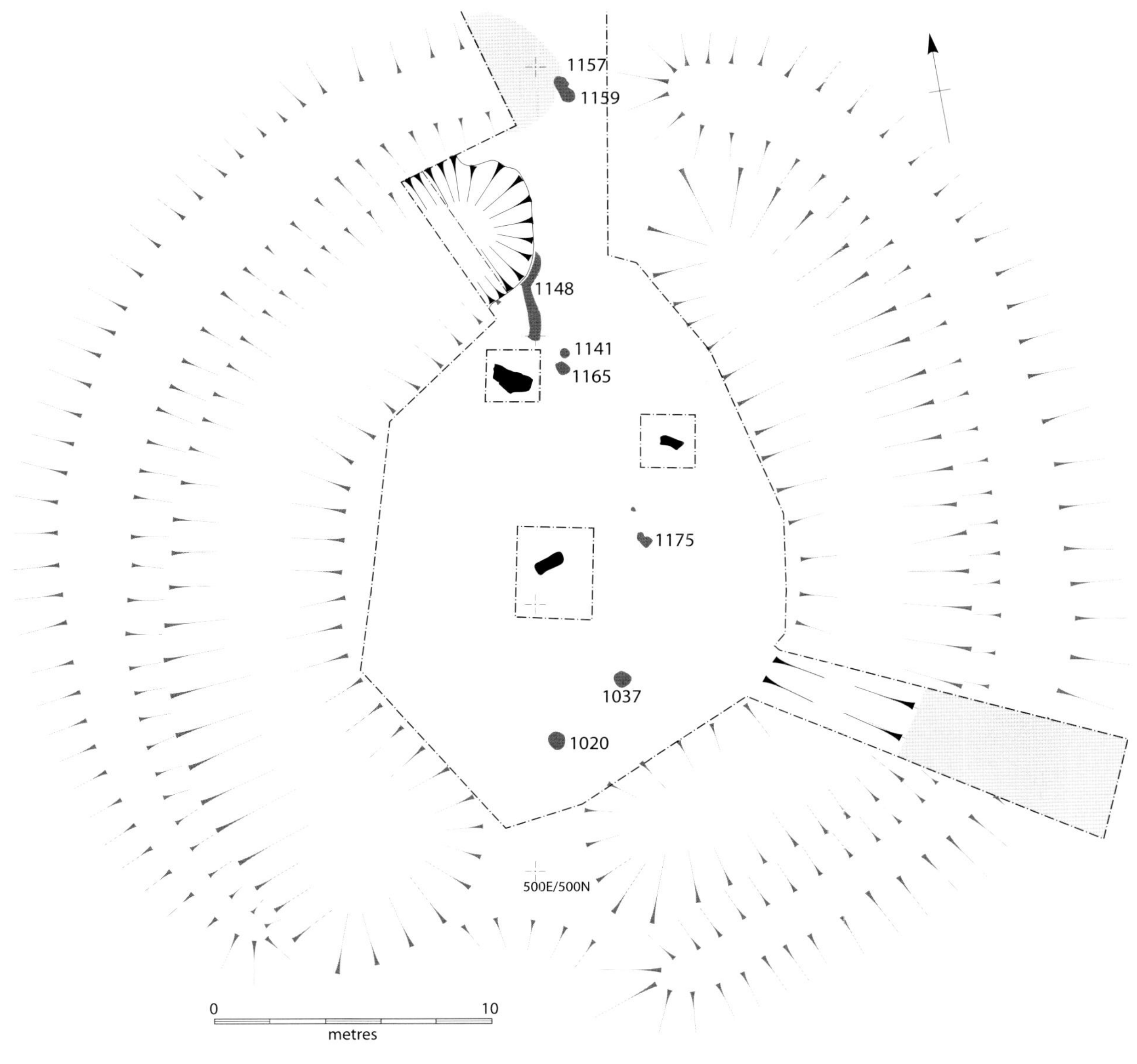

Illustration 1.31
Locations of the post-holes and the possible bedding trench (1148) excavated in 2005–6

socket. It may have been over-cut during the 1855 excavation. Dalrymple refilled it using rounded boulders, perhaps the packing for the adjacent standing stone. There were pieces of cremated bone in the filling of his excavation, and it may have been here that the vessels mentioned by Watt were found. The date of this discovery is the same as that scratched on a piece of window glass from this context.

Near the south entrance there was another possible pit (illus 1.28, 1031). It was oval in plan with steep sides extending to a depth of 75cm. There was no sign of a post pipe or any packing, but it was similar to the features found in the timber circle outside the monument.

Burials (illus 1.29)

Several of the features discussed already may have been associated with burials, in particular the irregular pit (1022) with parts of a Collared Urn. This section is concerned with three intact deposits which were missed during Dalrymple's excavation. Two were associated with the standing stone in the south-west part of the enclosure. The third was closer to the position of the shaft grave. There was also a concentration of cremated bone beside the western portal stone.

The first urned cremation was a cylindrical pit which cut through the edge of the south-western stone socket (illus 1.29, 1059). It was 30cm in diameter and 30cm deep. On its base was a small amount of charcoal. This feature had been backfilled with fluvioglacial gravel which overlay an inverted Vase Urn containing the cremated bones of a child. The vessel had been placed on top of two roughly circular pieces of granite which covered a small deposit of charcoal on the bottom of the pit. At 2σ a sample of bone from the urn is dated to 1890–1690 BC (SUERC-23673).

A second, deeper pit (illus 1.29, 1063) was located close to the stone socket. It was slightly oval in plan and measured 70cm by 80cm in diameter. It had been dug nearly a metre into the natural gravel and contained grey silts with occasional flecks of charcoal and lenses of sand. They formed a low 'dome' over the position of a massive granite slab which had been placed in the lower filling of the feature, surrounded on the east, north and west by an arc of eight small boulders. Apart from two grey pieces at the western limit of this

setting, their colours alternated between white and red. Immediately beneath these stones were lenses of sand, redeposited topsoil and larger pieces of charcoal, all of which were packed around an inverted urn. The vessel had been placed on the bottom of the pit and contained the cremated bones of a young woman together with a stone pendant. At 2σ a sample of bone from the urn is dated to 1950–1750 BC (SUERC-23675).

The other intact burial (illus 1.29, 1123) was close to the position of the shaft grave. Again it occupied a cylindrical pit 33cm in diameter and 50cm deep, the filling of which contained loose sandy material mixed with a dense deposit of charcoal containing a small number of boulders. It extended onto and around an inverted Collared Urn placed on the bottom of this feature (illus 1.30). It contained the cremated remains of a child and bones from another individual. The upper filling of the pit contained a few fragments from a different body, presumably collected together with the ashes from the pyre. At 2σ a sample of cremated bone from the urn itself is dated to 1930–1740 BC (SUERC-23674).

Finally, Context 1143 consisted of a concentration of burnt bone from the filling of Dalrymple's excavation just inside the western portal stone. This is where he

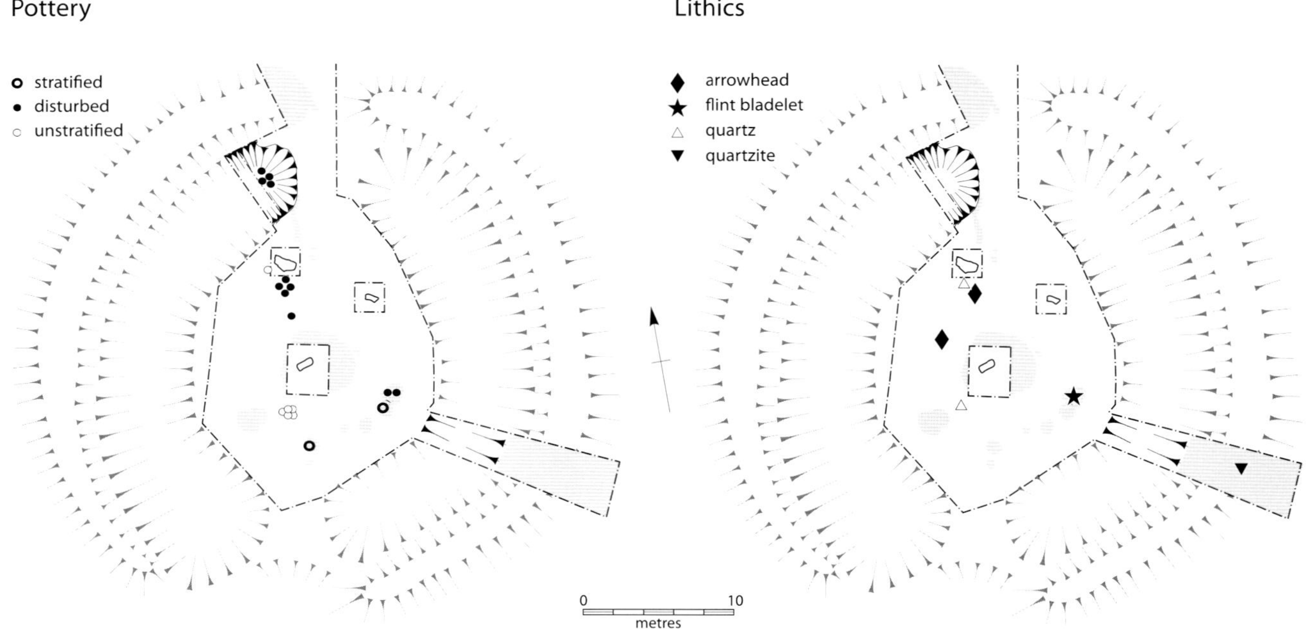

Illustration 1.32

Distribution of pottery (left) and lithic artefacts (right) recovered during excavation in 2005–6. The drawing is limited to material found below the disturbed surface layer of the site where these finds may have been dispersed

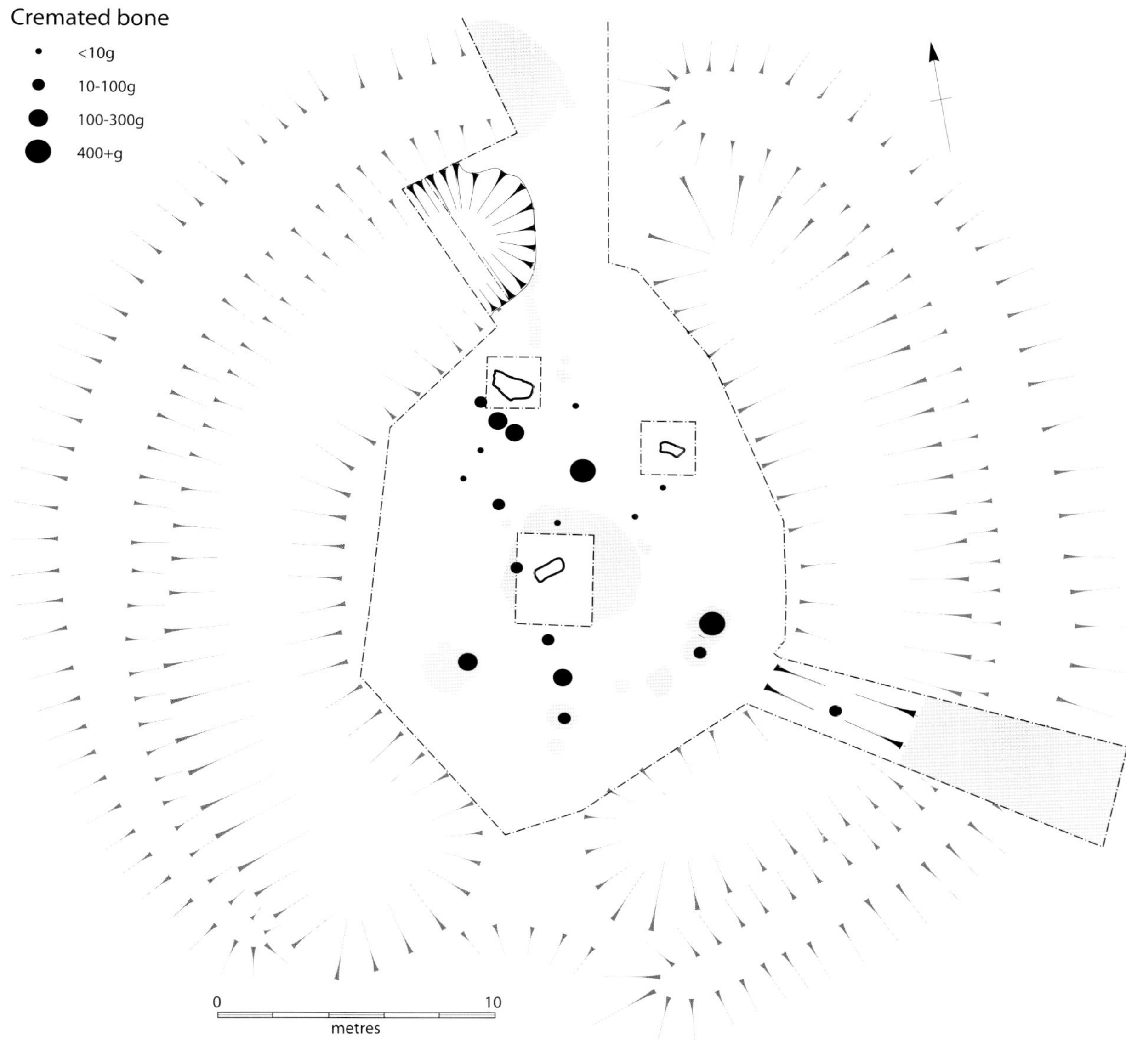

Illustration 1.33
Distribution of cremated bone found in the filling of the 1855 excavation. The three *in-situ* burials discovered in 2005–6 are shown in illus 1.14. The drawing is limited to material found below the disturbed surface layer of the site where these finds may have been dispersed

found a stone battle axe and urn in 1855. According to his account, there were three burials at the foot of the monolith. It cannot be certain that the bones found in 2006 came from the same deposits, but they do include the remains of two different people, an adult and a child. The redeposited material also included a burnt flint arrowhead which may have accompanied a body on the pyre. The topsoil beside the stone also contained part of a burnt bone pin. It could also have accompanied one of the burials recorded by Dalrymple.

The central shaft grave

This feature had been excavated and refilled. It was not possible to investigate it as Dalrymple had erected a decorated stone in its position. On the other hand, the surface of his excavation was cleaned and planned. The rim of a decorated Beaker was recovered; other parts of the same vessel were in the filling of Dalrymple's excavation along the southern lip of the pit. There was also a substantial slab of medium-grained granite which was 55cm long, 40cm wide

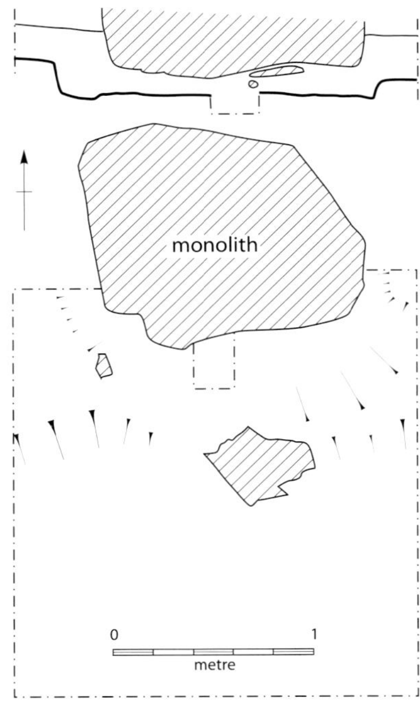

Illustration 1.34
Plan and profile of the sample excavation beside the extant monolith immediately south of the henge monument. The stone was flat-bottomed and did not require a socket

and 10cm thick. It might have been one of the end stones of the cist found here in 1855, although this cannot be proved as both items may have originated elsewhere on the site.

Post-holes (illus 1.31)
A line of post-holes extended between the entrances, diverging to the east as it passed the central shaft grave.

The character of these features changed according to the character of the natural gravel. Where this material was unstable it seems as if posts had been driven into the ground, but where the subsoil was more tenacious the uprights had been set in shallower pits dug for the purpose. Each of the three deepest sockets had been replaced in the same position, and one of the other post-holes was recut on two occasions. In contrast to the stone sockets, these features lacked packing stones.

The deepest post-holes were 60cm deep and had held posts approximately 30cm in diameter. They had been driven into the gravel and did not include any packing stones. In three cases they occurred in pairs, and in two instances the sockets were so close together

that one had almost certainly replaced the other. These features were virtually identical to one another. Three more sockets had been carefully dug. Context 1057 was nearly 50cm in diameter and 47cm deep but had been badly disturbed by rabbits. Beside it was a feature which may have been either a post-hole or a pit (illus 1.28, 1031). A more convincing post socket was in line with the southern entrance (1020). It was much better preserved. Although it was only 30cm deep, it had been recut on two occasions and held posts which were approximately 40cm in diameter. One of these had rotted *in situ* (or was cut off at ground level) before it was replaced. It is worth emphasising the point that the posts associated with the northern entrance may have stood to a greater height than their counterpart to the south.

The only dating evidence comes from the northern entrance where one of the double post-holes was cut through the buried soil and was sealed by sediments eroding from the end of the bank. A sample of charcoal from the latest growth of wood whose species could not be identified came from the uppermost filling where the two sockets converged. At 2σ it provided a date of 2290–2040 BC (SUERC-13996). This date can be compared with two of those from the land surface sealed by the bank.

Another feature may be related to the post sockets, although it lacked any direct dating evidence. This was a narrow slot or gully, 2m long and 55cm deep, which led from the ditch terminal in the northern entrance towards the position of the western portal stone (illus 1.31, 1148). It had a narrow flat bottom and it is uncertain whether it had held posts, although there was a possible socket close to the monolith at its southern end.

The distribution of the excavated material (illus 1.32, 1.33)
Apart from those finds scattered across the surface of the site, all the pottery, lithic artefacts and collections of cremated bones were given provenances in the field, whether they came from Dalrymple's excavation, from the surface of the natural gravel or from prehistoric features. All the pottery was within the area delimited by monoliths and stone sockets (illus 1.32) and, with only one exception, the same was true of the lithic artefacts (illus 1.32). The quantities of both were very small indeed.

In the case of cremated bone, which was much more prolific, every fragment came from the same area, with the sole exception of a tiny group in the filling of one of the Victorian trenches (illus 1.33).

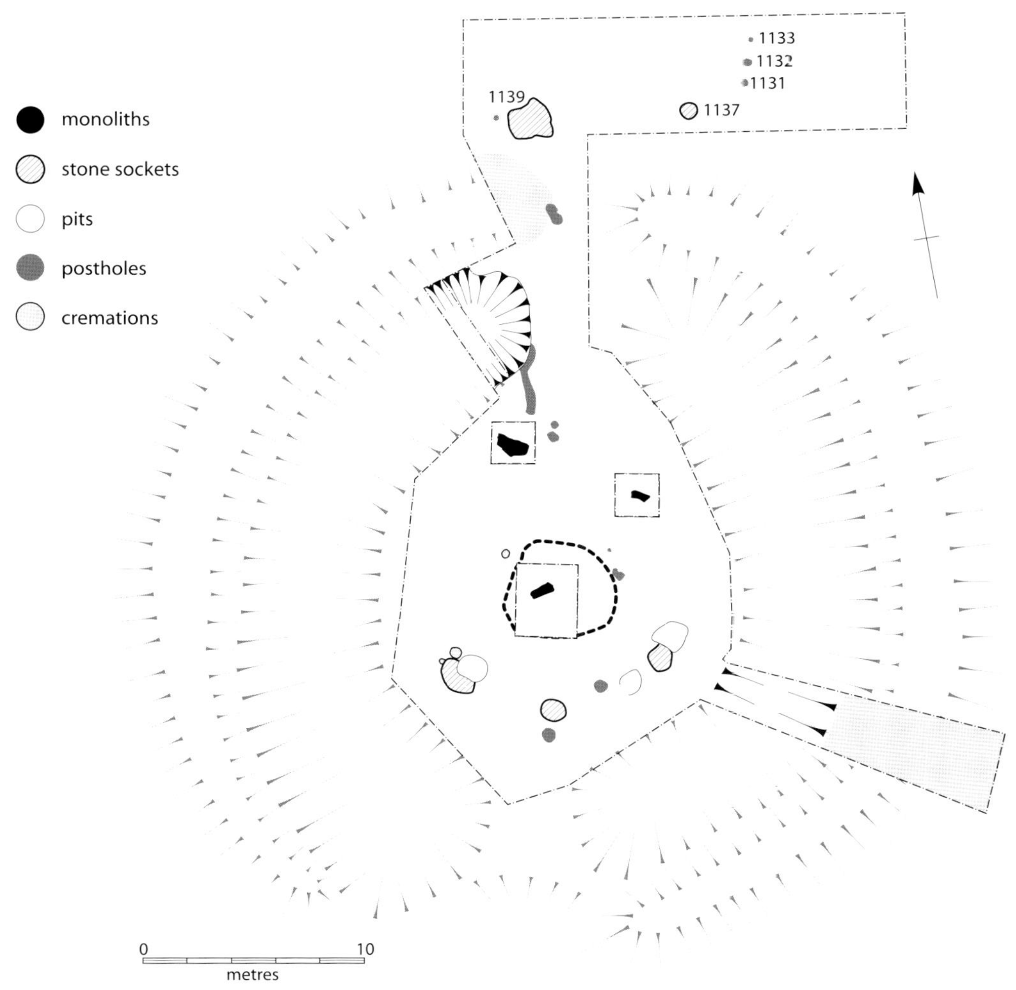

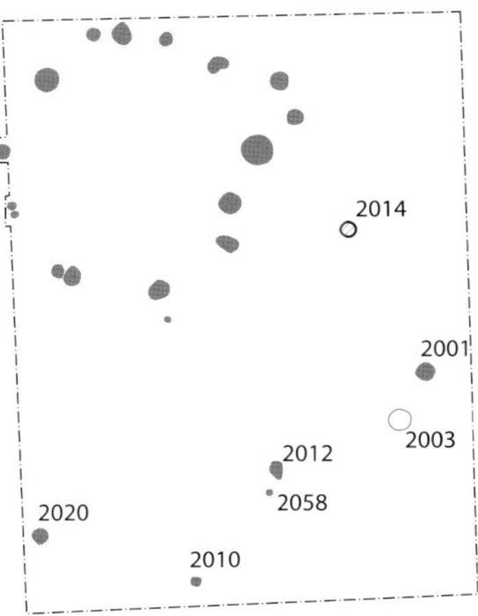

Illustration 1.35
Plan of the excavated features outside the northern and southern entrances of the enclosure. The extent of the timber circle is shown in dark tone. A detailed plan of this structure appears in illus 1.20

Details of the two of the excavated stone sockets belonging to the avenue: Context 1137 outside the north entrance; and Context 2003
outside the southern entrance

Illustration 1.37
General view of the 2006 excavation seen from the north with a deposit of rubble piled against the outer edge of the bank

Taken in combination, the different accounts of the 1855 excavation suggest that fifteen cremation burials were found, nine of them in urns. The distribution of material in the filling of the Victorian excavation suggests the position of at least two more concentrations of cremated human bone, one to the south of the shaft grave and the other to its north. Three undisturbed burials were found in 2005–6, suggesting a minimum number of deposits on the site of twenty, twelve of them in urns. In addition, the shaft grave contained an inhumation and at least one more cremation. Despite the damage caused in the nineteenth century, their distribution is very striking. Virtually all the cremated bone was inside the area bounded by the monoliths. There was little or no prehistoric material of any kind between the stone setting and the ditch of the henge, nor did it occur in prehistoric contexts associated with

the perimeter earthwork or in the areas excavated outside the northern and southern entrances.

Excavation outside the enclosure, 2006–7 (illus 1.34–1.42)

Monoliths and stone sockets

Before the main part of the project began the monolith immediately south of the monument was investigated by hand excavation. This was intended to examine its socket. The surrounding area had been ploughed, but it was important to record the setting of a standing stone that had not been disturbed. In the event it became clear that the stone had a flat base and did not require a deep foundation (illus 1.34). The monolith had remained in position due to its low centre of gravity and may not have been bedded in the subsoil. The

Illustration 1.38
Refittting fragments of one monolith and part of another from the rubble shown in illus 1.37

space between the stone and the gravel was probably reworked by roots and burrowing animals.

On the other hand, a stone socket (Context 2003) was found outside the southern perimeter of the henge. This was a steep sided circular pit 45cm in diameter and 30cm deep, with an upper filling of large boulders like those employed as packing inside the monument (illus 1.35, 1.36). It was similar to a larger feature excavated outside the northern entrance, but this was a metre in diameter and 95cm deep (illus 1.35, 1.37, 1.36). It was filled with similar material, and in this case there was evidence of severe compaction on the sides and bottom of the feature. In both instances it seems likely that an upright had been lifted out of the ground, leaving the packing to fill the hole. The quantity of stones in Context 1137 was so great that it is possible that the monolith had also been supported by a cairn: a practice that is known at sites like Balnuaran of Clava (Bradley 2000, 73–7).

There was another possible stone socket outside the northern entrance (illus 1.35, 1139). This was a large shallow pit which had been very badly disturbed by rabbit burrows. It was of a suitable size to have supported a standing stone. Beside it there may have been a small post-hole. Despite its poor condition, 1139 could have been the site of two features, one replacing the other, but so little remained that it would be wrong to place any weight on this interpretation.

The excavation of the northern entrance also encountered the deposit of stones that had been intended to build an enclosure wall (illus 1.37). It was found in the ploughsoil overlying the tail of the bank. Among the pieces recovered from this deposit were a series of fragments of psammite which could be

Illustration 1.39
General view of the sockets of the timber circle outside the south entrance at Broomend of Crichie

refitted to form a complete monolith 2m high, and two substantial pieces of granite which conjoined to form part of another (illus 1.38). Neither stone would have fitted the sockets revealed by excavation, although their position suggests that they were originally located on this side of the henge. Perhaps they once formed part of the northern section of the avenue.

Pits (illus 1.35, 1.39)

A round-bottomed circular pit 75cm in diameter and 47cm deep was excavated in the area outside the southern entrance (illus 1.39, 2003). It did not include any datable material.

Post-holes (illus 1.35, 1.39)

In the same area to the south of the henge there were five scattered post-holes (illus 1.35, 2001, 2010, 2012, 2020, 2058). They did not appear to belong to a single structure and produced no dating evidence.

Outside the northern entrance and close to an excavated stone socket there was row of three small post-holes between 40cm and 25cm in diameter and between 10 and 20cm deep (illus 1.35, 1131, 1132, 1133. They lacked any post pipes and did not include datable material.

The timber circle (illus 1.39–1.41)

The 2007 excavation was located outside the southern entrance of the henge and on the assumed course of its avenue. Its original objectives were to look for the positions of levelled monoliths and to investigate any associated deposits. In the event only one stone socket (2003) was identified. On the other hand, the work revealed a setting of substantial post-holes 9.5m in diameter.

There were sixteen post-holes in total, excavated to depths of between 13cm and 65cm in the natural gravel. There was no clear evidence of ramps. Where any evidence remained, the sockets had supported posts between 25cm and 40cm in diameter. Once the wood had been removed or decayed, the hollows that remained filled with fine sediment containing charcoal. No artefacts were associated with any of these features, but two samples of young wood from the top and bottom of one of the deepest post-holes (2048) provided

radiocarbon dates in the Early Bronze Age. At 2σ a sample of birch charcoal from the base of the feature gave a date of 1871–1642 BC (OxA-18252). A sample of hazel charcoal from the top of the weathering cone

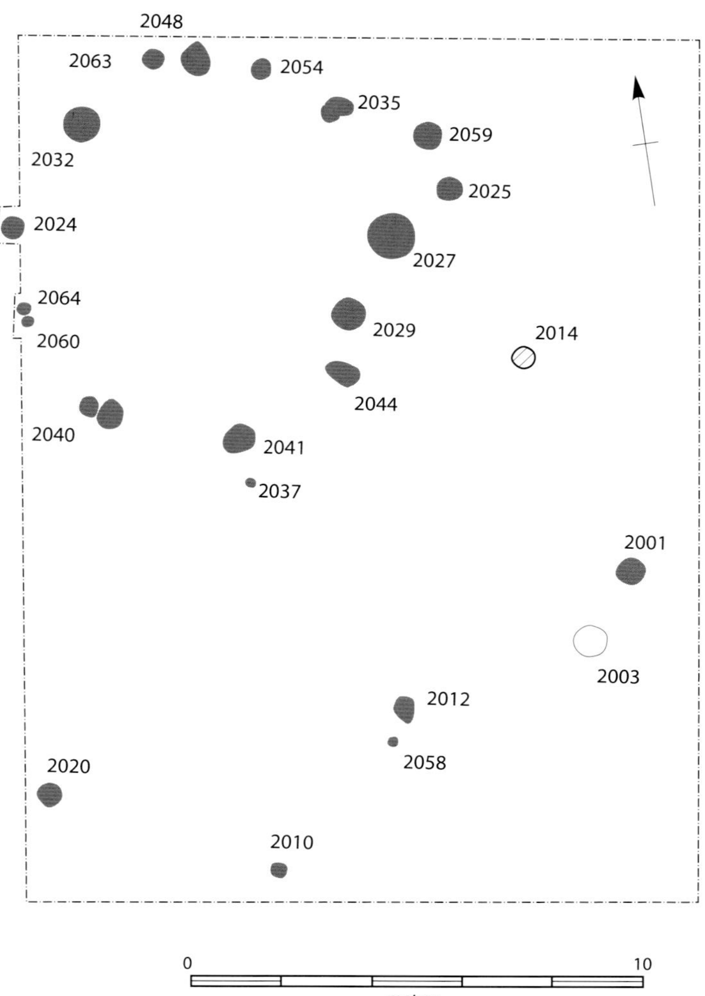

Illustration 1.40

Plan of the excavated area south of the henge monument, showing the positions of a stone socket (2014), an isolated pit (2003), scattered post-holes (2001, 2010, 2012, 2020 and 2058) and the sockets for a timber circle

is dated to 1694–1529 BC (OxA-12851). Comparison of these two dates suggests an interval of at least a century between the building of the structure and the last use of its site.

The great majority of the post-holes fall on the circumference of a circle 9.5m in diameter, but to the north-east two of them project from the line by

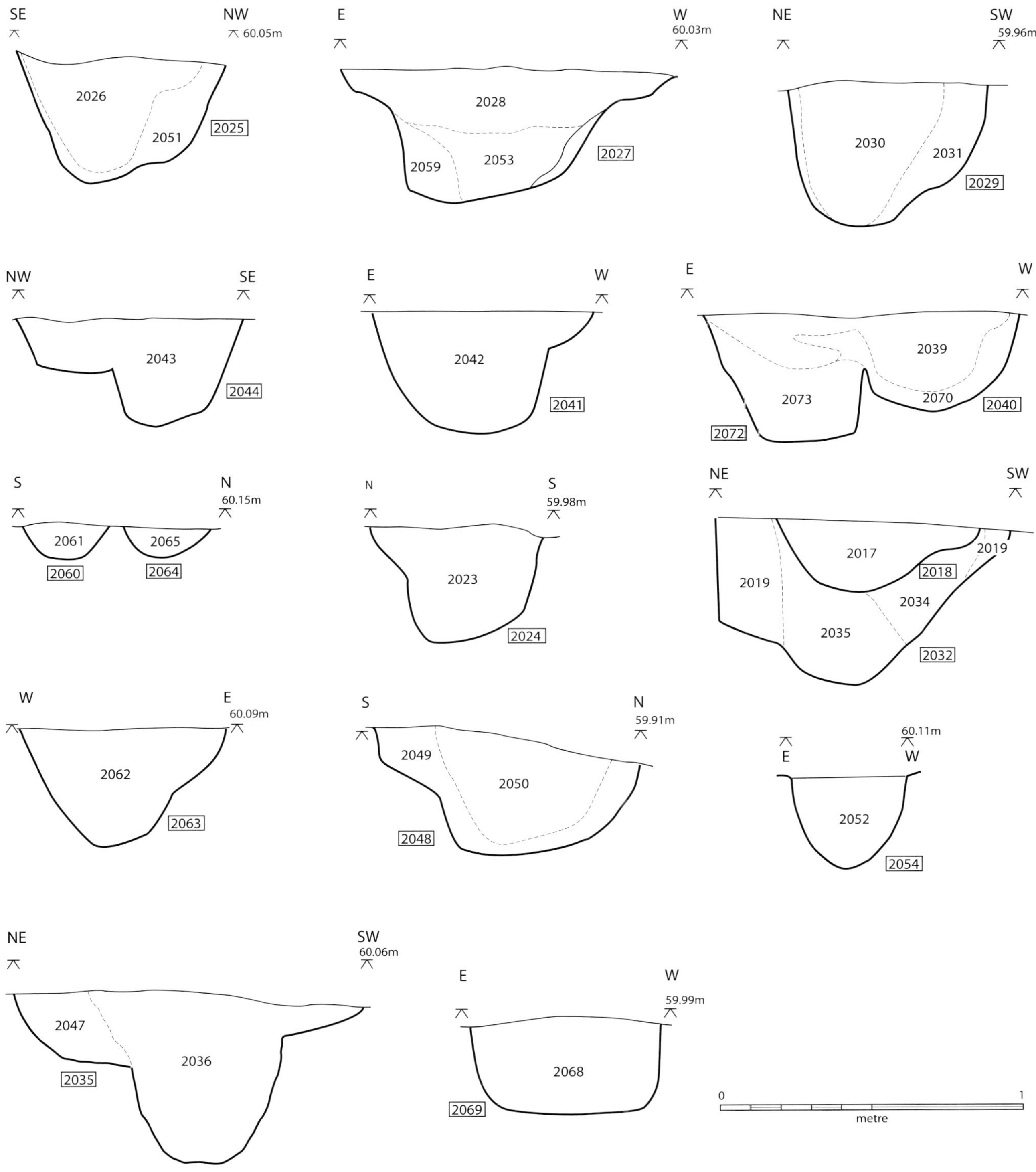

Illustration 1.41
Sections of the post-holes of the timber circle outside the south entrance of the henge

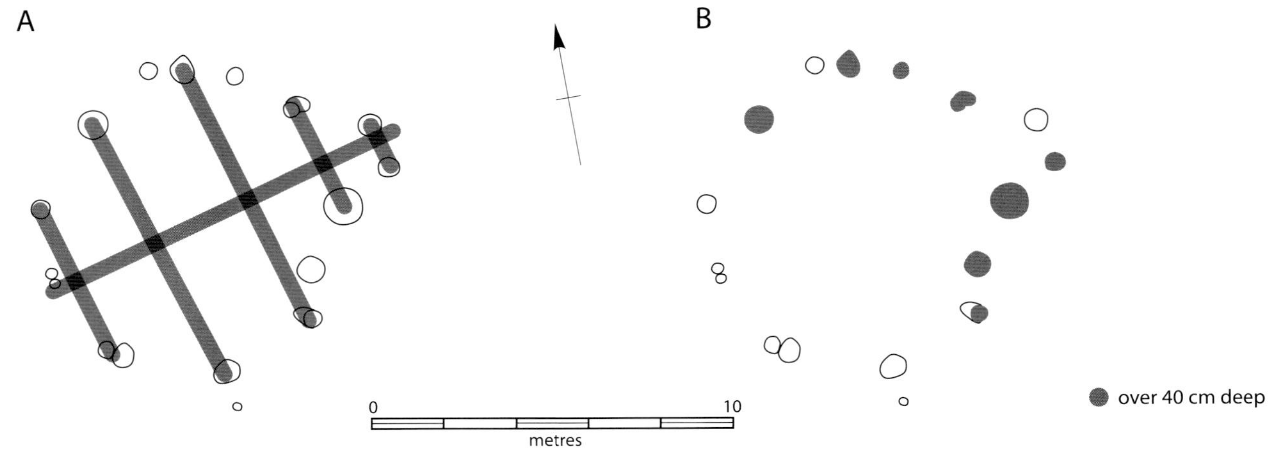

Illustration 1.42
(A) Post alignments in the timber circle, emphasising its orientation, and (B) the depths of the post-holes. The deepest sockets were towards the north-east

1.5m, suggesting an entrance 1.3m wide. The basic structure consists of five pairs of uprights on opposite sides of the building (illus 1. 40, 1.42). Away from the entrance structure they are placed at intervals of 2.4 or 2.8m. There are two unusually small post sockets at the south-western limit of the circle, but these were not quite on the axis of the entrance. Three posts holes, two of them set in unusually shallow sockets, did not conform to this scheme and may have held replacement timbers. The same could have happened where a pair of post-holes was excavated side by side, and this was obviously the case where a single socket was associated with two successive post pipes. The main evidence for this practice was found along the southern perimeter of the building.

Two other patterns can be identified (illus 1.42). The posts which were closest to the henge were more substantial than most of the others, while those to the south of the entrance were less robust. Although no land surface remained, the area of the timber circle was virtually level, yet there were striking differences in the depths of the post sockets. The deepest were towards the north-east, and the shallowest were to the south-west; in three cases posts in the shallower sockets had been replaced. Assuming that there is a consistent relationship between the length of the upright bedded in the soil and its height above the ground, it seems as if that the timbers were graded. The lowest were towards the south and south-west, and the tallest to the north and north-east. Such a pattern is commonly found in

stone settings, although the monoliths are generally taller towards the south and west (Bradley 2005, 106–7). In this case that configuration was almost exactly reversed.

The finds from the 2005–7 excavations, and finds from Dalrymple's excavations in the National Museums of Scotland (NMS) Collections

The artefactual finds from the 2005–7 excavations comprise sherds from a Beaker (Pot 1), three complete urns of a type perhaps best described as 'Collared/Vase Urns' (see below, Pots 2–4), sherds from three further urns (Pots 5–7), sherds from a burnt accessory vessel (Pot 8), a fragment of a burnt bone pin, one complete and one fragmentary burnt flint arrowhead, a few pieces of flint, quartz and quartzite and an incomplete burnt stone pendant.

The artefactual finds from Dalrymple's 1855 excavations that were acquired by the formerly named National Museum of Antiquities of Scotland (now NMS) in 1856 and 1865 comprise large parts of a 'Collared/Vase' urn (Pot 9); two sherds each from two further urns (Pots 10, 11); and a battle axehead. There is also the upper part of an urn (NMS X.EA 137), acquired from Watt in 1865, that is registered and published as having been found at Broomend of Crichie, but about whose provenance there is some uncertainty. This will be discussed below, under Pot 11.

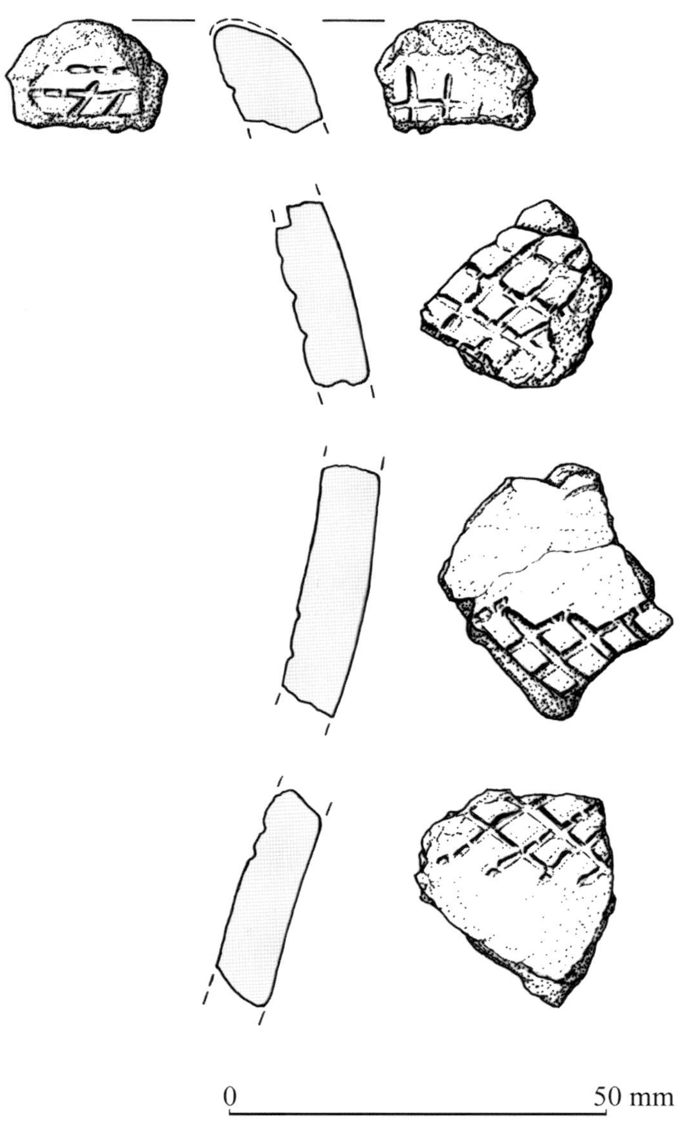

0   50 mm

Illustration 1.43
Pot 1 from excavation in 2005–6

The current location of the other urns found by Dalrymple's diggers – seven, according to Watt's account – is unknown, although parts of those urns may be represented among the sherds recovered in 2005–7.

The finds are described below by material and artefact type. No metal objects were found, and no copper staining on the cremated bones was noted, such as would indicate the former presence of a copper/copper alloy item.

Pottery

ALISON SHERIDAN

In the descriptions given below, all measurements are in millimetres, and abbreviations are as follows: E = estimated; Ht = height; L = length; RD = rim diameter; BD = base diameter; Th = thickness; W = width.

From the 2005–6 excavations

Pot 1 (illus 1.43) Twenty-six sherds and one fragment of a thin-walled, fine-textured Beaker: two conjoining sherds, and one sherd-plus-fragment conjoin, have now been refitted. Most of the sherds were found among unstratified, disturbed material near the shaft grave, while two sherds and the fragment were found in the filling of the south-eastern stone socket (C1029); the pieces show varying degrees of abrasion, with a few heavily abraded. Only a small part – perhaps around 5% – of the pot is present, but sufficient survives to show that this had been a sinuous-profiled and probably short-necked vessel with comb-impressed decoration arranged in zones of lattice design, interspersed with plain zones. The rim had been slightly everted and had probably been rounded. There is a zone of latticed comb impressions on its interior, and on the exterior two horizontal lines of comb impressions immediately below the rim form an upper boundary to the topmost zone of lattice design. There are at least three, and probably more zones of lattice design on the exterior, including one where the neck kinks out towards the belly and one on the belly; the lower belly is undecorated and the wall-base junction may have been gently pedestalled. One or more short combs, no wider than 1.75 mm, had been used to make the lattice design, and the closeness of the criss-cross lines varies from zone to zone. The rimsherd is too small to allow its diameter to be estimated, but the EBD is *c* 90 and the maximum diameter, at the belly, is 230mm; neck diameters of *c* 170 and *c* 140 have been measured. Wall Th ranges from 7.5 to 11. The exterior is markedly reddish; the core has a band, of variable thickness, of dark to blackish-grey (indicating a rapid firing); and the interior is light- to medium brown. Inclusions are sparse (up to 3% in density),

Illustration 1.44
Pot 2 from excavation in 2005–6

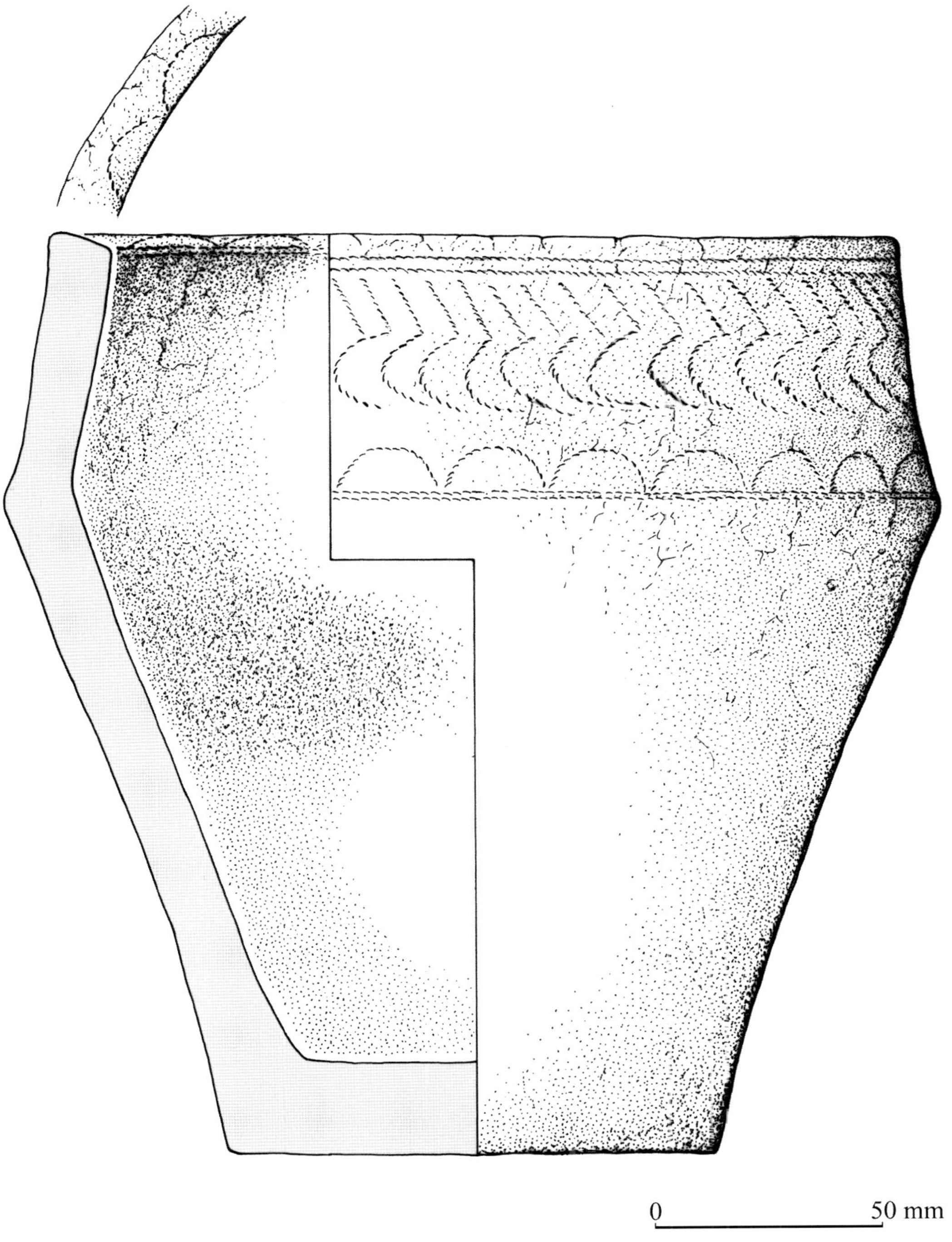

Illustration 1.45
Pot 3 from excavation in 2005–6

small (up to *c* 2 × 2mm), and angular and sub-angular fragments of several mineral types, including quartz/ite, a black mineral, a creamy mineral (?feldspar) and a speckled creamy and black mineral. The clay may well have been levigated. The surfaces had been carefully smoothed before decoration, and the exterior had been polished to a low sheen.

In terms of Beaker typology this would probably count as an 'S-profiled' Beaker (according to Needham 2005) and fall within Clarke's 'Northern' series of Beakers (Clarke 1970) and Shepherd's 'step 3' or perhaps step 4 (Shepherd 1986. Note that the use of interior decoration – a rare feature on Beakers in general in Britain – is echoed on several Beakers from north-east Scotland, including those of steps 5 and 6: ibid, illus 20). A Beaker of comparable shape and with zoned decoration including latticed comb impressions from Sandhole, Fetterangus, Aberdeenshire has been dated to 3845 ± 32 BP (2460–2200 cal BC at 2σ, OxA-V-2172-23: Sheridan 2007a, fig 11.3.6, 110). It is conceivable that this Beaker was broadly contemporary with the ones buried in the large cists in the cemetery on the sandbank to the south. Given the location and condition of the sherds, it seems likely that the Beaker may originally have been in the shaft grave cist, to be smashed and missed by the workmen.

Pot 2 (Context 1075; illus 1.44) Complete Collared/Vase Urn, found inverted in a deep pit, close to the south-western stone socket. The urn contained the cremated remains of a young adult, probably female, together with an incomplete and burnt stone pendant (see below); the bone was radiocarbon-dated to 3525 ± 35 BP, 1950–1750 cal BC at 2σ (SUERC-23675). Dimensions: Ht 291; RD 210–214; BD 100; Th *c* 12 on belly, 17 at base. Slender bipartite vessel, comprising a straight-walled neck/collar 73mm high, terminating in a low cordon, and below this an evenly tapering body. The rim is gently squared-off, with a very shallow internal bevel; the fairly narrow base is flat inside and out, with a continuously curving wall-base junction on the interior. The rim bevel and exterior of the collar have been decorated with twisted cord impressions. On the rim bevel these are arranged as a continuous running chevron, and on the neck a design featuring horizontal chevrons is framed between one upper and one lower horizontal line, and extends from just below the rim to just above the cordon. The design varies around the circumference but features sets of horizontal chevrons: starting at a point where two sets meet (and have the lower triangle

between them filled with two horizontal lines), there are – going clockwise – a set of ten right-facing chevrons; a set of twenty-two left-facing chevrons; a set of eleven right-facing chevrons; and a set of thirteen left-facing chevrons. The surfaces had been carefully smoothed and slipped on the exterior and interior, although lithic inclusions protrude through the surfaces, especially on the interior. The exterior is mid-brown with grey mottles; the core is not visible; and the interior is mid-brown with a black organic encrustation, extending up a third of the height, with sooty specks farther up. The lithic inclusions that had been crushed and deliberately added as a filler are mostly obscured, but where visible they seem to consist of angular fragments, up to *c* 10 × 4 in size, of a blackish-brown stone and of speckled black and white local granodiorite. (Specimens of the same stone from Pot 5 were identified as such by Dr Simon Howard, NMS Natural Sciences; it is likely to have been obtained locally.) Patches of white accretion on the rim are probably bone dust.

The stylistic affinities of this urn, and of the other urns, will be discussed below.

Pot 3 (Context 1065; illus 1.45) Complete Collared/Vase Urn, found inverted, and resting on two granite slabs, in a cylindrical pit cutting the edge of the south-western stone socket. It contained the cremated remains of a child, radiocarbon-dated to 3475 ± 35 BP, 1890–1690 cal BC at 2σ (SUERC-23673). Complete but for a short stretch of rim and upper neck. Dimensions: Ht 210; RD 187; max D (at base of neck) 204; BD 110; Th *c* 15 on belly, 22 at base. Bipartite vessel, comprising a straight, inclined neck *c* 62 high, kinking out to a fairly sharp carination; below that, the belly slopes a gentle curve towards a medium-width base that is flat on the inside and outside; the base-wall junction on the interior is a continuous curve. The rim is squared off and has a shallow internal bevel. The latter and the neck are decorated with twisted cord impressions. On the rim bevel these are arranged as arcs, while on the neck, framed by two horizontal lines top and bottom, there is a fringe of diagonal lines at the top; a row of C-shaped arcs along the centre; and a row of horizontal arcs at the bottom. The surfaces had been smoothed and slipped, but numerous lithic inclusions protrude. The exterior is medium brown with dark grey patches; the core, mid-grey, and the interior medium brown, becoming reddish-brown towards the base. There is a broad band of blackish encrustation running around the interior, extending in parts along the whole height of the wall but not covering the base. The lithic inclusions consist of subangular fragments of a fine-grained, speckled, slightly glittery micaceous variety of granodiorite, up to 8.5 × 6.5 and at a density of *c* 25–30%.

Pot 4 (Context 1124; illus 1.46)   Complete Collared/ Vase Urn, found inverted in a cylindrical pit close to the shaft grave and containing the cremated remains of a child, radiocarbon-dated to 3510 ± 35 BP, 1930–

1740 cal BC at 2σ (SUERC-23674). Complete, but has a horizontal crack around a fifth of the way up, probably running along a coil joint line. Dimensions: Ht 223; RD 195–198; max D (at bottom of neck) 237; BD 89; Th *c* 14 at rim bevel, 25 at base. Slightly squat bipartite vessel, comprising a collar-like neck, 75 tall and straight to slightly bulbous, kinking out at its bottom to a prominent cordon. The belly curves in, in a sinuous line, towards a flat, fairly narrow pedestalled base that is flat inside and out, its inner

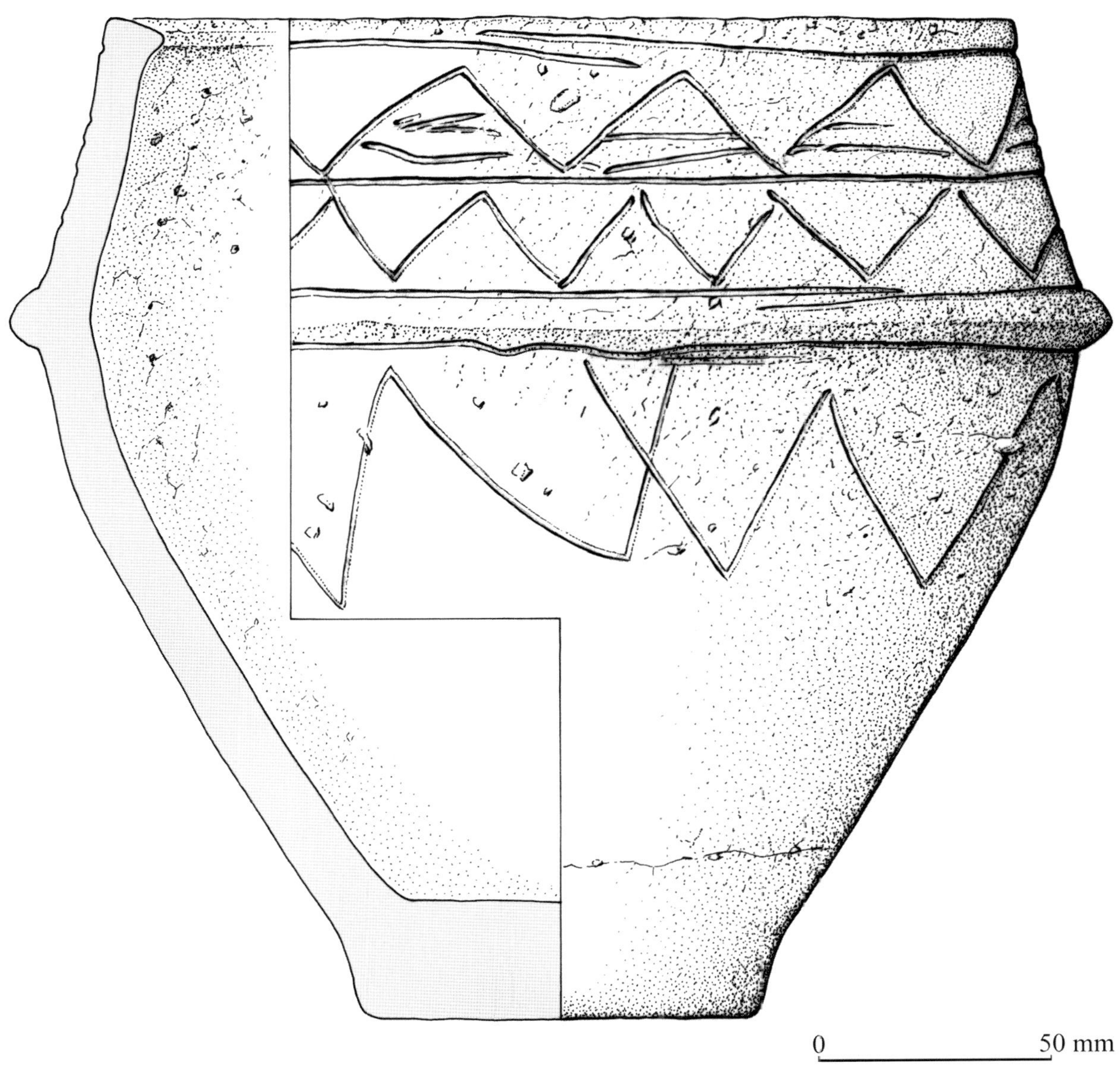

Illustration 1.46
Pot 4 from excavation in 2005–6

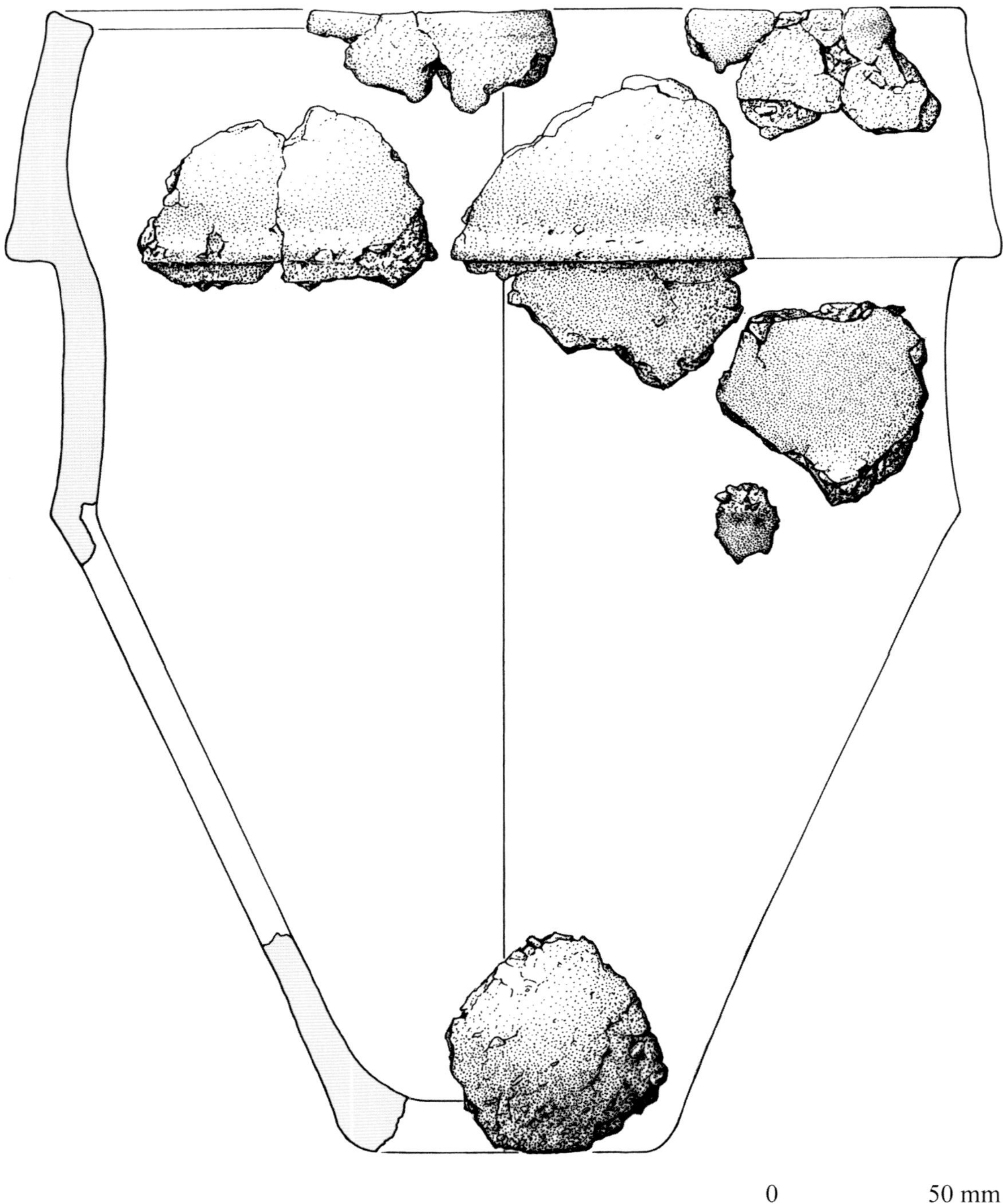

Illustration 1.47
Pot 5 from excavation in 2005–6

surface a continuous curve. The rim is squared off and expanded on the interior, and has a shallow internal bevel. The neck and upper belly are decorated with a fairly crudely executed design of incised lines, the lines up to 2mm wide. The neck has a panel featuring two rows of running chevrons, with single horizontal lines at the top and bottom framing them and with an untidy horizontal line separating them. At some points the two rows form a diamond design; elsewhere the points fail to meet. On the upper row, the lower triangles formed by the chevrons are filled by two horizontal lines. On the upper belly, below a single horizontal line running along the lower edge of the cordon, there is a deep running chevron design. Although the surfaces had been slipped inside and out, they are interrupted by protruding lithic inclusions. The exterior is mid-brown with patches of blackish, non-organic sediment. The core is obscured by sediment but is probably red-brown and dark grey. The interior is mid-brown, reddish and buff in places, and with mid-grey firing clouds. There is a tiny patch of possible organic residue on the interior at the base-wall junction. The inclusions comprise abundant angular and subangular fragments of black, and speckled black and white granodiorite, up to *c* 7.5 × 7.5, at an estimated density of 15–20%.

Pot 5 (mostly from pit Context 1022; illus 1.47)   Around ninety sherds, plus several fragments, constituting 10–15% of an undecorated Collared Urn. Most were found in pit 1022, beside the south-easterly stone socket, and it may well be that Dalrymple's workmen found the urn here and reburied it when it broke in pieces; the relatively slight degree of weathering of the fracture surfaces are consistent with such an interpretation. Dimensions: ERD *c* 270; max D (at bottom of collar) 290; EBD *c* 100; Th *c* 15 at neck, *c* 10 on belly; the urn may have been fairly tall. Tripartite, with a slightly bulbous, inward-sloping collar, at least 62 tall, that kinks out and overhangs at its base; a slightly concave, probably upright neck at least 50 tall, ending in a gentle carination; and a belly that may taper in a straight line to a narrow flat base. The base-wall junction on the interior is a continuous curve. The rim is slightly inturned, gently squared off, and has rounded, slightly expanded edges; it has a shallow, slightly dished internal bevel. The urn is undecorated. The surfaces had been carefully smoothed and coated with a thin slip, although some lithic inclusions protrude through the exterior, and rather more through the interior. Parts of the exterior

on the neck and belly have a low sheen, as though the pot's surface had been polished when leather-hard. The exterior is a reddish-brown, grading to a lighter reddish buff on the collar; the core is dark grey; and the interior varies from a mid grey to mid-brown and reddish-brown. There are small patches of blackish encrustation on the interior. The lithic inclusions consist of abundant angular fragments, up to 17 × 10.5, of the speckled variety of granodiorite as seen in Pot 4. One sherd from Pot 5 (SF 51) was subjected to organic residue analysis by Lucija Šoberl of Bristol University, using solvent extraction followed by gas chromatography, mass spectrometry and isotope ratio mass spectrometry. (A full report by Šoberl and Evershed is in the archive; the quotes below are taken from this report.) The sherd yielded an abundance of preserved organic compounds, with a lipid concentration of 68μg g^{-1}. The lipids confirmed the presence of degraded ruminant fat 'which could derive from meat or milk being prepared inside', although no compounds indicating cooking at over 300°C were detected, and experimental work is currently being undertaken to test whether the presence of such lipids could relate to the sealing of the pot's interior with milk upon firing. 'For the time being we have to interpret the results of lipid analysis from [this pot] with caution.'

Pot 6 (illus 1.48)   Two rimsherds plus around 50 body sherds, all undecorated, of an urn of indeterminate type. Most were found in the filling of the 1855 excavation just to the south of the north-western portal stone – the area that had previously produced the battle axehead (see below), Pot 9 and two un-urned deposits of cremated bone, according to Dalrymple. Whether Pot 6 had been associated with the battle axehead cannot be determined. The rimsherds are too small to

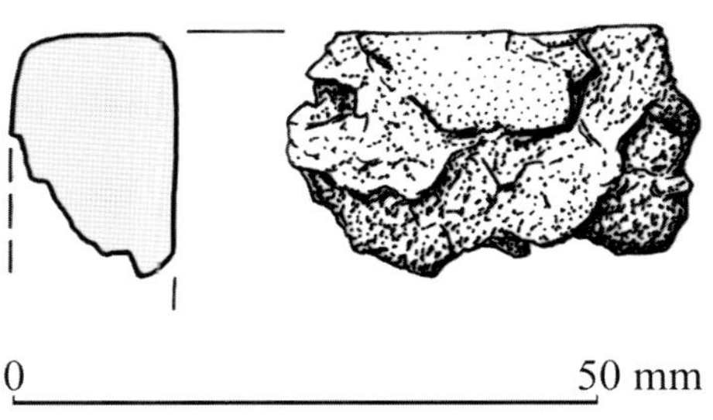

Illustration 1.48
Pot 6 from excavation in 2005–6

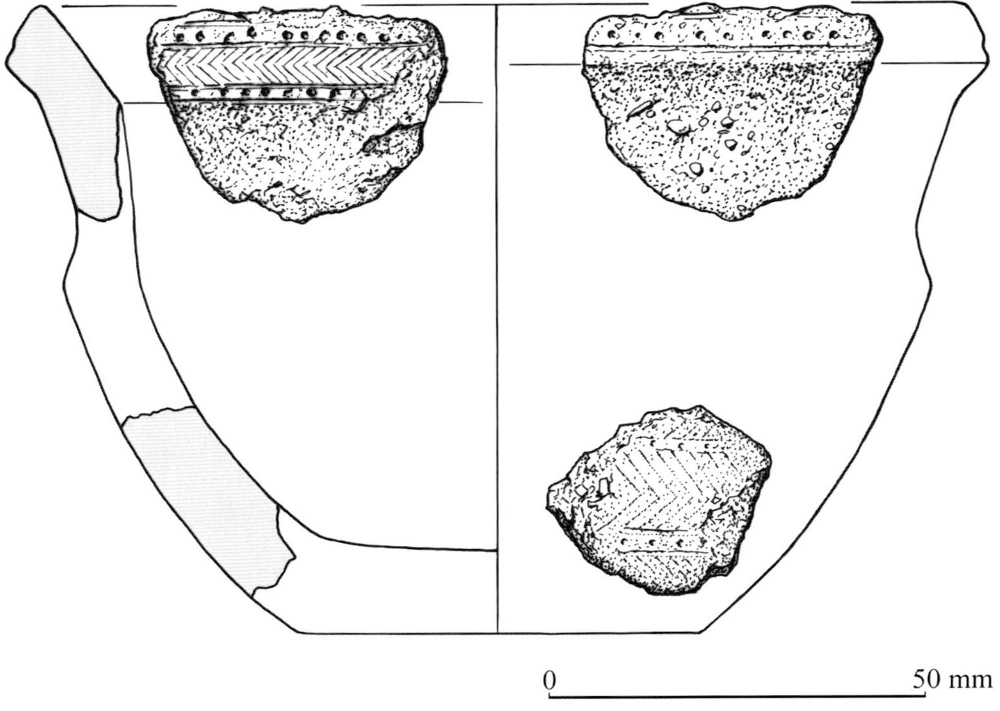

Illustration 1.49
Pot 8 from excavation in 2005–6

allow reliable estimation of the urn's diameter. Wall thickness is 13.5–14. The surfaces had been carefully smoothed and slipped, and parts (at least) of the exterior polished to a low sheen; some lithic inclusions protrude through the surfaces. The sherds are laminar, with a hackly fracture surface. The exterior is light brown and the core and interior are blackish. Patches of black organic encrustation are on the interior. Inclusions are angular and sub-angular fragments, up to *c* 21.5 × 9.5, of glittery, speckled, fine-grained black and white mica-rich granodiorite, at a density of 20–25%. One sherd from this pot was subjected to organic residue analysis, as described for Pot 5, by Lucija Šoberl. No organic compounds were detected.

Pot 7 (C1100, SF 201, not illustrated) Two conjoining (and now refitted) sherds from the tapering belly of an urn, found along with Pot 8 and a burnt pin fragment found in the filling of the 1855 excavation just to the south of the north-western portal stone. Th 16; E diameter at this point: 240. The sherd is small – only 38 × 35 – but it is clear, from its colour, texture and lithic inclusions, that it represents a different urn from the ones described above and below. The exterior and

interior surfaces are a light pink-orange brown and the core is salmon pink; the sherd had broken along a coil joint plane along its lower edge. The surfaces had been carefully smoothed, possibly by wet-smoothing. The fabric is fairly hard but heavily abraded, and lithic inclusions are sparse and small, with just one larger inclusion – a rounded fragment of a dark, slightly glittery stone, 5 × 3. The other inclusions comprise one piece of micaceous stone and several sub-angular fragments of a creamy mineral and a speckled whitish and dark mineral; all may have been present naturally in the clay.

It is impossible to determine the urn type from this small sherd.

Pot 8 (illus 1.49) Two sherds, from the rim and body of a burnt accessory vessel, found along with Pot 7 and the burnt pin fragment in the filling of the 1855 excavation just to the south of the north-western portal stone. ERD *c* 120; Th 7–12. The rim is slightly everted, with a deep straight internal bevel and a shallower external bevel; the overall profile cannot be determined, but it is likely to have had a flat base. The interior rim bevel is decorated with a

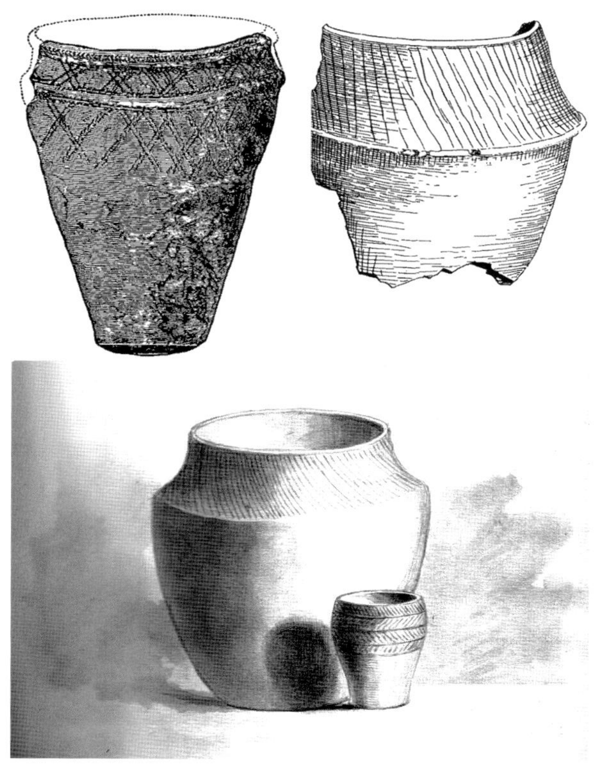

band of horizontal incised chevrons, framed top and bottom by single lines and by single rows of impressed dots beyond these. The exterior bevel has a row of similar impressed dots between two horizontal lines, and farther down the body two zones of horizontal chevrons are visible, framed once more by horizontal lines, and with a row of dot impressions between these lines. The surfaces had been fairly carefully smoothed. The exterior colour is partly obscured by burnt-on sandy sediment, but appears to be a pinkish-buff; the core is salmon pink and pale grey; and the interior is salmon pink on the body and pink-buff on the rim bevel. Inclusions are small (generally less than 2 × 2) and sparse (*c* 3%); they include a creamy mineral (?feldspar) and tiny mica platelets. See below for a discussion of comparanda.

Finds from Dalrymple's excavation
Pot 9 (NMS X.EP 1, plus four sherds from NMS X.EP 3: illus 1.50) Around two-thirds of an urn of Collared/

Vase type, found inverted, resting on a small flat stone and covered by a similar stone, just to the south of the north-westerly orthostat (position '3' in Dalrymple 1884, fig 1). Ht 238; RD *c* 220; max D (at bottom of neck) 230; BD 90; Th *c* 12.5. Slender bipartite vessel, slightly oval in plan, comprising a short, concave-walled neck/collar *c* 45mm high, terminating in a low cordon, and below this a body that tapers evenly to a fairly narrow flat base. The internal wall-base junction is a continuous curve. The rim, expanded at its inner and outer ends, has a straight, sloping bevel on its interior and a narrow vertical bevel on its exterior edge. These bevels, along with the neck and upper belly, are decorated with carefully made impressions of plaited cord; they are arranged in a criss-cross pattern on the neck and upper belly, with a pair of horizontal lines above and below on the neck. On the external rim bevel there is a band of narrow horizontal chevrons, framed above and below by a horizontal line, and on the interior rim bevel there are faint chevrons. The surfaces had been carefully smoothed and slipped on the exterior, and probably on the interior as well. The exterior is medium-brown, with a small patch of blackish-brown encrustation on the neck. The core is blackish-grey, and the interior is medium-brown and dark grey. The pot had been restored some considerable time ago, and this has both affected the interior colour and made it hard to detect whether there is a thin encrustation on the interior, as seems likely. The lithic inclusions consist of angular fragments, mostly small but some as large as 7.5 × 4.5, of blackish, glittery, fine-grained mica-rich granodiorite; some of the fragments have white speckles. The density is around 7–10%. One of the loose sherds in NMS X.EP 3 had broken along a coil joint line.

Pot 10 (Two sherds from NMS X.EP 3; not illustrated) Two sherds, from the tapering lower belly of an urn; their colour and texture indicate that they do not belong to any of the urns described above. The diameter at this point is *c* 200, and the wall Th, *c* 12.5. The surfaces had been carefully smoothed and probably coated with a thin slip on the interior and exterior. The exterior, and outer part of the core is light brown and slightly orange-brown; the rest of the core and the interior, black. There is a thin organic encrustation on the interior. The inclusions are of angular fragments of finer-grained black and white speckly granodiorite, up to 9.5 × 5, and at a density of 15–20%.

Illustration 1.51
Upper part of a collared urn apparently from the 1855 excavation at Broomend of Crichie. Photograph: NMS

Pot 11 (Two sherds from NMS X.EP 3; not illustrated)
One small sherd (26 × 23 × 12.5) plus a smaller, spalled sherd, from an urn with a greyish exterior. The larger of the two is decorated with diagonal incisions on its exterior. The surfaces had been carefully smoothed and the lithic inclusions comprise fine-grained, black and white speckled granodiorite, including one large fragment 14 × 7.5 in size. The decoration is very similar to that on NMS X.EA 137, the upper third of a collared urn that was acquired from Watt in 1865, a

decade after Dalrymple's excavations at Broomend of Crichie. It is registered in the Museum as having come from that site, and an illustration of it features in Coles' 1901 account of Dalrymple's excavation (as fig 31), in which it is stated that it came from beside the north-easterly orthostat (no 2 on his fig. 28). It matches the NMS X.EP 3 material not only in its decoration but also in its lithic inclusions. However, some uncertainty must remain over whether the urn had indeed come from Broomend of Crichie, as it bears a suspiciously close resemblance to an urn that had been found in at Tillybin, several kilometres away to the SSW, in 1834. By chance, a watercolour showing this urn and its associated accessory vessel recently came to light in an antiquarian notebook, and thanks to the kind offices of Iain Fraser of the RCAHMS, it is reproduced here as illus 1.50, beside a photograph (illus 1.51) and the line drawing of NMS X.EA 137. The resemblance is striking, and the estimated rim diameter of 9.5" (240mm) on the Tillybin illustration is close to the 200mm rim diameter of NMS X.EA 137. The Tillybin accessory vessel was acquired by the National Museum from the Watt Collection (NMS X.EE 27), so the urn may well have been in Watt's possession as well. It is possible that the provenance had accidentally been switched from Tillybin to Broomend of Crichie while the urn was in Watt's possession; alternatively, NMS X.EA 137 genuinely is from Broomend, and we are dealing with two virtually identical urns. The decorated sherd from NMS X.EP 3, acquired from Dalrymple (via the Earl of Kintore) in 1856, argues in favour of the latter. The question is unlikely to be resolved.

The 'Collared/Vase Urns' from Broomend of Crichie are of interest as they may form part of a regionally specific group of Early Bronze Age urns that do not fit comfortably within the traditional classification of either Vase Urns (also known as Food Vessel Urns) or Collared Urns, although they have features relatable to both design traditions – and indeed to some Cordoned Urns. It is for this reason that Cowie described Pot 9 as an 'atypical' Vase Urn (Cowie 1978, 103): it shares the generalised bipartite shape and the expanded bevelled rim form with Vase Urns, while its simple decorative scheme is more reminiscent of Collared Urns. Longworth chose not to include that pot in his *corpus* of Collared Urns (1984). The difficulty of pigeonholing these urns serves to remind us once more that urn design was not as rigidly constrained as the traditional typological scheme of 'Vase, Collared, Cordoned and Bucket Urn' suggests (Sheridan 2007b). The dates for the Broomend of Crichie urns suggest that they were made when Vase Urn design was dying out and when the Collared Urn design tradition had been adopted and locally adapted. Comparanda for the Broomend of Crichie Collared/Vase urns can be found within a 30km radius, at Seggiecrook (see below) and in the Haddo House Estates (NMS X.EA 191). As for the urn that fits more comfortably within the Collared Urn class, Pot 5, in terms of existing Collared Urn classificatory schemes, Pot 5 would fall within

Longworth's 'Secondary Series' (1984) and Burgess's 'Late' group (Burgess 1986). Comparanda include Grandtully, Logierait, Perth and Kinross (Longworth 1984, no 1997), whose associated cremated bones have been radiocarbon dated to 3580 ± 60 BP (GrA-21743, 2130–1750 cal BC at 2σ: Sheridan 2007b, 182).

Although represented by only two sherds, it is clear that the accessory vessel, Pot 8, is recognisable among the larger examples of this class of pot. A relatively local parallel is offered by the pot from Tillybin that accompanied the urn discussed above (illus 1.50); a more distant parallel is the burnt pot from Temple, Midlothian, found with a Collared Urn (Longworth 1984, urn no 1942). The fact that the Broomend of Crichie and Temple pots have been burnt suggests that they had been on the pyre. It has been suggested elsewhere (Sheridan 2007b) that accessory vessels may have been containers for the material (eg glowing embers) used to light the pyre, to be placed subsequently on the pyre.

Lithic artefacts

RICHARD BRADLEY

Illus 1.32 shows the distribution of lithic artefacts within the deposits disturbed in 1855. With one exception, they are confined to the area bounded by

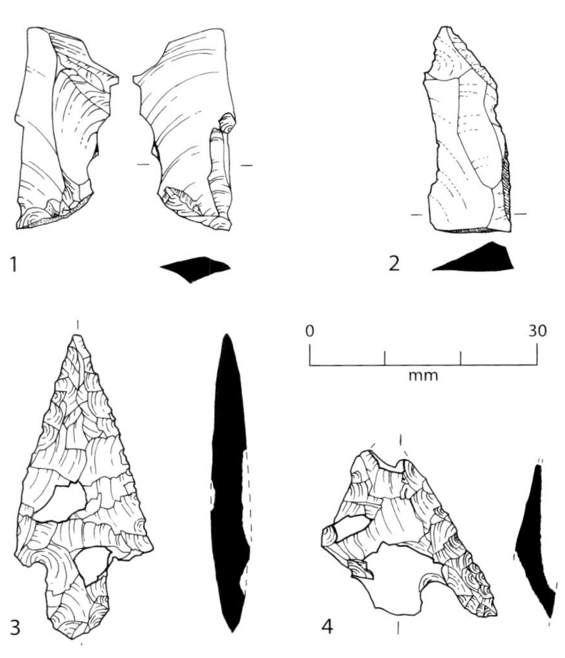

Illustration 1.52
Lithic artefacts from the excavation

Illustration 1.53
The stone battle axe from the 1855 excavation. Photograph: NMS

the setting of monoliths. A few more artefacts were scattered over the surface of the enclosure, but in this case their distribution is likely to be misleading. Three raw materials are represented: quartz, quartzite and flint.

The entire excavation produced two struck flakes of quartz and possibly three others, a tiny chip of the same material, and three irregular pieces from which flakes had been removed. There was one quartzite flake and possibly two others, a split quartzite pebble, and an irregular piece from which two flakes may have been detached. There is insufficient evidence to consider their date or technology.

There were also two narrow parallel-sided flakes (one of flint and one of chert), three other small flint flakes and two chips or spalls. The raw materials are similar to those represented among local surface finds in the collection of Inverurie Museum. Only the narrow flakes (illus 1.52, 1, 2) have any diagnostic characteristics as they were made by the same technology as the Early Neolithic artefacts recently published from Crathes (Murray, Murray & Fraser 2009, 101–2). It seems possibly that they are associated with the same phase of activity as the oldest group of radiocarbon dates from Broomend of Crichie.

Otherwise the only datable items are two flint arrowheads (illus 1.52, 3, 4) found in trenches originally excavated by Dalrymple. Both had been burnt and may originally have accompanied cremation burials. One (illus 1.52, 3) was found just beyond the western limit of the central shaft grave, but there is no evidence that it had originally been deposited in that feature. The other (illus 1.52, 4) was beside the western portal stone and may have accompanied one of the burials found there in the nineteenth century. Three candidates are mentioned in Dalrymple's report, one of them associated with a Vase Urn and another with a stone battle axe. Details of these artefacts are as follows.

Illus 1.52, 3: tanged flint arrowhead. It was originally worked on both surfaces but much of one face and small parts of the illustrated surface have been detached by spalling in a fire. The edges show clear evidence of serration. From Context 1125, an area disturbed by Dalrymple west of the central burial pit.

The size of this artefact allies it with Green's Sutton a type which is especially common in southern England. The evidence of serrated edges suggests a link which his Ballyclare type, but the arrowheads in this group are significantly larger than this example. The associations of both forms extend from the Beaker period into the full Early Bronze Age (Green 1980, chapter 6).

Illus 1.52, 4: fragmentary flint arrowhead, lacking its tip, one barb and the base of the tang. It was found in the filling of Dalrymple's excavation beside the western portal stone. It has been badly damaged by fire and one surface has flaked away almost completely. It is difficult to classify this artefact as the tang is incomplete, but its size and the form of the surviving barb link it to Green's Kilmarnock type which is particularly common in Scotland. This form has been found in association with Collared Urns, a Food Vessel and an Encrusted Urn and should date from the full Early Bronze Age (Green 1980, chapter 6). That would be consistent with the chronology of the other artefacts deposited close to the portal stone.

Stone battle axehead

ALISON SHERIDAN

NMS X.EP 2 (illus 1.53). From Dalrymple's excavations; found close to the foot of the north-western monolith (Dalrymple 1884, fig 1, stone 1, no 2). L 102; max W 76.5; Th 52; perforation diameter c 17 at its narrowest. Waisted, with a round, wide blunt blade, a narrower, rounded butt and a central shafthole that had been drilled from both sides. On the exterior, around each edge of the waisted area, are three incised grooves, each up to 1.5 wide. In the waisted area, around the perforation, there are facets on one side from its shaping, and on the other an abraded band, perhaps worn from contact with a haft. At the butt end are a few shallow batter-marks, suggesting that it may have seen some use. Its surface had been carefully smoothed but is naturally pocked. It is a bluish-grey colour, with a paler grey patch and a dark brown area on one side and larger brownish areas on the other. This variegation might reflect slight heat damage from its inclusion in the pyre, and the presence of hairline cracks plus a vertical crack across the narrowest part of the body on one side, with a corresponding crack around part of the body on the other, might be cited in support of this interpretation (although accidental post-excavation damage cannot be ruled out). If these characteristics do indeed indicate its exposure to fire, the relatively restricted extent of the damage could indicate that it dropped off the pyre at a fairly early stage. The rock type has been determined, through petrological thin-sectioning (ABN 149), as a metamorphic schistose rock containing andalusite, cordierite, muscovite, quartz and hornfels (Fenton 1983, 32), and it is typical of the local metamorphic schists (Simon Howard pers comm). It is likely that a river- or glacially-rounded cobble had been used.

The battle axehead is of a distinctive type which is named after this findspot (Roe's 'Crichie' group, in her 'Intermediate' series: Roe 1966). According to Malcolm Fenton's scheme (1983, 46–8, Appendix 1), it is a 'Northern Variant' with incised grooving. In Ireland, battle axeheads of this type are called 'Bann type' (Simpson 1990). This type of 'fancy' battle axehead would have taken longer to make than the 20–25 hours needed to make a less elaborate specimen; Fenton's experimental work has shown that incising a single line 130mm long and 0.5mm deep would have taken nearly an hour (Fenton 1984, 230). The object had clearly been a prestigious symbol of power

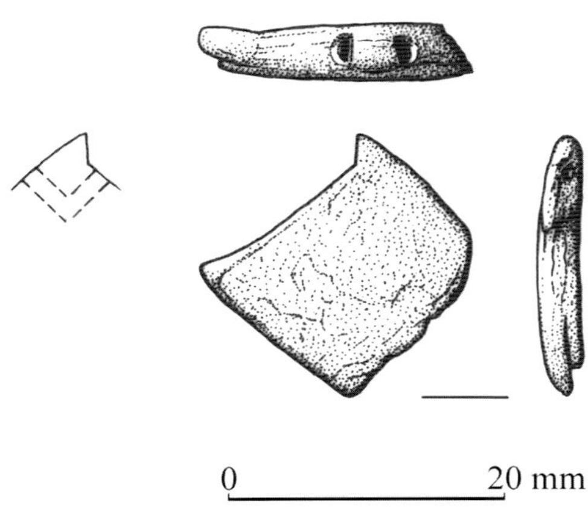

Illustration 1.54
Stone pendant from excavation in 2005–6

(Clarke *et al* 1985, cover, fig 4.10, 272). Two Scottish examples of this type – both associated with Collared Urns – have recently been radiocarbon dated as part of the National Museums' Scotland *Dating Cremated Bones Project*: one from Victoria Park, Glasgow, dates to 3435 ± 35 BP (1880–1640 cal BC at 2σ, GrA-24866) while one from Carwinning, North Ayrshire, has a virtually identical date of 3435 ± 45 BP (1880–1640 cal BC at 2σ, GrA-19421; Sheridan 2007, fig 14.10). These dates overlap at 1σ with those for the three dated urns from Broomend of Crichie.

Burnt stone pendant

ALISON SHERIDAN

Context 1075 (illus 1.54). Burnt fragment of a thin stone object with a V-perforation at one corner, probably a pendant. Found among the cremated bones of an adult, probably female, in Pot 2. It measures 16.2 × 14.6 × 3.3, and the perforations are slightly oval at their outer ends, one measuring 1.9 × 2.3, the other 1.9 × 2.6. One side – from which a large spall had broken away – is very slightly convex (and may have been the front), the other correspondingly concave, and the edges have been gently squared off. There are hints that the object had originally been diamond-shaped, and probably not much larger than its present form: two, possibly three of the original sides are present, and along one of these both ends kink out, suggesting that it had not been longer. The stone is dark grey and laminar, with whitish patches on its surfaces, caused by heat damage from the pyre;

it has been identified by Dr Simon Howard as a mudstone, and may well have been obtained locally, as fine-grained metamorphic rocks are associated with the local igneous rocks.

That this object is more likely to have been a pendant than a toggle fastener for a funerary garment is suggested firstly, by its lack of resemblance to the bone toggles that are known from Early Bronze Age deposits of cremated remains, and secondly, by the fact that a parallel – albeit not very close – is known from Seggiecrook, Kennethmont, just over 30km to the NW of Broomend of Crichie (Callander 1905, fig 1). Here, a small, subrectangular flat slate pendant around 37 × 23 in size, perforated at two of its corners along its long axis and with two incised lines running close to its edge, was found in a grave pit beneath the bottom of an urn. The latter, buried upright and full of cremated bone, resembles the Collared/Vase Urns from Broomend of Crichie, and a radiocarbon date of 3495 ± BP (GrA-19427, 1940–1690 cal BC at 2σ; Sheridan 2007b, 183) for its associated bone indicates it is contemporary with them. Both the Broomend of Crichie and the Seggiecrook pendants are very unusual within the canon of Early Bronze Age cinerary urn grave goods.

Bone pin fragment

ALISON SHERIDAN

Context 1100 (illus 1.55). Fragment from the shaft of a burnt bone pin, found along with sherds of

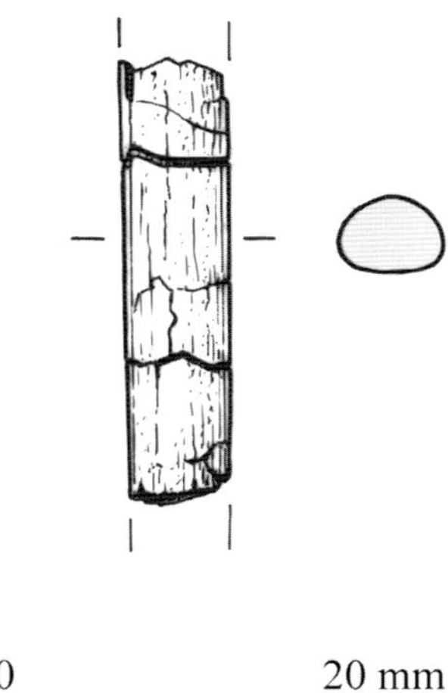

Illustration 1.55
Bone pin from the excavation in 2005–6

Pots 7 and 8 in Dalrymple's backfill beside the north-west portal stone; L 26.6, W 6.0–6.6; Th 5.0. The shaft tapers very slightly and is a rounded D-shape in cross section; the pin had probably originally been long and straight. Calcined; white in exposed subsurface, surface creamy-white and light grey, with hairline longitudinal cracks and deeper circumferential cracks. Made from a compact bone, probably a bovine long bone; it had probably been polished when new.

Pins such as this are not uncommon finds with deposits of Early Bronze Age cremated bone, mostly from urns, and the fact that they have been burnt indicates that they are likely to have been a fastener for a funerary garment. Alternative fasteners, also of bone, are toggles of various shapes; see Sheridan 2007, fig 14.11 for radiocarbon-dated examples of pins and toggles from Scotland.

Cremated bone

MARY LEWIS

Introduction

Three complete sets of cremated remains, excavated from urns in the laboratory, were analysed. In addition, material from come from a pit disturbed during Dalrymple's excavation. Context 1143 was a scattered cremation, and was examined to determine whether more than one individual was represented.

Methods

Initially, the assessment of the cremated remains aimed to establish if the remains were human or non-human, and the minimum number of individuals (MNI) in each urn. The skeletal assessment aimed at determining the age and sex of the remains, where preservation of the appropriate elements existed, and any manifestations of disease the individuals may have suffered. Additionally any information regarding the cremation techniques was collected.

Once it was established that the remains were human, they were sieved through a stack of sieves, with 9.5mm, 5mm and 1.5mm mesh sizes. The bone from each sieve was weighed and sorted into identifiable and non-identifiable bone. The identifiable bone was divided into five categories: skull, ribs and spine, upper limb, lower limb and unidentifiable long bone fragments. All identifiable groups of bone were then weighed and described in detail.

The expected weight of an individual cremation has been estimated to be on average 1625.9g, but can range between 1001.5g and 2422g (McKinley 1993). The extent of burning will dictate the level of fragmentation of the remains, and in most cases, the majority of bones are expected to have been collected from the funeral pyre (McKinley 1993). Gibson (1993) has suggested that the bones in Collared Urns rarely amount to a complete individual, and suggests that certain skeletal elements may have been lost due to excarnation prior to burning. The colour of the burned material can provide a guide to burning temperatures and may reveal information about cremation techniques (Mays 1998).

Results

FEATURE 1065: URNED CREMATION

The human remains weighed 490.64g, with 26% of the bone material identifiable to bone group. All of the bone groups were represented, suggesting a complete individual was placed in the urn. The weight of the urn contents is to be expected as it contained the remains of a young child. Dental development (Smith 1991) and the appearance of the coracoid process of the scapula (Scheuer & Black 2000) suggest the child was aged between 3–4 years. The bone was in good condition, with three different types of colouration. The majority of the material was creamy-brown, suggesting burning at temperatures under 300°C. However, fragments of scapula, first rib, humerus and ilium of the pelvis were coloured bright blue/white, indicating they had been exposed to much higher temperatures, up to 600°C. Some skull fragments were black. or charred, a feature that tends to occur when remains are burned at over 300°C.

FEATURE 1075: URNED CREMATION

The contents of this urn weighted 1635.73g, with 16% of the remains identifiable to bone group. The presence of the skull, teeth, torso, upper and lower body (including hard and feet) suggests that this was a complete cremation, with the majority of the elements collected after burning. There was no evidence of duplicate skeletal elements to suggest other human remains were included in the burial. Age and sex estimates were limited due to fragmentation, but the lack of evidence for joint disease associated with advancing age, and the fact that all of the teeth were completely developed, indicate a young adult. The small size of the remains, and the shape of the mandibular ramus, suggest a possible female.

The majority of the bone was creamy brown in colour, which indicates quite low pyre temperatures (under 300°C). However, the bones of the hands, feet and some rib shafts were blue-grey, suggesting that the some of the extremities reached temperatures of up to 600°C.

FEATURE 1123: URNED CREMATION

The contents of this urn weighed 1099.91g, with 40% of the remains identifiable to bone group. Skeletal elements from all areas of the skeleton were present, including bones of the hands and feet. It suggests careful collection of the majority of this individual after burning, although the presence of an additional child's right petrous portion and part of a right mandible suggest that some remains may have been collected from a previous cremation. The remains are those of a child. Examination of dental development (Smith 1991), and the morphology of the epiphyses (Scheuer & Black 2000) suggest that the child was between six and eight years of age when he or she died. There was no evidence of pathology.

As with the previous cremations, the majority of the bone was creamy-brown in colour, suggesting burning at low temperatures, however, the knee and some foot bones exhibited charring consistent with temperatures over 300°C, with the ribs and some hand bones being blue-grey. Once again, this suggests that, while the majority of the body burned under low temperatures, the extremities hit temperatures up to 600°C.

Above the urn in the filling of the pit was a small collection of charred human bone. This comprised skull fragments and a petrous portion of a child. The colour of the bones (brown-black) differed from those of the main burial, suggesting that these remains belonged to yet another child.

FEATURE 1022: CONTENTS OF DISTURBED PIT WITH SHERDS OF COLLARED URN?

Small Find 50 (48.29g) consisted of the cremated remains of a skull, long bones and one tooth root. Some of the remains belong to a juvenile, but it is not possible to be sure that all the material belongs to the same person. As with the other cremations, the creamy brown coloration suggests a low pyre temperature.

Small Find 60 (380.66g) appears to be the remains of an adult individual. Parts of the skull, upper and lower limb and hand and foot bones were present suggesting that this may have once been a compete cremation, but the weight confirms that much of the skeleton is now missing. All of the surviving material is creamy-brown. The remains were found with fragments of glass.

CONTEXT 1143: A CONCENTRATION OF BONE FROM THE FILLING OF DALRYMPLE'S EXCAVATION BESIDE THE WESTERN PORTAL STONE

The remains collected from Context 1143 were examined to identify whether the bones represented a single individual, or the amalgamation of a number of cremated burials. As with the other cremated material from this site, the remains were cream-brown in colour, suggesting that the remains were burnt to a low temperature.

The overall weight of the human remains (3821.65g) would suggest the presence of more than one person. McKinley (2000, 409) states that a maximum weight of 3000g has been recorded for undisturbed archaeological burials of single adults, and it is possible the material represents the bodies of only two people. The largest fragment was a long bone shaft of 76 mm, and the majority of the material (88%) was unidentifiable, with few joints or skull fragments to help with the identification of duplicated elements and to assist with estimating the Minimum Number of Individuals. The vast majority of material was adult, and no duplicate bones were observed. However, one fragment of pubic symphyses and a couple of carpal bones from the wrist (trapezoid and lunate) belonged to a non-adult, suggesting that this deposit had contained the remains of an adult and a child. The weight of the human bone is consistent with this theory.

Environmental evidence

Charcoal

KAREN WICKS

Despite the damage caused in 1855, three groups of charcoal samples were securely stratified.

The first came from underneath the bank in the northern entrance. The samples from the lower part of the buried soil were oak, hazel and alder. Those from its surface were hazel and heather.

Well stratified charcoal was also associated with the hollows left by the post of the timber circle. Here hazel predominated, with a smaller amount of beech.

Finally, charcoal was associated with the cremation burials excavated in 2005–6. Two were securely stratified and were interpreted as the remains of pyres introduced to the site together with the human bone. Details are as follows. A fuller version appears in the site archive.

The wood charcoal associated with the contents of Early Bronze Age urn in Context 1075 was dominated by Salicaceae (83%) ranking first in both frequency and weight. *Salix* (Willow) and *Populus* (Poplar) are genera that comprise the family Salicaceae. Their wood anatomies are very similar and as such are difficult (others would argue impossible) to differentiate on the basis of anatomy. In this study, wood charcoal with similar anatomical characteristics to *Salix* and *Populus* were recorded as Salicaceae and no further attempt to differentiate to genus was made. *Betula* sp. (Birch) was also recorded, ranking second in relative abundance by weight and frequency. Two species of *Betula* are native to north-east Scotland. Either *Betula pendula* (Silver birch) or *Betula pubescens* (Downy birch) could be represented in the wood charcoal assemblage as both taxa are anatomically indistinguishable. Wood charcoal overlying another Early Bronze Age urn in Context 1124 was also dominated by Salicaceae (67%), ranking first in relative abundance with respect to weight and frequency. Wood charcoal from *Betula* sp. was identified and recorded at slightly higher frequencies than Context 1075, again ranking second with respect to relative abundance by weight and frequency. Overall, species diversity is restricted to two taxa in the wood charcoal assemblage from Broomend of Crichie. Both Salicaceae and *Betula* sp. rank first in taxon ubiquity as both taxa are recorded in samples from each context described in this report.

The number of growth rings ranged from nine to seventeen (mean = 12 growth rings; standard deviation = 3.4) in samples of Salicaceae from Context 1075, providing an indication of the minimum number of years that the source plants were growing. Bark was preserved on one fragment of Salicaceae, marking the position of the terminal growth ring after a minimum of seventeen years of annual growth. Growth ring curvature ranged from moderately to weakly curved in the Salicaceae fragments, indicating that the wood probably originated from medium to large branches and/or trunk wood. Two growth rings with weak curvature were counted on the fragment of *Betula* sp. charcoal, representing a minimum of two years of growth in a medium to large branch or trunk.

The number of growth rings counted in samples of Salicaceae from Context 1124 ranged from four to fifteen years (mean = 11 growth rings; standard deviation = 4.7) and again exhibited weak to moderate curvature, probably derived from medium to large branches and/or trunk wood. Two fragments of Salicaceae also preserved evidence of hyphae, indicating that the assemblage derived, in part, from dead wood. Two fragments of *Betula* sp. with weakly to moderately curved growth rings indicate that medium to large branches and/or trunk wood with a minimum of six to seven years of growth were also incorporated in the charcoal assemblage.

Discussion

The results of the Broomend of Crichie wood charcoal analysis demonstrate that the cremation deposits are dominated by taxa from the Salicaceae family, deriving from species of *Salix* or *Populus*. The Broomend of Crichie wood charcoal assemblage provides a limited dataset with which to infer local habitat as the taxon diversity was restricted. Of particular palaeoecological interest is how the results of the wood charcoal identification compares with, and augments, the results of pollen analysis of buried soils at Broomend of Crichie (see p 71 below). Pollen analysis indicated a largely open environment at the time that the monument was constructed, with heathland habitats well established. Frequencies of *Salix, Populus* and *Betula* were low or absent from the pollen assemblages. Several explanations may account for the absence of these taxa in the pollen assemblages and their presence in the wood charcoal assemblage:

Pollen productivity and dispersal is relatively low for species of *Salix* that rely on insect pollination as a mechanism for sexual reproduction. As such, the spatial distribution and size of stands of *Salix* sp. in relation to sampling sites will affect the frequencies of *Salix* pollen recorded in pollen samples. *Salix* may have been present at Broomend of Crichie, perhaps growing as isolated stands in wet heath or along the river close to the site.

Preservation of *Populus* sp. in archaeological deposits is particularly poor due to the relatively thin exine (outer wall) of its pollen grain. Furthermore *Populus* pollen is readily corroded by aggressive chemical treatments during pollen sample preparation. As a consequence, pollen from *Populus* sp. is often under-represented in pollen diagrams. This taxon may have been growing perhaps as lone trees on drier ground surrounding the site.

Trees of *Betula* sp. are relatively prolific pollen producers with wide dispersal of pollen by wind. Low frequencies of *Betula* sp. pollen are an indication that rare isolated stands of *Betula* sp. may have been present in the surrounding environs or could represent a regional component of the pollen rain arriving at the site.

Some or all of the species described above were absent from the vicinity of Broomend of Crichie and wood was brought to the site specifically for use in cremation rituals, either as fuel or as artefacts (Campbell 2004, 30).

If the latter were true, one might expect superior wood types, such as *Quercus* (Oak), *Fraxinus* (Ash), *Prunus* (Cherry) and *Corylus* (Hazel) to have been incorporated in a wood charcoal assemblage associated with cremation rituals, such as has been found in other comparable deposits (Gale 1997, 82; Gale & Cutler 2000, 205; Campbell 2004, 270). In contrast, *Betula* and wood of Salicaceae are generally considered relatively poor fuels (Gale 1997, 82; Gale & Cutler 2000, 50, 236). Gale (1997, 270) argued that the selection of poor fuels for use in cremation rituals may be a reflection of the local availability of particular wood types and access to woodland, as appears to be the case at Broomend of Crichie. The pollen evidence indicates a lack of woodland cover prior to and during construction of the monument at Broomend of Crichie, while the use of Salicaceae and *Betula* sp. in Early Bronze Age cremation rituals at the site is perhaps an indication of their presence, albeit as insubstantial woodland in the surrounding environs. As such, an open heathland habitat, perhaps colonized by isolated trees of *Salix* sp, *Populus tremula, Betula* sp. and *Salix* sp. shrub stands, is envisaged.

The dominance of a single taxon in cremation pyres has been reported elsewhere and is often taken to indicate that one type of wood was deliberately chosen for the funeral pyre or that a single tree or shrub was burnt (Gale 1997; Thompson 1999; Campbell 2007). Furthermore, the selection of particular wood types for cremation pyres is often imbued with ritual or magical significance (Thompson 1999, 253; Campbell 2007, 30). Factors such as local availability of wood are considered to be of at least equal importance in terms of explaining the dominance of Salicaceae in the assemblage.

It has been reported elsewhere that charcoal found in association with cremation burials may have been hand-picked from the cremation pyre along with the skeletal remains selected for burial (Gale 1997, 82; Campbell 2007, 30). This suggestion is further substantiated by the absence of other taxa such as *Calluna vulgaris* (Common Heather). Other plant material such as twigs and grasses are likely

to have been used as kindling, along with timbers and large branches used as structural elements for the pyre (Campbell 2007, 30). *Calluna* burns rapidly, brightly and at high temperature, making it an ideal source of kindling (while being a meagre provider of sustained heat and light). This is because the stems of *Calluna* never grow much thicker than *c* 20mm, which causes it to burn quickly. However, its fast combustion provides a hot flame, allowing a rapid rise in temperature. It is ideal for use as kindling and would have been growing extensively in the surrounding environs and is likely to have formed an important component of the pyre. Its absence from the Broomend of Crichie wood charcoal assemblage suggests that perhaps one or two branches or pieces of trunk wood were removed from the pyre site for burial with the cremated bone.

Radiocarbon dates

Unidentifiable twig charcoal from Context 7 in the enclosure ditch:

Beta-2156 12   5200 ± 40   BP δ¹³C -24.7%
1σ cal BC 4040–3970   2σ cal BC 4060–3960

Unidentifiable twig charcoal from Context 7 in the enclosure ditch:

Beta-2156 13   4940 ± 40 BP   δ¹³C -24.3%
1σ cal BC 3760–3600   2σ cal BC 3790–3650

Charcoal of short-lived species, mainly hazel, from the base of buried soil under the bank in the northern entrance:

SUERC-13995 (GU 15255)   5239 ± 35 BP   δ¹³C −25.4%
1σ cal BC 4050–3970   2σ cal BC 4230–3960

Unidentifiable charcoal from the base of buried soil under the bank in the northern entrance:

SUERC-13990 (GU 15253)   5260 ± 35 BP   δ¹³C −25.2%
1σ cal BC 4230–3990   2σ cal BC 4230–3980

Charcoal of short-lived species, mainly alder, from the base of the buried soil under the bank in the northern entrance:

SUERC-13994 (GU 15254)   5000 ± 35 BP   δ¹³C −25.9%
1σ cal BC 3900–3700   2σ cal BC 3950–3690

Charcoal of short-lived species, mainly hazel, from the buried soil under the bank in the northern entrance. Stratified above GU 15253-5:

SUERC-13989 (GU 15252)   4910±35 BP   δ¹³C −28.3%
1σ cal BC 3710–3650   2σ cal BC 3770–3640

Unidentifiable charcoal, but from latest growth area. From the upper fill of Post-hole 1158 in the northern entrance:

SUERC-13996 (GU 15256)   3765±35 BP   δ¹³C −26.7%
1σ cal BC 2280–2130   2σ cal BC 2290–2040

Charcoal of short-lived species, mainly *calluna vulgaris*, from the surface of the buried soil beneath the bank in the northern entrance:

SUERC-13986 (GU 15249)   3665±35 BP   δ¹³C −25.0%
1σ cal BC 2140–1970   2σ cal BC 2140–1940

Charcoal of short-lived species, mainly *calluna*, from the surface of the buried soil beneath the bank in the northern entrance:

SUERC-13987 (GU 15250)   3625±35 BP   δ¹³C −25.3%
1σ cal BC 2035–1935   2σ cal BC 2130–1890

Charcoal of short-lived species, mainly *calluna*, from the surface of the buried soil beneath the bank in the northern entrance:

SUERC-13988 (GU 15251)   3520±35 BP   δ¹³C −00.0%
1σ cal BC 1900–1770   2σ cal BC 1940–1740

Cremated bone from urn in Context 1065:

SUERC-23673 (GU 18654)   3475±35 BP   δ¹³C −23.7%
1 σ cal BC 1880-1740   2σ cal BC 1890-1690

Cremated bone from urn in Context 1075:

SUERC-23675 (GU 18656)   3525±35 BP   δ¹³C −26.3
1σ cal BC 1910–1770   2σ cal BC 1950–1750

Cremated bone from urn in Context 1224:

SUERC-23674 (18655)   3510±35 BP   δ¹³C −23.3%
1σ cal BC 1890–1770   2σ cal BC 1930–1740

Beech charcoal from the bottom of Post-hole 2048 of the timber circle:

OxA-18252   3432±30 BP   δ¹³C −26.94
2σ cal BC 1871–1642 BC (1783–1662 BC at 76.1% probability)

Hazel charcoal from the weathering cone of Post-hole 2048 of the timber circle:

OxA-12851   3327±27 BP   δ¹³C -27.04
2σ cal BC 1694–1529

The dates fall into at least three groups. Those from the ditch are very similar to the dates from the base of the buried soil. They can be interpreted as residual material surviving from an episode of land use during the Early Neolithic period. Two of the samples from the surface of the buried soil overlap with the one sample from a post-hole in the entrance and may be associated with the removal of vegetation and the construction of the henge, for which a date between about 2150 and 1900 BC seems most likely. On the other hand, SUERC 13988 suggests a *terminus post quem* for the henge bank of 1940–1740 BC. That cannot be excluded, but the sample may have been intrusive and belongs to the same period as the three urned cremations found inside the enclosure. In turn, the timber circle outside the southern entrance was later in date than at least two of those burials.

Soil micromorphology

AMY POOLE & WENDY MATTHEWS

Introduction

Excavations in 2005 at Broomend of Crichie investigated an old land surface beneath the bank of the surviving earthworks and a section of the interior ditch. The results of this study will be discussed here in relation to previous investigations of earlier prehistoric monuments in the region, which have focused on investigating the environment and land-management prior to monument construction (Romans & Robertson 1975, 1983; Simpson & Davidson 2000), and, more recently, post-burial processes which may affect interpretations (Wilson 2000; Lancaster, Simpson & Davidson 2005). The excavations at Broomend of Crichie provide the opportunity to investigate how the site relates to the wider landscape prior to construction of the monument, through study of the buried soil below the earthwork, as well as post-depositional processes affecting preservation of materials at the site. Micromorphological investigation of the ditch sequence will examine post-construction questions on the period of use and abandonment of the monument.

This report begins by outlining specific questions relating to the bank and ditch sequences, and their wider significance. These questions are discussed in the context of previous micromorphological research at other Scottish monuments. The method of analysis is outlined in brief. Results from the bank and ditch are then summarised. These results are interpreted with regard to the life history of the buried surfaces, bank and ditch, and the results compared to the analysis of other old land surfaces beneath Neolithic and Bronze Age monuments in the east of Scotland.

Research questions

What information can be gained about the environment prior to construction of the monument?

Is there evidence for agricultural practices in this region prior to construction of the monument?

Is there any evidence to suggest a hiatus in agriculture practice prior to monument construction, as suggested at North Mains, Strathallan, Perthshire (Barclay 1983) and Balnuaran of Clava, Inverness (Simpson & Davidson 2000)?

How long was the earthwork actively in use? Was it constructed to mark a single event, or is there evidence that it was maintained over a longer period?

Research rationale

Current palaeoenvironmental evidence from north-east of Scotland indicates that birch, hazel and oak woodland was extensively cleared by the Early–Middle Bronze Age, with increasing evidence for agricultural activity (Tipping 1994; Edwards & Ralston 2003). Buried soils are often well preserved below earthworks and are a rich source of information on environment and past land-use throughout the United Kingdom (French & Lewis 2005). A number of Neolithic and Bronze Age buried soils from ritual sites in north-east Scotland have been examined using micromorphology, and are discussed below. Many of these monuments are situated on similar fluvioglacial parent materials, enabling comparison of soil properties and structure. The main focus of previous research and analyses was to determine previous land use and to investigate monument construction. The traces of land use that have been identified through micromorphology at these sites include clearance of vegetation by burning, cultivation, grazing/pasture, and truncation of the ground surface. Each of these traces has been identified using a range of different criteria. The evidence is not the same from one site to another and may be affected by a range of factors including climate, geology, soil type and post-depositional alterations. Importantly, the absence of evidence does not always mean that a process was not taking place.

The evidence and interpretations from each site previously investigated will be described in relation to the land-use process they represent. The processes are discussed in the chronological order in which they took place. For the purposes of this investigation 'clearance' represents the clearing of the land for monument construction, rather than the removal of trees and vegetation prior to cultivation, and hence discussion of this appears after the section discussing 'cultivation'.

Cultivation

The identification of cultivation using micromorphology is a much debated topic (Carter & Davidson 1998; Macphail 1998; Carter & Davidson 2000). Positive identification of past cultivation practices is currently reliant on field identification of large scale features such as lynchets, cultivation marks and soil horizon mixing, supported by micromorphology, pollen, phytoliths and biomarkers (Carter & Davidson 1998). Micromorphology has the benefit of being a multi-faceted approach in itself, a way of identifying organic matter, mineral components, pedological activity and sedimentary processes using a single method. It also lends itself well to integration with other disciplines (Canti 1995; Macphail & Cruise 2001) and in the interpretation of cultivation it contributes to a multi-disciplinary role as many markers for cultivation can be difficult to interpret in thin section. Debates focus on whether micromorphology can be used confidently to identify ancient arable agriculture; this technique is often best used in conjunction with other evidence (Carter & Davidson 1998; Macphail 1998; Carter & Davidson 2000). Soil type and geology have a major impact on what features are produced. Post-depositional alteration can have a considerable impact on what survives. It is important to note that on sites of abandoned cultivation given over to pasture, well developed textural features may be masked by later biological reworking (Wilson 2000). The debate is ongoing as to the role of micromorphology in the study of ancient agriculture (Carter & Davidson 2000). Micromorphology is increasingly being used to study experimental agriculture (Gebhardt 1995) and in reconstructing past landscapes in conjunction with other paleoenvironmental techniques (French & Lewis 2005).

Micromorphological evidence for identification of cultivation at Neolithic and Bronze Age sites in north-east Scotland has been interpreted on the basis of evidence for the mixing of horizons and the presence of clay coatings or oriented clays, from disturbance of the soil and translocation of fine materials. Buried soils below two sites, a barrow at Daladies, Angus and a burial mound at Fochabers, Morayshire both exhibited oak charcoal and oriented clays in their A horizons. This was interpreted as consistent with 'slash and burn' clearance of deciduous woodland followed by cultivation (Romans & Robertson 1975). The buried soil at Balnuaran of Clava (Simpson & Davidson 2000) included mixing of soil horizons and dusty clay coatings comparable to those seen at Strathallan and supported an interpretation of cultivation. Brown clay coatings in the buried soil at Fordhouse Barrow in Angus, could have been the result of cultivation exposing the soil to rainsplash, but the evidence was inconclusive. Cultivation ridges were uncovered beneath the henge bank of the Early Bronze Age mound at Strathallan, Perthshire during the excavation. These ridges were associated with a higher pH in the A horizon of the buried soil, possibly related to agricultural liming (Romans & Robertson 1983; Barclay 1983).

Abandonment

The free draining nature of the soils at these sites in north-east Scotland is likely to have led to the leaching of nutrients and a reduction in the quality of agricultural land, potentially leading to abandonment (Romans & Robertson 1975). The abandonment of cultivation in favour of grazing or pasture leads to the podzolisation of the soil, the creation of leached horizons and the formation of iron pans (Limbrey 1975).

At both Daladies and Fochabers the soil beneath the monuments is an acid brown forest soil, while those surrounding them are podzolized. This suggests that cultivation or land management was continuous until monument construction (Romans & Robertson 1975). At North Mains, Strathallan, a compacted A horizon was interpreted as evidence for grazing immediately prior to construction of the earthwork. An underlying well developed and undisturbed iron pan, and iron depletion pedofeatures suggest the beginnings of podzolisation and indicate the abandonment of cultivation some time before the monument's construction.

At Balnuaran of Clava a grey iron depleted mineral E horizon occurring below an organo-mineral A horizon containing depletion pedofeatures, is indicative of a well podzolized soil which had formed as a result of natural pedogenesis. Thus the land had not been maintained for some time before the monument's construction (Simpson & Davidson 2000).

At the sites where no conclusive evidence for cultivation was found, for instance at Fordhouse Barrow, Tomnaverie and Cothiemur Wood, the buried soils all show evidence of incipient podzolisation, suggesting that these areas were cleared of woodland, and then turned over to pasture or grazing prior to monument construction.

Clearance and ground preparation

A number of sites exhibit evidence for preparation of the ground prior to monument construction. At Balnuaran of Clava the presence of heated stones and trace charcoal in the uppermost horizon was interpreted as 'light burning' of the surface prior to

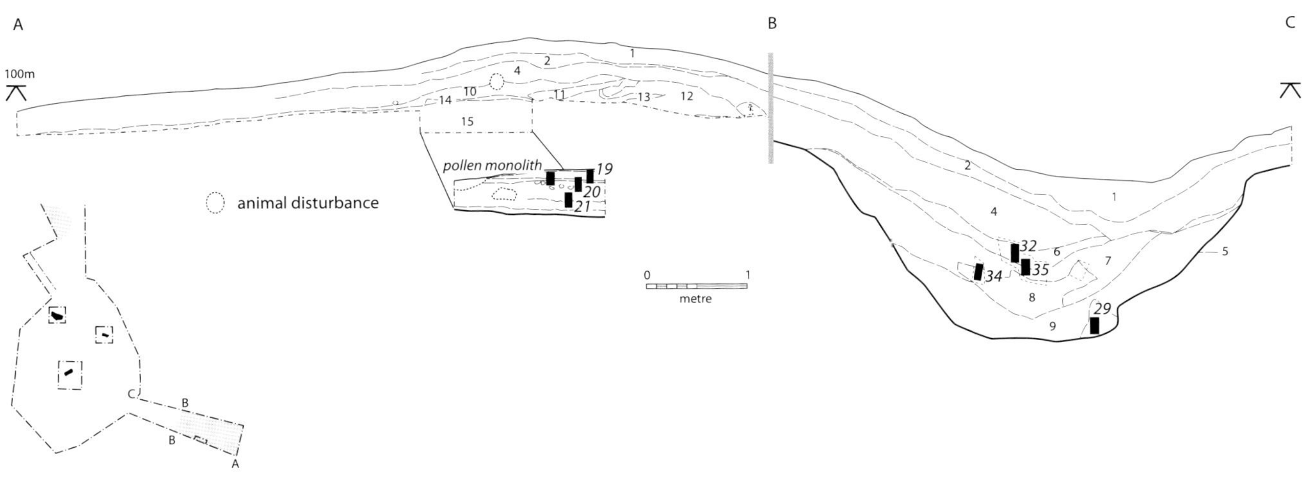

Illustration 1.56
The locations of the soil monoliths investigated

63

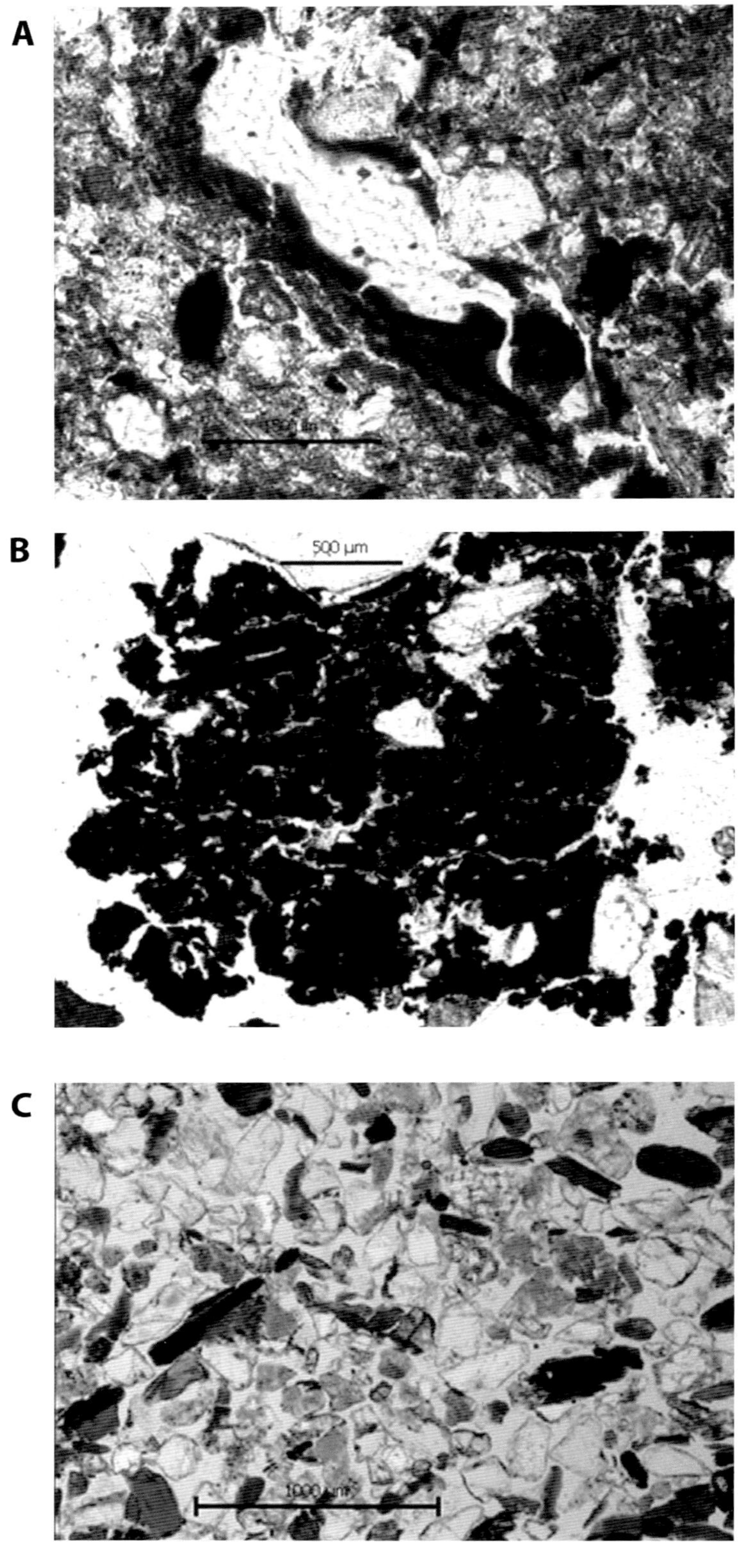

Illustration 1.57
Three thin sections of the buried soil at Broomend of Crichie. For details of these samples see the text

construction (Simpson & Davidson 2000). Evidence from the field and micromorphology at Tomnaverie suggest preparation of the ground by truncation and possible de-turfing. The mixing of dark brown and brown material suggested the remnants of an A horizon mixed with the B horizon. There was some evidence of disturbance, supported by the presence of matrix coatings (Lancaster *et al* 2005). At Cothiemuir Wood the sparsity of matrix coatings and the presence of charred plant tissue suggested that the surface vegetation had been cleared by burning (Lancaster *et al* 2005).

The investigations that have taken place on these sites provide a framework for the investigation of Broomend of Crichie.

Comparative examples and models for interpretation of the ditch fill are drawn from observations from the *Experimental Earthwork Project*; an earthwork constructed on chalk at Overton Down, Wiltshire in 1960, and an earthwork constructed on acid heathland at Wareham, Dorset in 1963 (Bell *et al* 1996). Explanations of the nature of the ditch collapse are also drawn from the work of Limbrey (1975).

Topography, geology and soil

The henge monument was sited on a gravel terrace along the edge of the River Don. The soils formed on these gravels of fluvio–glacial and morainic origin have a very coarse texture. The gravels consist mainly of granite, schist, gneiss and quartzite, and are rounded to sub-rounded from abrasion and water transport. The modern day soils at the site are of the Corby Series, a class of free draining iron podzol. The semi-natural vegetation is a dry heath community (Glentworth & Muir 1963).

Sampling and methodology

A total of seven undisturbed block samples for micro-morphological analysis were collected from two major sections through depositional sequences associated with the bank and the ditch (illus 1.55). In the area of the bank, three samples were selected from the buried soil profile and the overlying bank material (21, 20, 19). Four block samples were taken from the ditch (29, 32, 34, 35).

The micromorphology thin sections were prepared at the University of Reading. Moisture was removed from the samples by drying in an oven. The samples were then impregnated with resin under vacuum and cured before being cut, ground and precision lapped to 30μm (cf Courty *et al* 1989).

The thin sections were examined using a Leica DMEP polarising microscope, following the procedures of *The International Handbook for Thin Section Description* (Bullock *et al* 1985) and *Soils and Micromorphology in Archaeology* (Courty *et al* 1989). This allows for a systematic description of soil features such as minerals and components, microstructure and pedofeatures. A range of magnifications (×1–×400) and light sources (plane polarised, cross polarised and oblique incident) were used to obtain the description of each microstratigraphic unit, which are summarised in Table 1. The majority of rock and mineral assemblage encountered consisted of quartz, feldspar, quartzite, granitoid, schist and gneiss, and was consistent with the underlying geology of the area (Glentworth & Muir 1963). The overall particle size and percentage of each size class of mineral and rock has been recorded for each context. Three size categories have been used: 50–500μm which encompasses the very fine-medium sand sized grains, 500–2000μm which encompasses the coarse to very coarse sand sized grains, and >2000μm which encompasses the fine gravel size grains (Bullock *et al* 1985).

Results and interpretation

BURIED SOIL AND BANK SEQUENCE (ILLUS 1.56)

Slides 21, 20 and 19 represent the sequence of the buried soil and bank material making up the earthwork.

The buried soil horizon was marked by a thin layer of burnt material which was visible in the field. In thin section this horizon was 4mm thick. There was evidence for bioturbation in the form of channels with traces of roots and a small number of fungal sclerotia. The upper boundary between the burnt horizon and the base of the bank, however, was clear, and less reworked. The burnt material includes abundant charcoal and charred plant material (15–30%) in a lens 4mm thick, at the top of the soil profile, representing the pre-bank O horizon. Vertical cracks at and below this surface are evidence for shrinkage, and support the argument for *in-situ* burning (illus 1.56, A). This is most likely representative of light burning on the soil surface to clear vegetation. The soil itself exhibited no reddening as result of burning. Experiments into the effects of burning on soil by Canti and Linford (2000) indicate that reddening is not always the product of *in-situ* burning and is affected by many other factors including organic matter content, iron oxide content and water content. This burnt horizon appears to have been sealed by the bank very shortly after the burning occurred as the layer is well preserved, retaining an angular blocky structure, and showing no evidence of trampling or mixing, and bioturbation was limited once the substantial bank covered the ground surface.

The soil directly beneath the burnt horizon is light yellow brown in colour and appears to darken with depth. This could be interpreted as evidence for incipient podzolisation, although the soil mostly retains the appearance of an acid brown forest soil and there is no evidence for the formation of iron pans (Limbrey 1975). There is a continuation here of the vertical cracks observed in the burnt layer above. No translocated clay or iron coatings were observed in the buried soil that would be indicative of disturbance caused by cultivation. In the field, however, the buried soil was mixed with aggregates of the underlying paler yellow silty loam, and was interpreted as possibly disturbed and mixed by ploughing. This is potentially evidence of cultivation at some point prior to the earthwork's construction and is supported by the incipient nature of the podzolisation. The thin and compacted nature of the burnt A horizon could support an interpretation for grazing prior to monument construction, although the burning of this layer makes an assessment of the original thickness difficult. The A horizon of an acid brown soil is characteristically thin in nature, compared with that of a podzol or brown forest soil (Limbrey 1975).

The bank is constructed from unsorted, rounded to subrounded, medium sand and fine gravel, with no evidence of micro-layering or any orientation of coarse material in thin section. The mineral and rock assemblage in the bank is consistent with that of the local geology and is exposed in the sides and bottom of the ditch (slide 29), confirming that the bank was constructed from the gravels of fluvio-glacial and morainic origin into which the ditch had been cut. Sparse fragments of charcoal are also present. Bioturbation is evident in the form of channels reaching down into the buried soil and a small number of fungal sclerotia.

Slides 29, 32, 34 and 35 represent the ditch sequence containing three distinct episodes of infill.

The ditch was cut into the gravel terrace to a depth of almost 2m deep and was 5m wide. The gravel sequence exposed at the edge of the ditch comprises multiple layers of rounded fluvio-glacial

Pleistocene gravels of the Corby Association. These layers are not cemented and potentially unstable. The initial episode of infilling was a thin layer (5–8mm) of fine to medium sand. This layer represents finer material that was blown or washed into the base of the ditch, probably from the sides, immediately after construction (illus 1.56, B). Above this the infill is represented by a poorly sorted medium to coarse sand. This material was rapidly eroded or collapsed from the ditch sides. 20cm from the base of the ditch there were blocks of intact soil with turves, roughly 10×10cm in size, that closely resemble the buried soil profile below the earthwork. It suggests that these blocks may have eroded from the edge of the ditch. Erosion of the ditch sides is likely to have undermined the upper edges of the ditch, creating an overhang, which resulted in intact turves falling from the ditch edge, as independently observed at the experimental ditches and earthworks at Overton Down and Wareham (Bell 1996; fig 14.1–2, 234–5). In the ditch at Broomend of Crichie these blocks rest on top of the initial gravel infilling, and are covered by a second episode of infilling. The presence of these blocks at the same height within the ditch fill may indicate a period of stability within the ditch. The intact turf block is represented in thin-section 35 and is composed of a moderately sorted medium to very coarse sand and fine gravel. The block has a comparable soil structure and colour to the buried soil found under the bank. A low level of bioturbation is indicated by the presence of more recent cellulose plant remains in channels and fungal sclerotia. This may have occurred during the formation of the buried soil, rather than *in situ* in the ditch, as the same level of bioturbation is not evident in the surrounding fill.

The second phase of infill is made up of unsorted fine to coarse sand and a fine gravel, with little fine material, and is similar to the underlying ditch fill. In thin-section 34 the second infilling exhibits fine banding in the first 4cm. These could represent a series of in-washings from the exposed gravel terrace ditch sides brought down by rainfall, as the gravel bands also contain little fine material.

The top of the second major sequence of fill was sealed by a blackened organic layer 10cm thick with banded lenses of grey/brown aggregates. This layer marks a third phase in the history of the ditch, represented by a stabilisation of the ditch where the amount of humic material increased due to soil formation and the growth of vegetation; this interpretation is supported by the presence of desiccated plant remains. Coarse charcoal

Table 1
Broomend bank/buried soil sequence

	Thin Section No Unit No Deposit type Thickness (mm) Boundary (upper)	19 bank >100 not on slide	19 burnt horizon 4 abrupt/wavy	20 buried soil >110 sharp/wavy	21 subsoil >120 not on slide
Structure	Sorting	poor sorted sand in mod. sorted silt	unsorted	moderately sorted	moderately sorted sand and silt
	Microstructure	aggregate with cpv, planes and channels 30%	blocky partially accomodated with vughs & planes 20–30%	begins blocky becoming aggregates with cpv, planes and channels 30%	aggregate with cpv and planes 30%
	Coarse Material Orientation/Distribution	random/unreferred	random/unreferred	random/unreferred	random/unreferred
	c/f related distribution	intergrain aggregate	open intergrain aggregate/ embedded	intergrain aggregate	intergrain aggregate
Coarse Mineral >63μm	Overall Particle Size	medium sand and fine gravel	very fine to fine sand	fine to medium sand and fine gravel	fine to medium sand and fine gravel
	Overall Particle Shape	R–SR	R–SR	R–SR	R–SR
	Mineral/compound mineral % v.fine-medium sand 63–500μm coarse-v.coarse sand 500–2000μm fine gravel >2000μm	•••• •• •••	•••• ••	••• •••• •	•••• ••• ••
Fine mineral <63μm	PPL – Nature and Colour	organo-mineral/light yellowish brown	organic/very dark brown	organo-mineral/light yellow brown becoming light brown	organo-mineral/reddish brown
	XPL – Birefringence fabric and Colour	speckled/dark orange brown	undifferentiated/opaque	speckled/reddish brown	speckled/yellow brown
	OIL – Colour	yellow orange, some reddish orange and brownish orange	dark brown	yellow orange	yellow orange

Table 1
Broomend bank/buried soil sequence (*continued*)

		Thin Section No	19	19	20	21
		Unit No				
		Deposit type	bank	burnt horizon	buried soil	subsoil
		Thickness (mm)	>100	4	>110	>120
		Boundary (upper)	not on slide	abrupt/wavy	sharp/wavy	not on slide
Plant material		Charcoal	•	••	•	
		Charred plant fragments		•••		
		Fungal sklerotia	•	••	•	•
		Cellulose plant fragments				
		Desiccated plant remains				
		Phytoliths				
Pedofeatures		Amorphous organic (red)			•	
		Amorphous organic (yellow)	•			
		Amorphous organic (black)			•	
		Fe/Mn nodules	•		•	
		Clay intercalation (red)	•			
		Bioturbation	••	••	••	•
		Clay infillings/coatings				

PPL = plane polarised light, XPL = cross polarised light, OIL = oblique incient light, N/O = not observed

• = very few <5%, •• = few 5–15%, ••• = common 15–30%, •••• = frequent 30–50%, ••••• = dominant >50%

R = rounded, SR = sub-rounded, SA = sub-angular, A = angular

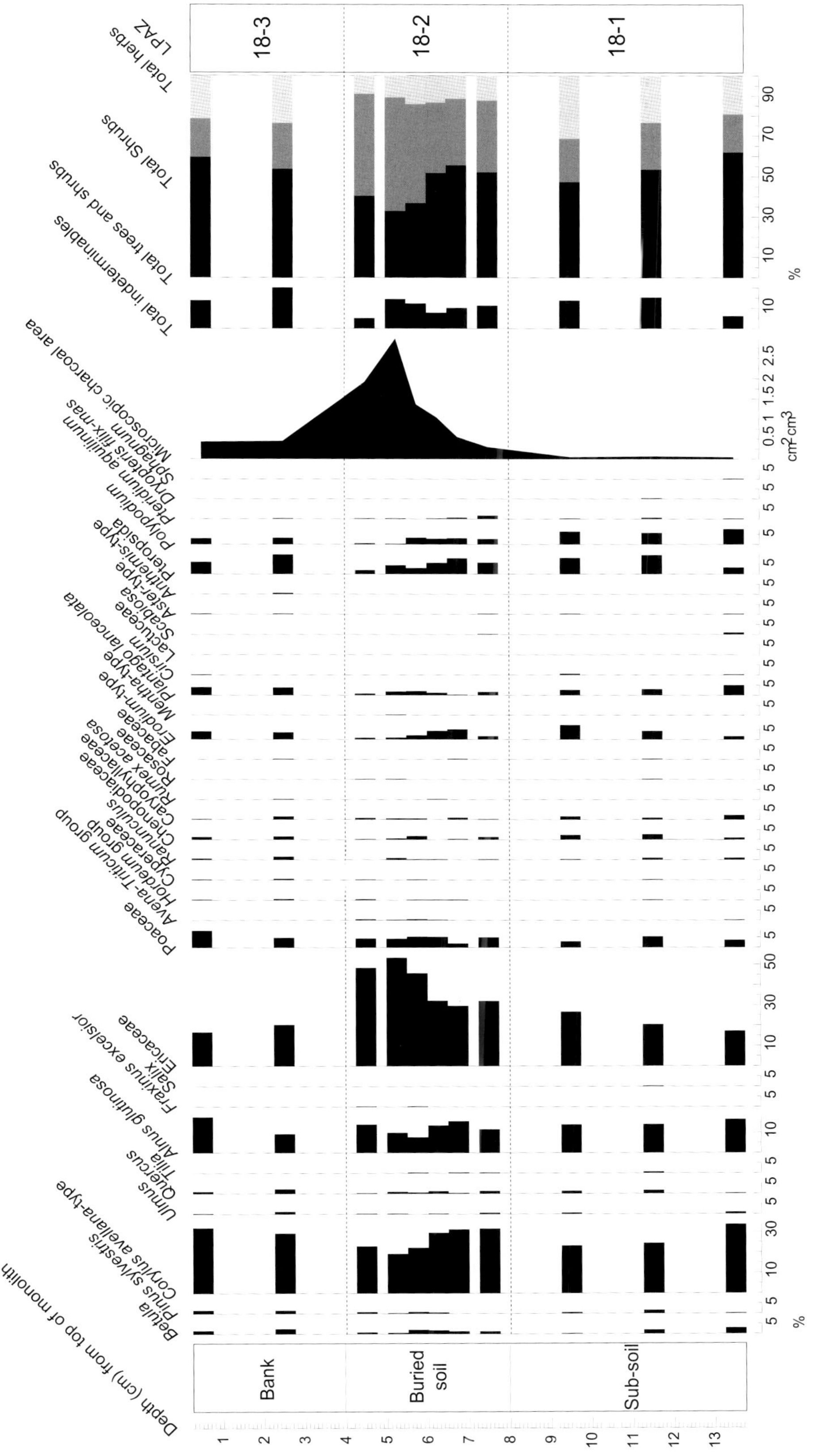

Illustration 1.58
Pollen from the buried soil and ditch at Broomend of Crichie

69

is present (0.5mm, 15–30%) and could represent burning within the monument or land management of the surrounding heathland after the monument's construction, although no other evidence exists to support this. The grey/brown lenses contained orange/yellow laminated clays infilling many of the channels and voids, and surrounding mineral grains (illus 1.56, C). This is evidence for disturbance in the subsequent layers. This observation supports the interpretation that the bank was demolished in the nineteenth century, the material being deposited into the ditch. This deposition rapidly created the fourth major fill sequence and caused the downward movement of clays.

Conclusion

The buried soil sequence provides some evidence to support an interpretation of past agriculture in the form of mixed horizons and an acid brown forest soil exhibiting incipient podzolisation. This is potentially indicative of cultivation for a continued period, not allowing the podzol to develop on the open landscape. The heavy leaching and loss of nutrients on the well drained parent material could have led to the abandonment of the land for cultivation. During this hiatus podzolisation began, and a heathland developed. The compacted A horizon is potential evidence for grazing, as seen at North Mains, although no soft iron pans were observed at Broomend of Crichie (Romans & Robertson 1975). The pollen evidence from the buried soil at Broomend also supports an interpretation of a pre-existing grazed and pastoral landscape that prevented regeneration of woodland. No other conclusive evidence exists in the micromorphology to support cultivation prior to construction. The pollen evidence supports an interpretation of a partially agricultural landscape (this volume pp 71–2).

This micromorphological interpretation of the environmental conditions at Broomend of Crichie is supported by pollen evidence for an open heathland with hazel scrub exhibiting probable evidence of anthropogenic manipulation by fire. The micromorphological evidence from Broomend of Crichie conforms to the broad pattern for northeast Scotland. Areas of woodland were cleared for cultivation. A hiatus in cultivation, perhaps due to drainage conditions leading to nutrient poor soil, was followed by a period of open grassland and grazing. The land was eventually cleared for monument construction, and the vegetation was removed by burning.

The ditch section showed three distinct phases of major infilling. The first phase of infilling was made up of the collapsing ditch sides as they were eroded and the ditch form stabilised, causing an overhang of the ditch edges and the eventual collapse into the ditch bottom of intact turves from the edge of the buried soil below the bank at the top of the ditch. The second infilling represented a slower accumulation of windblown material and material from the unstable bank, which covered the turf blocks and then stabilised, with soil formation and vegetation cover (Limbrey 1975). This was eventually followed by a fourth fill, interpreted as the deliberate destruction of the monument bank in the nineteenth century. This rapid infill of the ditch caused disturbance which led to the movement of fine material down the profile, creating the clay coatings and infilling in the channels and voids of the second fill.

The ditch was not obviously maintained after the initial construction period and most likely began to collapse and stabilise over a period of 20–50 years, on the basis of comparisons with experimental earthworks (Bell 1996, fig 14.1–2, 234–5). In the early Victorian period the bank may have been demolished and its remains deposited in the surrounding ditch.

Pollen analysis (illus 1.57)

ALEX BROWN

Introduction

Sections through the buried soil, bank and ditch were sampled for pollen and microscopic charcoal analysis. An initial assessment indicated that pollen was preserved in all but the primary fills of the ditch and was best preserved within the buried soil. It is very likely pollen within the ditch is mixed as parts of the bank, including intact turves from the original land surface, had collapsed into the ditch soon after it had been cut. Consequently, detailed analysis was undertaken only on the buried soil (monolith 18) where disturbance was minimal. The results of analysis help place the monument in a broader environmental and landscape context. Key aims of analysis were concerned with establishing the long-term land-use history of the site. Two specific questions are considered: (i) is there evidence for substantial vegetation change prior to the construction of the henge, and (ii) was the site situated within an agricultural landscape?

Method

Samples for pollen analysis *c* 1cm³ in volume were taken at intervals of 0.5–2cm from monolith 18. Two *Lycopodium* tablets were added to enable calculation of pollen concentrations. Samples were prepared following standard laboratory techniques (Moore *et al* 1991) and mounted in glycerol jelly stained with safranin. A minimum of 300 pollen of terrestrial species were counted for each level. Pollen percentages are calculated based on terrestrial plants. Ferns spores and *Sphagnum* are calculated as a percentage of terrestrial pollen plus the sum of the component taxa within the respective category. Identification of cereal pollen followed the criteria of Andersen (1979). Indeterminable grains were recorded according to Cushing (1967). The pollen diagram was produced using Psimpoll version 4.10 (Bennett 2002). Pollen zonation was achieved in Psimpoll based upon a comparison of binary splitting by sum of squares, optimal splitting by sum of squares and constrained cluster analysis (CONISS). Microscopic charcoal was quantified using the point count method of Clark (1982).

Results

Pollen and microscopic charcoal data from monolith 18 are described in the context of three local pollen assemblage zones. All depths are from the top of the monolith tin.

Buried soil sequence (monolith 18)

Zone 18–1 (14–8cm). High values for pollen of *Corylus avellana*-type (hazel), *Alnus glutinosa* (alder) and Ericaceae (heaths) suggest a environment of hazel-scrub and heathland, with alder growing on wetter soils. Arable and disturbed ground are suggested by occasional cereal-type pollen grains together with *Plantago lanceolata* (ribwort plantain), Chenopodiaceae (goosefoots) and *Erodium*-type (stork's-bill).

Zone 18–2 (8–4cm). This zone covers the buried soil, characterised by an increase from 6cm in Ericaceae and a decrease in *Corylus avellana*–type, associated with a significant increase in microscopic charcoal. The buried soil also contains significant quantities of macroscopic charcoal, suggesting burning of the surrounding environment favouring the expansion of heathland taxa. Local cultivation of cereals is suggested by the presence of cereal-type pollen grains of the *Avena-Triticum* group along with a range of herbaceous taxa characteristic of arable, grazed and/or

disturbed ground (*Plantago lanceolata*, Chenopodiaceae, *Ranunculus*).

Zone 18–3 (4–0cm). This zone corresponds to the henge bank that seals the buried soil. The bank will include a mixture of sediment and pollen from multiple contexts excavated during the construction of the ditch. The close similarity in pollen assemblage between zones 18-2 and 18-3 would support the hypothesis that the bank includes a predominantly mixed pollen assemblage redeposited from the buried soil and sub-soil deposits.

Ditch sequence

Five monoliths were taken from the ditch sequence for pollen analysis (monoliths 29–31, 34 and 36). Monoliths 29 and 34 cover the primary fill of the ditch. Monoliths 30, 31 and 36 were taken from bank deposits that collapsed into the ditch soon after the construction of the henge. Pollen in monoliths 30, 31 and 36 was uniformly poorly preserved and very likely substantially mixed. No further analysis was undertaken. A single sample from monolith 29 (sandy-gravel primary fill) produced no identifiable pollen. Of two samples taken from monolith 34, only one produced pollen (sample 34.1, 1–2cm).

The primary fill may include a substantial reworked pollen component, including sediments eroded and redeposited into the ditch. Reworked pollen will be mixed with a contemporaneous pollen component that, given the limited catchment of ditches, will most probably represent the local vegetation conditions immediately following the construction of the henge.

Sample 34.1 is dominated by *Corylus avellana*-type, *Alnus glutinosa* and Poaceae with low values for Ericaceae pollen compared to all other samples. The low values for Ericaceae could suggest that heathland plants had been largely cleared from around henge. Values for *Alnus glutinosa* and *Corylus avellana*-type are broadly similar in both the primary fill and top of the buried soil. Values for Poaceae and fern spores, however, are significantly higher in the primary fill, perhaps reflecting grasses and ferns growing within the ditch.

Discussion

The pollen data suggest that the vegetation environment prior to monument construction was largely open, dominated by a mix of hazel scrub and heathland with alder more frequent on wetter soils. Small quantities of cereal-type pollen imply that the monument was constructed in an at least partially agricultural landscape, with evidence also for pastoral and grazed land. Microscopic charcoal and pollen indicative of heathland increase towards the top of the buried soil, suggesting probable anthropogenic manipulation of the surrounding vegetation prior to monument construction. Heaths develop in areas cleared of woodland and are maintained through grazing pressure and burning. The microscopic charcoal and pollen data is strong evidence, therefore, for the potential management of surrounding heathland through the application of fire. The high values for Ericaceae pollen also imply sustained grazing, most probably as a result of the activities of both domesticated and wild animals.

The surrounding region is devoid of well-dated comparative pollen sequences (Tipping 1994, fig 2). However, the wider palaeoenvironmental picture from north-east Scotland suggests that woodland, dominated by birch, hazel and oak, was extensively cleared by the second millennium BC (Tipping 1994; Edwards & Ralston 2003). Correspondingly, evidence for agricultural activities increases, with a higher proportion of pollen indicative of cereal cultivation, pastureland and heathland. The pollen evidence from Broomend of Crichie conforms to this broad pattern.

Chapter 2

THE HENGE MONUMENT AT BROOMEND OF CRICHIE IN ITS LOCAL SETTING

RICHARD BRADLEY & AMANDA CLARKE

Introduction

This chapter has three objectives. The first is to synthesise the information from the recent excavation at Broomend of Crichie and to relate it to the nineteenth-century discoveries on the site. A second aim is to consider how the different structures on the gravel terrace were related to one another. As part of that discussion it revisits Ritchie's important study published in 1920. The third builds on both these themes to suggest how the monument complex developed and how it might have been used. Its relationship to other sites in Scotland and beyond is considered in Chapter 3.

The chapter is in four parts. The first considers the sequence of excavated structures at Broomend of Crichie and their dating. The second investigates their relationship to the features known from documentary sources and museum collections. A third section considers the development of the monument complex at a series of different time scales, while the fourth puts forward a new interpretation of the henge.

Establishing a sequence

Chronological relationships

There are only a few fixed points in the archaeology of Broomend of Crichie, but they are of vital importance for this account. There are the stratigraphic observations made during the excavation of the henge, and there is the chronological information provided by radiocarbon dating.

Two key points were established by excavation. The first is that one of the recut post-holes in the northern entrance was sealed by sediments eroding from the terminal of the bank. Either the post was related to the monument or it belonged to an earlier phase. A second observation is that one of the burial pits containing an urned cremation cut through the filling of the socket for the south-western monolith. In the same way, the central pillar must have been erected after the shaft grave had been refilled. No physical evidence of this relationship remained by

the time of Dalrymple's excavation, but Skene's illustration is unambiguous.

Within the limits of the technique, radiocarbon dating supplies other fixed points. There was activity of some kind during the early part of the Neolithic period, after which there may have been a hiatus of over a thousand years although the gravel terrace could have been cultivated and grazed. Activity really resumed in the second half of the third millennium BC. It is clear that the Beaker cists at the southern end of the gravel terrace were significantly earlier than the henge. The interval could have been several hundred years (Sheridan 2007a, 109, 110). At the same time there is evidence for the burning of vegetation before the enclosure bank was built. This activity seems to have taken place in between the use of the cist cemetery and the creation of the henge.

The samples from under the bank at the northern entrance provide only a *terminus post quem* for the construction of the enclosure, but it probably happened before the burials excavated in 2005–6 were deposited. There is also some evidence that the construction and use of the timber circle took place after the building of the earthwork. It seems have occurred as the use of the henge as a cemetery was coming to an end. That would be consistent with another line of argument. There is no direct dating for the battle axe found by Dalrymple beside the western portal stone, but artefacts of this distinctive form have a restricted currency in Scotland and those from secure contexts have radiocarbon dates between about 1850 and 1650 BC (Sheridan 2007b, 185).

It is harder to establish the date of the shaft grave which could not be re-excavated in 2005–6, but there are good reasons for attributing it to the same phase as the avenue, which changes direction at the position of the grave. It may have done so because it had already been excavated but there is no way of knowing this. What is clear is that a few sherds of a Beaker pot were found on the lip of this feature, and that all the finds of this character were confined to the area defined by the setting of monoliths. In fact two pieces of the same Beaker vessel were in the disturbed filling of a stone socket and another was in the top of the re-excavated shaft grave together with what was probably a cist slab. As Alison Sheridan has argued (p 46), they may be contemporary with the intact vessels found in the cist cemetery during the nineteenth century. In each case the cists were of similar proportions and construction; the same applies to the undated example beside the avenue at Allanshaw. David Clarke records that Beaker burials are associated with a number of shaft graves in Britain, not all of them covered by mounds, although he defines these features as pits over a metre deep (Clarke 1970, 452–3). One example which was nearly twice that depth was found at Nether Criggie not far south of Aberdeen (Kirk & McKenzie 1955, 1–6). It was associated with two Beakers and has a radiocarbon date at 2σ of 2280–2030 BC (OxA-V-2166-46; Alison Sheridan pers comm). A more striking comparison is with the shaft grave found by Canon Greenwell under Rudston Barrow 62 on the Yorkshire Wolds. It was of a similar depth to that at Broomend of Crichie and had two cists at the bottom. Again it was associated with Beaker vessels. Other features are shared by these two sites: the deposition of inhumations and cremation burials together in the primary phase; a thick deposit of rubble in the filling of the pits; and the presence of a layer of charcoal towards the surface (illus 2.1; Greenwell 1877, 234–45; Manby 1967; Pacitto 1972).

On the basis of these arguments a possible chronology would be as follows. The estimates are to the nearest 50 years:

4200–3650 BC	Neolithic activity on or close to the site of the later henge
3600–2400 BC	Intermittent grazing and possibly cultivation on the gravel terrace
2450–2150 BC	Establishment of a cist cemetery towards the southern end of the gravel terrace
2450–2150 BC	*Estimated* date for the central shaft grave
2150–1900 BC	Most likely *terminus post quem* for the construction of the henge bank; otherwise 1950–1750 BC
1950–1700 BC	Cremation burials inside the henge monument
1850–1650 BC	*Estimated* date for the battle axe deposited beside the northern portal stone
1850–1650 BC	*Terminus post quem* for the timber circle
1650–1500 BC	*Terminus ante quem* for the timber circle

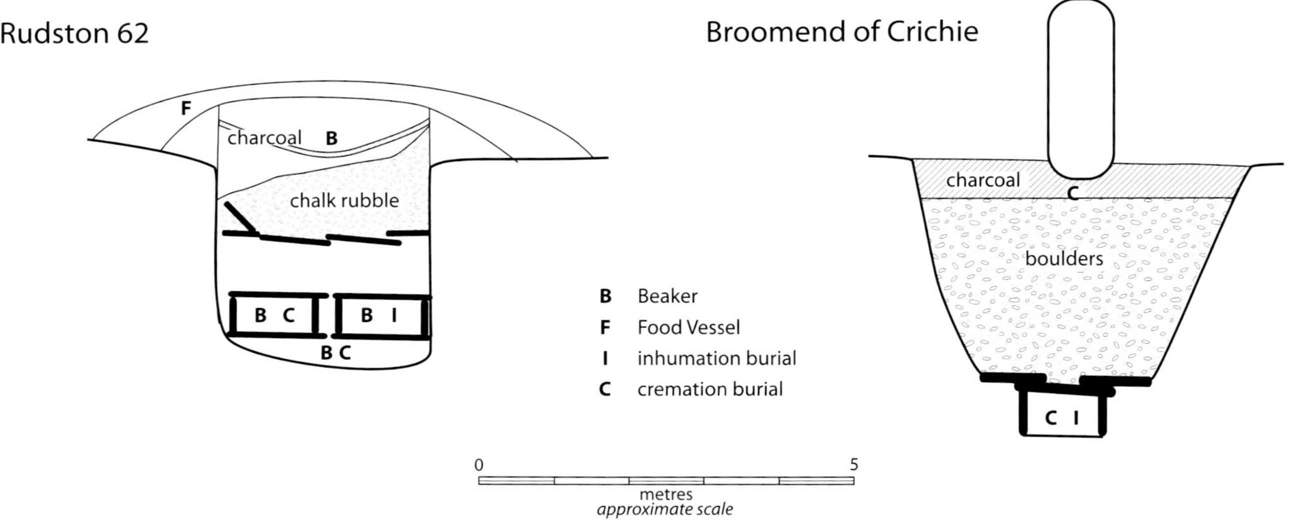

Illustration 2.1

Reconstructed section of the shaft grave at Broomend of Crichie based on the written account by Dalrymple 1884 plus his schematic section drawing. This is compared with the shaft grave at Rudston Barrow 62, based on the published account by Greenwell 1877, as interpreted by Manby (1967). The dimensions of the Rudston grave have been modified in the light of the excavation reported by Pacitto (1972). In each case there are discrepancies between the exact dimensions provided in different sources, and the scale on this drawing must be regarded as approximate.

Illustration 2.2
The monument complex at Broomend of Crichie showing the avenue and secondary burials referred to in the text. Air photograph by Moira Grieg, Aberdeenshire Council

Spatial relationships (illus 2.2)

Other interpretations can be based on the spatial relationships between different components of the monument complex. Here Ritchie's interpretation has been extremely helpful.

The avenue, the portal stones, the shaft grave and the earthwork

The course is of the avenue is of particular importance. To the north of the henge Ritchie (1920) reconstructed its position using two kinds of information (illus 2.3). The first was Maitland's statement that an avenue of paired monoliths ran between the henge monument and a stone circle which was later destroyed by quarrying. The second was a map made in 1780 which suggested that this monument had been about 50m NNE of the henge. If so, it would mean that the avenue followed a slightly different alignment from the southern section

that still survives. Ritchie drew attention to the dimensions of the northern stone circle as they were recorded in the eighteenth century. There was only one part of the quarry where such a large structure could have been removed in its entirety. It was on that basis that he estimated the position of the northern avenue. These details are important, for a stone socket and a row of three post-holes were found in 2006 on precisely the course he had suggested. There is no way of taking the argument further, for the remaining area north of the henge has been disturbed.

As Coles noted in 1901, the eastern portal stone is not in line with the northern entrance of the henge. On the other hand, it is aligned on the newly discovered stone socket, on the post-holes outside the monument, and also on the most likely position of the lost stone circle. To the south it is in line with two of the surviving components of the avenue as well as the stone socket excavated in 2007. It seems possible

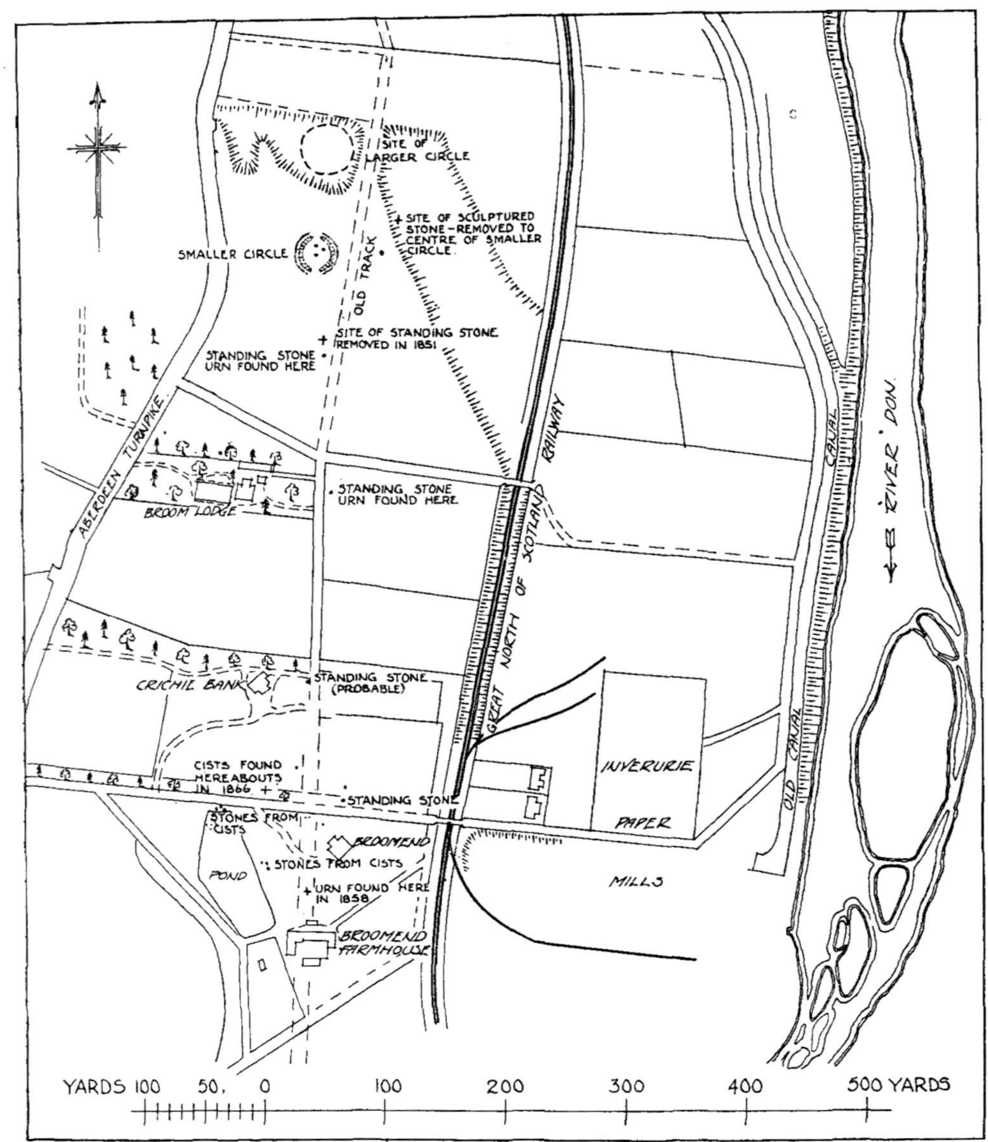

Illustration 2.3
James Ritchie's reconstruction of the Broomend of Crichie complex published in 1920

that they were all components of the eastern row of monoliths (illus 2.4).

If the eastern portal stone was originally part of the avenue, it would explain why the monolith is poorly aligned with the entrance of the earthwork. It could have been an earlier structure. One of the other monoliths inside the enclosure may also predate the henge, for it had been set in the ground with the aid of a ramp and had obviously been manoeuvred into position from the south. That would not have been possible if the ditch was already there.

This idea has significant implications, for the arc of standing stones conformed to the layout of the enclosure. It was laid out symmetrically around the southern perimeter of the henge and followed the edge of the shaft grave. In turn that feature was located in the centre of the monument midway between its entrances. If the stone setting was built before the

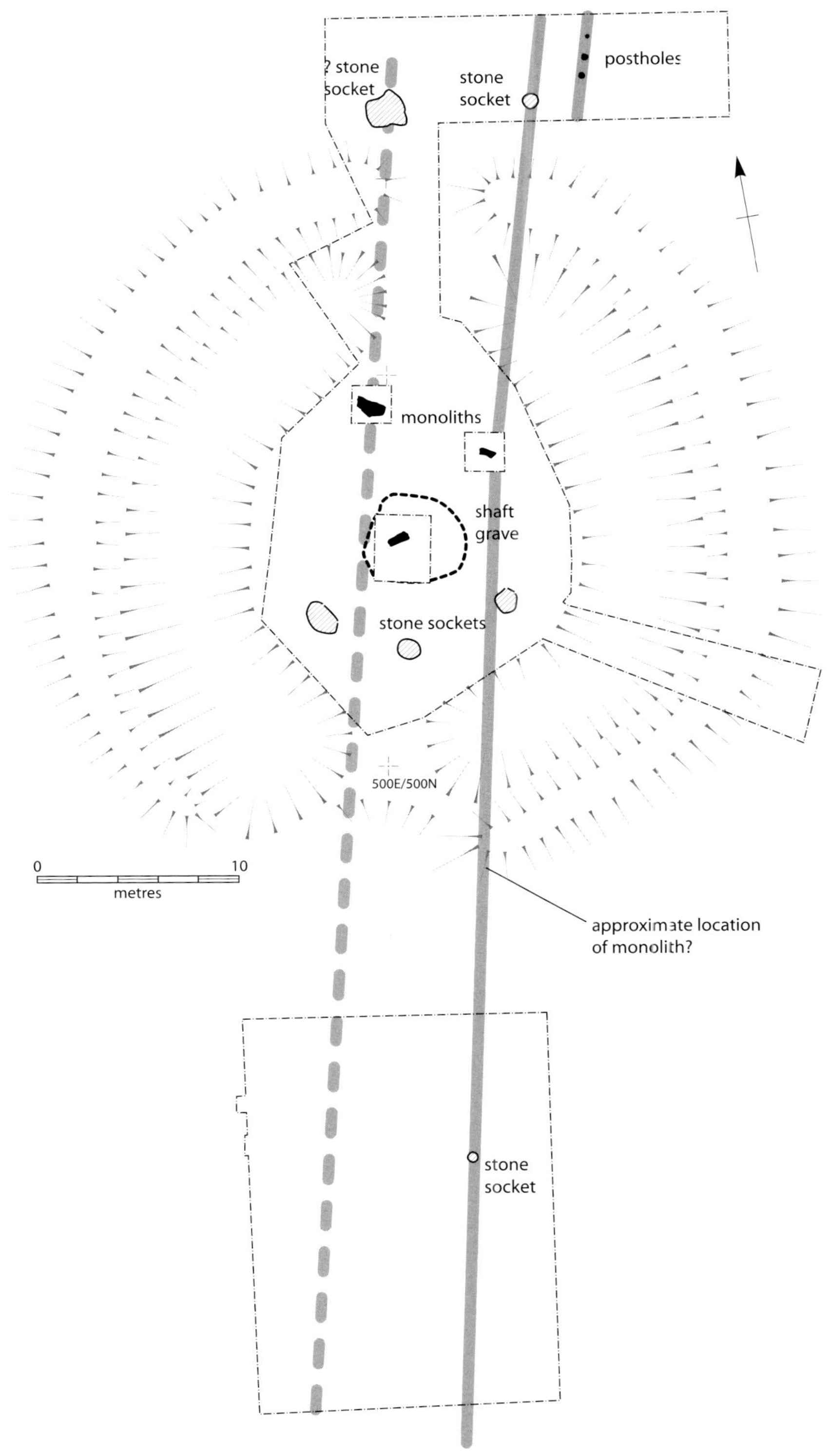

Illustration 2.4
A reconstruction of the avenue at Broomend of Crichie on the basis of excavation in 2005–7. The alignment suggested for the eastern side of the avenue continues southwards beyond the limit of the plan and includes the positions of two monoliths that still remain *in situ*. The western side of the avenue is largely hypothetical and the possible stone socket shown outside the north entrance was badly disturbed by rabbits. It is not certain that that it had held a monolith

earthwork, both could represent separate stages in accomplishing the same design.

That would not explain why the avenue changed direction at the position of the shaft grave. Here three possibilities arise. Firstly, the pit may have been earlier than the avenue, in which case the monoliths were aligned on the position of an existing burial. They were put in place to connect the stone circle to the grave, and to link the cist burial to those at the southern limit of the terrace. Alternatively, the avenue may have turned at a place which already enjoyed a special significance. The shaft grave may have been located there for that reason. A third possibility is that it was inserted into the course of the avenue after that structure had been built. There is no way of deciding between these interpretations, although parts of the same Beaker vessel were found in disturbed deposits on the edge of the shaft grave and in one of the stone sockets.

The nature of the stone avenue

If it is difficult to work out how the avenue was related to the shaft grave, the same problem applies to the earthwork enclosure. How were the henge and the 'cove' integrated with the course of the avenue? There are two possibilities to consider. The first is that the northern length of avenue predated the southern section. In that case it may have extended from the destroyed stone circle as far as the position of the shaft grave – the arc of monoliths would have formed its southern terminal. The other possibility is that the entire avenue was constructed in one operation, changing direction slightly at the position of the shaft grave. In that case the arc or 'cove' and the associated burial could have been inserted into an existing construction or they could have been already there.

In either case there are indications that the avenue was conceived as a unitary design. One clue is provided by the spacing of the monoliths, and the other by the distinctive ways in which raw materials were deployed. Two monoliths from the eastern line still remain in place and the locations of two others have been found by excavation. All these stones are located at intervals of between 18.5m and 20m, or at approximate multiples of those figures. That applies to the northern section as well as the main length south of the henge. It suggests that there were between forty and fifty monoliths, compared with the seventy or so postulated by Ritchie (1920, 159).

At the same time, it is notable that four of the surviving monoliths attributed to this feature – both

the portal stones and two others located due south of the earthwork – share a similar composition. They consist of substantial pieces of granodiorite. The remaining stones inside the henge were of other materials. At the same time, the stone sockets outside both the entrances were of similar proportion to those belonging to the cove. It seems possible that the builders of the avenue used massive stones and more slender monoliths in alternation; the spaces in between them may once have been occupied by posts, like those beyond the northern entrance. This tentative reconstruction has two implications: the same scheme was used both north and south of the henge, and it also applied to the three stones bounding the shaft grave.

The post-holes within the henge and the position of the shaft grave

The interior of the henge monument also contained a line of post-holes which extended between the entrances and skirted the position of the central burial. It seems likely that they held unusually high posts and were replaced on at least one occasion. The recut sockets in the northern half of the monument were strikingly similar to one another, perhaps because the posts had to be hammered into the natural gravel. They were supplemented by a shallow trench, with a possible post-hole at one end, which led from the entrance causeway towards the western portal stone.

How were those posts related to the earthwork of the henge? There were substantial sockets just inside each of the entrance causeways, both of them recut. They emphasised the long axis of the enclosure, and the feature sealed by the bank terminal in the northern entrance continued that alignment. The other 'double' post socket was offset from that axis and located on the edge of the shaft grave. It was directly opposite the centre of the enclosure. It seems as if the large recut post-holes were spaced at intervals of between 7.5 and 9m and divided the interior of the earthwork into four segments, all of exactly the same size (illus 2.5). Their layout conforms precisely to the outline of the henge, so either the posts were erected as the earthwork was built or they were set in the ground soon afterwards.

The alignment of large posts is poorly integrated with the arc of standing stones which flanked the central grave. At the same time those monoliths must have been erected before the earthwork was built. That suggests that the stone setting and the shaft grave were in place some time before the posts were raised.

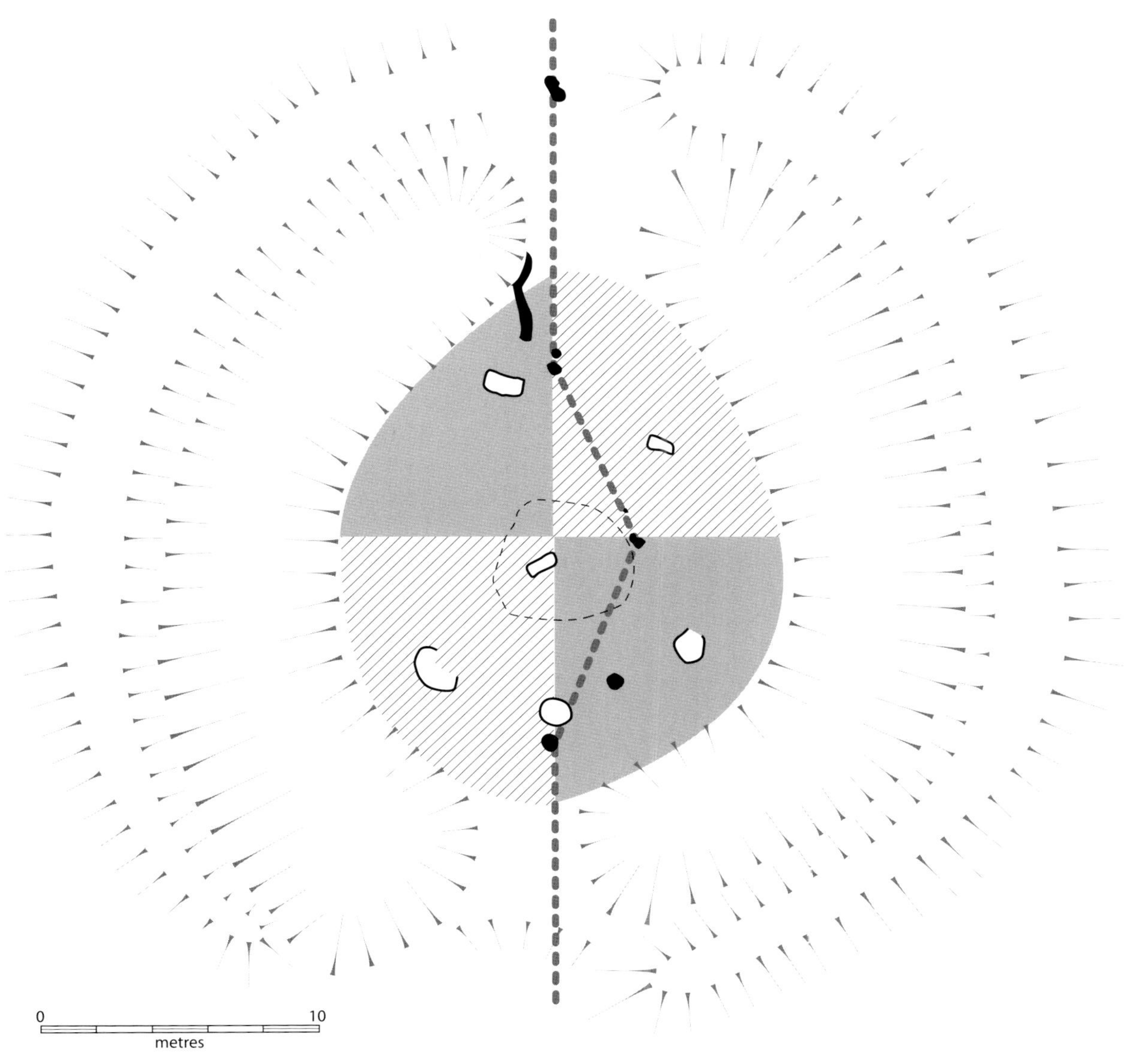

Illustration 2.5
The configuration of the re-cut post-holes associated with the enclosure at Broomend of Crichie. Together with a possible bedding trench, they appear to define a path leading between the entrances and skirting the position of the shaft grave. Their placing also divides the interior into four equal segments

The depths of the sockets suggest that the timbers were unusually tall. They could have been painted or carved and would certainly have drawn attention away from the monoliths that were already present. Skene says that the stones were between four and seven feet high. The simplest hypothesis is that each group of features belongs to a separate stage in the history of the monument. The standing stones were associated with the shaft grave and the avenue; the posts were an integral component of the later henge.

The timber circle and the avenue

One other relationship is worth considering here. Radiocarbon dates suggest that the timber circle postdates the henge. At the same time the position of this structure overlaps that of the southern avenue. Whilst it does not impinge on the stone socket excavated in 2007, it must have cut across the western row of stones. No trace of any monolith was found, but if a flat-bottomed rock had been employed it need not have been bedded in the ground.

The timber circle had a completely different axis from either the henge or the avenue. It may have been located just outside the southern entrance, but its porch was directed towards the ENE, past the earthwork boundary and towards the River Don. The posts were graded in height to emphasise that orientation. It seems as if it was built at a time when the original alignment of monuments was losing its significance, for there is no evidence of later prehistoric activity on the site.

Summary

These spatial relationships shed further light on the development of the excavated structures. Only a few points can be demonstrated with certainty on such a damaged site, but, in combination with the stratigraphic evidence and the radiocarbon dates, this evidence suggests the following possibilities:

- The henge monument was not the earliest feature on the site, as the portal stones in the northern entrance formed part of an older avenue.
- That avenue crossed the position adopted by the henge. It changed direction at the position of the shaft grave, which may have been contemporary with the rows of monoliths. Alternatively the grave could have been there already, or it could be a later addition.
- An arc of smaller monoliths was erected in the path of the avenue and emphasised the position of two burials in a massive cist.
- After the shaft grave was refilled, its position was indicated by the tallest monolith on the site.
- The bank and ditch of the henge reflect the positions of the stone setting and the central cist, but they were constructed when the monoliths were already in place.
- A line of large posts extended between the entrances of the henge and led past the position of the shaft grave. The uprights were replaced on at least one occasion.
- The positions of the posts reflect the layout of the henge. They emphasise its long axis and divide the interior into four equal segments.
- Early Bronze Age cremations were placed in pits beside each of the standing stones.
- After a period in which the henge was used for burials a timber circle was built outside its southern entrance. It cut across the avenue and instituted a new alignment towards the River Don.

The other components of the monument complex

So far the discussion has been based on the features investigated in 2005–7, as well as those revealed by Dalrymple 150 years earlier. They shed some light on the chronology of the excavated structures, but how were they related to those parts of this complex known from documentary sources and museum collections? This discussion involves some features that can no longer be investigated in the field.

The southern limit of the avenue

The first are the Beaker cists found in the nineteenth century. They were towards the southern limit of the terrace on which the monuments were built, and it seems likely that the establishment of the cemetery was one of the earliest activities on the site. Four cist burials were recorded at different times, three of which were large examples, while the fourth was significantly smaller than the others. According to the earliest account of their discovery, they were not buried in an artificial barrow or cairn:

> Some months since, Mr Tait, in making new road … had occasion to cut through a large natural bank or mound of sand and gravel. I examined the face of the bank, and satisfied myself that it was undisturbed since deposited there, in regular layers, by the action of water (Chalmers 1866, 111).

The siting of these burials follows a more general pattern among Beaker inhumations in north-east Scotland:

> [Short cists] with little or no covering mound … were usually placed in the crest of natural gravel knolls, often in small groups or cemeteries (Shepherd 1986, 12–13).

The first cist to be discovered was entirely empty, and all that is recorded is that 'it must have been of considerable size' (Chalmers 1866, 111). A second example contained two crouched burials which were identified as those of adult men belonging to the 'Ancient Caledonian race'. Their heads were towards opposite ends of the grave and both bodies were covered by 'a curious matty substance'. Behind each of them, 'at the back of the neck', was a complete Beaker. The other contents of the cist were a bone pulley ring, identified at the time as 'an ornament of rude nature', and a flint flake and two scrapers (illus 2.6; Clarke 1970, 360).

Illustration 2.6
The contents of Cist 1 in the cemetery at Broomend of Crichie. Photograph: NMS

A third cist came to light two months later. Like the example just mentioned, it was floored with waterworn cobbles and contained two flexed inhumations, those of an adult and a child. Both were covered by a distinctive deposit which was identified as hide. The adult body occupied the main part of the cist. 'At the back of this skeleton, about opposite the top of the thigh' was an upright Beaker vessel containing an unusual horn ladle; its handle was inside the pot. Behind the shoulder of the corpse there were two flint flakes (illus 2.7; Davidson 1866).

The infant burial 'was in the north-west corner of this kist behind the large skeleton ... [A] small urn was found in the corner behind this skeleton, and partly

Illustration 2.7
The Beaker and horn ladle from Cist 2 in the cemetery at Broomend of Crichie. After Davidson (1866)

fallen over' (Davidson 1866, 117). This was also a Beaker.

Finally, a much smaller cist was discovered alongside this burial. It contained part of a human skull but was not associated with any artefacts. The grave had not been constructed with the same care as the other ones and 'had no bottom or flooring of any kind' (Davidson 1866, 117).

The nature of these burials is better understood in the light of modern research. In two cases the bodies seem to have been covered by hides. A similar practice is recorded at two more sites in Aberdeenshire, one of them associated with a Beaker, and other with a Bowl (MacAdam in Watkins 1982, 126–7). It was not until 1882 that all four vessels from the Broomend of Crichie cemetery were illustrated (Anderson 1882, 455–7). Human bones from the burials have been dated by radiocarbon (Sheridan 2007a). At 2σ, the cist with the pair of adult inhumations has a date of 2470–2200 BC (OxA-15016), and the grave with an adult and child is dated to 2460–2190 BC (OxA-V 2166 34). They were among the earliest Beaker burials in northern Britain.

How were these burials related to the southern section of the avenue which appears to end about 50m to their east? Two points are important here. The surviving monolith need not mark the terminal of this alignment as the terrace extends a little farther before the ground falls away. On the other hand, that stone is set at right angles to the axis of the avenue. This would have been an ideal place to build another structure to mark the southernmost limit of the monument complex. Unfortunately, the surrounding area has been disturbed and until recently the obvious position for any such feature was occupied by a house. There seems no prospect of resolving the question.

Some of the cist slabs found in 1866 still survive. As Ritchie (1920) recognised, they were used to build a rustic bench on the edge of an ornamental lake (illus 2.8). They are relevant to this discussion because they consist of medium-grained granite – the same raw material as the nearby monolith. The stones could have come from the same source, and it is not impossible that they were collected at the same time.

One reason for taking this view is the discovery of an empty cist at Allanshaw, 300m south of the henge (Grieg & Shepherd 1993). It was beside one of the stones of the avenue and was similar in size and construction to the cists found in 1866. For that reason it may have been contemporary with the others (Table 1). Its position beside a monolith raises the possibility that the entire avenue was established during the Beaker phase.

Lastly, the southern section of the avenue evidently remained important into the Early Bronze Age as there are reports of inverted urns similar to examples from the henge. Like those found in the excavation, they were apparently closed by flat stones:

About three hundred yards [from the cists] Mr Tait found, some time since, three urns in a bank of gravel. These were not in kists, but each covered by a flat stone, and went to pieces on being disturbed' (Chalmers 1866, 111).

Illustration 2.8
The rustic seat built out of reused cist slabs near to the southern limit of the avenue

Table 2

A comparison of the two dated cist burials in the cemetery at the south end of the avenue (Crichiebank) with those at Allanshaw and inside the henge at Broomend of Crichie

	Crichiebank 1 *Beaker Inhumations*	Crichiebank 2 *Beaker Inhumations*	Allanshaw *No burial*	Broomend of Crichie *Inhumation and cremation*
External length	1.88m	1.65m	1.40m	1.52m
Internal length	1.60	1.27	–	1.22
Width	76–91cm	56–69cm	1.00 m	–
Depth	76cm	48cm	–	76cm
Clay luting?	Yes	Yes	Yes	No information
Associated with rounded pebbles?	Yes	Yes	Yes	Probably
Base slab?	No	Yes	No	No

Ritchie (1920) records similar burials beside two monoliths that still survive immediately south of the henge.

The northern limit of the avenue

The northern limit of the avenue raises even more problems for it was destroyed two hundred years ago. Ritchie's documentary research, combined with the result of the 2007 excavation, provided evidence that the alignment extended towards a large stone monument which was obviously circular in plan. The descriptions left by Aubrey and Maitland are difficult to understand, but this structure included several concentric rings of stones. It may have had some kind of cairn at its centre, and according to Maitland there was 'an altar of one stone with a cavity in the upper part'. He also says that there was 'was an artificial heap, or cairn, with a large flat stone on the upper part whereon to burn the sacrifices'. This can be compared with the recumbent stone which typifies a number of monuments in the region. The 'cavity' could have been a cup mark, while the three circuits of uprights might represent a setting of monoliths and both kerbs of a ring cairn. One indication that this might be correct is the orientation of the avenue that seems to have led from this monument. The first section was directed towards the SSW before it changed direction and ran due south towards the cist cemetery. That might be revealing as south-western alignments are typical of this kind of monument (RCAHMS 2007, 59–67). Other interpretations of its layout were considered in an earlier section of this chapter (above p 75).

The information contained in antiquarian accounts could also be relevant to the overall chronology of the site, for recent work suggests that recumbent stone circles are associated with Beaker pottery (Bradley 2005). It would mean that the avenue at Broomend of Crichie connected two structures or groups of structures that were in use at about the same time. Perhaps it was during the same period that the shaft grave was excavated, flanked by an arc of standing stones.

Summary

Taken together, documentary sources and the artefacts recovered in the nineteenth century suggest further observations concerning the chronology of the monuments:

- The Beaker cists may have been contemporary with the avenue, and it is possible that a further monument once existed at the southern end of that alignment.

- The empty cist beside a monolith at Allanshaw may have been contemporary with those discovered close to the southern limit of the avenue in 1866.

- The avenue may be contemporary with the shaft grave and the arc of monoliths along its southern edge. Alternatively, it could have been aligned on the position of an already-existing monument, or the burial could be a secondary feature.

- The northern limit of the avenue may have been the site of a recumbent stone circle

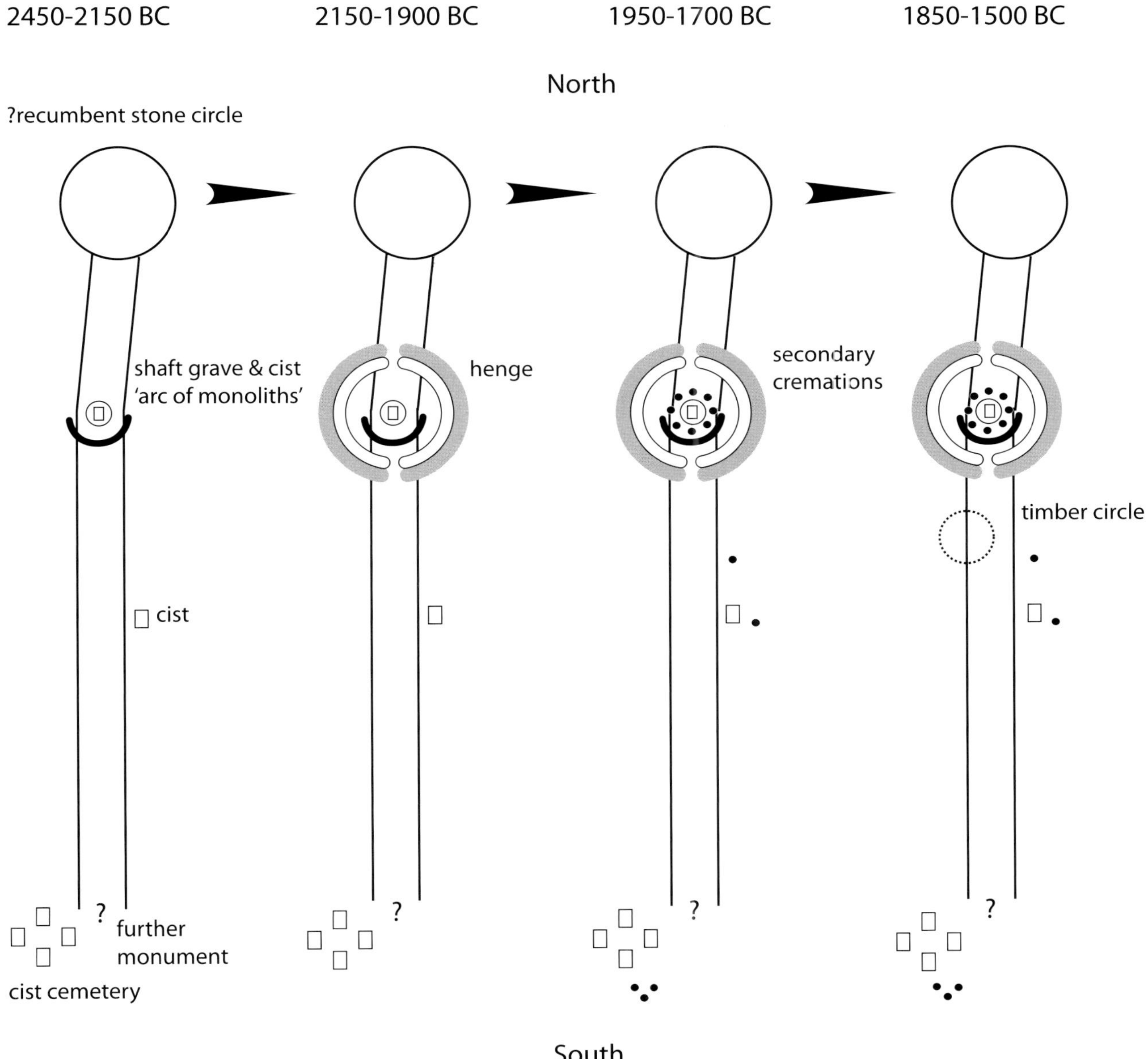

Illustration 2.9
The sequence of monuments and burials in the Broomend of Crichie complex, with their approximate dates

which was used at the same time as the cist cemetery.

- The alignment of the northern section of the avenue might reflect the orientation of a stone circle of this type, although other interpretations are possible.

- Like the cist cemetery and the putative recumbent stone circle, the shaft grave may belong to the Beaker phase. All three could have been in existence before they were linked together by an avenue.

Three histories of Broomend of Crichie (illus 2.9)

The features described so far were obviously related to one another, but the development of this complex did not proceed at an even pace. Some developments were sustained over a long period, while others have more of the character of 'events'. Before offering a new interpretation of the henge itself, it is important to distinguish between three different time scales.

Long-term developments

The gravel terrace at Broomend of Crichie provides evidence for an intermittent sequence of activity. Radiocarbon dates from a recent evaluation suggest that it began in the Mesolithic period (Murray & Murray 2007). Further dates from excavations in 2005–7 suggest that it continued into the early Neolithic phase: a suggestion that is supported by environmental evidence preserved beneath the henge. There was a period of more intensive activity in the second half of the third millennium BC. It began with the establishment of a cist cemetery, and from that time onwards the area was a focus for burials and monument building. The process continued until a developed phase of the Early Bronze Age. Then there was another hiatus until the first millennium AD when a symbol stone was erected near the henge. David Clarke has suggested that the stone was reused from the one of the prehistoric structures (2007, 38). According to Alexander Watt, a 'large urn' was found beside it, not far east of the henge (1865, 154).

A number of elements remained constant during the use of the gravel terrace. The monuments were arranged along a north–south axis running parallel to the Don. The importance of the alignment was emphasised by the creation of an avenue which connected three different components of this landscape, but there is no evidence that any of these features was orientated on a specific astronomical event. The river and the valley seem to have been the most important elements. At the same time few surface finds are recorded from the area occupied by the monuments, suggesting that their use may have been reserved for special occasions. Two pieces of burnt and worked flint were found in disturbed ground on the course of the avenue 130m south of the monument. On the other hand, more lithic artefacts have been found in Port Elphinstone a short distance to the north, and large numbers are recorded from cultivated land around Inverurie.

Another consistent feature is the way in which the monuments were used. In contrast to henge monuments in southern England whose roles changed in the course of their history (Parker Pearson & Ramilsonina 1998), almost every phase at Broomend of Crichie was associated with the remains of the dead. An early phase may be represented by massive cists associated with Beaker pottery, while the Early Bronze Age burials were mostly urned cremations. They were found inside the henge, but others were close to the long-established cemetery at the opposite end of the terrace. Burials of the same kinds were associated with individual components of the avenue. It seems possible that some of the cremations were placed inside stone structures, but, to judge from antiquarian accounts, they were significantly smaller than the cists of the Beaker phase.

Medium-term developments

There are other features of this complex which remained consistent over shorter periods. One was the importance of stone settings. They comprised an avenue, some kind of cove, and what was most probably a recumbent stone circle. All were closely related to one another. An alignment of paired monoliths may have linked that stone circle to another setting whose position was eventually enclosed by the earthworks of the henge. It seems possible that those monuments were used in succession.

Another development which extended over the medium term was the construction of cists containing inhumation burials. Those at the southern end of the avenue were associated with Beaker pottery and the example in the centre of the henge may be of the same date. There was also an association between standing stones and cremations. This is found in every part of the complex for which records exist. The duration of this practice remains uncertain, but it seems possible that it lasted little more than a century or as long as 300 years.

The post alignment inside the henge had a significant history, too. It seems to have extended between the entrances and formed a link between three different features: the north-west ditch terminal, one of the portal stones and the position of the shaft grave. The uprights were of considerable proportions and all of them were replaced. Obviously, it was not an ephemeral structure.

Finally, the same argument applies to the timber circle outside the southern entrance, but in this case the posts which were replaced were among the least substantial components of the building.

Short-term developments

There are three developments which must have taken place over a short period, or periods, of time.

The first was the excavation of the shaft grave, the construction of a cist and its burial beneath a deposit of rubble. That was followed by the raising of the tallest standing stone on the site. Unfortunately, the only sources of information are accounts of the 1855 excavation. Even so, certain points are clear. The shaft occupied much of the central area of the site and had been dug to a depth of about 3.3m. It must have cut through lenses of unstable fluvioglacial gravel and sand, and its sides could not have remained exposed for long before it collapsed. It would have been difficult to construct a cist on the bottom of such a shaft, yet it must have happened before the pit began to fill with silt. It is not known where the rubble used to fill the grave had come from, nor is it clear what happened to the spoil taken from the shaft. One possibility is that it was ramped around its western edge where few artefacts or subsoil features were found during the recent excavation. At some stage a monolith was raised over the infilled grave, but there is nothing to indicate when that happened.

An equally rapid development would have been the construction of the henge. Again the ditch was cut up to 3m through layers of sand and gravel and from the outset its sides would have been unstable. In fact they began to give way almost immediately, for little or no attempt was made to maintain the stability of the earthwork. What applies to the ditch of the monument applied to its bank as well. There is evidence that it was steep and narrow and that it had been built immediately outside the ditch, with the result that its inner edge was soon undercut by erosion. The problem was made even worse by the peculiar structure of the monument where the deepest section of ditch was associated with a particularly narrow length of bank. The structure

must have been vulnerable from the start, and it soon gave way. Again this process could not have taken long.

The last feature of note was the creation of the timber circle. Its construction signified a change in the character of this complex. It was built of timber, not of stone. In that respect it contrasts with the other circular monuments on the site. It was not associated with any finds of cremated bone and was built across the line of the avenue. The orientation of the post circle was completely different from that of the structures that had preceded it. This obviously applies to the henge and the avenue, but it may also contrast with the disposition of the burials inside the earlier monument. Most of the cremations had been in the western half of this enclosure, with a significant number of deposits around the south-west monolith. The stone battle axe was found beside the western portal stone, and even the central cist followed an east–west alignment. Many Bronze Age monuments in northern Britain were orientated towards the moon or the sunset and show a special emphasis on the south and west (Bradley 2005, 108–9). Now that alignment was reversed, and the latest structure at Broomend of Crichie faced the opposite way. It was directed towards the river where the sun would have risen in late February and August but does not seem to have been orientated on a specific solar event (Douglas Scott pers comm). Mr Scott also advises that 'there are times when the full moon would have risen between the eastern post-holes near the autumn equinox'.

An interpretation of the henge monument

The construction and use of the henge represent only one period in the sequence at Broomend of Crichie, but it was this monument that provided the focus for excavation between 2005 and 2007. Now that it can be seen in its wider setting, how should the site be interpreted?

In order to answer this question it is necessary to study its earthwork – the defining characteristic of any henge – in relation to the other prehistoric features: the stone avenue, the cove, the shaft grave, the central monolith, the line of posts and the cremation burials. So far the discussion has considered the order in which they were made. Is it possible to say more about the ways in which they were used?

Broomend of Crichie encapsulates some of the characteristic features of this kind of monument – and those of structures of similar appearance elsewhere in northern Britain. What these earthworks share is a distinctive sequence of construction and a common architectural form. As Chapter 3 will show, they are also linked by an association with human remains. It distinguishes them not only from earlier buildings of the same type, but also from better known sites in southern England.

One of the striking characteristics of the monument is how completely the distribution of artefacts and cremated bone focuses on the small area delimited by the standing stones. It hardly extends as far as the perimeter earthwork, or into either of the areas investigated outside the entrances. The same applies to the evidence of excavated features: cremation burials and pits. Again they are virtually contained within the area bounded by the avenue and the arc of standing stones. Everything focuses on the position of the shaft grave in the middle of the enclosure. That would have been still more obvious when the central point in the interior was marked by the tallest monolith. It was directly in line with the entrances and would have obstructed the view between them. That was not the case when it was first erected, as the grave is probably older than the henge.

Several of these features are closely related to one another, whatever the precise order in which they were built. The arc of stones described as a cove provided a monumental backdrop to the shaft grave, just as the central pillar indicated the position of the burial. The earthwork of the henge was laid out around these features, and the long axis of the monument surely emphasised their importance. The southernmost monolith of the stone setting was in line with the southern entrance and could have impeded movement through the enclosure. The same was true of the tallest standing stone. The eastern portal stone does depart from this scheme, but that may have happened because it formed part of an avenue which predated the other structures.

Two observations are particularly revealing. Not all these elements were constructed simultaneously. They were established in sequence and the order in which they were built was obviously important. At the same time some of these processes may not have taken long. For the reasons explained earlier, the shaft grave must have been filled in soon after it was dug. The earthwork of the henge was equally unstable, and there is evidence that it collapsed at an early stage. It follows that the use of both these features was extremely short-lived. How were they related to one another?

It is possible that the stones of the avenue were put in place at about the same time as the 'cove'. That is because the avenue changes direction at this point. Similarly, the arc of monoliths flanked the position of the shaft grave, and these components may have been created together, most probably during the Beaker period. The raising of a central monolith completed the plan of the stone setting, although it was never a 'circle'.

Perhaps these components of the site can be interpreted as the stage setting for a lavish funeral and for the rituals that took place afterwards. A great effort was made to dig the central grave and to emphasise its position by raising a standing stone. More effort went into making a monumental cist and covering it with a deposit of boulders which had to be introduced to the site. Those events must have taken place over a short period.

Another period of intensive activity followed some time afterwards when the bank and ditch were built, their course echoing that of the earlier arc of monoliths. The shaft grave was in the centre of that enclosure, midway between its entrances. Its position was marked by the tallest standing stone on the site. Until the filling of the pit had settled, this would have been surrounded by a circular expanse of rubble. The north-western ditch terminal was directly linked to a line of posts extending around one side of this feature.

The construction of such an enormous earthwork divided the shaft grave and the stone setting from the area around them and virtually concealed them from view. If the 'underground cairn' reported by Dalrymple separated the dead from the living, the bank and ditch served the same function, but in a different way and probably at a different time. Like the recumbent stone circles which were constructed around older cairns, it seems to have 'closed' the monument. In another respect the sequence was very different. Whilst the central cist was no longer displayed, the henge could still be visited. That is why it was provided with entrances. Cremations were deposited there during the Early Bronze Age. Their presence may have acknowledged the special significance of the people buried in the shaft grave.

Even then there may have been constraints on how the site could be used. One of those entrances was remarkably narrow, and it may be no accident that in this part of the site the ditch was unusually deep and the bank was unusually high. The other entrance, to the south, was aligned on the position of the cove, and even here access was restricted. That is evident from the post setting which links the causeways in the ditch and leads around the position of the shaft grave. It may have prescribed the appropriate route between the openings in the bank. The cist and its contents could no longer be seen, but the position of the burial was marked by a standing stone, and the path respected the grave. By that stage the site had changed its character entirely. The cove may have provided the setting for an elaborate funeral, but this happened only once. The subsequent history of the monument was concerned with commemoration and with the continuing respect paid to the dead.

That sequence sheds new light on mortuary ritual in north-east Scotland. When Ian Shepherd discussed this topic in 1986, he distinguished between the concentration of Beaker burials and finds of early metalwork in Buchan, and a group of henges farther to the south (cf Needham 2004). He suggested that they provided evidence for two different kinds of society. Powerful individuals or 'Big Men' were commemorated by cist cemeteries, while communities in which political authority was exercised through public rituals were associated with earthwork enclosures. The latter were considered to be a Neolithic form of monument.

It is true that north-east Scotland contains an exceptional concentration of Beaker burials and that some of these appear exceptionally rich, but the contrast that Shepherd identified can be expressed in a different way. The largest of the henges, Broomend of Crichie, was not a Neolithic monument. In fact it was no earlier than these graves. At the same time, there are indications that the earthwork on that site was first used after a nearby cist cemetery and was constructed to enclose an older shaft grave. Both the elements that he discussed in 1986 – a Beaker cist cemetery and a henge – occur together at Broomend of Crichie, where the earthwork enclosure seems to have been the last major monument on the site.

Perhaps the distinction that Shepherd made can be expressed in a different way. The cist cemetery, of which Broomend of Crichie is an early example, was the burial place of selected individuals. The positions of the deposits in this cemetery may not have been marked by conspicuous monuments, while the location of the shaft grave was emphasised by no fewer than four standing stones. People would have been aware of it as they moved along the avenue between the cemetery and a stone circle. The construction of the henge took that process further, for it screened the site of the grave from the surrounding area and defined a route leading past an important monument to the dead. In time, further burials were deposited beside the foot of the standing stones. The construction of the henge emphasised the continuing significance of the dead, but it also played a part in the ceremonies at which they were remembered.

Chapter 3

BROOMEND OF CRICHIE IN ITS WIDER CONTEXT

RICHARD BRADLEY

The interpretation of Broomend of Crichie and its associated monuments was based on a mixture of excavation, surface observation and documentary evidence and can never be much more than the preferred hypothesis among several competing versions. It is unlikely that further material will come to light without fresh excavation. On the other hand, some parts of that interpretation are reflected in the archaeology of other monuments.

This chapter is divided into three sections. The first considers sites in the same area as Broomend of Crichie and the features they share in common. The second discusses monuments and monument complexes in other parts of northern Britain in the light of the fieldwork reported here. Finally, the last section attempts to place these separate elements in their wider context in the Early Bronze Age.

Local comparisons

The re-excavation of Broomend of Crichie may shed light on four other monuments in Aberdeenshire, all of them excavated some time ago. The first of these projects took place at two sites near Kintore: Fullerton and the Hill of Tuach (Stuart 1856, xx–xxi; Watt 1865, 151–3; Coles 1901, 218–19). Like the work considered in Chapter 1, it was undertaken by Dalrymple. In the earliest account of these projects one of the sites was compared with Broomend of Crichie, but it was not until Fred Coles's work half a century later that Dalrymple's plan of the Hill of Tuach was published.

Two more accomplished projects were undertaken in the 1930s by Howard Kilbride-Jones. The first was on the 'enclosed cremation cemetery' at Loanhead of Daviot, which is located beside the better known recumbent stone circle at the same site (Kilbride-

Loanhead of Daviot

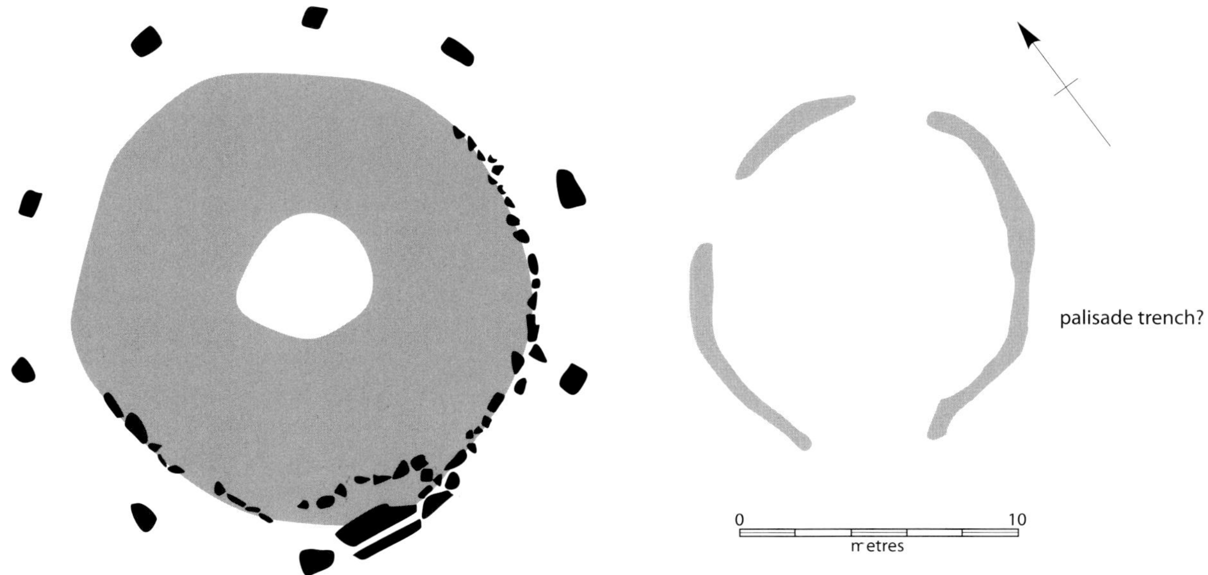

Illustration 3.1
Outline plan of the two neighbouring monuments at Loanhead of Daviot. After Kilbride-Jones (1935 and 1936)

Loanhead of Daviot

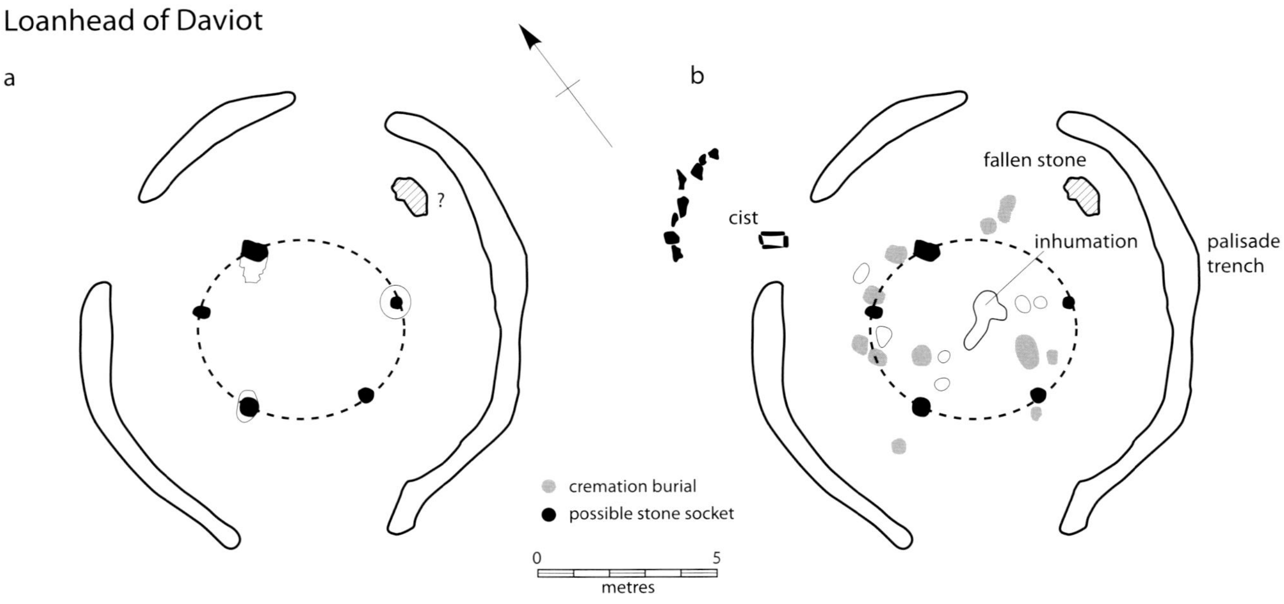

Illustration 3.2

Possible stone sockets inside the 'enclosed cremation cemetery' at Loanhead of Daviot (a) and (b) the putative stone circle in relation to the positions of an inhumation burial and a series of urned cremations (shaded)

Jones 1935, 1936), and the other was at Cullerlie (Kilbride-Jones 1935). In this case the results of the projects were not compared with one another and it is only the new work at Broomend of Crichie that makes this possible. Because Kilbride-Jones's work was of a high standard, it is with his excavations that the discussion begins.

Loanhead of Daviot (illus 3.1, 3.2)

Loanhead of Daviot is known for two different monuments, both of them excavated in the 1930s (Kilbride-Jones 1935, 1936). The recumbent stone circle was discussed in detail in an earlier publication (Bradley 2005, 100) and for that reason only the bare outlines need be summarised here. The monument probably witnessed three phases of activity. The first was the construction of a ring cairn over a burnt land surface. In a second phase, which may have followed soon afterwards, a circle of stones was erected to enclose this structure. When it happened, the kerb of the original monument was truncated. Then it was rebuilt to integrate the cairn with a recumbent stone and its flankers. This phase was probably associated with Beaker pottery. The structure did not undergo further modifications until the Late Bronze Age when a pit was excavated in the centre of the site. It contained

a quantity of pottery and a large number of cremation burials.

When Kilbride-Jones's excavation extended into the area east of the standing stones it encountered a second monument which was investigated and published separately. It was of approximately the same size as the recumbent stone circle but was bounded by two arcs of rubble, set in a discontinuous gully. Together they formed an approximately circular enclosure about 13m in diameter, with two wide entrances facing one another to the north and south. The interior of the enclosure had been heavily burnt, as had the sides of the 'ditch'. Within it there were three kinds of feature. At its centre was an irregular area with some unburnt bones belonging to a man of about 40. There was no dating evidence, but ranged around it were a large number of pits, most of which contained cremations. Like those at Broomend of Crichie, they were associated with Collared Urns and Vase Urns. Kilbride-Jones's report was remarkable because it provided sections or profiles of all these features. The majority resemble the simple cremations at the latter site. All but one of the vessels had been inverted and, like those at Broomend of Crichie, two of these urns were placed on top of a flat stone. The mouth of the one upright vessel had been closed by another slab. The cremated bones were those of adults and children, and the remains of more than one person were sometimes deposited together.

The published section drawings identify a few more subsoil features. They were not associated with burials of any kind. Their profiles are similar to the shallow sockets found at Broomend of Crichie. It seems possible that the 'cremation cemetery' included a setting of monoliths. That possibility is strengthened by considering their distribution, for they form an arc in the western half of the monument; to the east there is evidence for greater disturbance by the plough and similar features might not have survived so well. The excavation plan also depicts a large horizontal stone which might once have stood upright, although this could only be substantiated by excavation. This evidence suggests the former existence of a circle of monoliths. It would have been roughly 6m in diameter and occupied the central part of the enclosure.

Taken together, the components of the 'enclosed cremation cemetery' achieve a certain coherence. The rubble 'dyke' should probably be reinterpreted as the remains of a palisade trench containing packing stones. If so, it can be compared with similar but smaller monuments at Streethouse in north Yorkshire (Vyner 1988), Whitton Hill in Northumberland (Miket 1985), and perhaps with an enclosure at Bleasedale in Lancashire where waterlogged posts survived (Varley 1938). The enclosure at Loanhead of Daviot defined a circular space and was breached by two main entrances. Although these gaps were wider than their counterparts at Broomend of Crichie, both monuments have much in common, although one was defined by a massive earthwork and the other may have had a wooden perimeter. Inside the enclosure at Loanhead of Daviot there could have been an irregular setting of monoliths. They would have been less substantial than their counterparts in the recumbent stone circle, and that may be why they have disappeared. In the centre of the monument there seems to have been an inhumation burial. The putative setting of standing stones was directly associated with groups of cremation burials whose forms and associations resemble those at Broomend of Crichie. Only two of the burials in the 'cremation cemetery' were outside the possible stone setting. There was also a small cairn associated with a cist on the eastern limit of the enclosure. It contained a Food Vessel bowl. Kilbride-Jones considered that it was more directly associated with the recumbent stone circle, but it occupied a gap in the perimeter of the 'cremation cemetery' and the two structures may have been built simultaneously.

How were the monuments at Loanhead of Daviot related to one another? There is disagreement about the exact sequence on the site, but it is clear that the recumbent stone circle was associated with Beaker ceramics and that its reuse as a cemetery took place during the currency of 'flat-rim ware', most probably in the Late Bronze Age (Bradley 2005, 100–2). By contrast, all the burials in the neighbouring monument were found with Collared Urns and Vase Urns. They should be later in date than Beaker ceramics although their overall chronologies could overlap. This suggests that the two structures were most probably built and used in succession, the slighter enclosure supplementing or even replacing an already established monument. Virtually the same sequence is suggested at Broomend of Crichie, where there is documentary evidence for the existence of what was probably a recumbent stone circle a short distance north of the surviving henge. In turn the excavated structure at Broomend of Crichie was organised on similar lines to the 'enclosed cremation cemetery' at Loanhead of Daviot and both sites were perhaps of similar date.

Cullerlie (illus 3.3)

The slighter enclosure at Loanhead of Daviot contained a variety of deposits, but it seems clear that at its centre

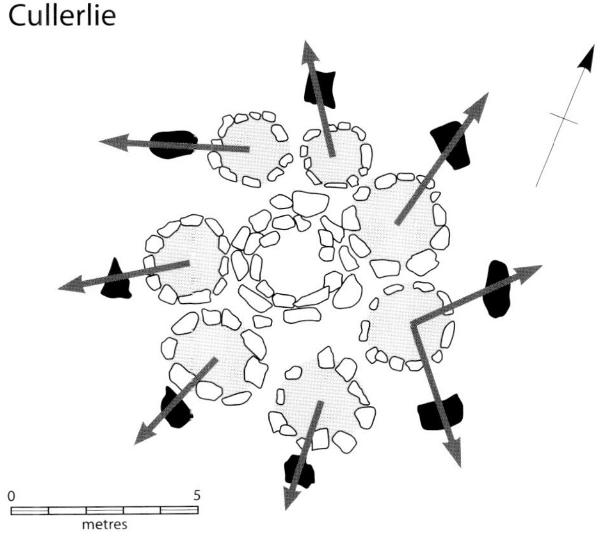

Illustration 3.3
Outline plans of the stone circle and small kerbed cairns at Cullerlie, emphasising the pairing of these structures and the individual monoliths

93

there was a complete or partial inhumation and that the cremations were ranged around it. The same was true at Broomend of Crichie, although all too little is known about the primary burial in the shaft grave. Space was organised in a strikingly similar manner at another monument excavated by Kilbride-Jones: the standing stones of Cullerlie (Kilbride-Jones 1935). Unfortunately this site is poorly dated, but again its distinctive features are best paralleled at Early Bronze Age monuments. The construction of the site on a platform recalls the evidence from recumbent stone circles. So does the evidence of fire, which was also present on both sites at Loanhead of Daviot. Another link with better dated monuments is the presence of a cup mark on one of the stones.

There are three components to the site at Cullerlie. The perimeter of the monument consists of a ring of eight monoliths and is approximately 11m in diameter. Just inside the circle of uprights there was a ring of seven small cairns, each with its own kerb. Towards the west there is a gap in this arrangement which may have marked an entrance to the monument. Five of the stone settings were associated with finds of cremated bone. The centre of the site was occupied by an eighth cairn which was considerably larger than the others and also associated with a cremation burial. Cullerlie had a lengthy history and it seems likely that the stone circle was in place before the other features were added. That is because the lower parts of the uprights had been affected by fire, while the small structures built within its area overlay a burnt land surface.

Again the organisation of the site recalls important features of Broomend of Crichie. There are a limited number of monoliths — significantly fewer than the twelve found in recumbent stone circles — and most of them were accompanied by a cremation burial or burials close to the inner edge of an upright stone. There was a larger structure of the same kind in the centre of the ring. It could have been the equivalent of the early shaft grave at Broomend of Crichie. It even seems possible that the cremations at both sites were secondary to the settings of standing stones.

There is a possible explanation for the difference between the standing stones at Cullerlie and the henge at Broomend of Crichie. The earthwork enclosure was constructed on a river terrace where a considerable ditch could be excavated. In places it was dug 3m into the gravel: about the same depth as the central grave. The standing stones at Cullerlie, however, were located in a damper environment and the site was partly enclosed by a swamp. In the circumstances, it was impractical to dig substantial pits or ditches, so, with only two exceptions, all the structures were above ground.

Instead of the small burial pits at the foot of monoliths at Broomend of Crichie, at Cullerlie there were stone settings containing cremated bone, and the place of the central grave was taken by a larger structure of the same kind. A possible comparison is with a pair of sites near Kilmartin. The principal stone circle at Temple Wood (Scott 1989) and the Ballymeanoch henge (Craw 1931) both contained cists with Beaker pottery, but the site that was closer to water (Temple Wood) lacked major subsoil features. Ballymeanoch, however, was located on a well drained terrace and here an earthwork was built.

The Hill of Tuach and Fullerton

A third local comparison is between Broomend of Crichie and two unusual monuments near Kintore. One was on the Hill of Tuach. This structure was also investigated by Dalrymple, although there is only limited information on what he found there (Stuart 1856, xx–xxi; Coles 1901, fig 6). That must be combined with more recent surveys of the surviving earthwork which has been disturbed since his excavation took place (illus 3.4). Accurate plans are provided by Fred Coles (1901, fig 5), the Royal Commission (RCAHMS 2007, fig 5.19) and an unpublished survey by Alexander Keiller in the National Monuments Record. All three supplement Dalrymple's own sketch plan which was first published after his death.

The enclosure is defined by an external bank and a wide internal ditch and encloses an area just over 7m in diameter. At present there is one substantial stone in its interior, but it may not be in its original position. It is represented in all the twentieth-century surveys, but when the enclosure was investigated by Dalrymple the site included six monoliths. They were approximately concentric with the earthwork and defined a space about 4.5m across. Like those at Broomend of Crichie, the stones were not placed at equal intervals. It is uncertain whether there been an entrance through the bank and ditch. Dalrymple did not observe one, but a section of the earthwork is currently occupied by a field wall. On the other hand, the enclosure was built on sloping ground and would have commanded a view of the Midmill long cairn on the skyline. Such a striking visual connection could hardly have been ignored.

Hill of Tuach

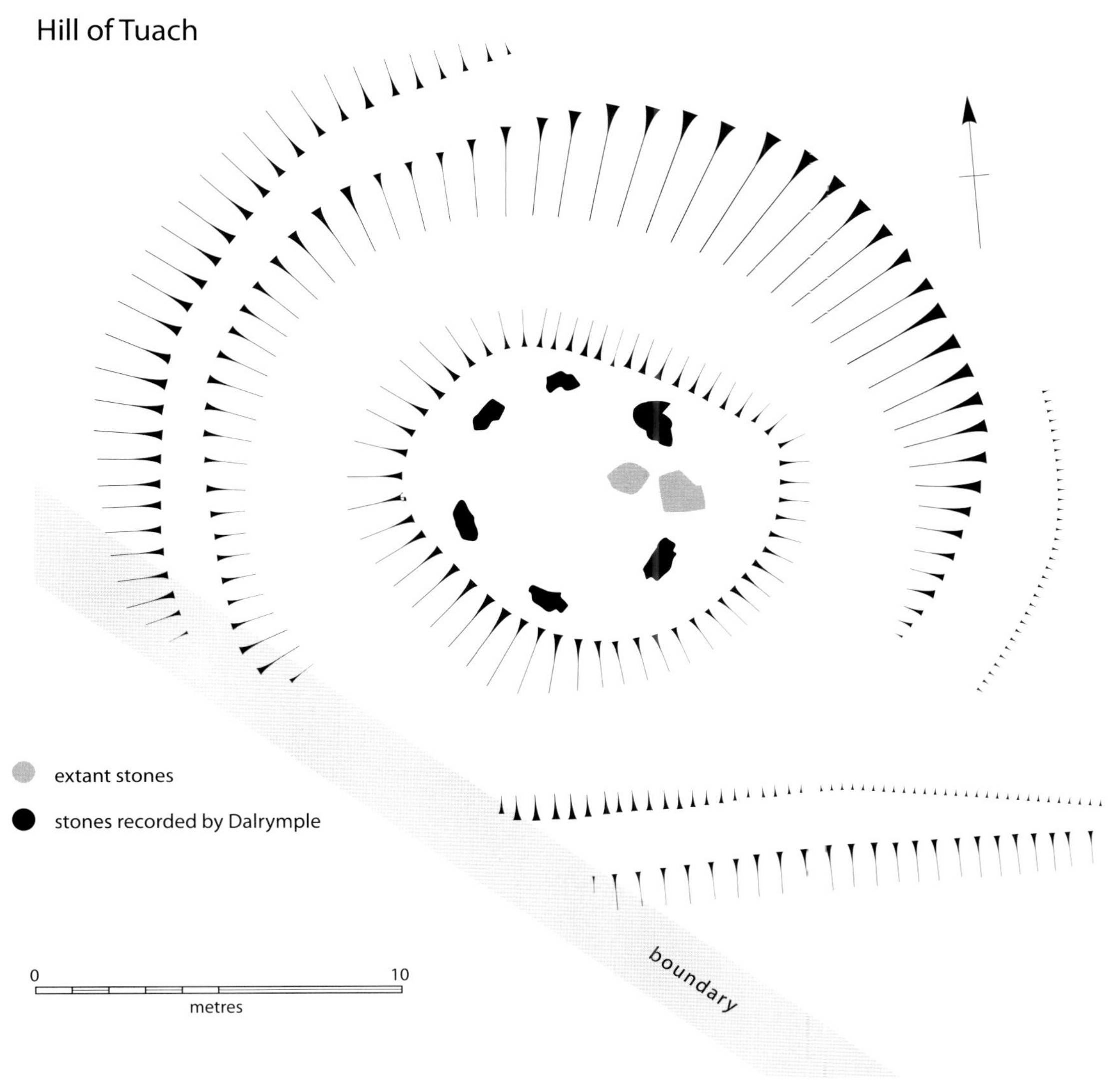

Illustration 3.4

A reconstruction of the monument on the Hill of Tuach, Kintore. The positions of the monoliths recorded by Dalrymple are shown in black and are based on a drawing first published by Coles (1901). The two large stones that remain on the site today are shown in dark tone and may not be in their original positions. The plan of the earthwork combines information from Coles (1901), RCAHMS (2007) and an unpublished survey undertaken by Alexander Keiller in 1927 held by the National Monuments Record of Scotland

Dalrymple investigated part of the ditch. It was nearly 4m wide, but he says little about it. Inside the enclosure there was what the excavator called a 'cromlech'. This was probably the remains of a central cist or setting of slabs and was associated with three cremation burials. Five more were found at the foot of the monoliths, three of them in inverted urns. Like similar deposits at Broomend of Crichie, they were in pits located on the inner side of the standing stones. Two of the urns were covered by flat slabs. Both were associated with one of the monoliths on the north side of the monument. John Stuart compared this evidence with that from Broomend of Crichie where a battle axe was deposited beside the north-west portal stone. The pottery from Tuach includes Cordoned Urns, and there were also fragments of bronze. Radiocarbon dates for this ceramic style suggest that the monument was used during the later part of the Early Bronze Age and was probably constructed after the henge at Broomend of Crichie.

There was a comparable site not far away. A small monument at Fullerton shares some of the same characteristics, although it is even more damaged. Again it was investigated by Dalrymple, but no plan of his excavation survives (Coles 1901). It was certainly defined by a ditch which enclosed a circular area about 8.5m in diameter and seems to have had an external bank, although that feature may have been built to enclose a recent tree plantation. It is not known whether there was an entrance. It originally contained a setting of seven monoliths, with a central grave containing burnt and unburnt bone. As at Broomend of Crichie, that deposit was surrounded by a series of cremation burials, some of them in small cists.

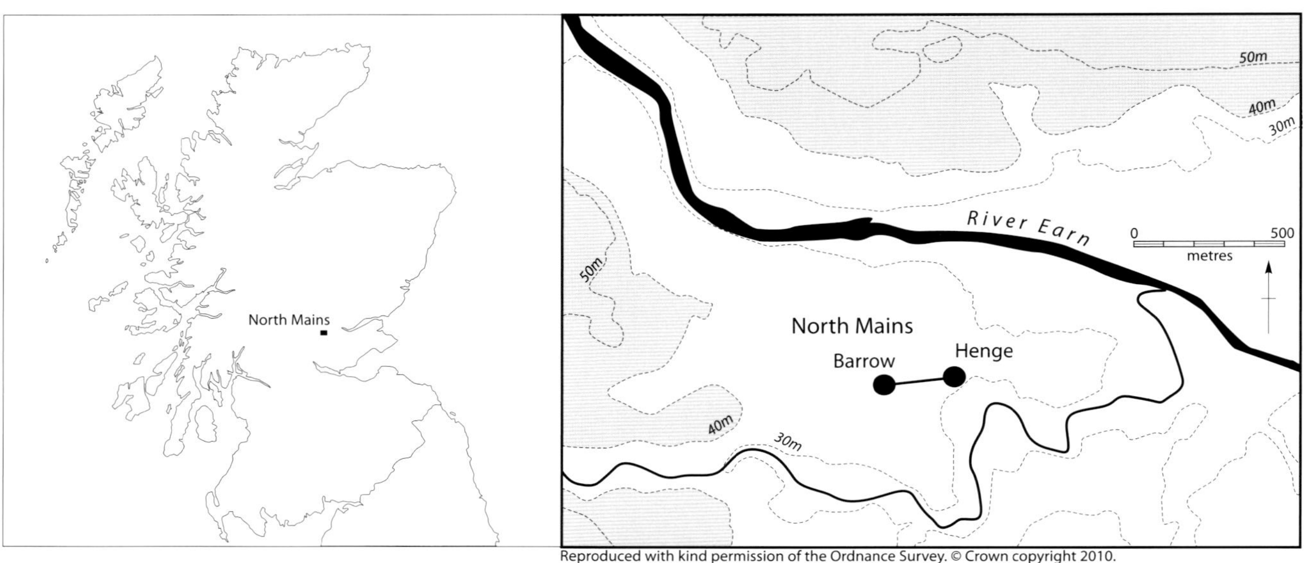

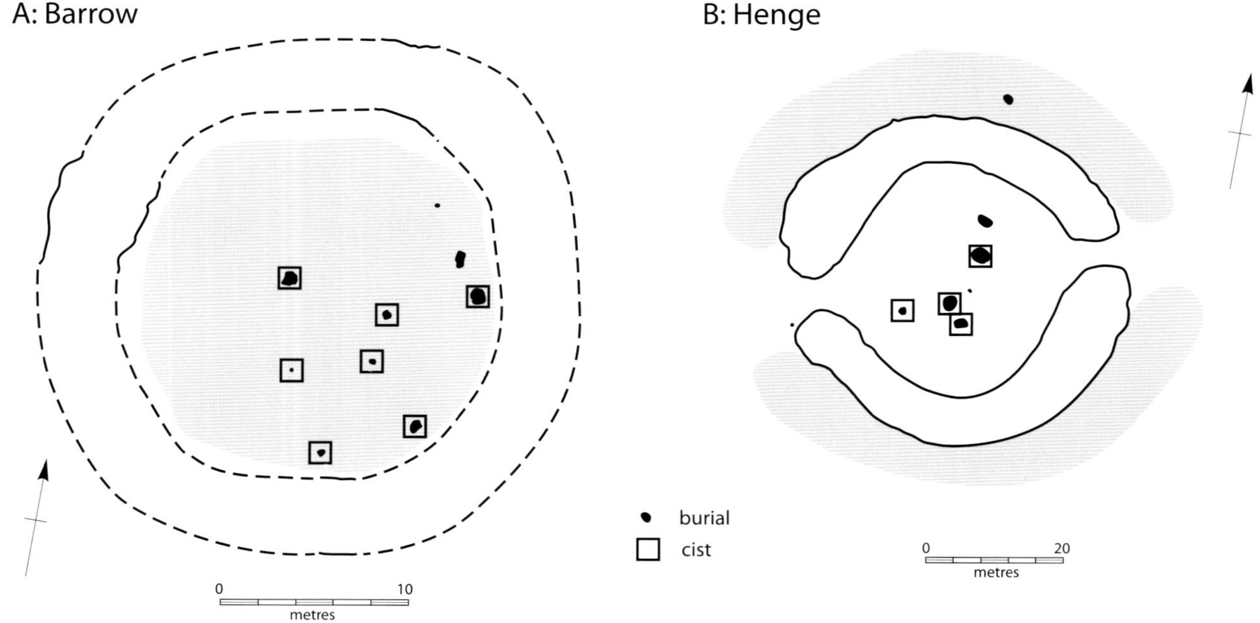

Illustration 3.5
The relationship between the henge and the nearby round barrow at North Mains, Strathallan, with details of the excavated Early Bronze Age burials associated with both sites. Information from Barclay (1983)

Despite the early date of these excavations, enough is known to suggest some links between the sites. Those connections were not recognised by the excavator himself, so it seems unlikely that he was led astray by his own expectations. All were circular enclosures defined by a broad ditch and, in at least two cases, by an external bank. There was a pair of entrances at Broomend of Crichie but at Tuach the ditch is continuous, although a causeway could have been removed in antiquity. Two of the enclosures contained stone settings that were broadly similar in plan. At both sites cremations were deposited at the foot of the uprights. They were always located on the inside of the stone setting. At the centre of Broomend of Crichie there was a shaft grave and at Fullerton the central grave may have contained the same mixture of cremated and unburnt bones. In each case they were surrounded by a series of cremation burials. On the Hill of Tuach the centre of the monument was occupied by an arrangement of slabs associated with three burials. Although the monuments were obviously of different ages, it seems as if the henge on the Hill of Tuach (and possibly the monument at Fullerton) were miniature versions of the older structure a few kilometres away.

The enclosures at Fullerton and on the Hill of Tuach are little known because Dalrymple never published reports on his excavations there. The same does not apply to the standing stones of Cullerlie or the 'enclosed cremation cemetery' at Loanhead of Daviot, both of which have seemed completely anomalous in the archaeology of the Early Bronze Age. Perhaps the re-excavation of Broomend of Crichie helps to place each of these monuments in a wider context, for whatever their chronological relationships, they seem to have been local expressions of similar ideas.

Wider comparisons

There are a few excavated monuments in northern Britain and Ireland that provide evidence for a sequence like that at Broomend of Crichie. So does Alex Gibson's excavation at Dyffryn Lane in Wales, the results of which will soon appear in print (Alex Gibson pers comm).

In some ways the most informative excavation was at a site mentioned in the introduction to this study: North Mains, Strathallan. This henge monument has a most distinctive character.

North Mains (illus 3.5)

The henge itself was a massive circular enclosure with two entrances which seemed to enclose a pair of timber settings of Late Neolithic date (Barclay 1983). Both were slightly oval but had different long axes from one another. When the site was first investigated the excavator, Gordon Barclay, postulated a period of secondary reuse in which it provided the focus for an Early Bronze Age cemetery. An unaccompanied cremation was identified, sealed when the bank was built, but until it became possible to date such burials directly by radiocarbon it seemed likely that it was Neolithic. Now it is known that it was deposited during the Early Bronze Age, at the same time as the cemetery was established. It follows that the timber circles had never been enclosed and that the henge was actually associated with the graves. In fact it was aligned on a large round barrow, 250m away, which contained more burials of the same period.

At North Mains there was no central grave like that at Broomend of Crichie, but the Early Bronze Age burials inside the henge were arranged on either side of an axis extending between the entrances. The larger burial pits were closer to the middle than the others. The forms of several of these graves are more complex than the surviving deposits at Broomend of Crichie and include a number of cists. The chronologies of the two sites can be compared with one another. At 2σ the directly dated cremations at Broomend of Crichie extend between about 1950 and 1700 BC, and the earthwork monument most probably has a *terminus post quem* of 2150–1900 BC. Only one of the prehistoric burials inside North Mains is closely dated. At 2σ its age is between 2150 and 1940 BC (GrN-24863) and the cremation sealed by the bank provides a *terminus post quem* for its construction of 2140–1960 BC (GrN-24007).

The two sites share another feature. The henge at North Main was aligned on the position of an enormous round barrow, and both monuments contained burials of similar character. Something similar happened at Broomend of Crichie where urned cremations were buried inside the henge and also around the site of a Beaker cist cemetery, 450m away. If one focus was provided by the bank and ditch, the other seems to have been 'a large natural mound' (Chalmers 1866, 111). At North Mains the two groups of burials were linked conceptually by the alignment of the earthwork enclosure. At Broomend of Crichie the connection

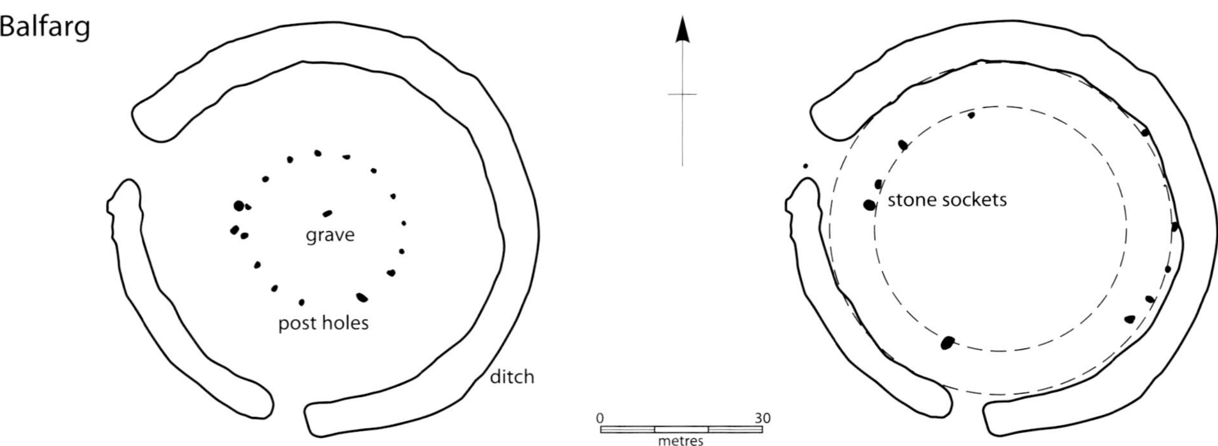

Illustration 3.6
The relationship between the principal post circle, the stone setting, the Beaker grave and the earthwork at the monument excavated by Mercer (1981) at Balfarg

between these places was made explicit by the existence of an avenue.

Balfarg (illus 3.6)

A second well known site was excavated by Roger Mercer at Balfarg (Mercer 1981). This was by no means well preserved and it was not easy to establish the plans of the structures inside the henge. There are many possibilities, from the severely minimal to more ambitious schemes. Two points are accepted by all the commentators on the monument. It contained both a timber setting and one or more circuits of stones; there was also a late Beaker grave towards the centre of the enclosure. In the absence of stratigraphic evidence it is difficult to work out the history of this monument. At first sight the structures developed according to the sequence that has long been proposed for similar earthworks in England. First came a circular enclosure with two entrances; it contained at least one timber circle and possibly more. There followed a ring, or perhaps two concentric rings, of standing stones and, finally, the grave.

There are problems with this scheme, for some of the monoliths were located so close to the enclosure ditch that it is hard to see how that they could have been erected if the earthwork was already there. At the same time, the principal timber circle was precisely concentric with that feature, suggesting that they were used together and may even have been constructed simultaneously. That is entirely plausible, but it raises the possibility that the conventional sequence from timber circle to stone circle should be reversed, so that the earliest feature on this site would have been the stone setting. In that case the principal timber circle – and presumably any other rings of posts – would have been a secondary development. Moreover, the grave is approximately central to the henge and also in line with its entrances. Its position does not conform so well to the outline of the stone setting. One indication that the timber circle might be late in the sequence is Mercer's argument that the individual posts were graded in height towards the west. This is a particular characteristic of Chalcolithic and Early Bronze Age stone settings in northern Britain. It would also be consistent with the occurrence of the grave, which at 2σ has a date of 2130–1880 BC (OxA-13213; Sheridan 2007a).

This interpretation raises as many problems as it solves, for the sockets of the timber circle contained sherds of Grooved Ware and were associated with radiocarbon dates in the early third millennium BC. That leaves three possibilities to consider. The first is to accept that dating evidence and to conclude that the ditch of the henge had filled up so rapidly that there was no problem in placing substantial monoliths along its edge. The second is to follow the suggestion that the stone circle predated both the ring of posts and the henge and to accept the Late Neolithic date assigned to the timber monument. That is not impossible as such large stone settings are supposed to be among the oldest structures of their kind (Sheridan 2004c).

Dun Ruadh

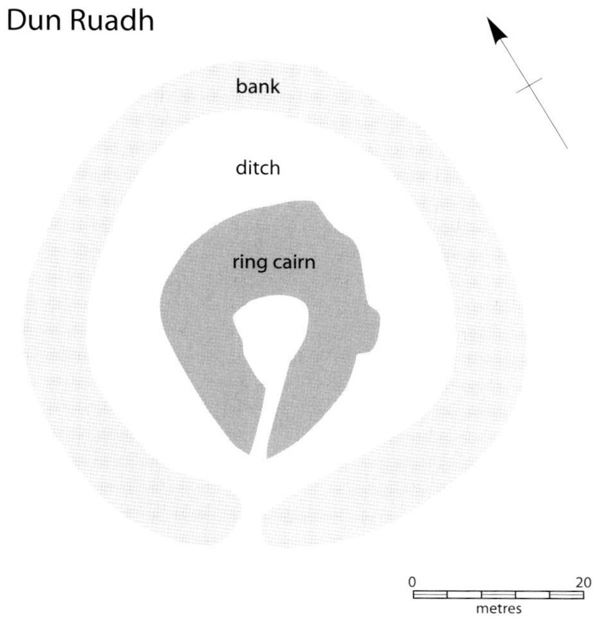

Illustration 3.7
Outline plan of the henge monument and associated ring cairn at Dun Ruadh, County Tyrone. Information from Simpson, Weir and Wilkinson (1992)

A third option is to consider whether the pottery and charcoal samples had entered the post sockets as residual material from the land surface through which they had been excavated: an idea first suggested by Alex Gibson (pers comm). There was a concentration of Neolithic material in the vicinity as this is mapped in the excavation report. There is no way of telling which interpretation is correct.

Dun Ruadh (illus 3.7)

Another source of information is one of the few henge monuments excavated in Ireland: Dun Ruadh in County Tyrone (Simpson, Weir & Wilkinson 1992). In this case a ring cairn was enclosed by an earthwork with an internal ditch and a single entrance. The site has been investigated on two occasions, and the most recent project concluded that it was a Neolithic henge. The ring cairn inside it was associated with cist burials containing Irish Bowls and was assigned to a later phase than the earthwork itself. That need not be correct. The bottom of the ditch provided a radiocarbon date at 2σ of 2140–1940 BC (UB-3047), but it was based on a bulk sample of bone and unidentified charcoal and could have included material that was earlier than the

construction of the monument. In any case the date is Early Bronze Age rather than Neolithic. The bank has a *terminus ante quem* at 2σ of 1880–1700 BC from a burial dug into its surface, but that particular grave was not associated with any pottery (UB-3048). When the excavation took place such estimates would not have raised a problem, but Anna Brindley's recent work has shown that cists were associated with Irish Bowls between 2160 and 1920 BC (Brindley 2007, 165–77 and 238–51). The vessels found at Dun Ruadh belong to the earlier stages of their evolution, narrowing the likely range to 2160–1980 BC. In the circumstances it is just as likely that the henge enclosed an older monument, or that it was constructed around the cairn while it was still being used for burials. Again the evidence recalls the sequence at Broomend of Crichie.

It is worth making a further point. All three monuments discussed so far had complex structural sequences, and in some cases there is more than one way in which they can be understood. Even so, it may be more than a coincidence that most of the radiocarbon dates that have been quoted here fall in the Early Bronze Age. In that respect they are similar to those from Broomend of Crichie.

Cairnpapple (illus 3.8)

Similar arguments apply to a number of other monuments. One of these was Cairnpapple where an internal circuit of posts or stones followed a different course from the bank and ditch (Piggott 1948). It seems as if it was conceived as a slightly oval arrangement of uprights with a single entrance to the south. Its long axis was echoed by an enigmatic arrangement of shallow pits recorded in Stuart Piggott's excavation. Within this enclosure a series of shallow holes defined a semicircular setting of posts or monoliths. These features were associated with cremation burials, one of which has been dated by radiocarbon to the Middle Neolithic period (Alison Sheridan pers comm). Piggott considered these features to be similar to those defining the limits of the monument and it is possible that both groups formed parts of a single structure. If this is correct, it would have been one of the earliest examples of its kind. The bank and ditch at Cairnpapple had a separate alignment from that monument, the difference amounting to about seven degrees.

The axis of the henge is important in another way, for the principal Beaker grave was directly opposite a change in the structure of the bank along the eastern perimeter of the monument. The height

Cairnpapple

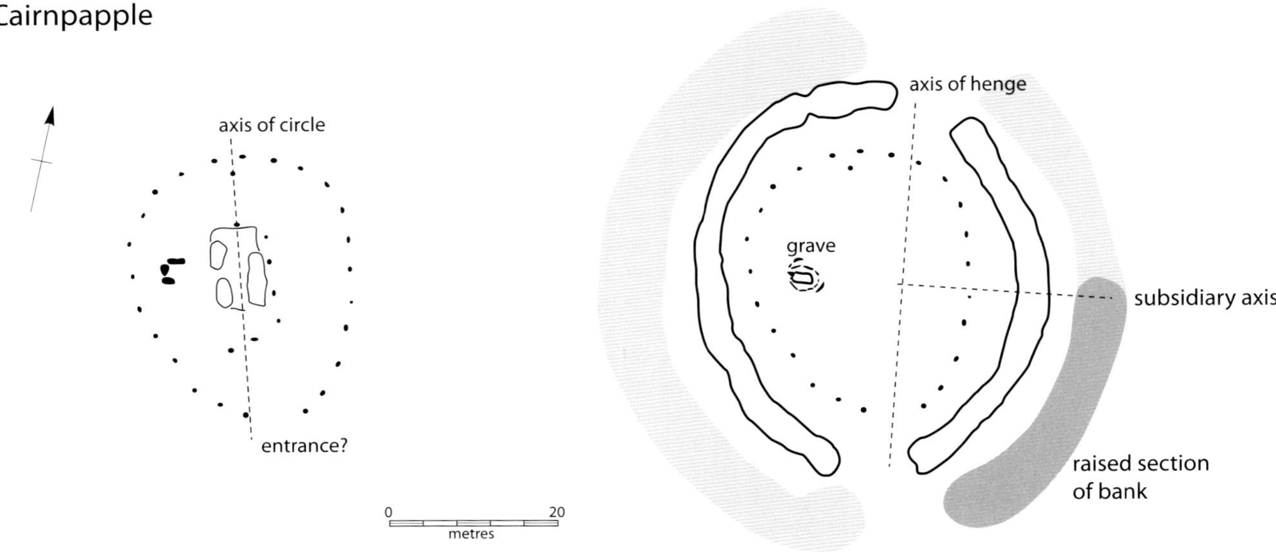

Illustration 3.8

A reconstruction of the sequence of monuments at Cairnpapple: (left) an early phase defined by a setting of posts or monoliths, an arc of post-holes or stone sockets, and two 'coves'; (right) the relationship between the primary structure and the henge, emphasising the changed alignment of the monument, the position of the principal Beaker grave, and the structure of the enclosure bank on the eastern perimeter of the site. Information from Piggott (1948)

of the earthwork increased at this point, effectively dividing the interior of the enclosure in two. That might suggest that these features were related to one another, but this presents a problem as the principal Beaker burial replaced an older cove whose date is entirely unknown. It may sufficient to suggest that the henge was built some time after the setting of posts or stones and that it *might* have been contemporary with that burial.

Arbor Low (illus 3.9)

Cairnpapple has always been compared with the northern English henge of Arbor Low. Although the stones on that site have fallen, John Barnatt's account of the site makes it possible to discuss the original form of the monument (Barnatt 1990, 31–9). Again the course of the earthwork perimeter does not conform to the original positions of the monoliths. Another point of comparison is that the site contained another cove, albeit a much larger structure than its counterpart at Cairnpapple.

The circuit of monoliths at Arbor Low is strikingly similar to the early enclosure at Cairnpapple and both can be characterised as 'egg-shaped' settings. In each case the best candidate for an entrance is at the most constricted point in the circuit. The long axis of Arbor Low echoes the alignment of the cove on the same site. Although the stones have fallen, it is possible to estimate their original heights. It suggests that the tallest uprights were to the south and that most of them were located to the west of the long axis of the monument: a feature that is more familiar on Scottish sites (Burl 2000). The other monoliths which seem to have been unusually high were by the possible entrance.

As happened at Cairnpapple, the later henge was not symmetrical with the stone setting. To the west the monoliths are 4 to 4.5m inside the inner edge of the ditch; to the east the equivalent figure is 6m. Again the two enclosures had different axes and the orientation of the henge differs from that of the stone setting by about fourteen degrees. The cove did not conform to the long axis of the henge. Another link with Cairnpapple is that the bank was higher in the part of the monument approached through a narrow entrance. By contrast, the earthwork loses height on either side of the other causeway. The same happened at Broomend of Crichie.

It seems possible that the earthwork of the henge at Arbor Low was built some time after the stone setting and that its construction involved a change to the alignment of the monument. Dating evidence is extremely limited, but St George Gray found a barbed and tanged arrowhead on the base of the ditch (Gray 1903, 471–3). That suggests that the earthwork was not constructed before the Beaker period. Again a comparison with Cairnpapple seems to be justified.

Ballymeanoch, Cairnpapple and Arbor Low

Broomend of Crichie can be compared with other henge monuments on a more specific level. Three excavated sites combine its main characteristics. Each has two opposing entrances, and all are directly associated with mortuary monuments.

One feature that links these sites is that they have two entrances which are rather different from one another (illus 3.10). At Broomend of Crichie the northern entrance is unusually narrow, while its counterpart is wider and commands a vista down the valley towards the position of the cist cemetery. The narrower entrance was marked by some of the tallest posts on the site; a less prominent post occupied the equivalent position to the south. An important point is that the width of the entrance is defined by the extent of the bank, rather than the causeways in the ditch whose dimensions compare closely with one another. It follows that similar evidence is unlikely to

be recognised at sites that have been mapped by air photography. On the other hand, the same pattern can certainly be identified at two well known monuments, Arbor Low and Cairnpapple, and has also been claimed at Ballymeanoch, although the wider entrance is towards the south in the Royal Commission's plan and in Craw's much earlier survey it is to the north (RCAHMS 1999, 24; Craw 1931). Such details matter because they shed light on how these places might have been used. If Craw's interpretation is the right one, the principal entrance at Ballymeanoch faced the main concentration of monuments in Kilmartin Glen. On the other hand, if the Royal Commission plan is correct – and the site was badly disturbed by the time it was undertaken – the principal axis led away from these sites.

That particular problem cannot be resolved without excavation, but it is true that each of the entrances at Cairnpapple and Arbor Low commands a very different view over the surrounding area. The narrower entrance at Cairnpapple faces a largely undifferentiated area of high ground to the south of the monument, while its northern entrance, which is significantly wider, overlooks a considerable area extending beyond the Firth of Forth. The effect is so obvious that specific landmarks are identified on a modern signboard. Exactly the same observations apply to Arbor Low.

Arbor Low

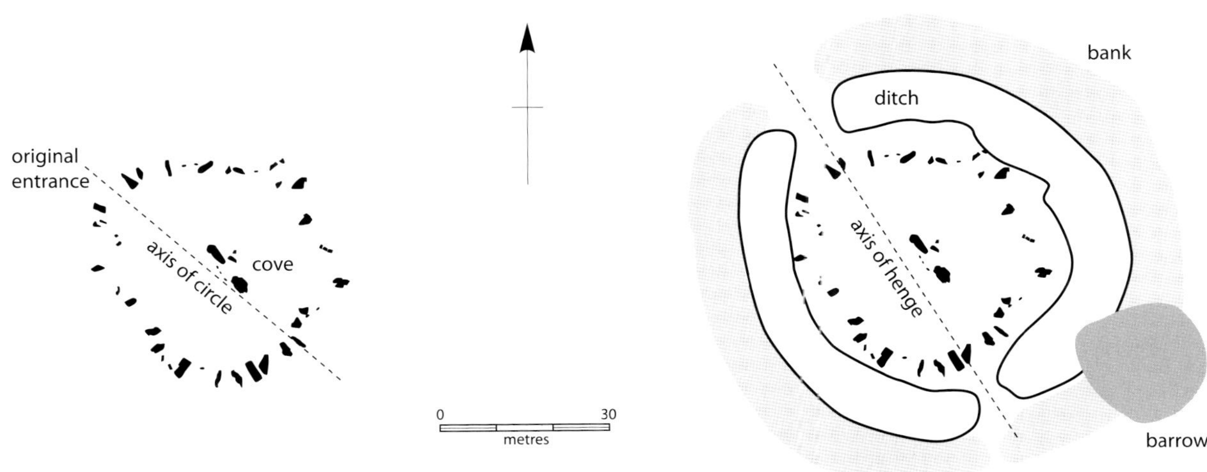

Illustration 3.9

A reconstruction of the sequence of monuments at Arbor Low: (left) an early phase defined by a setting of monoliths and a 'cove'; (right) the relationship between the primary structure and the henge, emphasising the changed alignment of the monument and the location of a round barrow apparently superimposed on the bank. Information from Gray (1903)

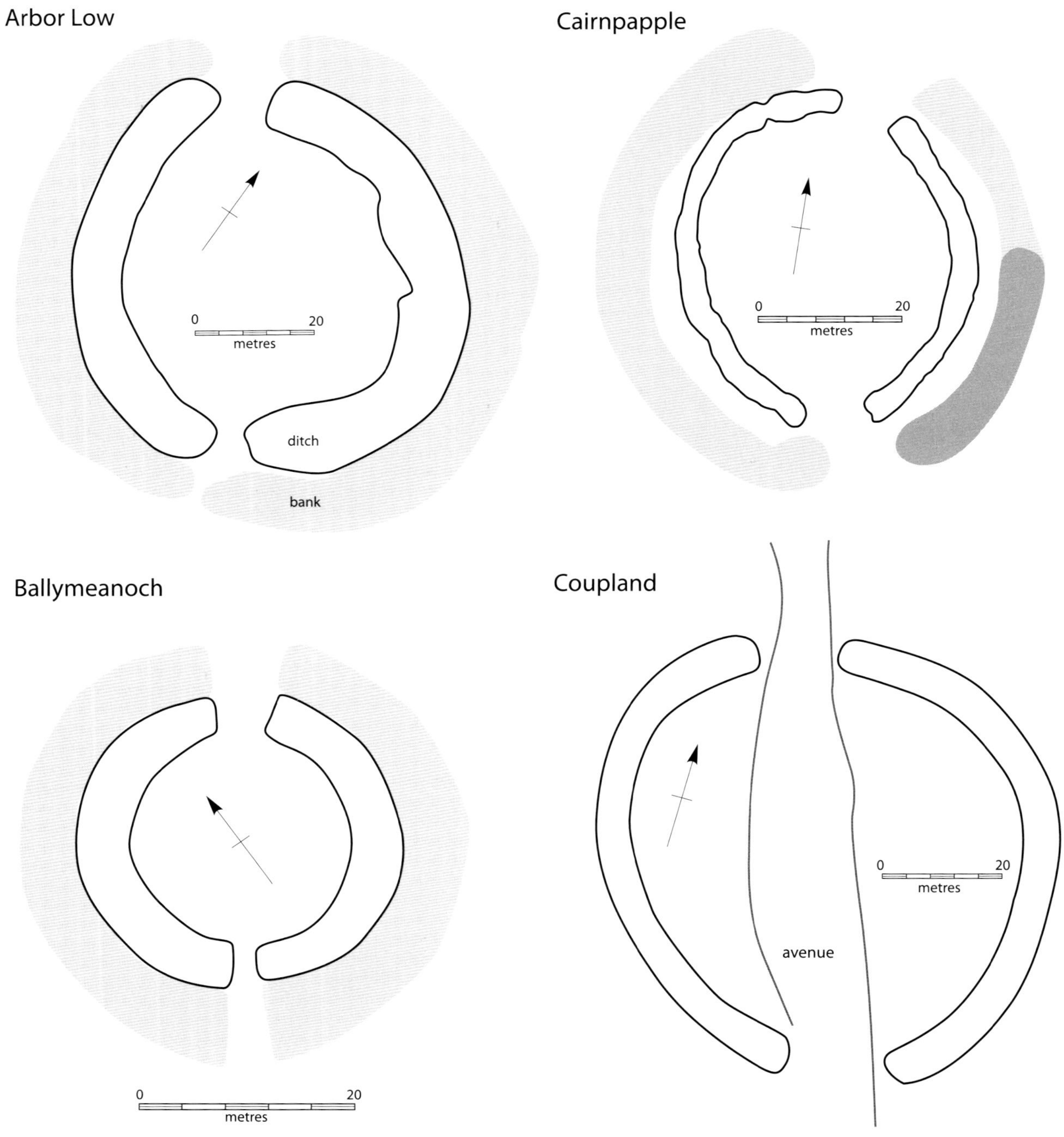

Illustration 3.10
Outline plans of four henge monuments with one wide and one narrow entrance. The plan of the enclosure at Coupland also includes a section of the ditched avenue. Information from Gray (1903), Craw (1931), Piggott (1948) and Atkinson (1950)

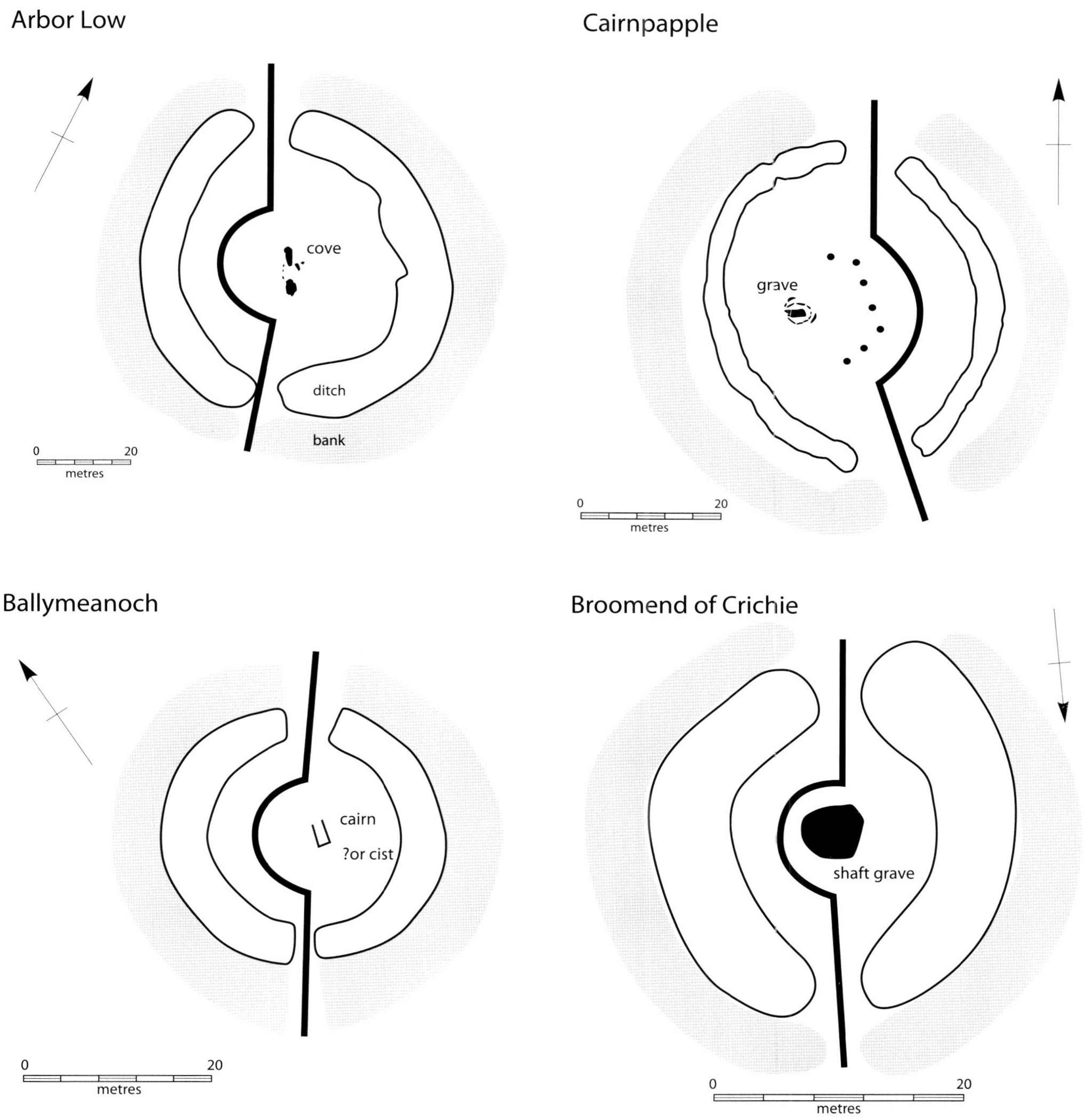

Illustration 3.11

Outline plans of four henge monuments with one wide and one narrow entrance, showing how the routes across the enclosures may have skirted the positions of mortuary monuments in the central area. In the case of Broomend of Crichie and Ballymeanoch this reconstruction uses two early plans – those of Coles 1901 and Craw 1931 – to estimate the extent of the banks before they were damaged by the plough. In the case of Cairnpapple it also assumes that the arc of Neolithic features excavated by Piggott held stones that still remained in position when the henge was built. Information from Gray (1903), Piggott (1948), Craw (1931) and Coles (1901)

The monument was built across the contours so that its comparatively narrow southern entrance looks out on a blank expanse of gently sloping ground, while its wider counterpart commands a large segment of the Derbyshire Dales. Perhaps the sizes of the entrances reflect the number of people who were using them. It is possible that they came into the enclosure one at a time. The extent of the wider landscape was not revealed until they reached the other side of the monument. The Scottish stone circle at Croft Moraig contrives a similar experience (Bradley & Sheridan 2005).

The interpretation of these monuments assumes a special significance because they have another feature in common with Broomend of Crichie where a line of posts extended between the entrances and skirted the position of the shaft grave at its centre. That had the effect of dividing the enclosure into two unequal sections. The same division of space could be represented at Ballymeanoch, Cairnpapple and Arbor Low (illus 3.11).

At Arbor Low those entering the enclosure through the narrower entrance would be unable to cross the centre of the monument because it was occupied by the 'cove'. Instead they would have made a slight detour to the left before approaching the wider opening in the earthwork. The same would be true at Broomend of Crichie where the route seems to be prescribed by a series of wooden uprights. According to Craw's description of the site, it might also have happened at Ballymeanoch where the direct route between the entrances seems to be blocked by a cairn associated with two cists, one of them containing a Beaker. In this case the argument is harder to substantiate as the site is disturbed, but a similar arrangement might have been followed at Cairnpapple where an arc of features identified by Piggott as stone holes has been dated to the Middle Neolithic. It occupies the western half of the enclosure and defines the outer edge of an area containing a cove, a series of shallow pits, a grave and a monolith. Their precise sequence is not clear, but it would be hard to explain why these features were

Weston

Muir of Ord

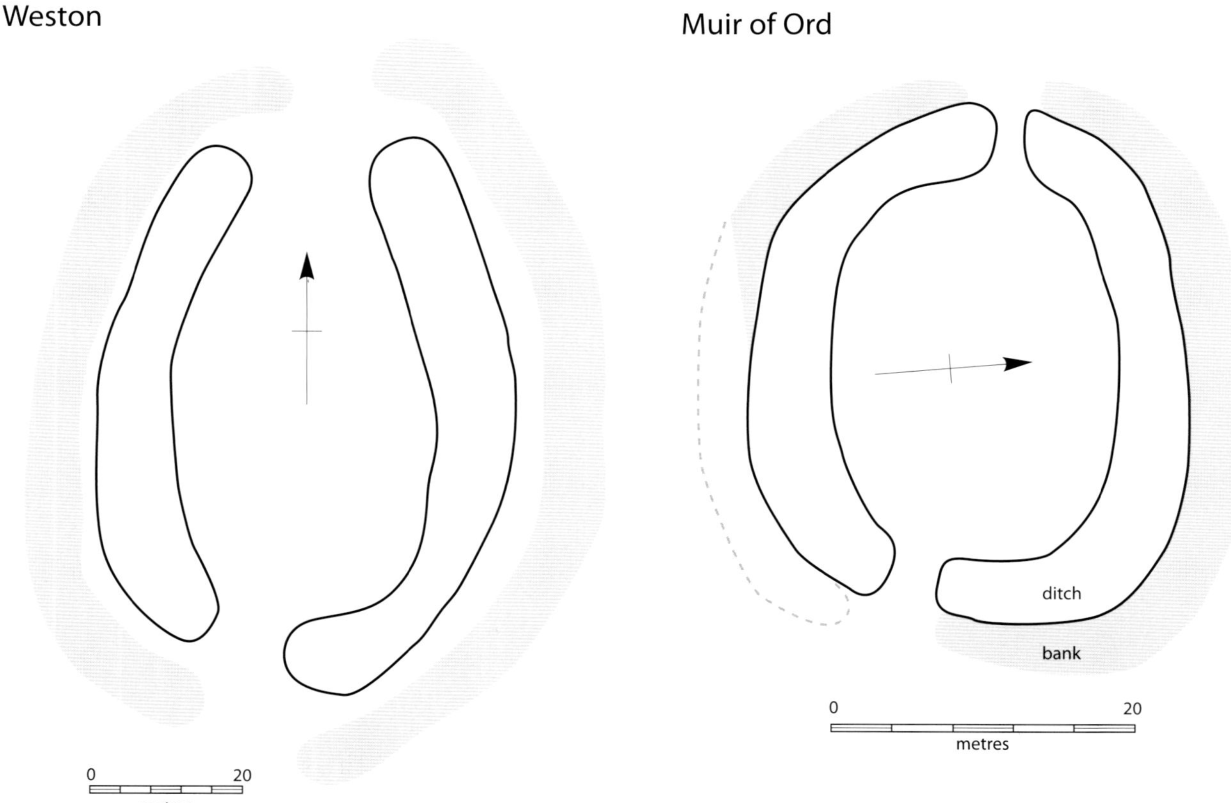

Illustration 3.12
Elongated henges with two entrances at Weston and Muir of Ord. Information from Harding and Lee (1987)

so closely related to one another unless the Neolithic features held standing stones; had they been post-holes, their positions would surely have been lost long before the Beaker period (cf Barclay 1999, 25, 39). Whatever the solution, the pattern of movement at Cairnpapple was rather different from that on the other sites, as someone moving between the narrow entrance and the wider one would have been obliged to turn right rather than left. Again it is uncertain at what stage the earthwork was built, but in every case it seems as if visitors entering these enclosures were expected to file past monuments to the dead.

At Arbor Low and Broomend of Crichie there is another indication of how the interior of the henge might have been subdivided, for in each case the earthwork perimeter is significantly wider on one side of the monument than the other. At Arbor Low the enclosure ditch is noticeably broader towards the east, while exactly the opposite pattern occurs at Broomend of Crichie. In several cases the outline of the monument is asymmetrical and creates the same effect by another means. In Scotland that happens at Cairnpapple, Broadlea, Muir of Ord and Weston (illus 3.12; Harding & Lee 1987, 346, 384, 367, 401), and in northern England it occurs at Arbor Low. A related development was the elongation of some of the enclosure plans, from an approximately circular outline to an oval whose long axis extends between the entrances. This effect was created to varying extents, from the slightly elongated layout of Cairnpapple to the longer, narrower outlines of the Scottish sites of Normangill and Weston (Harding & Lee 1989, 398, 401).

A further detail links two of these monuments. The position of the shaft grave at Broomend of Crichie was marked by a standing stone in the centre of the enclosure. An unusually large Beaker grave at Cairnpapple is also associated with an isolated monolith. Although it has been interpreted as the sole survivor of the cove which predated the burial, it is clear that the erection of the stone disrupted the kerb around the edge of this grave. The monolith must have been erected *after* the pit had been excavated and probably after it had been filled. Surely it was used to mark the position of the body. It remained in place until a large part of the monument was buried beneath a cairn.

The Milfield Basin

Similar arguments apply to the excavated monuments in the Milfield Basin, across the English border in

north Northumberland (Harding 1981; Miket 1985). They have a surprising number of features in common with the sites discussed so far. Harding's account of the henge monuments in this complex provides information on seven separate earthworks, no fewer than four of which had central pits. Of course this is based partly on the evidence of aerial photographs, and in such cases no chronological relationship between these features can be inferred.

These small henges are widely distributed, but three of them are connected by an earthwork avenue defined by parallel ditches. It skirts two of the enclosures and runs across a third, extending through both its entrances. Although it has been reinterpreted as a droveway linking a series of stock compounds, there seems no reason to depart from the original excavator's conclusions (Edwards 2007). Nor is there sufficient justification to backdate any of these structures to the beginning of the Neolithic period.

In some ways the configuration of the avenue is particularly relevant to this discussion. It runs across the interior of the Coupland henge, dividing it in half. Richard Atkinson's survey shows that the entrances of the monument were of quite different widths from one another (Atkinson 1950). This feature seems to have influenced the course of the avenue which is broader to the south of the monument than it is immediately to the north (illus 3.10).

Two of the other henges have been excavated and share certain points in common. Milfield South enclosed a large pit partly bounded by wooden posts which was located inside one of its entrances but offset from central axis of the monument. The base of this feature was lined with stones and may have been a grave, but this interpretation cannot be confirmed as the soil would not preserve unburnt human remains. The pit contained a cup-marked stone and provided a series of radiocarbon dates extending between about 2300 and 1750 BC. After the initial filling had accumulated, its position was marked by an upright post (Harding 1981, 977–9).

Milfield North was excavated on a larger scale (Harding 1981, 101–15). It had four main elements (illus 3.13): a henge monument with two principal entrances, one of which was wider than the other; a ring of shafts which surrounded the earthwork enclosure; a setting of much smaller features which defined the interior space; and a series of substantial pits, two of which contained a cist or a stone setting. The largest pit was in the centre of the monument midway between its principal entrances.

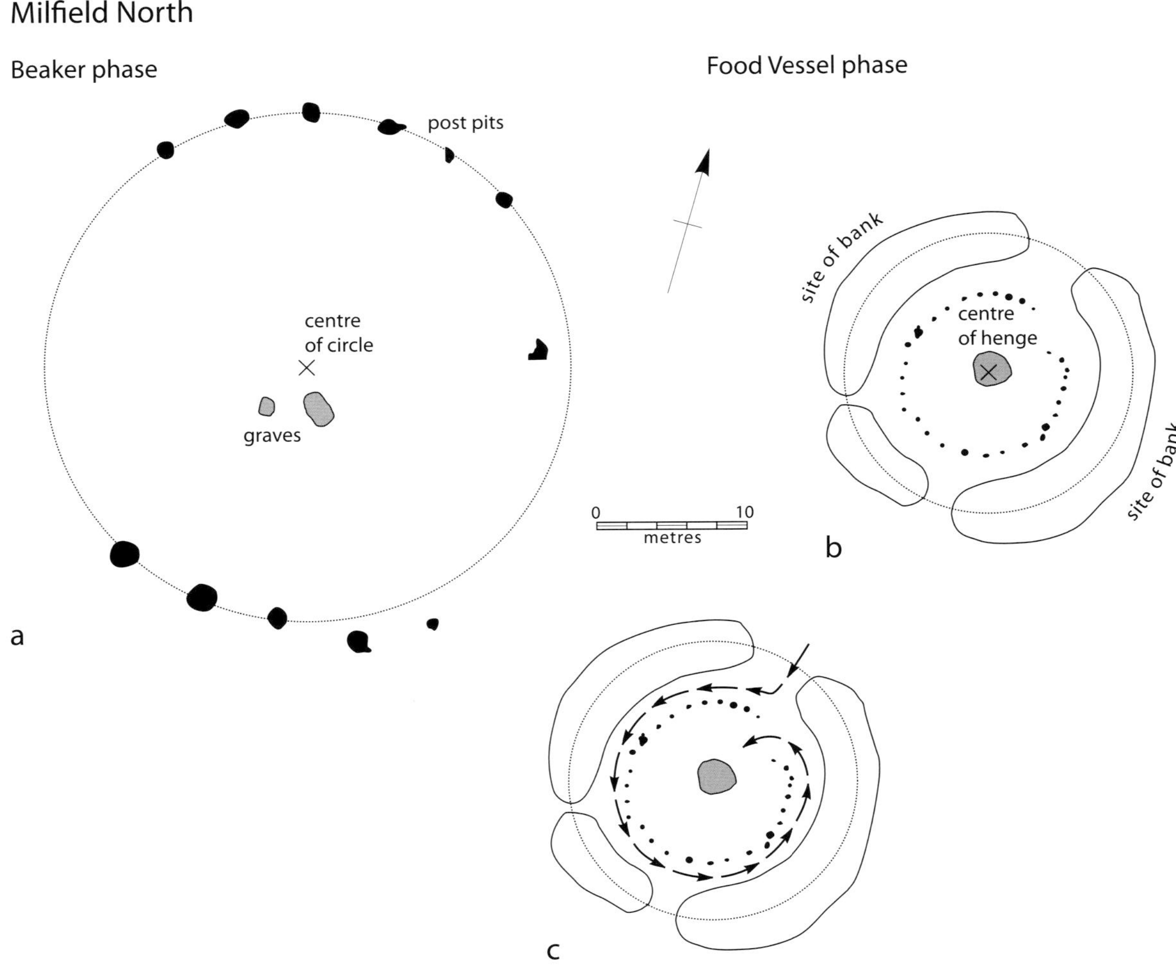

Illustration 3.13

A reconstruction of the sequence at Milfield North. In the Beaker phase a ring of posts may have enclosed the position of a burial. In a subsequent phase, associated with a Food Vessel, this structure was replaced by a circular henge monument with two entrances, a possible grave, and a ring of small pits or post-holes which blocks one of the entrances. The drawing suggests a path leading between the northern entrance and the position of the burial. Information from Harding (1981)

There are indications of a complex sequence on this site. As Alex Gibson (2004a) has pointed out, the bank of the henge would have covered the positions of some of the external shafts, suggesting that it was built at a later stage in the development of the site. Those shafts, which probably held posts, are laid out in a ring which is not quite concentric with the course of the excavated ditch. Close to the true centre of this circle there may have been two graves, one of them associated with a Beaker. By contrast, the exact centre of the earthwork that succeeded it was indicated by a feature associated with a Food Vessel. The presence of an entire pot in its filling suggests that it could have been a second burial, but again no bone survived. To judge from the section drawing, there may have been another marker post. The filling of this feature produced a radiocarbon date at 2σ of 2300–2040 BC (HAR 1199).

The pit at the centre of the henge was enclosed by a circle of smaller features. Their function is uncertain although they are exactly concentric with the earthwork of the henge, suggesting that both were conceived at about the same time. There is a further complication. Their circuit acknowledges the position of one of the entrances, but on the other side of the monument it cuts across the axis of the causeway and impedes access to the interior. Perhaps people coming from that direction were obliged to turn left and to follow a 2m wide path in between these features and the edge of the ditch. Only then could they enter the inner space.

That is not unlike the situation inferred at sites like Cairnpapple.

Three characteristics of these monuments recall the evidence from Broomend of Crichie. The first is the presence of some kind of avenue extending

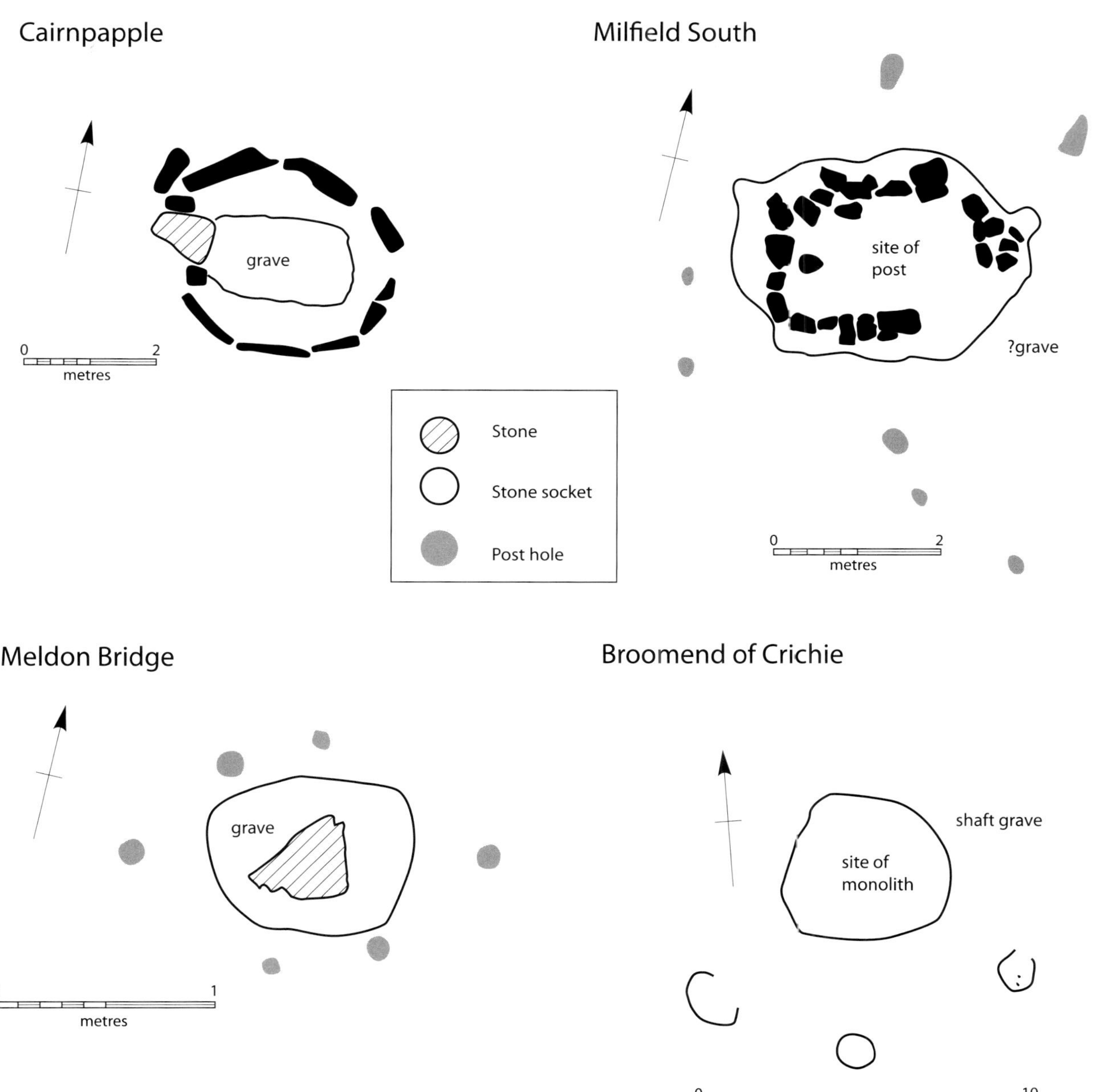

Illustration 3.14
Plans of three Beaker/Early Bronze Age graves marked by posts or monoliths, compared with the evidence from Broomend of Crichie. Information from Piggott (1948), Harding (1981) and Speak and Burgess (1999)

across the landscape to link different monuments to one another. It is particularly striking as this feature crosses one of the henges and extends beyond both its entrances. That also happens at Broomend of Crichie where the sequence of construction is different, but at most other sites in Britain an avenue leads into a monument and goes no further. Another point of similarity is the relationship of this feature to the entrances of the Coupland henge, for in this case the avenue changed its width.

A second link between Broomend of Crichie and the henges of the Milfield Basin is the presence of large pits inside these monuments. They are likely to have been associated with inhumation burials, but this cannot be proved. What is apparent is that the sites of one, and probably two, of the graves were indicated by substantial posts (illus 3.14). The large feature in the centre of Milfield North occupies the equivalent position to the shaft at Broomend of Crichie and dates from between 2300 and 2040 BC. In fact this may a little early as the radiocarbon sample was not identified and may have included old wood; the presence of a Food Vessel in the pit suggests that it was not filled before 2100 BC (Sheridan 2004a). A similar feature was excavated inside the palisaded enclosure at Meldon Bridge in southern Scotland where the position of a cremation burial was indicated, first by marker posts and then by erecting a monolith. It is associated with a radiocarbon date, unfortunately on oak charcoal, at 2σ of 2900–2100 BC (GU-1039; Speak & Burgess 1999, 26–8).

Lastly, the arrangement of smaller pits inside Milfield North could have been intended to guide the movements of participants around the positions of the graves. That is by no means certain, nor is it clear whether these features had held posts, but there may be a link between the organisation of space on the site and the way in which the interior of Broomend of Crichie was structured. There is not enough evidence to take the discussion further.

Arminghall, Broomend of Crichie and the problem of 'coves'

One of the problems of interpreting Broomend of Crichie is the belief, which goes back to John Aubrey, that the monoliths inside the enclosure formed a 'circle'. That idea certainly guided Dalrymple's excavation, and it has influenced subsequent accounts of the monument. Fieldwork in 2005–7 showed that his reconstruction was incorrect. Instead of a ring of

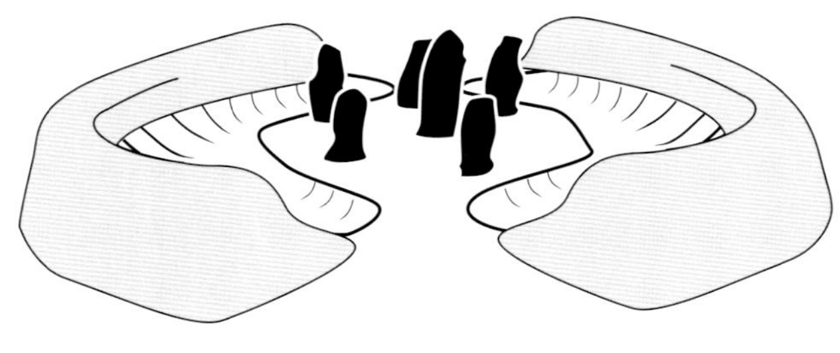

Illustration 3.15

John Skene's drawing of the stone setting inside the henge at Broomend of Crichie before the removal of four of the standing stones (reproduced by permission of NMRS). This is compared with Margaret Mathews's three-dimensional reconstruction of the monument, using the positions of the stone sockets excavated in 2005. The profiles of the stones are taken from Skene's illustration. The only significant difference between the two illustrations is that Skene shows the portal stones arranged symmetrically on either side of the north entrance to the earthwork enclosure. That was incorrect, as those monoliths remain in their original positions today

stones arranged at equal intervals, it indicated that the two that still survive were more closely associated with the northern avenue. Three other monoliths formed an arc around the position of the central shaft grave, with a fourth marking the position of the burial. Allowing for the misalignment of the portal stones and the entrance causeway, that is what is depicted in John Skene's drawing of 1832 (illus 3.15). Three of the stones were equidistant from one another but the alignment did not continue any further. If they are to be compared with other monuments, the frame of reference ought to be the 'cove' rather than the stone circle (illus 3.16). Unfortunately, coves form an extremely disparate group and examples of this type of structure are scattered widely across space and time (Burl 1988a). Moreover they range from a small timber structure like that at Ringlemere to enormous stone constructions such as those at Arbor Low, Avebury and Stanton Drew (Needham, Parfitt & Varndell 2006, 17–30).

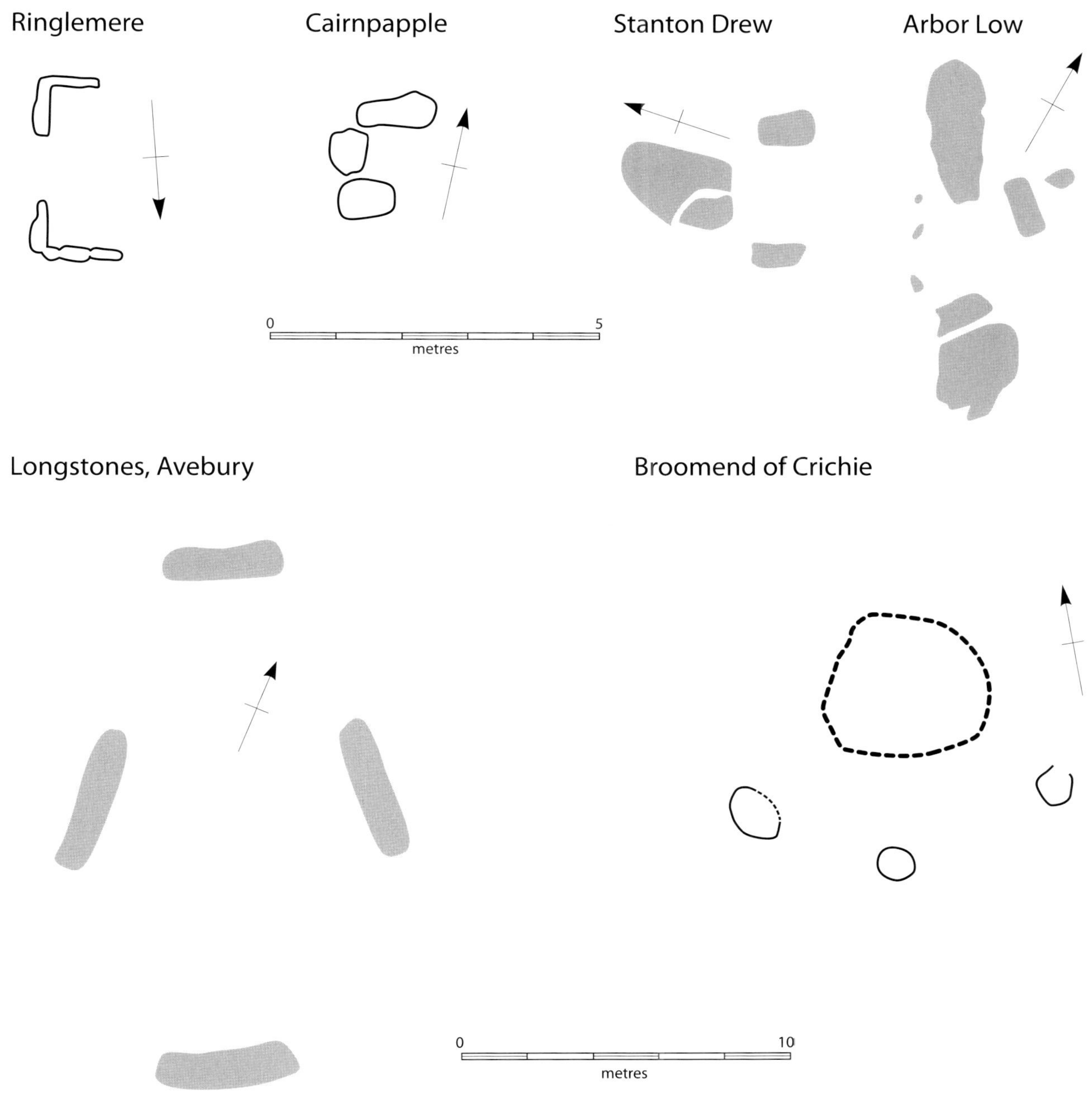

Illustration 3.16

Outline plans of a series of structures that have been described as 'coves'. Subsoil features are shown in outline and stone structures in light tone. Information from Burl (1988a), Gillings, Pollard, Wheatley and Peterson (2008) and Needham, Parfitt and Varndell (2006)

A more productive approach is to consider the distinctive forms of these structures (illus 3.17). They may be rectangular, square or oval and are sometimes aligned on other features, such as the entrance of a henge or a stone circle. A few examples are associated with human bones. Whilst they can define a restricted space, most examples are open on one side. That is certainly true at Broomend of Crichie where the stone setting runs continuously across the southern entrance and is open to the north. The same configuration is more clearly illustrated at the unusual English site of Arminghall (Clark 1936). Here the age of the timber

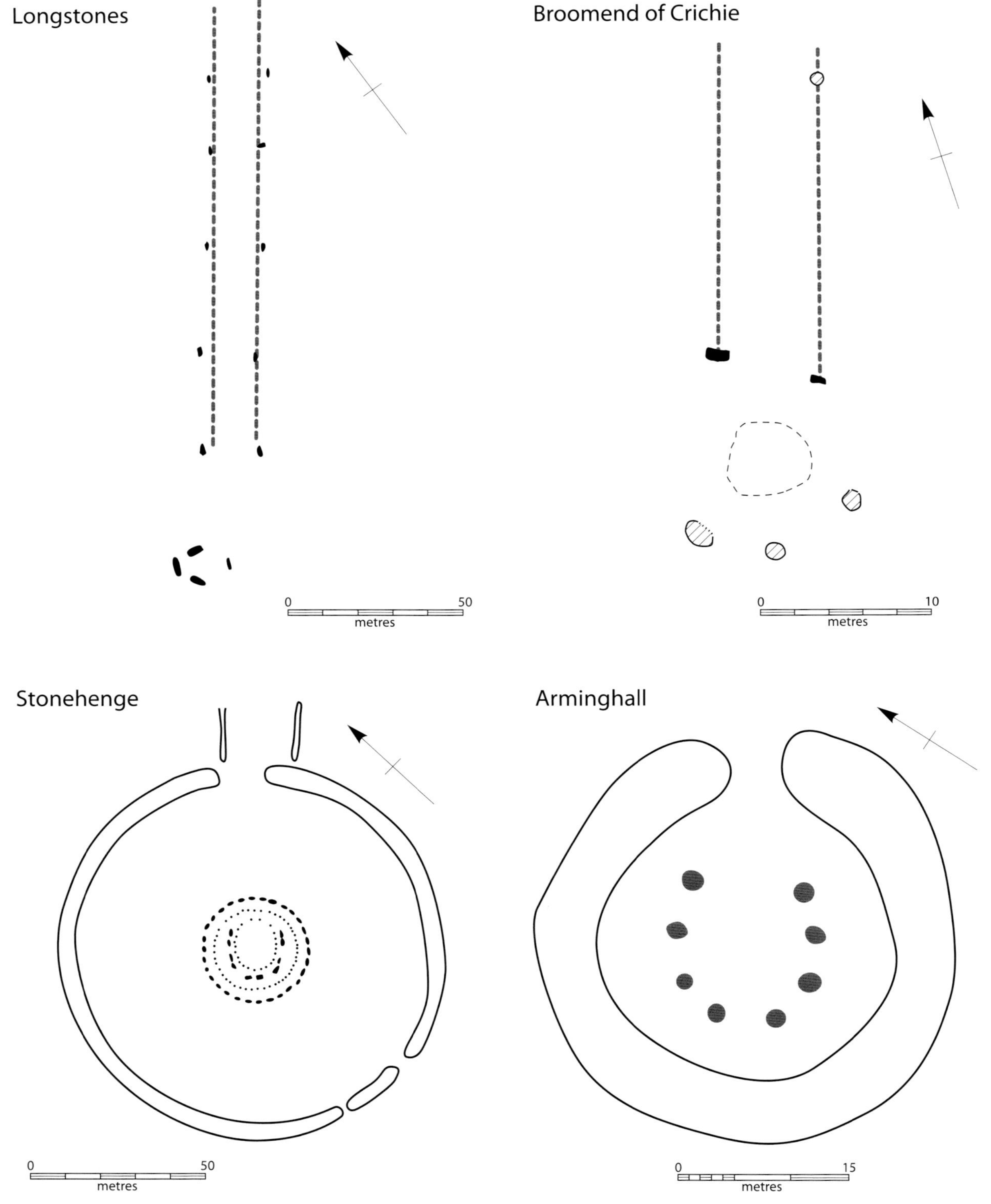

Illustration 3.17
The relationship between 'coves' or other horseshoe-shaped stone settings and the avenues at Avebury, (Longstones), Broomend of Crichie and Stonehenge. The drawing also shows the horseshoe of massive posts inside the henge at Arminghall. Information from Gillings, Pollard, Wheatley and Peterson (2008), Cleal, Walker and Montague (1995) and Clark (1936)

monument is not known since the only radiocarbon date may be on mature wood, but it is clear that again the uprights defined a horseshoe-shaped interior. The bank and ditch were built sometime afterwards but respected the position of its entrance. Sherds of rusticated Beaker were deposited during this phase.

There is also a site where an avenue ran up to a cove. This happened at the Longstones, on the Beckhampton Avenue at Avebury. The authors of a recent monograph make an interesting comparison with the layout of Stonehenge, for that is another monument – albeit a grander one than Broomend of Crichie – whose internal structure was dominated by an oval of monoliths (Gillings, Pollard, Wheatley & Peterson 2008, 124–8). That setting forms the focus for an earthwork avenue and, like many stone monuments in northern Britain, it is graded in height towards the south-west.

Broomend of Crichie and the problem of timber circles

It is unnecessary to discuss the timber circle in much detail as monuments of this kind in Scotland have recently been analysed by Kirsty Millican (2007). This particular example falls within their distribution, and another example has been excavated at Kintore, not far to the south (Murray & Murray 2008). On the other hand, the structure at Broomend of Crichie has some unusual features that ought to be emphasised here.

The first is its date. It was built and used during or just after the period of use of the henge, at a developed stage of the Early Bronze Age. That is not unprecedented, but the sites quoted in Millican's article nearly all belong in the third millennium BC. It is clear that this kind of building had a much longer currency. For example, there are Bronze Age dates from two structures of this kind at Kilmartin Quarry (Terry 1997). A second striking characteristic is its association with an older monument. It was located just outside the southern entrance at Broomend of Crichie and overlapped the likely position of its avenue. A similar development occurred at Kilmartin where the earliest structure was a Neolithic cursus. There was also a timber avenue on the site.

The post circle at Broomend of Crichie seems to have been provided with a porch, but in this case it was clear that the uprights were bedded in the gravel to different depths, with the result that the structure was probably graded in height from south-west to north-east. It is striking that this is the opposite of the pattern found in local stone settings and in the timber structure excavated by Mercer at Balfarg. The post setting at Broomend of Crichie would have been difficult to roof. It may look like a roundhouse in plan, but it must have played a more specialised role.

Broomend of Crichie in its Early Bronze Age context

In some ways the deposits at Broomend of Crichie are laid out as if they were underneath a barrow. This idea obviously influenced Dalrymple whose workmen laboured to no avail digging deep holes in the middle of other stone circles. Despite their lack of success, the comparison remains a useful one. It is pursued in detail in the final section of this chapter which tries to characterise the distinctive features of Beaker/Early Bronze Age henges in the north of Britain.

One observation is so important that it often goes without comment. Henge monuments had a long history which began at the start of the third millennium BC, but only the later examples were constructed during a period in which round barrows and round cairns were common. Although a few Late Neolithic monuments are associated with cremated bones (Parker Pearson *et al* 2009, 25–7, 31–3), it is only those built after the introduction of Beakers that belonged to a world where monuments were designed specifically for mortuary rituals. That remained the case well into the second millennium BC.

Two other developments may have happened over the same period and, taken together, they provide the basis for distinguishing between an earlier tradition of henge building which is essentially Neolithic, and a later tradition which is both Chalcolithic and Early Bronze Age. The first was the replacement of timber structures by stone settings. This could occur on a single site, but the later monuments contain rings of monoliths which lacked any wooden predecessors. Timber circles were still being built, but they are less common inside henges. The evidence from Broomend of Crichie illustrates this point. Here a stone setting was enclosed by a massive earthwork, while the post circle that replaced it was located on open ground outside one of the entrances to the enclosure; unlike the henge, it did not include any cremated bone. The increasing importance of stone monuments may be related to an emphasis on the dead. As Parker Pearson and Ramilsonina (1998) have observed for southern England, timber structures are sometimes associated with evidence for feasting and inhabitation. Stone circles, on the other hand, produce few finds apart from human bones.

Another development has long been claimed in the literature, although the evidence for this interpretation is rather limited. It is sometimes suggested that henges with two entrances are later than those with only one (Harding & Lee 1987, 34). The idea can easily be exaggerated, for single-entrance monuments were certainly built in the Bronze Age, but it does suggest that monuments with two opposed entrances had a distinctive role. That is true of several sites discussed in the earlier part of this chapter – Arbor Low, Cairnpapple, Ballymeanoch, North Mains, Milfield North – and Broomend of Crichie itself. All could date from the Chalcolithic and the Early Bronze Age and are probably associated with burials.

It is worth stepping back from the details of the henges themselves to consider the decisions that people must have made in dealing with the dead. Although there were general developments like those considered earlier, many of these decisions would have been formed on a local level, and some could even have been specific to individual sites or regions. That may account for the idiosyncratic character of the monuments near Broomend of Crichie. What options were available to those conducting a funeral? When they are better understood, it will be easier to view the developments at henge monuments in a wider context.

Some of those decisions are easy for archaeologists to identify. Funerals may have involved inhumation or cremation, and sometimes the two rites were practised at about the same time. The shaft grave at Broomend of Crichie, for instance, contained an unburnt body together with cremated bone. In other cases those rites may have been favoured during different phases, with a tendency for inhumation to be more common in an earlier period than cremation (Garwood 2007). The distinction between the two rites could also be expressed in the organisation of a cemetery. At Loanhead of Daviot, Fullerton and Broomend of Crichie the central grave contained an inhumation while cremation burials were ranged around it, but not necessarily at the same time. Inhumation graves normally contained one body, although this was not always the case. Cremations, on the other hand, might occur singly or could contain a mixture of different deposits within the same container.

To make the discussion clearer this account will treat these burial rites separately, although it is obvious that they were sometimes used in the same places and

even at the same times as one another. In the case of an unburnt corpse there were many decisions to make. One of the first was whether the body should be accompanied by grave goods and, if so, which items were to be selected and how they would be organised in the ground. Was the body to be deposited in a simple grave, and would the pit be shallow or deep? Would it contain a wooden coffin, an arrangement of stone slabs, or would the deceased be housed inside a cist? Could the grave be reopened to admit further deposits? If a cist was to be constructed, would it be closed by a simple capstone, or would it be sealed by a disproportionately large or heavy cover? To some extent these questions are concerned with access to the corpse. It might have been important to protect it from later disturbance, but it could have been equally necessary to prevent the deceased from returning to the community. Again the central grave at Broomend of Crichie illustrates this point. An unburnt body had been placed inside a cist on the bottom of a very deep pit. The filling of the shaft included a layer of boulders: a feature that has been identified on three other sites in Scotland (Henshall 1963, 151–2). In such instances the dead really were cut off from the living.

An equally wide range of choices was available to those cremating a body. Should the corpse be accompanied by any grave offerings? Were those artefacts to be burnt with the body, or might they be added to the burial at a later stage? Could the ashes of several different people be combined? Would the dead be buried on the same site as the pyre, and would their remains be placed in a simple pit, an urn or even a cist? If a pottery vessel was used it would be important to decide whether it should be buried upright or turned upside down. Again there were many options. The pits in which the ashes were placed could be unusually deep ones and sometimes access to the human remains was impeded by covering the burial with a boulder which would be difficult to move. Individual urns might be sealed by a slab or even contained within a setting of stones. All these options were followed at Broomend of Crichie. Again it seems to have been important to separate the dead from the living and to keep them in their graves (Bradley & Fraser 2011). That is very different from the practice of bone circulation that is suggested at other sites (Gibson 2007; Brück 2009).

A second set of decisions concerned the positioning of a burial. A few graves appear to be genuinely isolated, but many more occur in groups which can be described as small cemeteries. Again several options were available and different communities appear to have made their own choices. The graves could have been entirely unmarked or their positions could be indicated by low mounds or cairns, upright posts, standing stones or by a combination of these features. The extent of the cemetery might be defined by some form of enclosure, or the separate deposits could be buried underneath the same monument. Not every grave had to be treated in the same way. Thus the locations of certain deposits could be highlighted, while others were lost to view. The positions of particular burials could be emphasised by building a structure over or around them, while some remained outside it. Again there was considerable diversity.

There is a fundamental difference between mounds or cairns, and enclosures: one that is very relevant to the interpretation of henge monuments. Mounds might be constructed in a single operation or they could have been built incrementally, perhaps over several phases. In some cases the surface of the monument was breached as new graves were excavated. For a while the positions of older deposits would have been remembered, but they were rarely marked. As a result it is not known whether successive burials cut through one another by accident or by design. There are even cases in which a substantial monument seems to have been built to close off all the burials beneath it (Last 2007). After its initial construction it remained entirely unchanged.

By their very nature enclosures are open rather than closed and people can go inside them, moving between the positions of one burial and another. Often the locations of individual deposits are indicated, perhaps by a standing stone. At Broomend of Crichie, for instance, every monolith had least one burial at its foot, and the same may have been true of the some of the uprights in the avenue. It is possible that visitors could interpret the relationships between people in the past by considering how the positions of different graves reflected one another. If the same had happened during the construction of barrows and cairns, the process would have left little trace on the surface of the monument. The most that could be seen was the relationship between the structures in the same cemetery.

In principle, all the burials inside the enclosed cemeteries were equally accessible. This has a direct bearing on the peculiar character of Early Bronze Age henges. A ring cairn is a relatively modest structure and it would have been possible to see inside it even when no entrance was provided. That would remain the

case unless the interior was filled with rubble during a secondary phase. Similarly, stone circles are essentially permeable monuments. Even if there were prohibitions on entering them on the wrong occasions, it would be possible to view their full extent from outside. But henges are completely different. Even though their earthworks may have enclosed monuments of both these kinds, the construction of the bank and ditch changed their configuration entirely. That is why it is so important to establish whether they were unitary conceptions or whether the earthwork restricted access to places that had originally been open.

How did the building of the earthworks affect the use of these sites? It is easy to postulate a structural sequence, but much more difficult to discuss how it was played out in the past. The phasing of particular monuments depends on the apparent mismatch between the outlines of the stone and timber circles and the configuration of the surrounding earthworks (Gibson 2004a). In some cases they do not have a common centre, and at times there would have been practical problems in erecting the uprights once the ditch had been dug. Examples of these problems have been mentioned already. A second problem arises where henge monuments are associated with avenues. A recent study has pointed out how rarely such features lead directly into those monuments; instead they appear to be misaligned by several degrees, with the result that the bank and ditch impede access to the interior (Gillings, Pollard, Wheatley & Peterson 2007, 122–3). Broomend of Crichie is a case in point. In each instance the simplest explanation is that these structures did not conform to the same design as they were built during different phases.

That may satisfy the prehistorian's eagerness to identify a sequence, but it does not explain why the same 'mistakes' were made in the design of so many different monuments. Perhaps it would be more appropriate to ask whether these subtle changes of alignment were intended to restrict access to the interior or to contain any powerful forces inside it. An obvious comparison is with some of the burials inside these enclosures which were held in place by massive cist slabs or by the digging of unusually deep graves.

That is where the constructional details of these earthworks have an important contribution to make. Why were comparatively small areas of ground cut off by such wide ditches, and why were those ditches located inside the bank? Why were certain of the entrances unexpectedly narrow, and why were they occasionally flanked by the highest sections of the bank? The effect was surely to conceal the interior from people outside the monument and to achieve the maximum seclusion for those permitted to enter it. The existence of stone or earthwork avenues suggests they may have done so in procession, and a few sites provide indications that their movements around the interior of the enclosure may have been equally constrained. That could also be the implication of the pairing of a narrow with a wider entrance. All these features are represented at Broomend of Crichie.

The introduction made the point that public rituals often involve the inversion of patterns familiar in daily life (Turner 1969). For a period the participants separate themselves from the everyday world and flout the conventions on which social life depends. Often they do this in seclusion, in special places and on special occasions, but once this liminal phase is over they return to society, subtly transformed. In some cases they have taken on new identities.

That hypothesis attempts to explain the characteristic structure of henge monuments, but it does not specify the contexts in which such places were used. Were they employed sporadically or on a regular basis? Can the associated artefacts shed any light on these questions?

It is here that the distinction between timber and stone monuments may be particularly informative. As mentioned earlier, some of the timber circles are associated with large numbers of artefacts and animal bones, but on the whole they are not found with many human remains. The forms of the wooden buildings recall those of Neolithic dwellings but on such a large scale that it seems inconceivable that they were ever roofed. Perhaps they were thought of as the 'houses' of entire communities. That is certainly suggested by current excavations at Woodhenge and Durrington Walls (Pollard 2010; Thomas 2010; Bradley in press).

Most of those structures date from the middle to late third millennium BC. There is some evidence that, like the earliest stone circles, they may have been aligned on the sun at the turning points of the year. The related monuments of Stonehenge and Durrington Walls seem to be associated with both the winter and summer solstices, while the entrance of Woodhenge was aligned on the midsummer sunrise (Bradley in press). One possibility is that these places were where calendrical rituals were performed every year. They are among the rites of passage considered by Arnold van Gennep (1909).

The henges and stone circles of the Metal Age in northern Britain appear to have different associations. Most examples include graves. There is less to suggest an association with seasonal gatherings, and where there are celestial alignments they are not precise. If anything, these monuments face towards the position of the summer moon and perhaps the setting sun (Bradley 2005, 109–11). There is little or no evidence of feasting and, despite their considerable volume, the ditches are virtually free of artefacts. The same applies to the interior. On excavation the commonest finds are human bones and the vessels that accompanied or contained them.

It is tempting to suggest that such monuments were used in mortuary rituals. They were obviously involved in the burial of the dead, but it may be that they played an equally important role in their subsequent commemoration. That is why they had to remain accessible. Again van Gennep's account of the rites of passage may be helpful here. Perhaps these monuments were used in rituals connected with inheritance and succession. They could even have been where local leaders were inaugurated: a practice that was associated with earthworks of similar form in the Irish Iron Age or perhaps the Early Medieval period (Newman 1998). By contrast, barrows and cairns may have denoted a more distant conception of ancestry. That may be why it is unusual for henges to be replaced by burial mounds. For the most part these structures played quite different roles.

That was evidently true at Broomend of Crichie even though there were burials inside the monument and at intervals along its avenue. The shaft grave must have been particularly significant as the henge was constructed around it, although this probably happened at a later date. The ceremony for which the enclosure was built may have taken place only once, but the site was obviously visited for a long time afterwards. It is clear that this half-hidden arena was a special place. Not only was it screened from its surroundings by an enormous earthwork, it provided a stage on which remarkable events could occur.

PART II

Excavations in Sutherland and Caithness and their implications

Chapter 4

THE EXCAVATION OF THREE SMALL MONUMENTS IN SUTHERLAND AND CAITHNESS

Introduction

Part I was concerned with a single monument, Broomend of Crichie and its wider implications, but the final phase in the sequence on that site introduced some completely new elements. Towards the end of the Early Bronze Age a small timber circle was built outside the entrance to the henge. Its position seems to have cut across the line of the pre-existing avenue and the structure was set out on a new alignment. The posts were graded in height towards the north-east and its entrance faced the River Don. Unlike the earlier henge, it was not associated with any artefacts. The earthworks considered in Part II of this study share some of the same characteristics.

Chapters 1 to 3 studied a single monument complex and its wider implications. By contrast, Chapters 4 to 6 concern three sites which were much smaller and were excavated on a limited scale. It is not always clear whether there had been other structures of the same date in the vicinity and so they are more difficult to interpret. On the other hand, all these earthworks share important features in common. As Chapter 5

Illustration 4.1
The earthwork enclosure at Pullyhour before excavation

will explain, they also resemble unexcavated enclosures distributed over a wider area of Northern and North-eastern Scotland.

The excavations were undertaken for very different reasons. Work at Lairg formed only part of a larger investigation of a prehistoric landscape threatened by road building (McCullagh & Tipping 1998). The excavation at Loch Migdale also formed part of a wider investigation and included the underwater investigation of a crannog. This was undertaken for a television programme, and work on the site was limited to three days (Videotext Communications 1993). Excavation at Pullyhour was different again. It was planned as a research project designed to date a small henge monument in the north of Scotland and to consider the ways in which it might have been used. The work proceeded with no external pressure and the site could be recorded in greater detail than might otherwise have been the case.

In this chapter all three sites are treated separately, but the remarkable monument at Lairg is also studied in relation to excavated structures in its vicinity. That is not possible for the sites at Pullyhour and Migdale. The shared features of these three monuments also need highlighting, and they are considered together with the characteristics of a series of enclosures that have not been investigated in the field. To avoid burdening the reader with too much information, they will provide the subject of Chapter 5.

The excavation of a small henge monument at Pullyhour, Halkirk, Caithness

HUGO LAMDIN-WHYMARK & RICHARD BRADLEY

Introduction

The Pullyhour henge survives as a well preserved earthwork located in rough pasture on the side of a valley overlooking the Thurso River (illus 4.1; RCAHMS 1911a, 42). The earthwork had a single south-facing entrance and an extant external bank, surrounding a broad ditch and a small oval interior (illus 4.2, 4.3). The local landscape is rich in archaeology with activity from the late Mesolithic onwards. The henge was exactly aligned on the remains of large, probably Neolithic, cairn on the opposite bank of the river (Leosag cairn, NMRS: ND15SW 4, NGR 11624 53821). There had also been a standing stone (Myatt 2003, 18; NMRS: ND15SW 8, NGR: ND 115 542) to the south of the monument and an undated cist

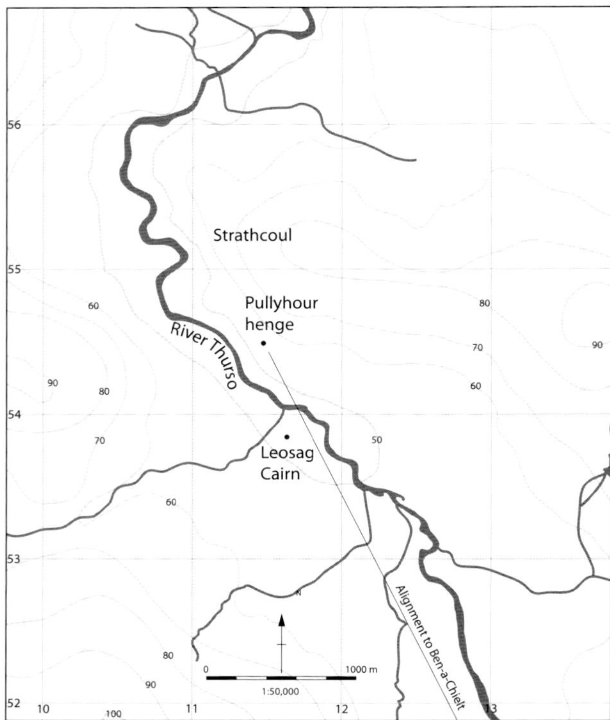

Illustration 4.2

The location of the excavated monument at Pullyhour. Reproduced with kind permission of the Ordnance Survey. © Crown copyright 2010

burial to its north (NMRS: ND15SW 14, NGR: ND 1146 5467).

Location, geology and topology

The Pullyhour henge (NMRS: ND15SW 3) is located in the valley of the Thurso River at NGR ND 11473 54478, 5km SSW of Halkirk, Caithness. The site is at approximately 56m above OD on a south-west facing slope, which gently falls towards the river (illus 4.2). The surface geology was a highly variable glacial till. The deposit was typically light to mid yellowish brown and was largely composed of sandy clay with gravel and pebbles, but lenses of unconsolidated sand were present on the northern edge of the excavation. The deposit also included some larger rounded to sub-angular rocks up to 40cm in diameter. The underlying solid geology, encountered only at the base of the ditch, consisted of impermeable mudstones of the Caithness Flagstone Group (Middle Old Red Sandstone).

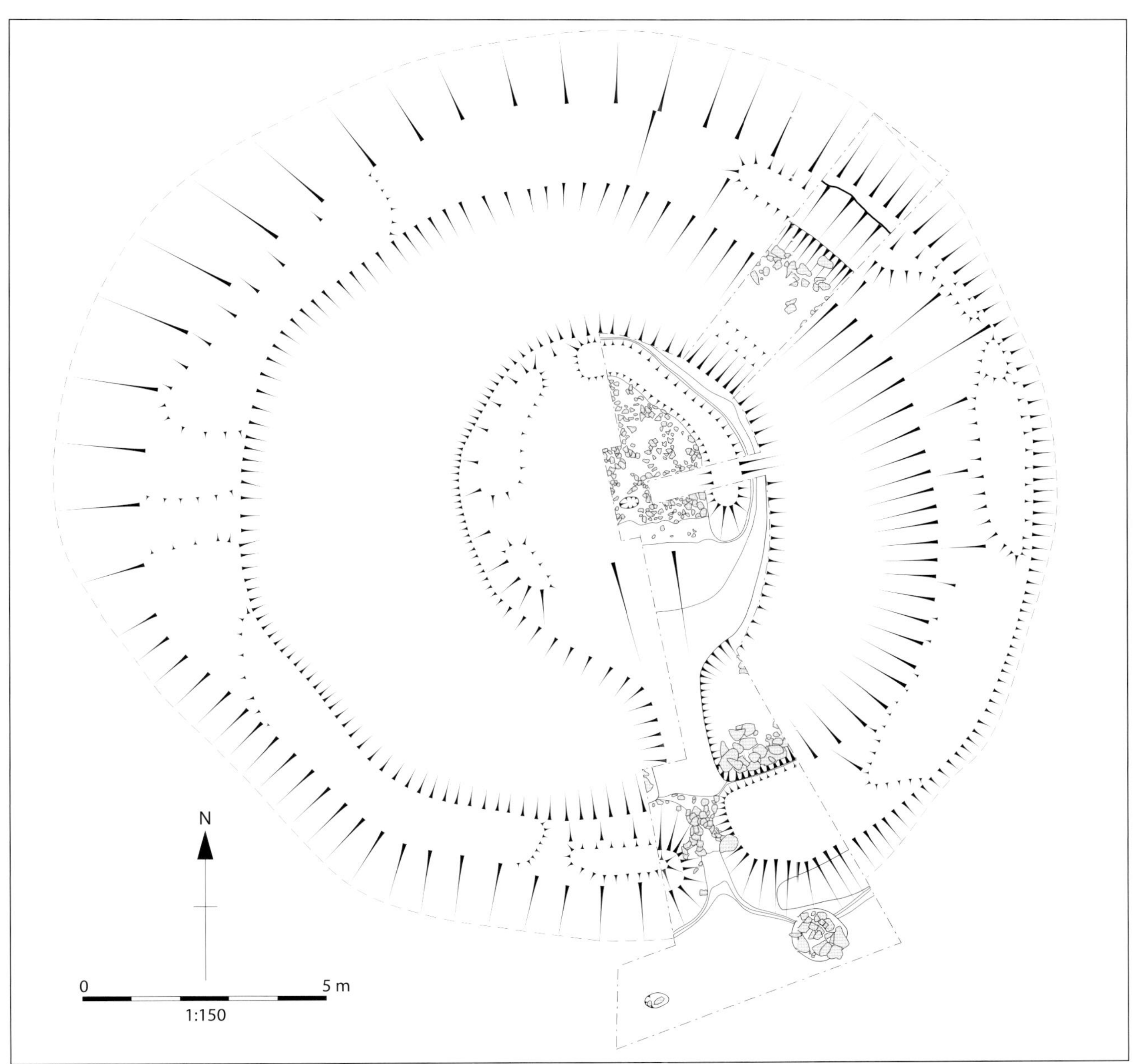

Illustration 4.3
The earthwork enclosure at Pullyhour, showing the extent of excavation in 2008

Excavation methodology

The excavations at Pullyhour were undertaken over three weeks in late March and April 2008. The excavation methodology was formulated to establish the key relationships, phasing and the character of activity within the henge with minimal disturbance to this well preserved monument. Two sections were excavated through the ditch and bank: one through the eastern terminal of the entrance and the other toward the back of the monument; because part of the site was prone to flooding the latter was located in the comparatively dry north–eastern quadrant. Approximately 50% of the interior of the monument on the eastern side was excavated, but only sample sections were excavated though a smaller bank on the

Illustration 4.4
The earthwork enclosure at Pullyhour showing excavation in progress in 2008

inner lip of the ditch (illus 4.3, 4.4, 4.5). A 50cm wide baulk was maintained, running east to west across the site. An area was also opened in front of the monument. Originally this area was confined to the eastern half of the entrance, but it was extended to the west to examine the entrance blocking and search for external post-holes. The entrance revetment and blocking were recorded *in situ* and left undisturbed.

Pre-monument environment and activity

Palaeosols

A thin palaeosol was preserved by the construction of the external henge bank and was observed in both excavated sections. The soil consisted of a friable mid brown sandy silt subsoil ('B'-horizon), which was *c* 5cm thick and a dark black greasy, organic, clay turf-line ('A'-horizon), which was 2 to 3cm thick. The turf-line beneath the banks exhibited a distinctive pattern of desiccation cracks that had filled with sand from above. The thin soil profile and well defined turf-line indicate that the soil had not been disturbed by agriculture. This interpretation is supported by soil micromorphology (p 137 below). The turf-line was rich in micro-charcoal and a piece from the north-east bank section yielded an AMS date of 1620–1450 cal BC at 2σ (OxA-3257). No artefacts were recovered from the soil preserved beneath the external banks.

The late Mesolithic scatter

The excavation of the subsoil (7) in the centre of the monument yielded seventy-five lithic artefacts, including six late Mesolithic microliths. The lithics formed a discrete scatter covering an area about a metre in diameter, with a lower density of artefacts in the surrounding area; no flintwork was recovered from the subsoil beneath the external bank (illus 4.6, 4.7). This distribution pattern, combined with the fresh condition of the lithic artefacts and lack of evidence for agricultural activity, indicates that the scatter is probably *in situ*, although it is likely that the artefacts were deposited on an extant land surface and have been vertically displaced through the soil profile.

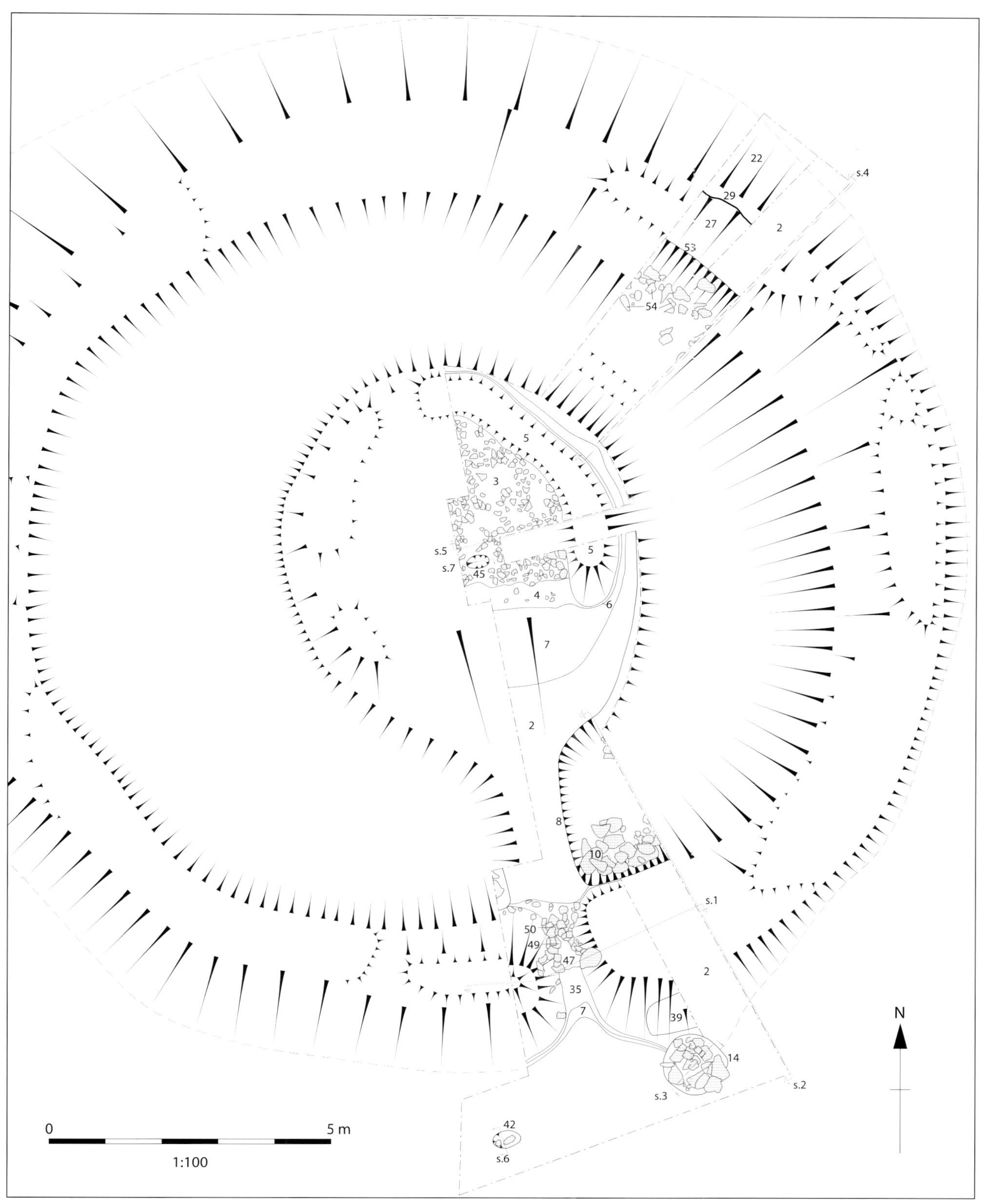

Illustration 4.5
Detailed plan of the excavated area at Pullyhour, showing the locations of individual contexts and section drawings

Illustration 4.6
Vertical view of the excavated area at Pullyhour

The scatter comprises seventy-five lithic artefacts (illus 4.8) that were predominately manufactured from beach pebble flint, although several pieces of chert/quartzite (also from a pebble source) and two chips of quartz were also present. The assemblage was dominated by small flakes and chips. A high proportion of the lithic artefacts were burnt (22–27%), but these artefacts were distributed throughout the scatter and do not indicate a specific location for the fire. It is notable that an area 40cm in diameter in the middle of the main concentration is virtually free from artefacts. This may suggest a central focus to the scatter, such as a fire or perhaps the location of a single seated individual. The limited size and distribution of the scatter may indicate that the activity at this location was comparatively brief and was perhaps focused on limited flint knapping for the maintenance of toolkits.

The Pullyhour henge

The circular enclosure: Phase 1

The date of 1620–1450 cal BC obtained on charcoal from the turf-line preserved beneath the bank provides a *terminus post quem* for construction of the Phase 1 enclosure. The first phase monument was circular, measuring *c* 17–18m in external diameter, and comprised a penannular ditch with a 1.25m wide entrance facing south (56) and an external bank (57); the enclosed area was circular and measured 7m in diameter. The ditch (56) was broad and shallow. It was 3m wide and between 42 and 58cm deep and had a flat base. Its sides were steeper towards the outside and shallower towards the interior of the monument (illus 4.9, 4.10, 4.11; sections 2, 4). The deepest area of the ditch was upslope to the north-east, and the shallowest area was located by probing in the south-eastern quadrant. This indicates that the ditch was cut into the slope and had an almost level base. The glacial till (2) through which the ditch was cut is not free draining and it is likely that the feature held water under all but the driest conditions.

The first phase bank (57) had a regular convex profile (illus 4.9, 4.10). For the most part it was 2.1m wide and 48cm high, but for approximately 2.5m on each side of the entrance its width increased to *c* 3m. Here it was slightly lower (42cm high) and had a flat top (illus 4.9, sections 2, 4). The bank terminals were squared, mirroring the ends of the ditch, but have weathered to a sub-rounded profile. The entrance is very restricted and is only 40cm wide. The bank

Illustration 4.7
The central area of the enclosure at Pullyhour during the excavation of the Mesolithic artefacts

exhibits two construction layers (illus 4.9, sections 2, 4). The lower layer (26 and 36) was a turf stack, presumably comprising turves from the surface area of the ditch. In the eastern terminus the turf stack measured 22cm high, while in the north-east section its height was 24cm. The second overlying layer (27, 48, 38) comprised redeposited clay, gravel and sands from the glacial till. The construction of the ditch probably also yielded numerous glacial erratics measuring up to 40cm in maximum dimension. These stones were found against the external edge of the ditch (10, 54) and could have lined the inner face of the bank. They may have been pushed into the ditch when the monument was closed (see below).

The interior of the monument was circular, measuring *c* 7m in diameter, and was devoid of contemporary archaeological features, although the buried soil sealed beneath the internal bank belonging to the second phase had a covering of yellow-brown

sediment which seems to have been obtained from the bottom of the ditch. It may have been intended to colour the surface of the monument. No artefacts can be assigned to this phase, although two flint flakes from the topsoil may be considered as broadly contemporary with the monument (p 133 below). The paucity of features and material culture associated with this phase, combined with the absence of wear to the pre-monument soil where it was exposed in the entrance, may indicate a comparatively brief period of activity before the monument was abandoned.

Elaboration and reconfiguration: Phase 2

A second phase of monument construction occurred at Pullyhour after a period of inactivity that allowed a soil horizon to develop over the original bank (illus 4.9, 4.10, section 4). The soil horizon (29) was a dark brownish black, greasy, sandy clay, 3cm thick. A fragment of charcoal from this layer has been dated to

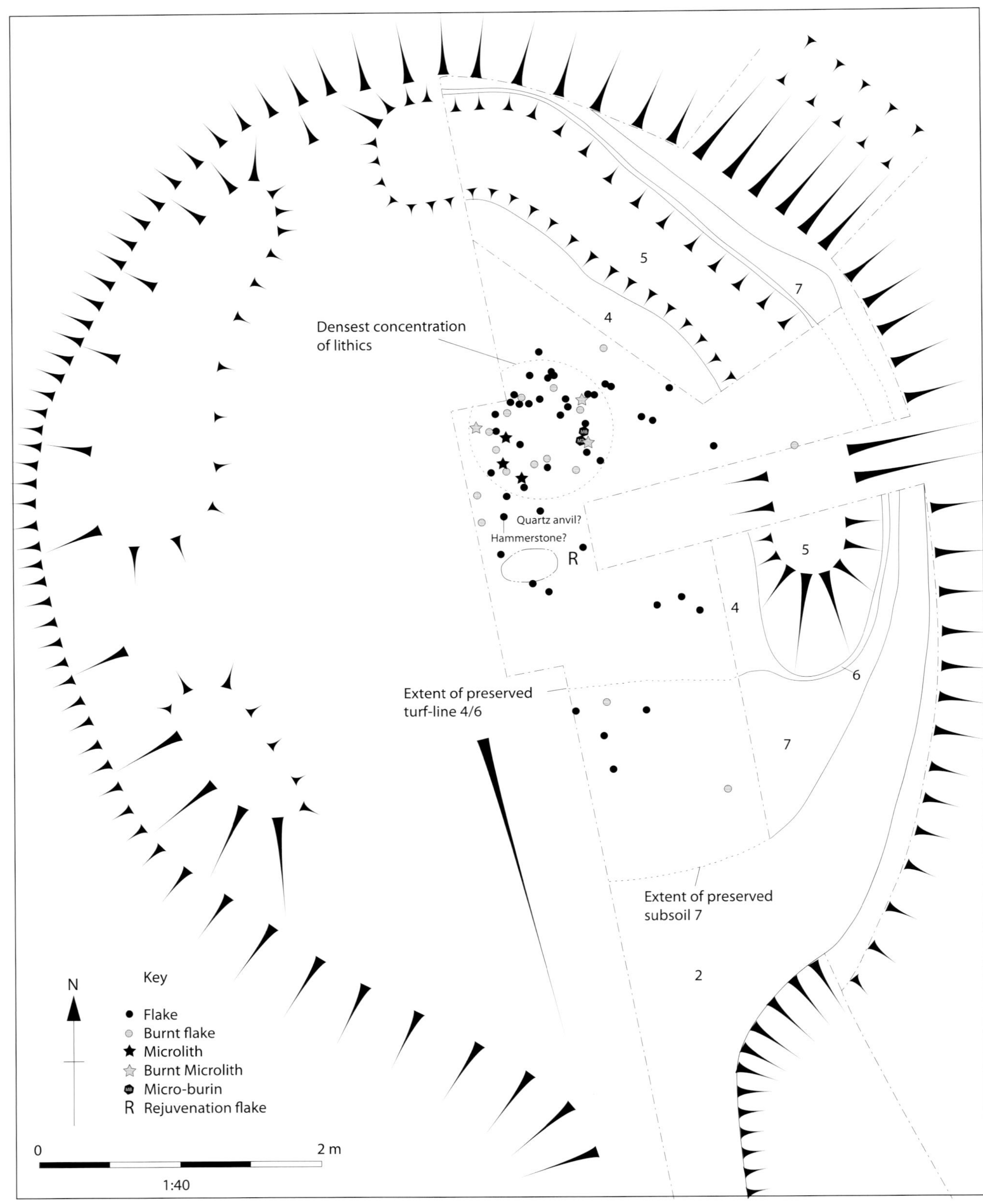

Illustration 4.8
Distribution of lithic artefacts in the excavated area at Pullyhour

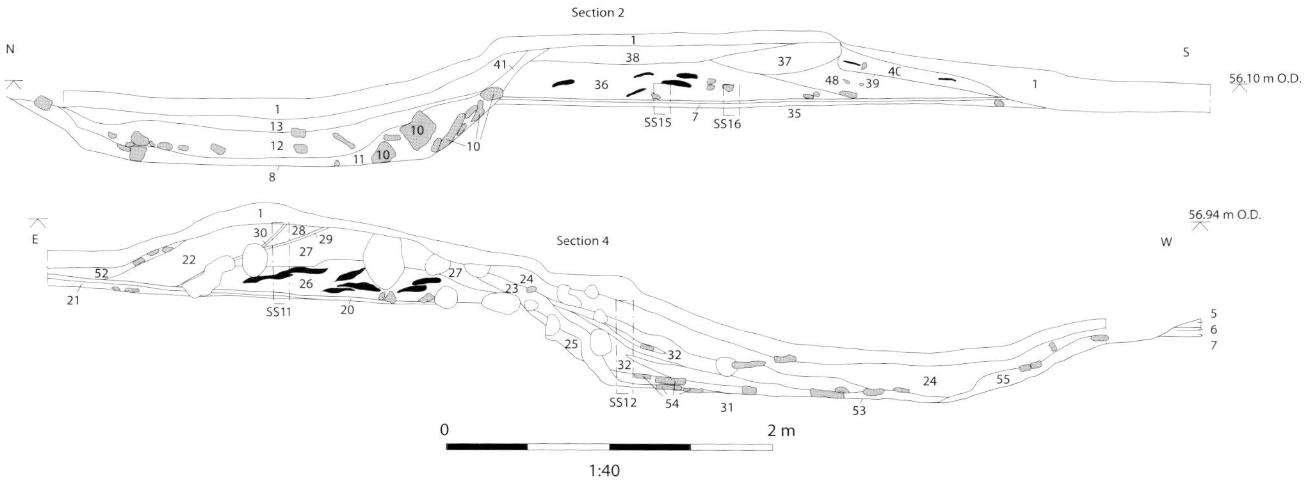

Illustration 4.9
Sections of the earthwork enclosure at Pullyhour

Illustration 4.10
Section of the bank at Pullyhour on the north-east side of the enclosure

1369–1126 BC at 2σ (OxA-18156), providing a *terminus ante quem* for the construction of the first phase bank and a *terminus post quem* for the construction of the overlying second phase bank. Pollen from this soil (29) and the soil preserved in the monument's interior (4, 6) indicate that the landscape continued to be dominated by heathland and grassland, but that less hazel scrub may have been present; this could suggest some clearance (see pp 137–41 below).

The second phase of construction involved remodelling of the ditch, bank, interior and entrance (illus 4.11). The inner edge of the ditch on the west and east sides was recut (58), forming an oval interior, measuring 7m long by 6m wide, with a NNW–SSE long axis. The external bank was raised irregularly, to a maximum preserved height of 55cm, with significant deposits placed on the outer edges of the western and eastern banks, widening the earthwork by *c* 40cm to *c* 2.5m. In the north-east section, the secondary bank is entirely composed of re-deposited glacial deposits,

indicating that any ditch fills that had accumulated since the first phase were probably not removed. The western terminal was also raised, while the flattened top of the eastern terminal was retained (illus 4.9, 3, 6). A small horseshoe-shaped bank, which has a break to the NNW and a possible slight break to the west, was also constructed in the interior (60). This bank, which was just 50cm wide and 10cm high, was constructed from redeposited glacial gravel and further reduced the interior area to 6.5m by 3.75 m. The area within the bank (60) was also paved with small flat fragments of white sandstone, which measure up to 10cm across (3).

Similar pieces of stone were also used to construct a low dry stone wall (49) on each side of the entrance, revetting the bank and further constricting access to the interior (illus 4.4, 3; illus 4.12). Two courses of this stonework survive to a height of *c* 15cm. They extend for 1.10m on each side of the bank terminals (illus 4.12). The entrance between these stones was

Illustration 4.11
Section of the ditch at Pullyhour on the north-east side of the enclosure showing the layer of rubble against its outer face

Illustration 4.12
The entrance to the enclosure at Pullyhour looking out through the bank terminals. The unexcavated kerbs can be seen together with a small setting of stones blocking the causeway

between 10m and 30cm wide. This revetment has not been securely dated. While similar materials had been employed during Phase 2 on other parts of the site, it is conceivable that this construction belongs to the first phase. The outer face of the eastern terminal was also remodelled by cutting back the bank (39) and revetting it with a turf stack (illus 4.9, section 2, Context 40). The turves used were thick and dark and differ from those in the preserved soil horizon.

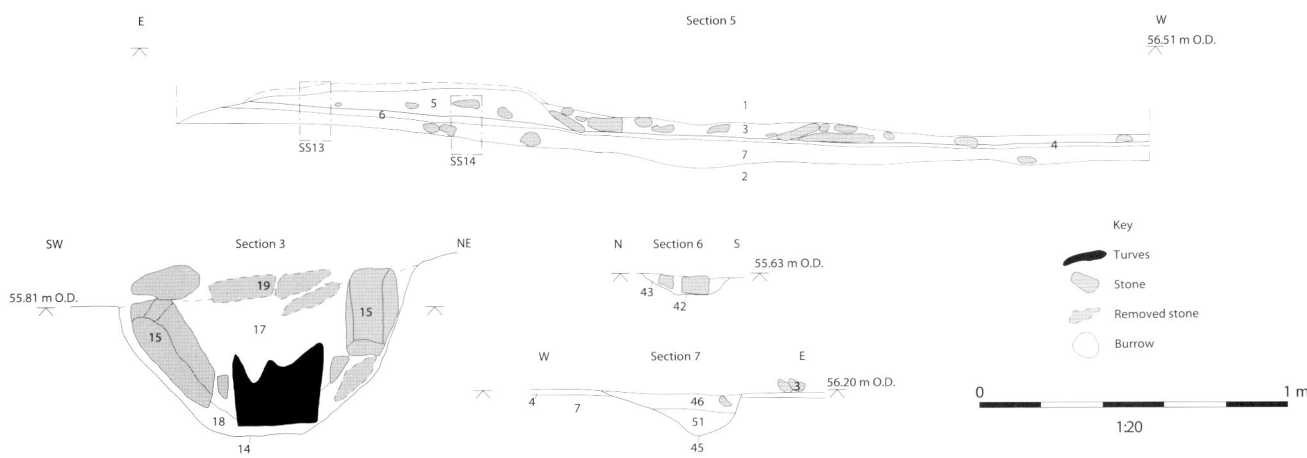

Illustration 4.13
Sections of features in the interior at Pullyhour plus the post sockets outside the entrance

Illustration 4.14
Vertical view of the large post-hole cut through the bank beside the south entrance

Outside the entrance were two post-holes of different sizes, one substantially larger than the other. The larger post-hole (14) cut through the primary bank and was circular with steep sides and a flat base, measuring 1.08m in diameter and 60cm in depth. The post-hole was packed with glacial stones measuring up to 30cm in maximum dimension (15). At the base of the hole the stump of the post had been preserved (illus 4.13, section 3; illus 4.14, 4.15). The post was badly eroded and hollow (illus 4.16). It was 27cm diameter and survived to a height of 27cm, but the stone packing shows that the post can never have been more than 32cm in diameter. The post has been identified as pine, a species which became extinct in Caithness at the end of the Neolithic period. It has been radiocarbon dated to 2573–2348 BC at 2σ (SUERC-20-320). This means that the post must have been extracted from a bog and was of considerable antiquity when it was erected. The second post-hole (42) was oval and measured only 38cm by 21cm; it was only 8cm deep and cannot have held a substantial upright (illus 4.13, section 6).

Another small post-hole was located at the centre of the monument. This post-hole (45) was oval and measured 45cm by 26cm. It was 13cm deep (illus 4.13, section 7). The similarity in size and form of post-holes 42 and 45 may indicate that are related and belong to Phase 2, although independent dating is not available. Significantly the alignment from the small centre post (45) through the large post-hole (14) respects the new NNW–SSE axis of the oval interior, the NNW gap in the horseshoe bank (60) and the low turf-revetted section of the bank terminal to the SSE. This alignment is directed towards distant hilltop, Ben-a-Chieltn (illus 4.17). The alignment from the centre post (45) though the second small post (42) is not directed at any obvious landscape feature, but in conjunction with post-hole 14 these posts frame the view of the Leosag Cairn to the south and the position of the full moon at midsummer (illus 4.18).

Illustration 4.15
Section of the large post-hole cut through the bank beside the south entrance

Illustration 4.16
Views of the bog pine post set into the earthwork bank at Pullyhour

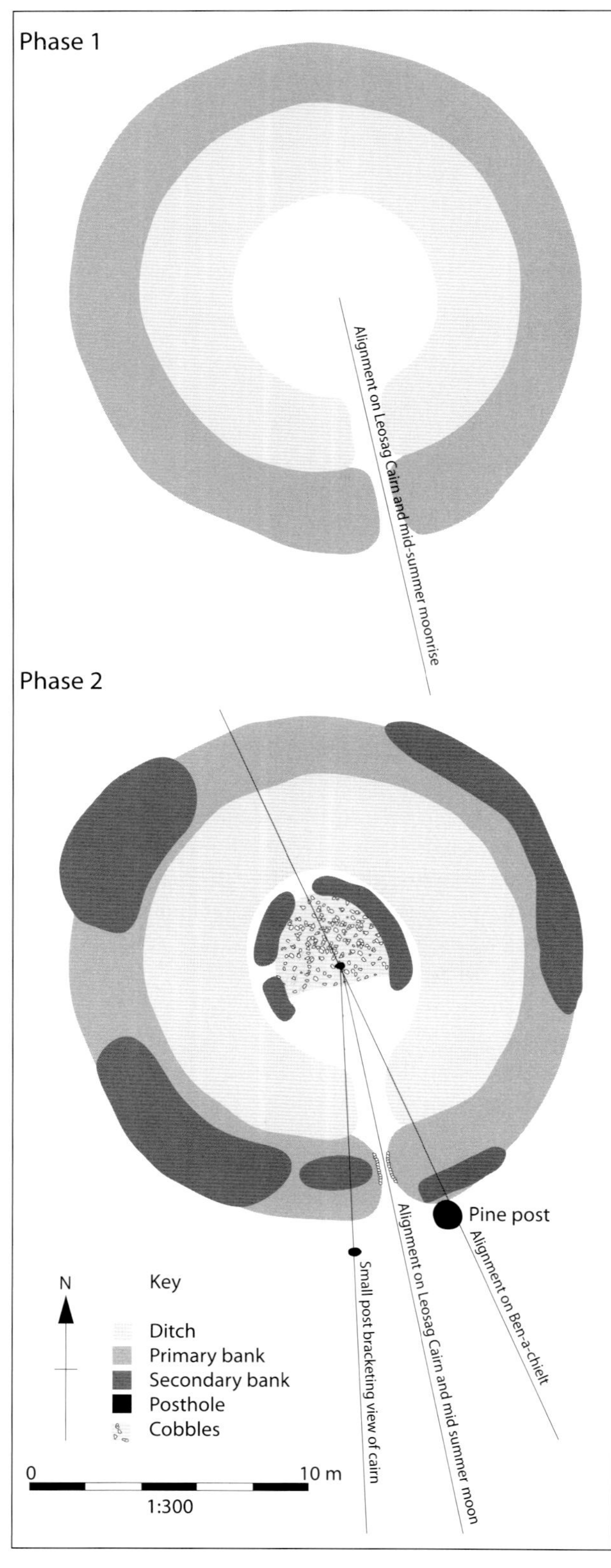

Illustration 4.17
Phase plan of the enclosure at Pullyhour, showing the changing alignments of the monument

Closing and abandonment: Phase 3

In the final phase of activity the monument appears to have been decommissioned. It may have immediately followed the previous activity. The closing of the monument involved the blocking of the entrance, removal of the large standing post and possibly pushing the stone revetment of the bank into the ditch.

The entrance was neatly blocked by laying two layers of stone over the causeway and the low wall revetting the bank. This feature covers an area of 40cm by 40cm and is 6cm thick. It must represent a symbolic blocking of the enclosure rather than a physical obstacle (illus 4.12). The large stones that may have lined the in edge of the bank may also have been pushed into the ditch, although they could originally have been deposited on the inner edge of the ditch or have slumped into this position. The post (16) in large post-hole (14) was removed, leaving no trace above ground. Because the stump of the post still survived, it must have either been cut or snapped, perhaps after it had begun to rot. The act was accompanied by some force, as one of the large packing stones was removed and smashed into nine fragments, of which eight were thrown back into the hole above the post (illus 4.13, section 3, Context 19).

The ditch fills comprise a series of dark tenacious clay silts, with some gravel and occasional pieces of stone resulting from erosion of the bank (illus 4.9, sections 2 and 4). The silting of the ditch was a gradual process, probably occurring over many centuries although no dating evidence was recovered. Pollen from the ditch is dominated by grassland at the base of the sequence, giving way to heathland higher in the fills. The ditch contained some potential indicators of agricultural activity, including pollen from the *Hordeum* group high in the sequence. The latter may reflect post-medieval agriculture relating to the settlement at Pullyhour (see p 140 below).

Artefactual evidence – Lithics

HUGO LAMDIN-WHYMARK

Introduction

Eighty lithic artefacts were recovered from the excavations, and a further three flints were collected from the surface in close proximity to the monument. Seventy-five of those from the excavations were recovered from a palaeosol preserved in the interior of the monument (subsoil 7). These lithics derive from a discrete *in situ* artefact scatter dated to the late Mesolithic

Illustration 4.18
A reconstruction of the Pullyhour monument, emphasising its relationship to the Leosag cairn and the rising midsummer moon. Visualisation by Douglas Scott, reproduced with his kind permission

through the presence of six microliths, including three scalene micro-triangles. The remaining five lithic artefacts comprise two small chunks of quartz, two flint flakes from the topsoil (1) in the interior of the monument, and a flint flake from the central post-hole (45, fill 46). These lithics are considered to be contemporary with the monument, with the exception of one of the flakes from the topsoil (1, SF3) which is comparable to artefacts from the Mesolithic scatter.

Raw material

The Mesolithic lithics from subsoil 7 are predominately manufactured from flint, but six flakes and a micro-burin have a coarse texture and are probably manufactured from a chert or quartzite. In addition, two chips of quartz and a quartzite flake were present. The Mesolithic flint was typically light grey or light greyish brown, but a dark grey flake and an orange-brown flake were also present. The chert/quartzite varied in colour from light brown to orange-brown.

Six flints and one chert/quartzite flake exhibited worn cortical surfaces, indicating that they were collected as small pebbles from a fluvial source. One of the cortical surfaces exhibited chatter marks suggesting that the pebbles originate from beach deposits. The two flint flakes that are probably contemporary with the monument are manufactured from an orange-brown flint with small white-grey inclusions. One of the flakes (SF 60) exhibits a chattered cortex, indicating that the flint was again collected from a beach. Three of the pieces of quartz and the quartzite pebble exhibit worn surfaces suggesting that they derive from fluvial or glacial deposits; the two small quartz chips from Context 7 are of indeterminate origin.

Condition

The lithics are in fresh condition, with the exception of a flake recovered from a stream near the monument which exhibits slight post-depositional edge-damage. The Mesolithic assemblage from subsoil 7 includes a

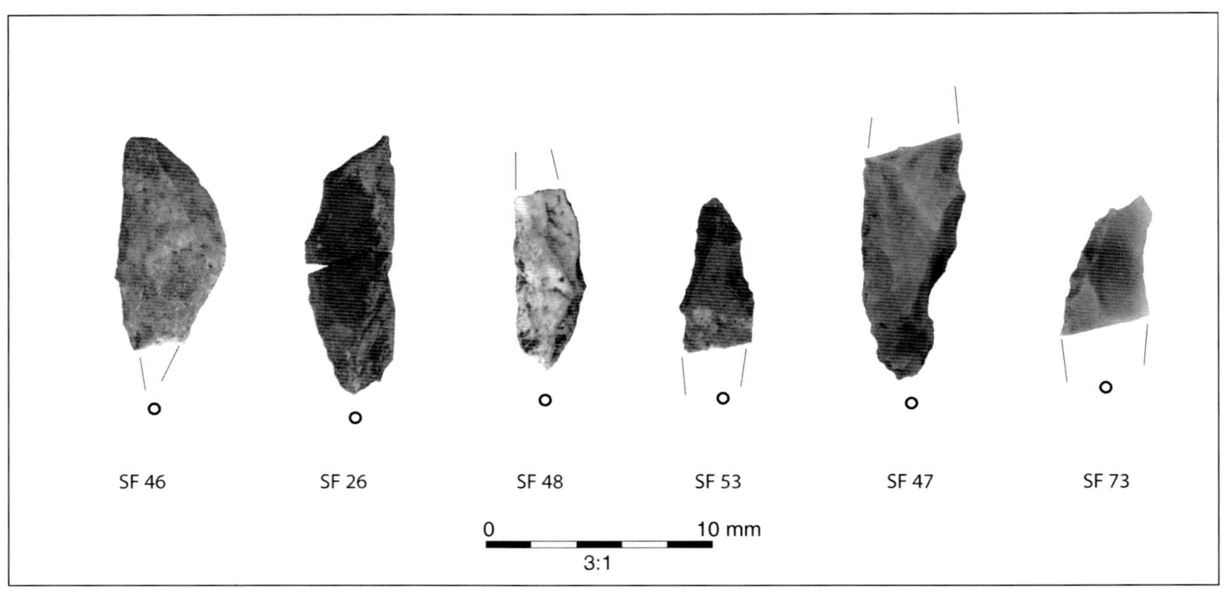

Illustration 4.19
The excavated microliths from Pullyhour

high proportion of broken artefacts (41–51.3%) and burnt artefacts (22–27.5%). The lithics are free from surface cortication, but a light orange iron-staining is present on a couple of artefacts.

The late Mesolithic assemblage (illus 4.19)

In total, seventy-five lithics were recovered from subsoil 7 and a comparable flake was recovered from the overlying topsoil (1, SF 3). This assemblage is predominately composed of small flakes and chips (flakes <10 mm²), with the largest flake measuring just 22mm in length by 18mm in width. Several of the chips appear to have derived from the same grey flint core, although it is apparent that flakes from several different cores are present. The platforms, where present, are plain or punctiform and the majority of flakes exhibit platform-edge abrasion. This suggests that the flakes were struck from a simple platform, perhaps the surface of a split pebble, with some care and consideration. A small platform-edge rejuvenation, measuring 10mm by 9mm by 2mm thick, further reflects a considered reduction strategy; while only a minor adjustment, this removal would have altered the form of flake removals from the core face. The flake debitage present appears to represent a mixture of flakes brought to this location from elsewhere, alongside chips from a brief knapping event that perhaps produced no more than a few flakes. No cores were present, suggesting that none was

exhausted at this location and that they were retained for further working elsewhere. A possible quartzite hammerstone, weighing 114g, was recovered at the edge of the main scatter, but as a water-worn pebble it is difficult to distinguish any slight edge-damage from natural abrasion and the identification must remain tentative. A large water-worn piece of milky quartz, weighing 296g, was also recovered to the south of the scatter. This piece has not obviously been worked, but a flat surface may have been used as an anvil.

The retouched component of the assemblage comprises six microliths and two micro-burins. The retouched artefacts are described fully below:

SF 26. Scalene micro-triangle (Jacobi 1978, 7a1). Burnt, but complete with a modern break. 12mm long by 4mm wide and 1.5mm thick. The bulb was not removed using the micro-burin technique.

SF 46. Scalene micro-triangle (Jacobi 1978, most comparable to 7a1). Complete except for slight modern damage to the proximal tip. 10+mm long by 5mm and 1.5mm thick. The left hand side exhibits straight slight-abrupt edge retouch and the proximal right hand side exhibits an oblique truncation to form a point.

SF 47. Proximal fragment of a microlith. The proximal end exhibits an unsuccessful attempt to remove the bulb using the micro-burin technique.

The bulb was subsequently removed by retouch, leaving a slight notch on the right hand side. 11.5 + mm long by 4mm wide and 2mm thick.

SF 48. Scalene micro-triangle (Jacobi 1978, 7a2). Burnt and broken; a modern break has removed the tip. 8mm + long by 3mm wide and 1.5mm thick.

SF 53. Distal fragment of a microlith. The left and right hand sides exhibit slight abrupt retouch that converges to a distal point. 7mm + long by 3mm wide and 1.5mm thick.

SF 73. Proximal fragment of a microlith. The right hand side exhibits slight abrupt edge retouch. The bulb was slight and was removed without using the micro-burin technique. 4mm long by 7mm wide and 1.5mm thick.

SF 9. Distal micro-burin on a light brown chert blade. This flint is larger than the majority in the assemblage. It was over 27mm long, 10mm wide and 3mm thick, and the distal end converges to a point. This raises the possibility that this artefact was used as a tool, for example a projectile point, and may have arrived at this site as a finished implement.

SF 54. Proximal micro-burin. A small but classic example measuring 6mm long by 6mm wide and 2mm thick. The notch is on the right hand side.

The Bronze Age assemblage

Two flint flakes and two chunks of quartz are tentatively assigned to the Bronze Age phase of activity. A side trimming flake of an orange-red beach pebble flint with white inclusions, measuring 21mm long by 15mm wide and 6mm thick was recovered from the central post-hole (45, fill 46, SF 60). A second flake of a comparable raw material was recovered from topsoil (1, SF 1) on the northern edge of the internal platform. This flake is much larger than the Mesolithic artefacts, measuring 25mm long by 23mm wide and 8mm thick, and appears to have been haphazardly struck from a simple platform without preparation of the platform-edge. This flake exhibits some possible use-damage. The two pieces of quartz comprise one chunk (SF 75), weighing 1g, that was recovered among the stone cobbling (3) in the centre of the monument, and a second chunk, weighing 16g, that was recovered while cleaning the southern entrance.

Other lithics

In addition to the lithics from the excavation, three flints were recovered on the surface close to the monument. A molehill 8.5m east of the entrance yielded a small burnt and broken chip (SF 78), while a second molehill 11m to the west of the entrance produced a broken bladelet of light-grey brown pebble flint. It was over 22mm long, 6mm wide and 2mm thick (SF 76). A broken blade-like flake of orange-brown flint was recovered from the bed of a stream, *c* 50m SE of the monument and alongside the road. These flints are not intrinsically datable, but the bladelet probably dates from the Mesolithic.

Discussion

The lithic assemblage contains components from two distinct periods: the late Mesolithic and the Bronze Age. The Mesolithic assemblage, including all the diagnostic artefacts, largely derives from a small *in situ* scatter preserved in the palaeosol (subsoil 7). The majority of the artefacts fall within a sub-circular area *c* 1m in diameter, but the central 50cm of this area is almost free from artefacts. This may suggest the scatter may be the product of a single individual seated in the centre of this area. The scatter appears to indicate limited flint knapping and the production of at least one microlith. The broken and burnt microliths may represent elements discarded while repairing a tool, or pieces that were embedded in the quarry and burnt during cooking. The burnt artefacts indicate that a fire was probably present, but these pieces are spread throughout the scatter and do not indicate its location. For that reason the debris may have been subject to limited movement, although this may have occurred as part of the activities around the scatter. The size and distribution of this scatter indicate comparatively limited activity, potentially of relatively short duration.

Radiocarbon dates

Unidentifiable charcoal fragment from the surface of the Phase 1 buried soil:

OxA–3257   3257 ± 28 BP $\delta^{13}C$ −26.71
1σ cal BC 1610–1490   2σ cal BC 1620–1450

Unidentifiable charcoal fragment from the surface of the Phase 2 buried soil:

OxA–18156   2988 ± 26 BP $\delta^{13}C$ −27.4
1σ cal BC 1292–1142   2σ cal BC 1369–1126

Outer rings of bog pine post (Context 16):

SUERC–20–320   3965 ± 30 BP $\delta^{13}C$ −25.5
1σ cal BC 2565–2463   2σ cal BC 2573–2348

Soil micromorphology

AMY POOLE

Excavations at Pullyhour in 2008 investigated the old land surfaces preserved beneath two phases of the henge monument. The first buried soil was under the external henge bank, and the second was preserved below a small horseshoe-shaped bank constructed at a later date within the interior of the original henge. The results from the micromorphology on these two buried horizons will be discussed here.

Research questions

What information can be gained about the environment prior to the monument's construction?

Is there any evidence of land use prior to monument construction?

Are there any discernable differences between the buried soils represented by the two phases of monument construction?

Topography, geology and soil

The henge monument is located in the valley of the Thurso River. The surface drift geology here is boulder clay. The underlying geology is the Wick beds of the lower Caithness flagstone group. The soil is of the Thurso association and consists of the poorly drained Thurso Series of non-calcareous gleys (Crampton 1914).

Sampling and methodology

Two undisturbed samples were available for micromorphological analysis. Sample 15 (13 × 8cm) represents the buried horizon from the first phase

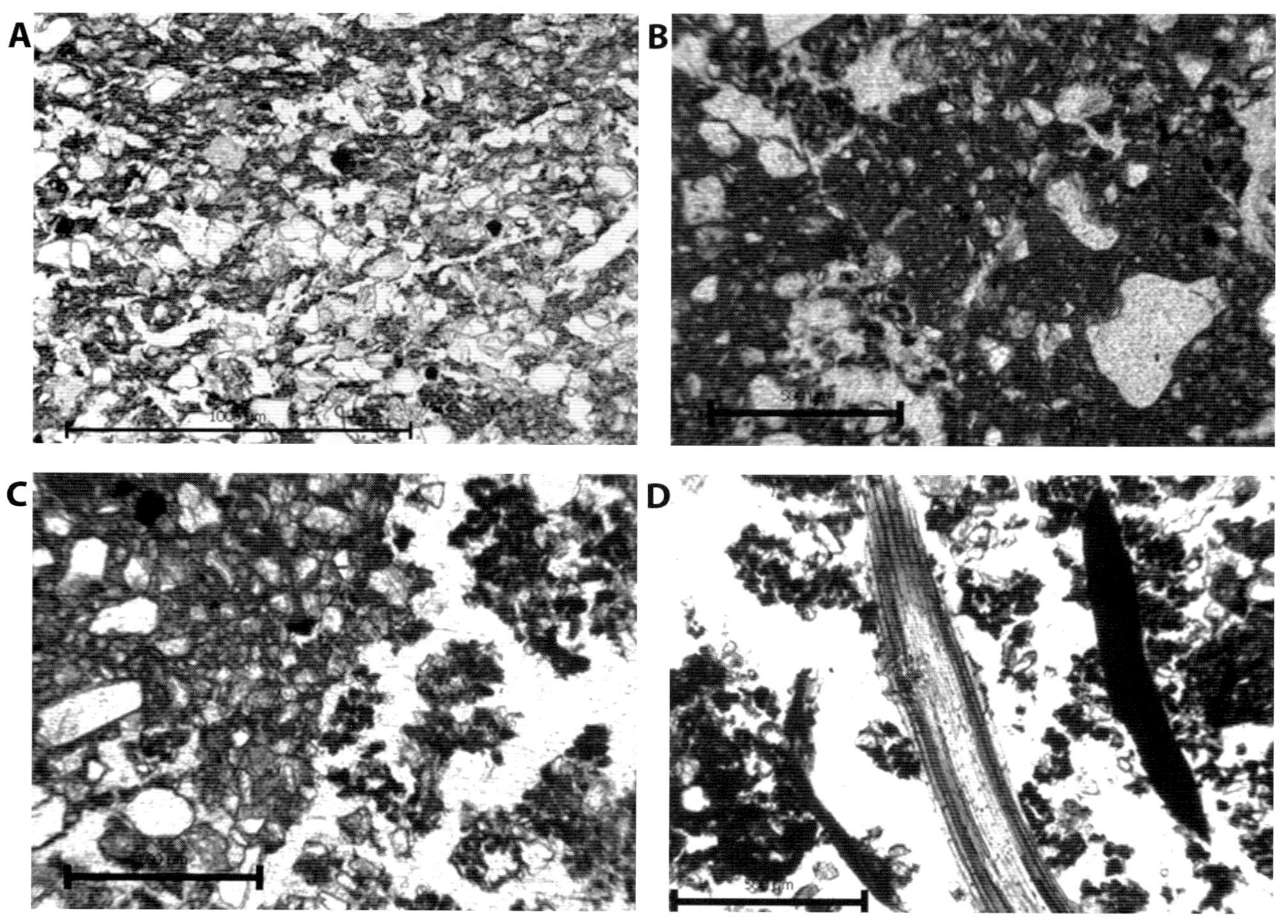

Illustration 4.20
Thin sections of the buried soils at Pullyhour. For details of these samples see the text

of construction and was taken from the north bank section. This sample encompasses the buried soil, the organic turf layer and the bank material. Sample 13 (13 × 8cm) represents the buried horizon from the second phase of construction and was taken from the horseshoe-shaped bank in the interior of the henge. This sample encompasses the buried soil, the organic turf layer and the bank material above.

The methodology used here for slide manufacture and investigation is the same as that used for Broomend of Crichie (see p 61 above).

Results (Table 3)

NORTH BANK SECTION

The sediments in this thin section (15) represent the primary construction phase on the site.

The subsoil (2) consists of a moderately sorted fine to medium sand. The fine material is organo-mineral and yellowish brown in colour. There is evidence for fungal sclerotia (5–15%) and preserved plant remains (<5%). The horizon was very disturbed by channels caused by bioturbation (15–30%), which often contain red and brown aggregates.

The buried soil (7) consists of a moderately sorted fine to medium sand 10–15mm thick. The fine material is organo-mineral and yellowish to reddish brown in colour. The coarse material shows some linear orientation to the turf line above (illus 4.20, A). Charcoal and charred plants are present in small quantities (<5%). The horizon is disturbed by channels caused by bioturbation (10–20%). There is evidence for fungal sclerotia (5–15%). Vertical cracks, the results of wetting and drying, indicate fluctuations in the water table.

The turf line (35) is 10–15mm thick and discontinuous across the section. It is organic and dark orange brown in colour. Micro-charcoal and charred plant remains (200–500μm) are present (<5%). This horizon is very disturbed by channels and planes (30–40%), the result of bioturbation, which often contain a little very fine to fine sand-size particles.

The overlying bank material (36) is an unsorted very fine to medium sand. In the first 10mm above the turf line there are visible linear bands of coarse material, oriented to the turf line below. The fine material is light brown in colour. Some channels are lined with red oxidised material. Rock fragments 5–10mm in length exhibit iron depletion rims. The bank is disturbed by bioturbation, channels and planes (30–50%). There is also evidence for ferruginous plant remains (<5%),

fragments of modern roots (<5%), and fungal sclerotia (<5%).

All contexts are badly disturbed by bioturbation, making interpretations a little difficult. The bank is not thick and the buried soil, underlying soil and bank material all show evidence for wetting and drying in the form of vertical cracks, and there are signs of oxidation along channels and cracks indicated by reddened fine material. Rare fragments of charcoal and charred plant material are most likely windblown; no other evidence suggests clearance by burning prior to the construction. There is no evidence to suggest cultivation or any other disturbance at the site prior to the monument's construction. The turf layer and the buried soil beneath the bank were both thin and compacted, potentially indicating grazing on the site prior to the construction of the monument (Romans & Robertson 1975). On the other hand, it is not certain that the compaction occurred before these deposits were buried.

INTERIOR HORSESHOE BANK SECTION

The sediments in this thin section (13) represent the second phase of construction on the site.

The subsoil (2) exhibits very similar characteristics to the subsoil present in the north bank section. It consists of moderately sorted fine to medium sand, but includes some fine gravel. The fine material is organo-mineral and light brown in colour. There are common ferruginised plant remains (15–30%) and few modern root fragments (5–15%). Bioturbation is evident in the form of channels (30–40%). Some fungal sclerotia are present (<5%).

The buried soil (7) is 10–30mm thick. It consists of a moderately sorted very fine to medium sand. The fine material is organo-mineral and light brown in colour with some areas of reddish brown. There is a small amount of charcoal present (<5%). Well preserved plant remains are common (15–30%). Bioturbation is evident in the form of vertical channels (20–30%) and fungal sclerotia were present (<5%). There are vertical cracks in the upper part of the buried soil, the result of wetting and drying processes.

The turf line (6) is 10–20mm thick and discontinuous across the thin section. It is organic and reddish black in colour. Well preserved plant fragments are common (15–30%) and there is considerable disturbance from bioturbation in the form of channels and planes (30–50%), some containing red aggregates.

Directly above the turf layer in the second phase of construction is a horizon that does not appear in

Table 3

Pullyhour Micromorphology

		15	15	15	15
Thin Section No		15	15	15	15
Unit No		2	7	35	36
Deposit type		natural	buried soil	turf line	bank
Thickness (mm)		>50	10–15	10–15	>30
Boundary (upper)		smooth/diffuse	smooth/clear	wavy/clear	not on slide
Structure	Sorting	moderate to unsorted	moderate	unsorted	unsorted
Structure	Microstructure	vughs, planes and channels 20–30%	planes, vughs and channels 10–20%	planes and channels 30–40%	channels, planes and vughs 20–30%
Structure	Coarse Material Orientation/Distribution	random/unreferred	some parallel linear orientation to turf line above	random/unreferred	some bands of material oriented to turf line
Structure	c/f related distribution	embedded	embedded	embedded	embedded
Coarse Mineral >63µm	Overall Particle Size	very fine to medium sand	fine to medium sand	very fine to fine sand	very fine to medium sand
Coarse Mineral >63µm	Overall Particle Shape	SR–SA		R–SR	R–SA
Coarse Mineral >63µm	Mineral/compound mineral % v.fine-medium sand 63-500µm	•••••	•••••	•••	•••••
Coarse Mineral >63µm	coarse-v.coarse sand 500-2000µm	•••	••		••
Coarse Mineral >63µm	fine gravel >2000µm	••	•		•
Fine Mineral >63µm	PPL – Nature and Colour	organo-mineral/yellowish brown (patches of reddish brown)	organo-mineral/yellow–red brown	organic/dark orange brown	organo-mineral/light brown
Fine Mineral >63µm	XPL – Birefringence fabric and Colour	undifferentiated/dark brown	undifferentiated/dark brown	undifferentiated/opaque	speckled/orange brown
Plant material	Charcoal		•	••	
Plant material	Charred plant fragments		•	•	
Plant material	Fungal sklerotia	••	••		•
Plant material	Modern plant roots				•••
Plant material	ferrunginized plant remains	•	••		•
Pedofeatures	Amorphous organic (red)				
Pedofeatures	Amorphous organic (yellow)				
Pedofeatures	Amorphous organic (black)	•	••		•
Pedofeatures	Fe/Mn nodules				
Pedofeatures	Bioturbation	•••	•••	•••	••••

PPL = plane polarised light, XPL = cross polarised light, OIL = oblique incient light, N/O = not observed

• = very few <5%, •• = few 5–15%, ••• = common 15–30%, •••• = frequent 30–50%, ••••• = dominant >50%

R = rounded, SR = sub-rounded, SA = sub-angular, A = angular, spv = simple packing voids, cpv = complex packing voids the first phase of construction (5). Although severely disturbed by bioturbation, areas that have remained undisturbed show a compacted structure of fine material, yellow-brown in colour with very fine to fine rock and mineral grains (illus 4.20, B). The fine material is embedded with the mineral grains and large areas contain no voids. The boundary with the context above is heavily mixed by bioturbation. There are many channels (30–50%) containing brown and red aggregates (illus 4.20, C), the remains of modern roots (200–500µm, 15–30%), and ferrunginised plant remains (500–1000µm, 5–15%; illus 4.20, D).

The bank material (5a) overlying this compacted layer consists of an unsorted very fine to medium sand and a fine gravel. The fine material is mostly aggregates of red and brown with frequent voids (30–40%). Some areas are more embedded, whereas others are loose aggregate. Organic matter is present, both yellow and red. Large rock fragments show iron depletion rims. The horizon is very disturbed by bioturbation (>50%). Modern plant remains are common (15–30%).

All the contexts were disturbed by bioturbation. The internal bank was very low and the buried soil and the turf line in the second buried horizon show similar properties to those from the primary buried horizon. The buried soil and turf line provide evidence of a fluctuating water table, although not as much in the underlying soil. The buried soil and the turf line were both more uneven than in the primary phase and showed no evidence for linear banding or orientation. The fine yellow compacted layer, which was not present in the primary phase, showed a massive structure, with no voids where undisturbed by bioturbation. The structure of this layer is not consistent with any other contexts in either the primary or secondary phase, although the minerals and rocks are consistent with that of the local geology. The layer seems to be composed of material that has been removed from the base of the ditch during construction and deposited within the henge after the construction of the primary monument. This material has been compacted during the life of the henge and later covered by a small bank during the secondary construction phase. The upper boundary of this deposit contains no evidence of burning or other land use, although it is heavily mixed by bioturbation. The bank material above was far more mixed and disturbed than the primary phase. Only a single fragment of charcoal was found, most likely windblown and not indicative of any *in situ* burning in the interior of the monument prior to the secondary phase of building. The turf line and the

buried soil are less compacted in the secondary horizon than in the primary horizon, potentially indicating a difference in the treatment of the ground surface in the interior of the henge after the construction of the first earthworks.

CONCLUSION

The buried soil sequence from Pullyhour indicates that the environment prior to the monument's construction was open land; a compacted A horizon is potential evidence for grazing. A little charcoal present is indicative of anthropogenic manipulation of the surrounding landscape, but there is no evidence for *in situ* burning. There is no evidence for cultivation at the site. The buried soil and underlying soil layers show evidence for wetting and drying consistent with a fluctuating water table.

The buried soil beneath the second phase of construction is consistent with that from the first phase. The humic turf layer in the secondary phase exhibits less compaction than that in the primary phase, evidence that no grazing took place inside the enclosure. Inside the earthwork and sealed by its internal bank is a context that is not present in the primary phase. It has been interpreted as a compacted surface lain down in the interior of the henge following the primary construction. The surface is yellow brown in colour. The rock and mineral inclusions are consistent with the local geology, and the deposit is most likely composed of material that was removed from the base of the ditch during construction. The structure of the deposit differs from the buried soil and the underlying subsoil in particle size and microstructure due to mixing and compaction.

Pollen analysis

ALEX BROWN

Introduction

On-site examination of several sections of the monument was undertaken with the view to taking samples for pollen analysis. Two monoliths (illus 4.9) were sampled from section 4 (illus 4.21). Monolith 11 covers both primary and secondary phase buried soils. Monolith 12 covers the adjacent ditch sediments which are considered to have accumulated after the monument went out of commission. Analysis focused on the buried soils with the aim of establishing the land–use history and environmental context of the site. It investigates two specific questions:

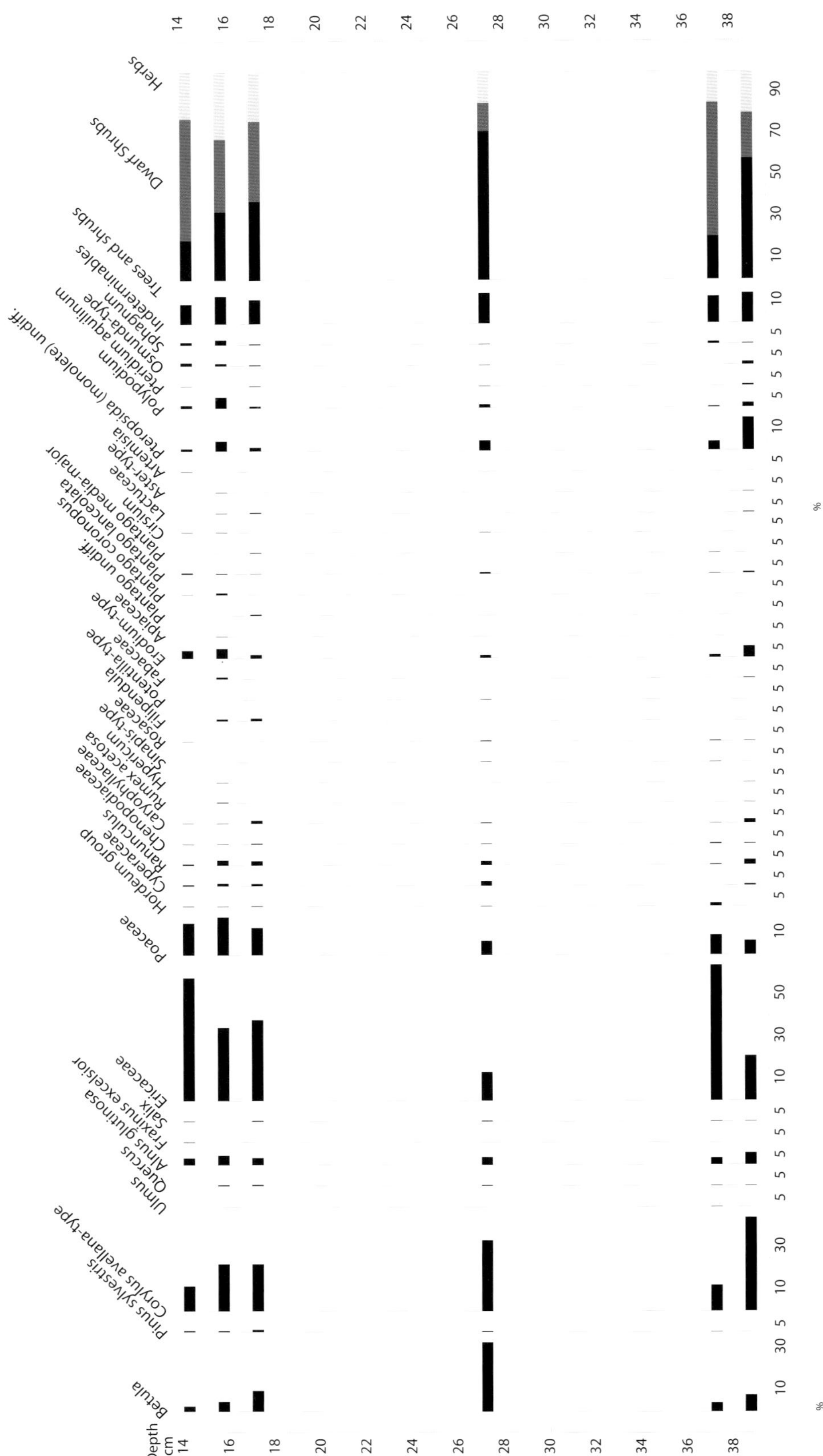

Illustration 4.21a
Pollen from the bank at Pullyhour

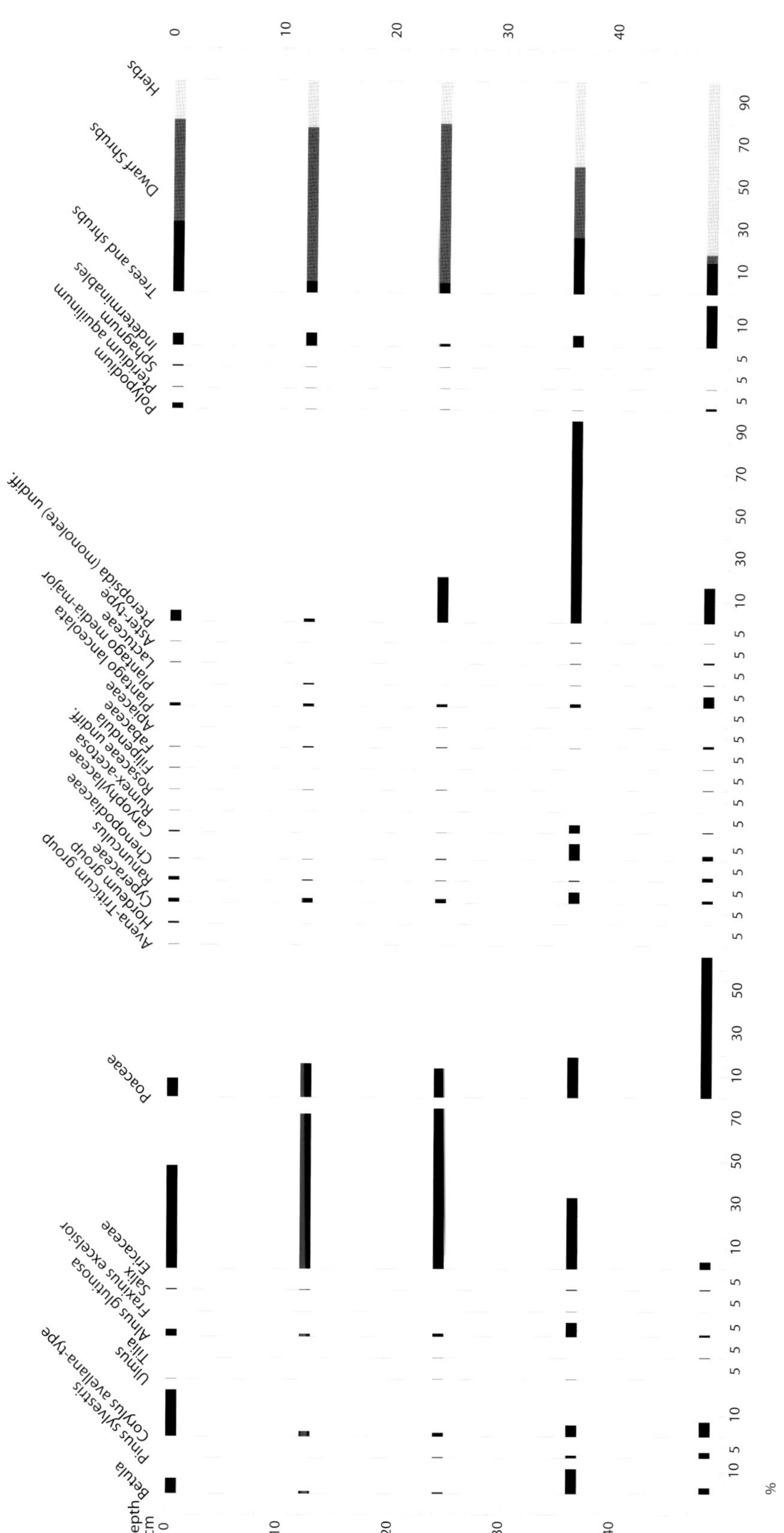

Illustration 4.21b
Pollen from ditch at Pullyhour

Was the circular enclosure of Phase 1 constructed in an actively settled landscape?

Was there any significant alteration in landscape between the first and second phase buried soils?

Analysis of the ditch fills was undertaken to determine whether there is evidence for activity in the landscape after the monument fell out of use.

Results

The pollen method follows that used for Broomend of Crichie in Chapter 1. Pollen diagrams were not zoned because of the small number of samples analysed.

Monolith 11 (primary and secondary phase buried soils) (illus 4.21)

Primary phase buried soil (39–37cm). The two samples from the primary phase buried soil are characterised by contrasting pollen assemblages. *Corylus avellana*–type dominates the basal sample, while Ericaceae dominates the upper sample, suggesting a reduction in hazel scrub and an increase in heathland communities prior to construction of the first phase circular enclosure. Arboreal pollen values are otherwise low, with *Alnus glutinosa* and *Betula* more frequent on damp soils. The occurrence of small values of *Erodium*-type pollen and other herbs (*Ranunculus*, Chenopodiaceae, Caryophyllaceae, *Plantago lanceolata*) suggest areas of arable, pasture and/or disturbed ground. Occasional cereal-type pollen grains of the *Hordeum* group may derive from one of several species of wild grass that constitute the majority of this group, and cannot be taken as certain evidence for cultivation.

Turf (27–26.5cm). A single pollen sample was analysed from a turf fragment within the deposits of the first phase bank. The pollen assemblage is superficially similar to the base of the primary phase buried soil, but includes significantly more *Betula* and less Ericaceae. The differences in pollen values for *Betula* and Ericaceae may reflect a degree of heterogeneity in pollen assemblage within different parts of the buried soil. Alternatively, pollen from deposits of significantly earlier date, indicative of open *Betula-Hazel* woodland, may have become incorporated into the bank deposits.

Second phase buried soil (18–14cm). Three samples were analysed from the second phase buried soil. Ericaceae dominates, increasing significantly within the top of the buried soil, with lesser values for *Corylus avellana*-type and Poaceae. The high values for Ericaceae suggest

a heathland-dominated vegetation, perhaps analogous to *Calluna vulgaris-Erica cinerea* heath still common in oceanic parts of Scotland (Rodwell 1991). The range of herb pollen (cf Poaceae, *Erodium*-type, *Ranunculus*-type) most probably reflect plants growing within and around the monument, for example, on the bank and within the enclosure and ditch.

Monolith 12 (ditch) (illus 4.21b)

Five samples were analysed from the ditch. The ditch sediments are considered most likely to have accumulated after the site was abandoned. The basal sample (48–49cm) is dominated by Poaceae, most probably reflecting grasses initially colonizing the ditch. In subsequent samples, values for Poaceae decline sharply, while Ericaceae values increase significantly, indicating the dominance of heathland vegetation around, and very likely encroaching onto, the site. Pteropsida spores also increase sharply (36–37cm), derived from ferns growing within the vicinity of the site. Heath and scrubland are suggested from the top of the sequence with high values for Ericaceae and *Corylus avellana*-type. A single cereal-type pollen grain of the *Avena-Triticum* group in the latest filling of the ditch implies comparatively recent cultivation of cereals within the vicinity of the monument.

Discussion

The pollen data suggest that the vegetation environment prior to and during the use of the monument was largely open, dominated by heathland and hazel scrub, with alder and birch on wetter soils. Cereal-type pollen grains of the *Hordeum* group may derive from wild grasses rather than cultigens, and are not absolute proof of cereal cultivation in the landscape surrounding the monument. The dominance of Ericaceae pollen in the buried soils suggests the development of heathland, either through sustained grazing or expansion of wet heath in waterlogged areas (that is, peat-forming communities).

There are few comparable pollen sequences from the landscape surrounding Pullyhour with which to set the monument into a wider vegetational context. Tipping's (1994) synthesis of the environmental evidence from Scotland indicates open birch-hazel woodland in Caithness and Sutherland. An increasingly open landscape is indicated during the mid- to late-Holocene at Cross Lochs (Charman 1994) and Loch Winless (Peglar 1979), with decreasing values for tree pollen. Microscopic charcoal at both sites, and from sites in the far north of Caithness (Robinson 1987), provide evidence for probable anthropogenic impacts on the landscape from the Mesolithic onwards. The pollen evidence from Pullyhour corresponds to the broad palaeoenvironmental pattern from northern Scotland.

Interpretation

HUGO LAMDIN-WHYMARK & RICHARD BRADLEY

The Mesolithic phase

The late Mesolithic flint scatter at Pullyhour can be added to a limited, but gradually increasing, corpus of Mesolithic sites in Caithness. A small Mesolithic flaked stone assemblage was recovered from the palaeosol beneath the Camster Long cairn, located to the east, but the assemblage was mixed with an early Neolithic assemblage, making it unsuitable for comparison (Wickham-Jones 1997). More recently fieldwalking projects, including the Caithness Fieldwalking Project, have identified several discrete Mesolithic scatters. These include three scatters at Loch Scarmclate (Stuart 1998; Pannett 2002a) and another site at Loch Watten (Pannett 2002a). A further surface scatter at Oliclett has been investigated by excavation, and a substantial assemblage of *c* 1100 lithic artefacts was recovered (Pannett 2002b). These artefacts were predominately of pebble flint, but a small number of quartzite artefacts were also recovered. These raw materials were considered to have been collected from local beaches (ibid, 16), and this pattern of raw material procurement is comparable to that observed at Pullyhour. Moreover, comparable microlith forms are present, including scalene micro-triangles (ibid, fig 8). The scatters at Pullyhour and Oliclett, however, dramatically differ in size and artefact density. From the available evidence Pullyhour appears to mark the location of a brief episode of activity, while the substantial scatter at Oliclett appears to result from extended or repeated episodes of occupation. At present it is not possible to speculate further on settlement patterns in Caithness.

The Bronze Age phase

The construction of the henge occurred in an open environment and the site was carefully aligned on the Leosag Cairn on the other side of the Thurso River and also on the rising full moon at midsummer. The small central area was bounded by a ditch containing water. Only a limited number of individuals could have participated in activities within the enclosure, but the design of the henge would allow their actions to be observed from outside the monument. The practices undertaken in the henge left no archaeological trace, but it seems possible that the interior was surfaced with yellow-brown soil to create a striking visual effect. The absence of wear to the entrance indicates that the use of the earthwork may have been brief or sporadic.

The second phase of construction elaborated the monument, and by reshaping the interior and erecting three posts a new alignment to Ben-a-Chielt was incorporated. The significance of this distant hill is unclear, but the area around this landmark was certainly the focus of considerable prehistoric activity. The interior was surfaced with white stones, and similar material was used to line the entrance. This evidence recalls the use of quartz at earlier monuments (Darvill 2002). Again the activities at this place left little archaeological trace although two flints, including one from the central post-hole, may be contemporary with the monument.

The closure of the monument was a significant event. It involved the removal of existing post alignments and the blocking of the entrance. The stones lining the inner edge of the bank may have been pushed into the ditch at this stage. There is no evidence of later activity on the site.

The wider implications of this project are considered in Chapter 5.

An evaluation of the henge monument at Loch Migdale, Sutherland, 2003

ANDREW FITZPATRICK & PHIL HARDING

Over three days in 2003, three sites at the head of Loch Migdale were surveyed and evaluated as part of the Time Team television series. The sites were the putative henge monument, a hut circle some 280m north-east of that monument, and a probable crannog in Loch Migdale (Wessex Archaeology 2003). Only the excavation of the henge is reported here.

Topography and geology

The topography of Loch Migdale valley is undulating and the henge is located on a low knoll in a valley bottom, 80m from the shore of the Loch, and at 40m OD (illus 4.22). The knoll, which is dry, is surrounded by poorly drained, boggy channels that flow into the Loch. The lower slopes by the edge of the Loch are rough moorland with gorse, but areas higher up are set to pasture. There is a series of clearance cairns in

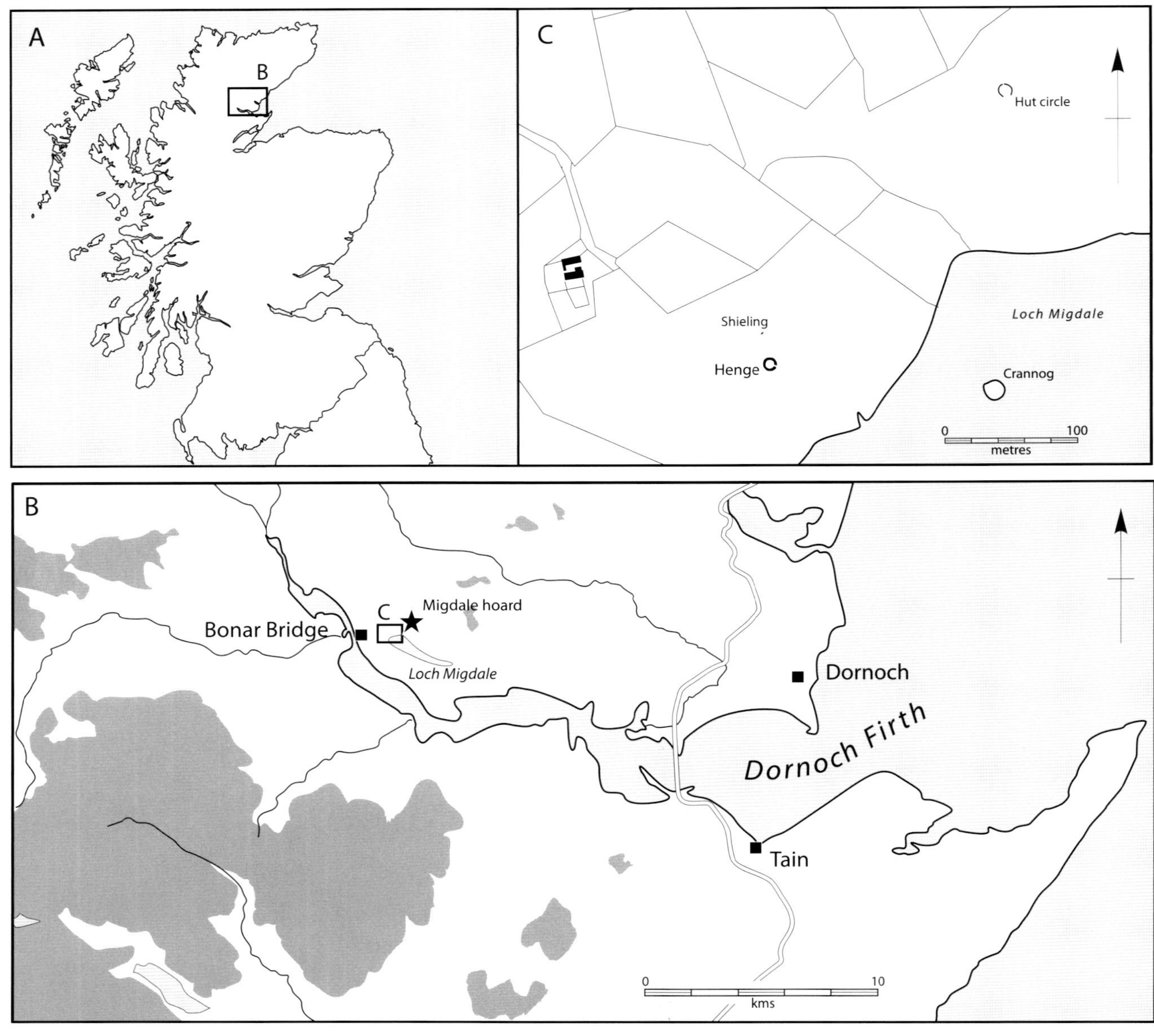

Illustration 4.22
The location of the Migdale henge and nearby sites, including the findspot of the Early Bronze Age Migdale hoard. OS data B and C: Reproduced with kind permission of the Ordnance Survey. © Crown copyright 2010

the surrounding area. A kilometre to the ENE is the findspot of the Early Bronze Age Migdale hoard which gave its name to a distinctive phase of metalworking.

The henge monument

The site has been recorded since the early twentieth century (RCAHMS 1911b, 26) but was first identified as a henge by Woodham (1953) who undertook a small excavation in 1970. The monument is 12m in diameter, enclosing an area of 175 sq m, and consists of a level circular platform, with an internal diameter of 6.7m that is surrounded by a well defined internal penannular ditch 1.1m wide and 0.2m deep. What may be a re-cut of the ditch is evident over most of its course. The external bank is 1.2m wide and 0.2m high. The bank is broken by a gap and a narrow causeway across the ditch, 0.6m wide, on the south-east.

The 1970 excavation (illus 4.23 and 4.24)

Dr Anthony Woodham's excavation was not published but his site drawing and notes show that the south-east quadrant of the monument was examined with an extension, approximately 1m square, to include the centre of the site. He also extended the trench to bisect and define the entrance causeway including the western bank and ditch terminal, although he did not excavate either of them. A section, approximately '3ft' wide, was excavated through the bank 3m south of the entrance but the ditch was not excavated.

The peat turf that covered the site was approximately 15cm deep, beneath which was a patch of 'black earth with charcoal', forming a rim 'about 3ft wide' around the central area. A scatter of quartz chips was discovered in the ditch at the southern edge of the monument, but no further finds or features were found. There

was no evidence of either pits or post-holes. The test trench across the bank revealed a selection of stones, interpreted as a continuous revetment encircling the bank. Beneath the peat and darker earth across the monument was yellow sand, interpreted by Woodham as natural geology. Embedded in this sand in the central test pit were two stones, again interpreted as natural features.

The 2003 excavation

The objective of fieldwork in 2003 was to re-excavate Woodham's trench and to extend it by approximately 0.75–1m to reveal a limited area of undisturbed stratigraphy and to expose clean sections. Any previously unrecognised internal features were to be excavated and the ditch terminals were to be examined to interpret fully the entrance. The section through

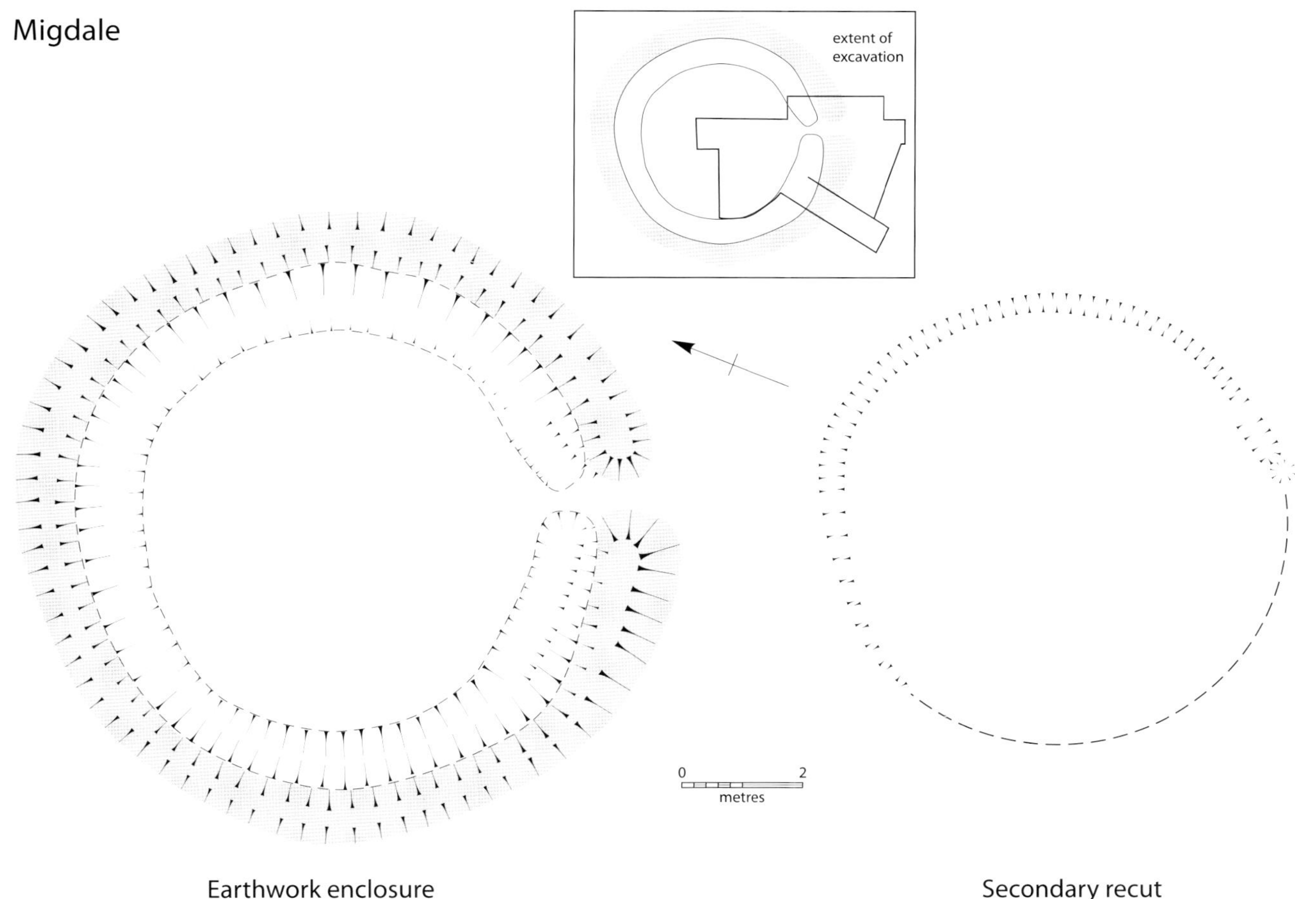

Illustration 4.23
The successive enclosures at Migdale, showing the extent of the excavated area

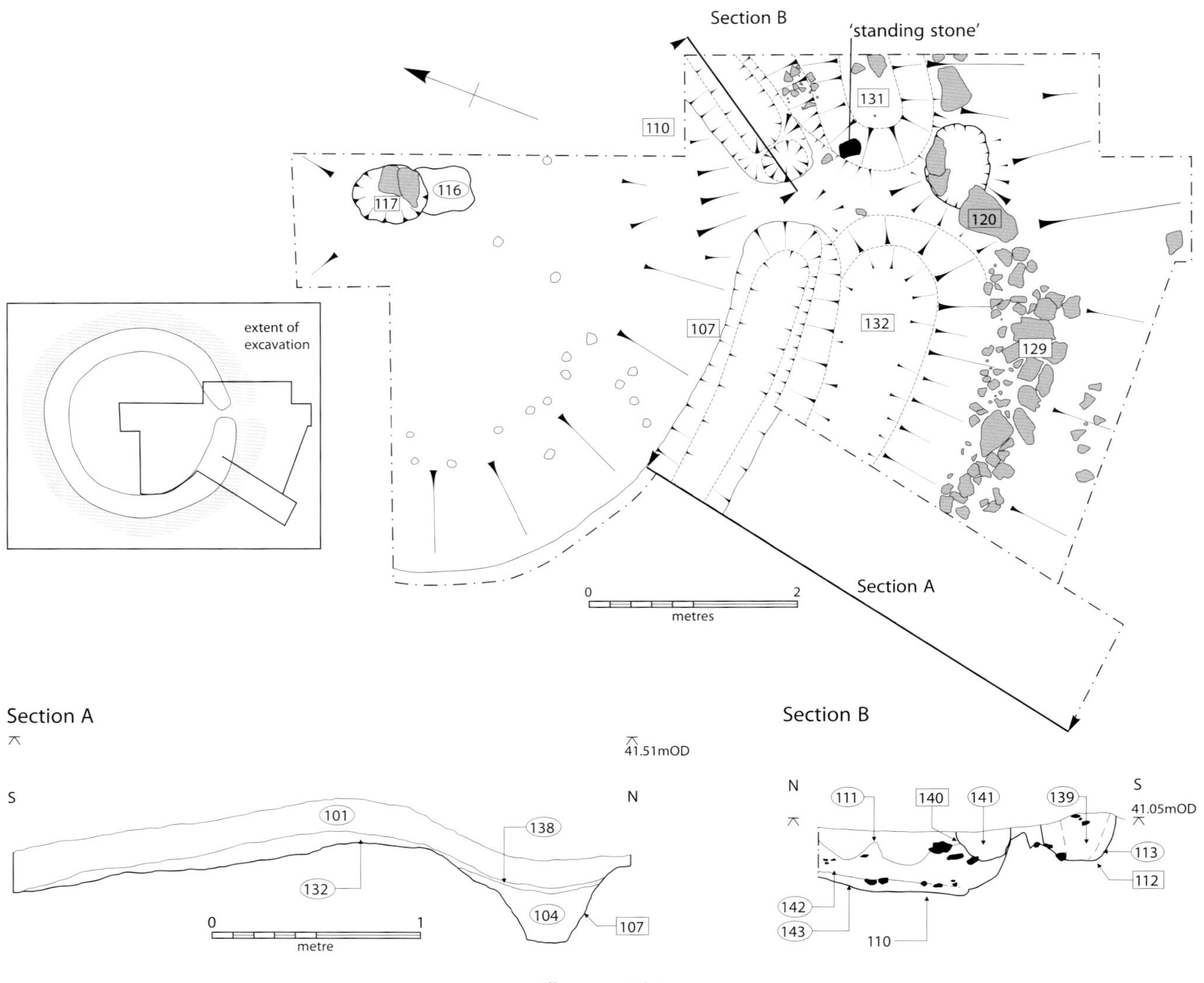

Illustration 4.24
Detailed plan of the excavated area at Migdale and sections of the perimeter earthwork

the bank, as excavated in 1970, was re-excavated and recorded. No other parts of the bank were removed in order to restrict the damage to the upstanding earthwork.

The geophysical survey was undertaken with gradiometry and a small area of resistivity was carried out over the henge. Very few anomalies were discovered within the henge. Anomalies typical of natural responses were present, while ferrous responses in the data could be due to modern debris or igneous inclusions within the soil or drift (GSB Prospection 2003).

The topsoil was a mid to dark brown, well sorted peaty soil, 15cm thick on average, and represented a soil profile associated with well established unploughed pasture. Most features were filled with dark brown or grey-brown sandy silts derived from the bedrock. These fills were frequently peaty.

Within the henge, the trench measured approximately 4m east–west and 4m north–south, including an extension to the north-west around Woodham's excavation in the centre of the monument. The trench was also extended to the south to incorporate Woodham's section through the bank and to expose the entrance area. This provided a trench area of 35 sq m, representing *c* 20% of the total area.

The area of the 1970 excavation was visible across the monument, and removal of the turf revealed a veneer of backfilled material (137) overlying the natural sand deposits in the interior of the henge. Beyond the areas of the former excavation the stripped area comprised a well developed turf in a well sorted dark brown peaty topsoil, 15cm thick. A thin black manganese-enriched subsoil below the turf may have been the dark horizon identified by Woodham, which he interpreted as evidence of burning.

The interior

In the centre of the henge the two stones found by Woodham were relocated and found to form packing stones of a large post-hole (117), which lay 50cm east of the true centre of the henge. This feature was sub-circular in shape, measuring 70cm north-south by 55cm east-west, and was 22cm deep with moderately sloping sides and a flat base. A probable post pipe (136), approximately 17cm in diameter, filled with brown sandy silt lay to the north-west of the packing material (135), which included large sub angular boulders 25cm across. An area of fire-reddened/heat affected natural subsoil (116), approximately 45cm in diameter extended away from the southern edge of the central post-hole. There was no charcoal or ashy deposit, and none was noted by Woodham. It is likely therefore that this represents a single event of burning *in situ*.

A number of shallow circular stake holes were identified in the excavated quadrant of the henge. They were on average 10cm in diameter and 7cm deep with steep sides and concave bases and were filled with light brown silty sand. Although it is possible to postulate a number of possible alignments, including lines radiating from the central post-hole, there is a clear ring of stake holes, 20–25cm apart, concentric with and approximately 1.2m inside the inner lip of the ditch. There are no stake holes facing the general direction of the entrance.

The ditch and bank

Both terminals of the internal ditch were sectioned, and segments of the ditch, *c* 1.5m long, were excavated. The western terminal (107) was 70cm wide at the surface, 36cm deep and tapered to a profile 45cm wide at the base of the weathering cone, with steeply sloping sides and a flat base 20cm across. It was filled with undifferentiated mid grey-brown sandy silt (104), which was capped by a veneer of material (138), 4cm thick, derived from the slumped bank. Only a few of

the tiny quartz chips that Woodham had found were rediscovered in the backfill. There were no other finds.

The eastern terminal (110) was of similar depth and profile. The undifferentiated primary fill (143) was sealed by a deposit of material (142) that was derived from the bank to the south and by an upper layer of peaty sand (111) that might represent a re-cut of the ditch. A possible post-hole (140), 30cm in diameter and 15cm deep with steep sides and concave base, appeared to have been cut subsequently through the tertiary peaty sand, into the ditch terminus. There was no apparent post pipe, although stones in the fill may represent packing. There were no finds from the ditch or the post-hole.

A large oval post-hole (112), which it was thought might post date the construction of the henge was found immediately west of the lip of the ditch terminus in the edge of the causeway. It was 40cm long, 35cm wide and 23cm deep with steep sides and flat base and was filled with a central pipe (139), approximately 17cm in diameter with well defined light yellow brown sandy silt packing (113) around the edge.

The outer bank was revealed and recorded in a single section exposed by re-excavating Woodham's bank section on the western side of the entrance. The bank survived as a well defined feature, approximately 1.4m wide and 25cm high, although the upper 15cm were formed by the overlying topsoil. The core of the bank consisted of a low mound of dark brown sandy silt (132) with frequent stones, approximately 10cm across, derived from the construction of the ditch. It survived as a bank 1.4m wide and 20cm high. No trace of an old ground surface survived below the bank. The entrance between the banks was formed by a gap approximately 60cm wide. A single, recumbent, stone that originally stood in stone hole 118, protruded through the tail of the east bank.

Around the outer edge of the bank were large sub-angular stone blocks (129), up to 40cm across, behind which there were smaller stones averaging 10cm across. It is unclear whether this kerb was contemporary with the use of the monument or whether it derives from more recent field clearance. It was visible in the eastern section of Woodham's trench but not in the western one and it is uncertain whether it extended around the entire circumference of the bank or whether it was designed to enhance the entrance. It wrapped around the western terminal of the bank. Only the extreme western tip was exposed on the east side, although it appeared to continue beyond the entrance as a slight earthwork step, which lay outside the outer tail of the bank.

The entrance gap in the bank was filled by a large oval stone hole (118), which had originally held a standing stone (120) which was snapped and recumbent in front of the stone hole. The stone hole, which lay towards the outer edge of the bank, measured 92cm long, 60cm wide and 30cm deep with steep sides and a flat base. The stump of the broken stone (120) was positioned against the north edge of the hole and was packed with large stones in a matrix of very dark silty loam. The top of the standing stone (120), which measured approximately 60cm long, had snapped at approximately ground level.

Calculations made from the reconstructed alignment formed by the axis through the central pit (117) and stone (120), which, if they were contemporary, equate to 120° magnetic, or roughly south-east. Calculations made independently by Douglas Scott indicate that the entrance aligns with where the sun rises close to the spring and autumn equinoxes, 21 September and 21 March. A notch in the horizon in the hills at the far

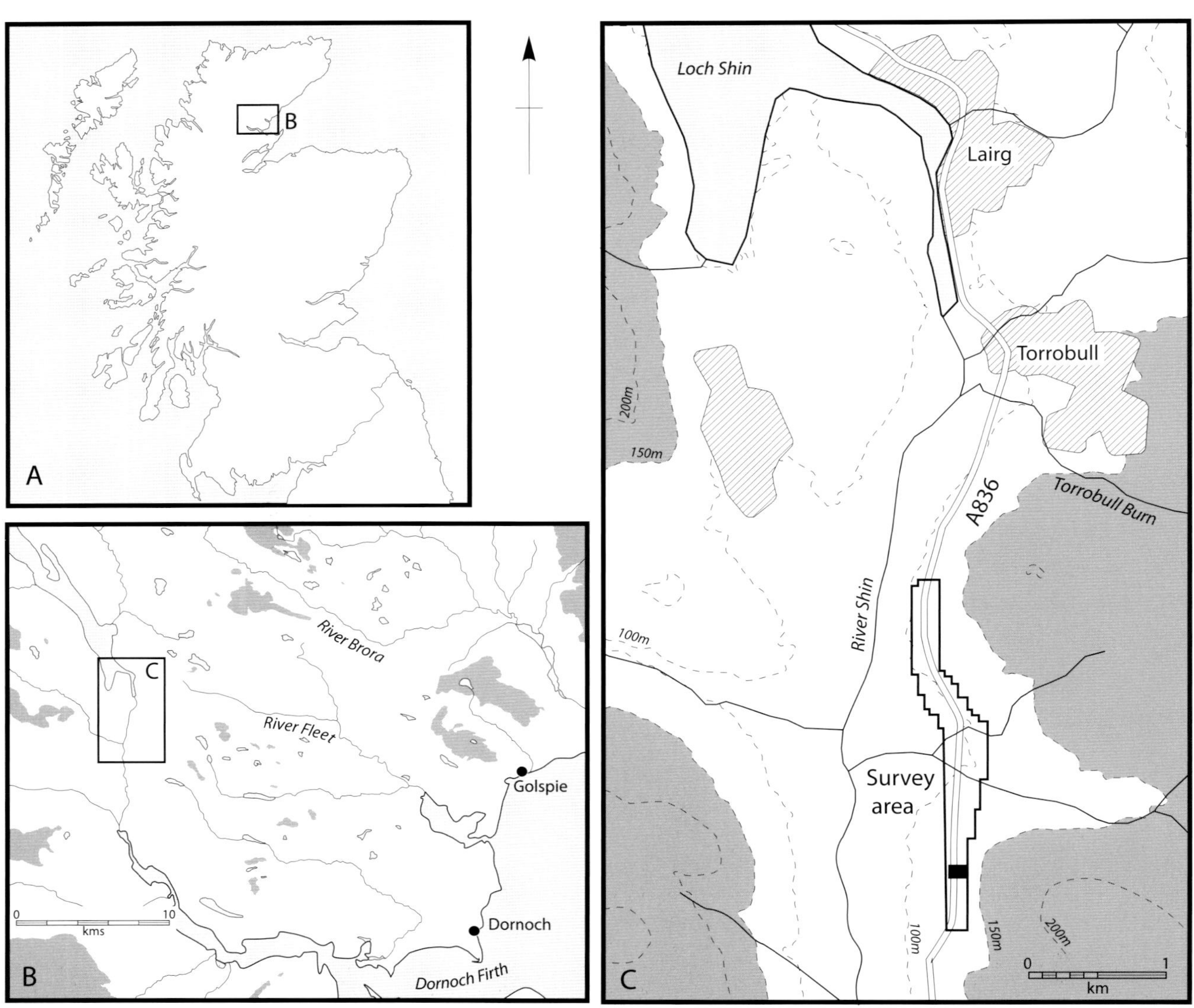

Illustration 4.25
The location of the excavated monument at Lairg. OS data B and C: Reproduced with kind permission of the Ordnance Survey.
© Crown copyright 2010

end of Loch Migdale (Migdale Rock) coincides with the position of the sunrise about a week before or after the modern equinoxes.

Interpretation

Re-examination of the putative henge in Area 1 broadly supports Woodham's original interpretation (Woodham 1953), but the age of the earthwork remains unknown. The only charcoal found in the excavation came from the position of the uprooted standing stone. It was very eroded and unsuitable for radiocarbon dating. Inside the enclosure there may have been a ring of stake holes, and perhaps a radial division. There was also a central feature that may have held a post. The same area produced evidence of burning.

The standing stone at the entrance would have effectively blocked access to the interior with its presumed upright in the central pit. This may have been deliberate and an integral part of the way that the monument was used. Alternatively it may indicate

a reworking of the monument with which post-hole 112 within the lip of the eastern ditch terminal and the possible stone kerb 129 might be contemporary. Similarly, what appears to be a gully in the top of the ditch may indicate that a fence replaced the earthwork.

The ditch may have refilled rapidly and never amounted to a significant barrier. The bank, however, may have been revetted by a kerb on the outside, but the deposit of rubble may have been a product of more recent field clearance. This could not be established in such a small excavation.

The excavation of a ditched enclosure at Achinduich Farm, Lairg, Sutherland

RODERICK McCULLAGH

The small henge described below was discovered during the course of a watching brief on road construction works in January 1996. It was located within poor pasture on the farm of Achinduich, some 3km south of

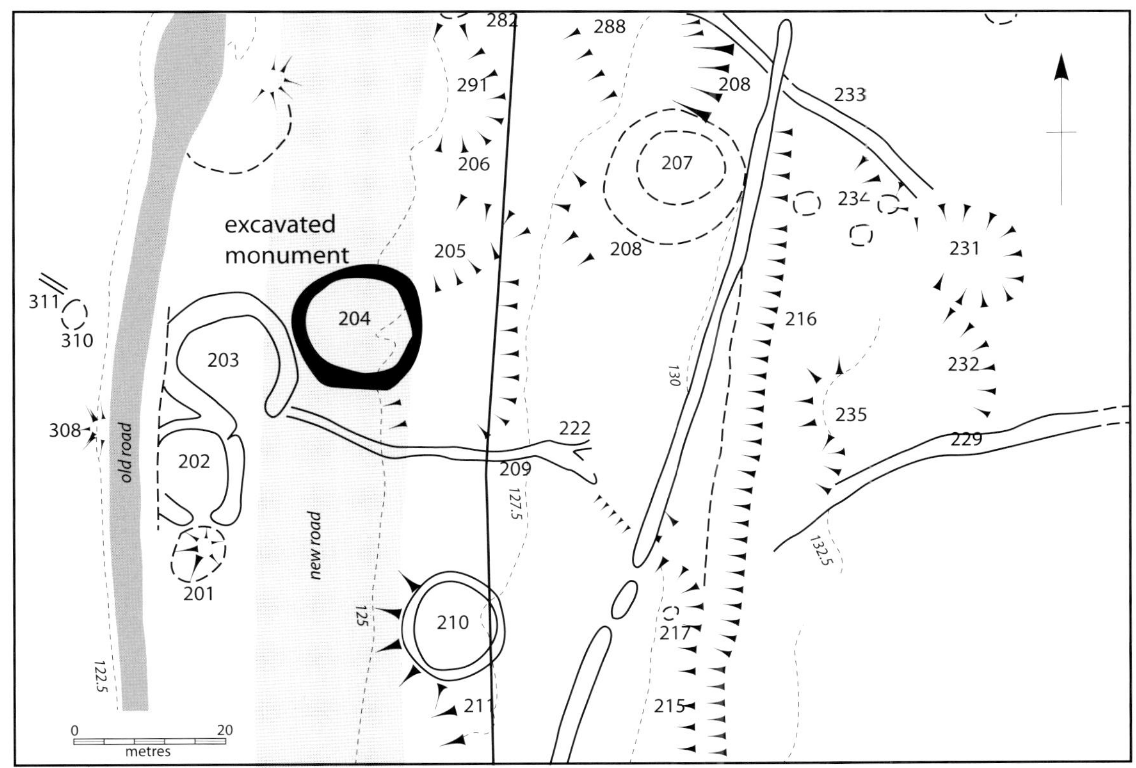

Illustration 4.26
Pre-excavation survey of the excavated monument at Lairg and nearby features. The ditched enclosure is indicated in black

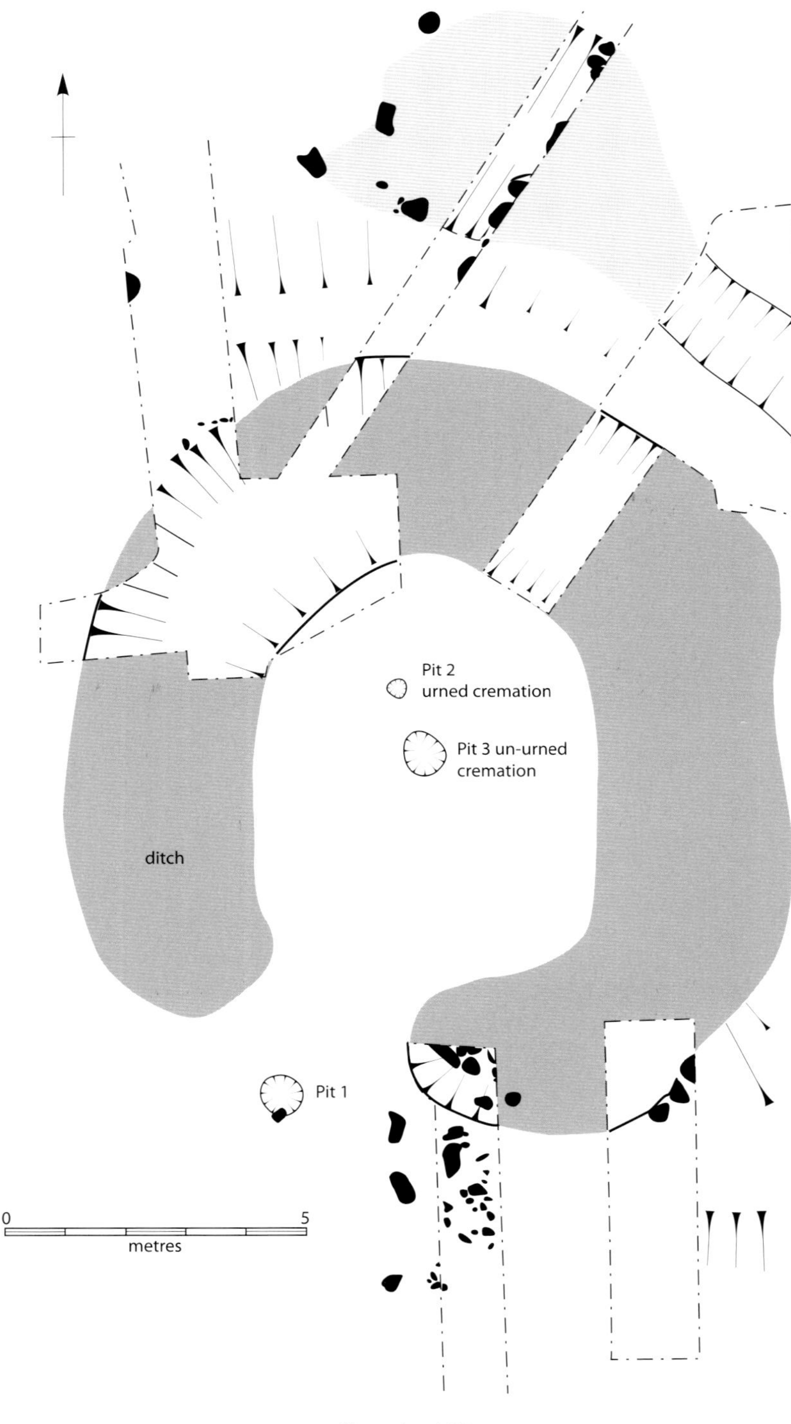

Illustration 4.27
Plan of the features revealed during the watching brief at Lairg

Lairg, Sutherland (NC 5820 0092; illus 4.25). An initial note was published in *Discovery and Excavation in Scotland* 1996 (AOC Archaeology 1996). The site is listed by the RCAHMS as NC05SE9 and by the Highland Council Archaeology Service as MHG12804.

Before this final phase of fieldwork took place, extensive field survey, in 1988 and 1989, and excavation, in 1990, 1991 and 1994 had mapped and explored the remains of successive phases of land-use and settlement from the Neolithic to the nineteenth century AD (McCullagh & Tipping 1998). This work will now appear unusual in that it was undertaken prior to the final route selection; the road planners had identified a broad corridor of land but not the exact road line. This 3km corridor included extensive remains of prehistoric and later settlement and no route could be devised that avoided all the remains. The mitigation work could not prejudge which monuments would one day be conceded to the roadline; instead, the project aimed to investigate the landscape corridor to obtain a representative sample of what might eventually be destroyed. The project sought to establish a chronology for, and to characterise, this sample and to calibrate it to a reconstruction of Holocene vegetation change. The watching brief on the construction work in 1996 was designed as a safety net to catch the unforeseen.

So in the winter of 1995−6 our previous experience in this landscape led us to believe that we would be unlikely to encounter any sites with the potential for substantial quantities of new information. We also had confidence that a watching brief could deal adequately when any small–scale or insignificant remains were revealed by the construction work.

On that extremely cold morning in January 1996, the contractor's bulldozer had pushed through high, rank heather in which the 1988 survey teams had identified a series of small hut-circles. The first warning came with the sight of burnt bone exposed in the smooth blade-scraped, sub-soil surface. Engineering work was halted on this section, Historic Scotland found emergency funds and a four-person excavation team moved in.

In 1988 the site was located within an area of very rank tall-grown heather; this had militated against detailed recording. As illus 4.26 shows, the site (labelled 204) had been recorded as lacking any clear entrance; the form of the bank on the northern arc was indistinct. On its eastern (upslope) side, the bank abutted a lynchet-like break in slope (illus 4.26, 205); on its western side the bank almost touched the bank of a putative dwelling (illus 4.26, 203). In January 1996 this view was utterly changed: the deep heather had gone, as had most of the detail recorded in 1988. The bulldozer's work had created a marked scarp on the eastern edge of the road line, coincident with the pre-existing break of slope, and a levelled road track.

The site confronting the excavation team comprised the fairly level, shaved surface of the mineral sub-soil across the easement of the road cut. Rapid cleaning of the exposed track surface revealed that the bulldozer had removed almost all of the upstanding elements of the monument. What remained (illus 4.27) comprised:

- a penannular ditch with a causeway to the south-west;

- a short segment of a bank on the upslope edge of the site covering part of the circuit of the penannular ditch;

- two pits within the northern half of the space enclosed by the ditch;

- a third pit located within and central to the causeway;

- an arc of a second ditch beyond and concentric to the northern edge of the penannular ditch.

Ground water spewed onto the site from the upslope cliff, and the generally mottled and, in places, gleyed exposed ground surface was evidence of generally poor surface water drainage in this area. During the excavation the ground was constantly wet and the stratigraphy within the ditches was only accessible through constant pumping.

Although the fill of penannular ditch was visible on the surface, its boundaries were indistinct because of poor-drainage soil effects, surface water and ice. So the investigation proceeded by a series of sections to define the boundaries around the circuit. Generally the ditch was about 3m across and up to 1.5m deep. It had been cut with near vertical sides through the till and had penetrated the fractured and weathered surface of the underlying bedrock. The space defined by the pennanular ditch was almost rectangular in plan, measuring approximately 5.8m (east to west) by 7.4m (north to south).

Within the four profiles cut into the ditch fills the ditch had been back-filled with coarse angular stone which resembled the fragmented bed rock through which it had been cut. To judge from surface appearance this was the case around the whole of the ditch. The spaces between many of the angular stones in the ditch were devoid of sediment, which we interpreted as evidence that the ditch had been back-filled relatively quickly.

Despite the appalling conditions for excavation, it was possible to identify a low ridge running concentric to the outer lip of the ditch on its northern side. In section, the material forming the ridge resembled the till through which the ditch had been cut and, at its base, there was a slightly browner, silt-textured sediment. This ridge was interpreted as a relic of the bank seen in survey, and with a relic of the pre-existing ground surface preserved beneath the bank's footprint. The width of putative pre-bank soil in section (approx 80cm) suggested that the bank had been fairly narrow – but there had been some slumping of bank material onto the rock infill of the ditch. The absence of the ridge around the full circuit was thought to be caused by more vigorous ground clearance by the bulldozer on the southern and western sides of the site.

The gap between the terminals of the pennanular ditch measured 2.6m. At the centre of this gap and almost on the circumference of the outer edge of the ditch was a shallow stone-filled pit (Pit 1), which measured 20cm across and 60cm deep. Excavation showed the pit to contain a circular setting of large stones, which we interpreted as the surviving packing for a large timber post. The ground surface between the ditch terminals had survived the bulldozer's blade; it was slightly dished or hollowed with numerous small rounded and slightly polished stones. This was interpreted as a lag deposit from which the fine fraction had been removed through wear. There was no evidence, other than proximity, to link this possible post-hole to the entrance and, if the radiocarbon dates are to be believed, the post was erected many hundreds of years after the construction of the ditch.

Taken as a whole, these strands of evidence were interpreted as indicating that the gap between the ditch terminals had provided access on many occasions to the interior. Without a clear idea of how it might have functioned, we guessed that the post-hole may have been the remains of a gate.

Returning to the 1988 survey drawings, it seemed likely that the bank had completely encircled the interior with no break in the circuit. Unfortunately none of the survey photographs and the aerial photographs could corroborate this observation. If the survey was correct, we could find no evidence to help us determine when this putative entrance had been closed.

The interior space within the pennanular ditch had been quite badly disturbed by the bulldozer. Only two features were detected. The first (Pit 2) measured 45cm in diameter and was 20cm deep. Pit 3 measured 60cm in diameter and survived to a depth of 15cm. Pit 2 contained the remains of an upturned Cordoned Urn. Through its broken base – probably broken by the bulldozer – cremated bone was visible. The Cordoned Urn and its contents were wrapped in the field and later excavated whole in laboratory conditions, allowing for precise excavation, sieving and sub-sampling. Samples from the two cremations have produced radiocarbon dates at 2σ of 1620–1450 BC and 1690–1510 BC respectively (SUERC-29044 and 29045). Pit 3 contained cremated human bone which provided a date at 2σ of 1690–1520 BC (SUERC-29043). It also contained two pieces of worked burnt flint.

Because of the constant water ingress onto the excavation, the area to the north of the north of the penannular ditch was cleared in preparation for the cutting of a ring drain. This surface cleaning revealed a segment of another ditch. In plan, it was difficult to discriminate between fill and 'natural' but a section cut through this feature demonstrated that it was approximately 1m in depth and 1.4m wide. Although far from unequivocal, it seemed, at least on the basis of one section, that this outer ditch post-dated the construction of the bank.

In summary, the excavation revealed the remains of a small henge-like enclosure within which were two pits containing cremations. The ditch had not been filled by natural weathering – instead it seems possible that little time elapsed before it was deliberately back-filled. A narrow earthen bank ran around the outside of the penannular ditch but, at some time after fairly prolonged use, the gap through the bank was closed.

At some stage during or after the use of the interior, the bank became degraded and, in part, collapsed inwards over the already infilled ditch. At some stage in this process, another ditch was cut around the northern side of the enclosure, possibly to serve as a drain. There is reasonable evidence to suggest that land-use and settlement continued (perhaps with some breaks) in this locality well into the first millennium BC and without further degradation of the monument.

Cremated human bone

J L McKINLEY

Analysis of the cremated bone followed the writer's standard procedure (McKinley 1994). Full details are presented in the archive report. The cremated bone from both pits was in good condition without evidence of post-depositional degradation.

The bone within the Pit 2 Cordoned Urn, weighed 2299.1g and represented the remains of two individuals: a young subadult (*c* 14–15 years), probable female and an adult male of *c* 18–30 years.

Pit 3 contained 1244.3g of bone representing a single adult, probably female (31–45 years).

In neither burial was there evidence to suggest a deliberate selection of specific parts of a cremated skeleton. In the urned burial (Pit 2) the cremated bones of the two individuals were entirely mixed.

Various indicators of infection were present (for example, Schmorl's nodes in the urned assemblage and periosteal new bone growth on fragments of tibia and fibula shaft in the Pit 3 individual) but the specific disease could not be identified. Other non-specific bone lesions were present in the bone assemblages from both pits, as were osteophytes (new bone growth at joint margins) and exostoses (new bone at tendon or ligament insertions). An example of a relatively common developmental anomaly (in modern populations) was a large mandibula tori (new bone growth) which was found on the right inner surface of the lower jaw (the right lingual body) of the Pit 3 individual.

The recovered bone represents about 70–80% of the possible total of cremated skeletal remains. This level of recovered bone is matched by only two of the seven other cremations recovered in the course of the fieldwork at Lairg (Table 4). Beyond the burial within the henge-like structure these is no other indicator of special treatment, except that dual burials, as in Pit 2, are relatively rare. It is not possible to determine which individual, if either, was the primary burial and there was no available evidence to help determine whether the two individuals buried in Pit 2 were contemporary with one another.

In the burials from Pit 2, within the urn, 78.3% (by weight) of the bone was greater than 10mm and the maximum size recorded was 112.2mm. Slightly lower figures were obtained from the unurned (Pit 3) burial: 65.6% was greater than 10mm and a maximum of 82mm. The likely explanation for this difference is the greater protection afforded by the Cordoned Urn itself. There is no evidence of deliberate fragmentation in either pit assemblage. Within the urn, some sorting of the bone was evident, with more smaller bones and fragments in the lower levels. As the urn was inverted, this sorting is unlikely to have occurred before burial and is probably the product of slow post-depositional sorting by soil fauna and flora. The presence of pyre debris within the urned assemblage suggests that the cremated bone was transferred to the urn close to the pyre, and the high proportion of larger bones suggests that the urn was not carried very far before it was buried within the henge.

Carbonised plants

D RANKIN

The complete sample assemblage from the field-work and from the laboratory excavation of the Cordoned Urn was wet sieved with both the flot and retent sub-samples being hand sorted in laboratory conditions.

With the exception of wood charcoal, no plant macro-fossils were recovered from the sieving process. No plant impressions were observed in the fabric of the Cordoned Urn.

The charcoal consisted of alder (*Alnus glutinosa*), birch (*Betula* sp.), hazel (*Corylus avellana*) and oak (*Quercus* sp.). Two of the three samples submitted for radiocarbon dating were single species; the sample from Pit 1 contained only hazel charcoal, and the putative buried soil under the bank contained only oak charcoal. The charcoal accompanying the cremations in the urn (Pit 2) comprised alder birch and hazel.

The Cordoned Urn from Pit 2

ROSEMARY COWIE

The base and lower body of the Cordoned Urn were destroyed by the bulldozer. What survived represents about 75% of the original urn (illus 4.28). Reconstruction showed the urn to have originally stood

to a height of 32cm; it was cylindrical in shape with an irregular circumference; at the rim the diameter varied from 26 to 27cm. The rim form is simple, with a narrow, 1cm bevel showing finger indentations. The rest of the pot is undecorated except for two pinched cordons at intervals of 2cm and 10cm from the rim edge respectively. Iron pan deposits in some surface cracks indicated that the pot had not been in perfect condition when buried.

The fabric of the urn contains numerous talc inclusions of up to 7mm in length. The urn had been fired to a pale greyish brown, while the core and inner surfaces were an unoxidised grey. Fire-clouding was present on the upper body, between the cordons for about two-thirds of the circumference, and may indicate that the vessel was fired upside down. There are no obvious signs of coil joins, so manufacturing technique is uncertain. There is a small area of sooty residue on the interior but its cause is not known.

This urn, like the majority of Scottish urns, has a simple profile. It lacks any decoration, but it belongs within a small subset (7% of the total) of the Scottish assemblage (Waddell 1995, 118). This urn also fits in with all of the Scottish Cordoned Urns (150 in total) which are exclusively from funerary contexts (Waddell 1995, 113) and mostly found inverted over a cremation (cf Morrison 1968, 81–2). As a group Cordoned Urns are the predominant type of cinerary vessel from northern Scotland with five, including this one, known from Sutherland. Unlike the Lairg example, with its dual male and female cremations, most Cordoned Urns are associated with a single adult male cremation (Waddell 1995, 118).

Some Cordoned Urn pottery may have had a use before deposition with a cremation. Examples include Cordoned Urn 2 from Ratho, East Lothian (MacSween 1995, 89–90) and the Cordoned Urn from Culbin Sands, Moray (Walker 1967, 97). With this in mind, the talc-tempered fabric used in the Lairg Cordoned Urn is also a distinctive feature of local domestic assemblages, including those from the contemporary domestic sites excavated at Lairg (MacSween & Dixon 1998). Neither the Cordoned Urn nor the domestic pottery have been examined in thin-section but visual inspection did reveal a strong degree of similarity especially between the Cordoned Urn and vessels 71, 102, 139 and 154 from the excavation of the settlement (MacSween & Dixon 1998, 139–44). This may therefore be a case of a local fabric preference adapted to produce a vessel form to suit a specific ritual orthodoxy.

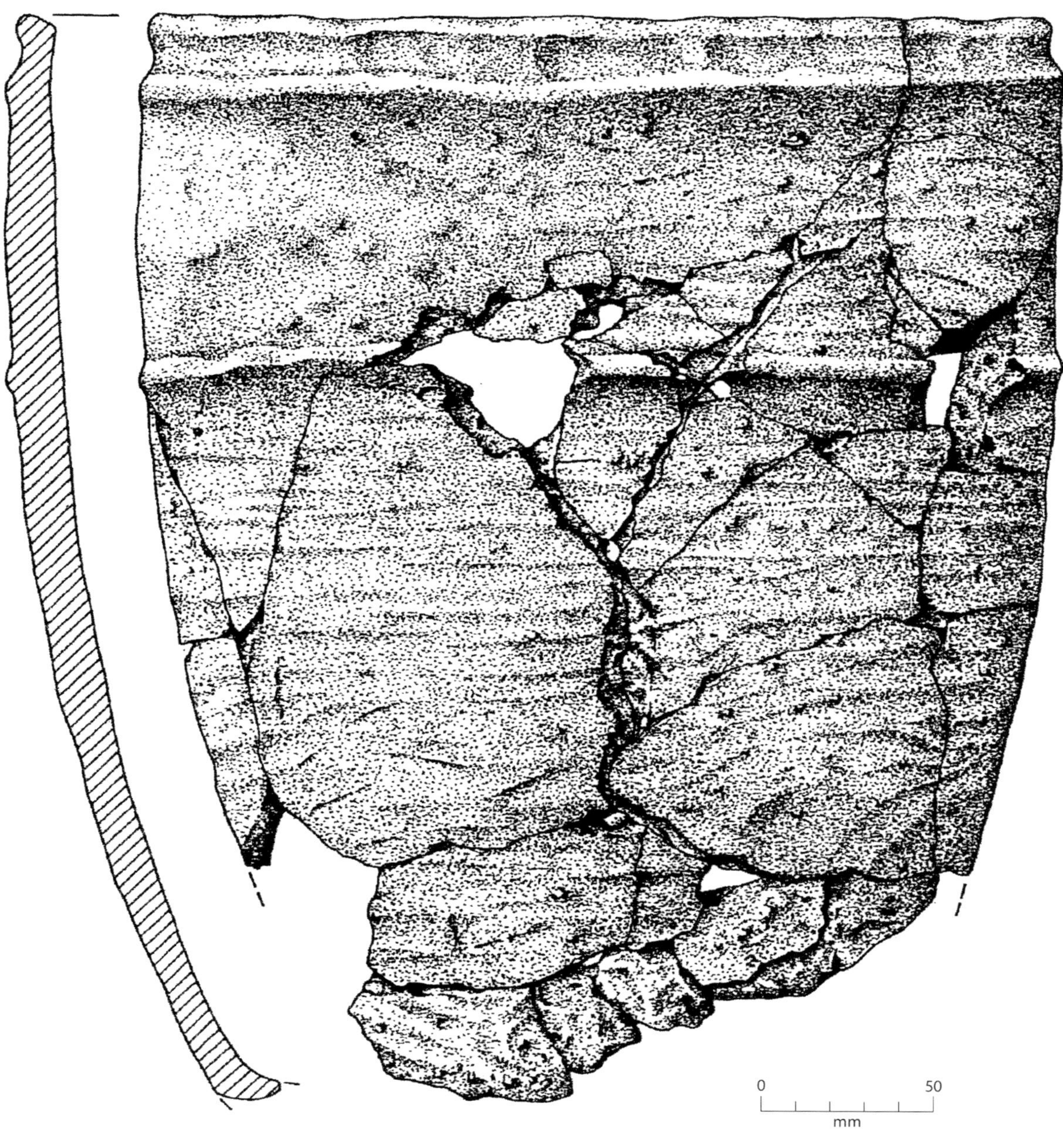

Illustration 4.28
The Cordoned Urn from the enclosure at Lairg

Worked stone

THOMAS REES

Two pieces of worked flint were recovered from amongst the cremated bone of the unurned burial (Pit 3). Both pieces were extensively damaged by burning; only one piece was identified to type, a small thumbnail scraper.

Sixteen pieces of worked quartz or quartzite were recovered, of which eleven came from amongst the ditch fill. None of these pieces displayed clear evidence for deliberate modification but edge damage was apparent on some. Similar worked quartz pieces were found fairly evenly distributed amongst all classes of monument at Lairg, in contexts associated with either construction (for example, wall cores) or abandonment, rather than contexts associated with site-use (Finlayson 1998, 139). It therefore seems likely that this material was the primary source of cutting or chopping tools, but each piece probably had only a very limited use life and would be discarded indiscriminately when no longer useful. Worked quartz thus forms an almost ubiquitous signature for human use of the area without much inherent functional or chronological information.

Radiocarbon dates

Three radiocarbon dates were obtained after the excavation. During the preparation of this monograph three more dates were obtained on samples of cremated bone: a technique that has developed more recently. The first three dates were from wood charcoal. With the benefit of long hindsight, the number of samples was not adequate and in one case the type of sample submitted now seems unwise (GU-7273 was obtained from a multi-species sample rather than single entity sample). That is why, in 2010, Historic Scotland funded the dating of three more samples from the excavation.

Charcoal samples

Pit 1 Post-hole at the entrance. The date was derived from a single sample of hazel from the fill of the putative post-hole:

AA-26222 2325 ± 60 BP $\delta^{13}C = -24.8‰$
1σ cal BC 406–380   2σ cal BC 751–241

Pit 2 Cordoned Urn Cremation. The date was derived from mixed species containing charcoal of alder, birch and hazel from the fill of the pit:

GU-7273 3000 ± 60 BP $\delta^{13}C = -27.0‰$
1σ cal BC 1383–1137   2σ cal BC 1420–1040

The date was derived from a sample containing only oak charcoal taken from the putative buried soil under the enclosing bank:

AA-26223 3150 ± 60 BP $\delta^{13}C = -25.3‰$
1σ cal BC 1514–1328   2σ cal BC 1600–1270

Samples of cremated bone

F. 0005. Unassociated cremation burial from the interior of the enclosure:

SUERC-29043 3320 ± 30 BP $\delta^{13}C = -26.1‰$
1σ cal 1640–1530   2σ cal BC 1690–1520

Pit 2. Cremated bone from Cordoned Urn (male):

SUERC-29044 3260 ± 30 BP $\delta^{13}C = -29.4‰$
1σ cal 1610–1490   2σ cal BC 1620–1450

Pit 2. Cremated bone from Cordoned Urn (probably female):

SUERC-29045 3315 ± 30 BP $\delta^{13}C = -27.9‰$
1σ cal 1630 - 1530   2σ cal BC 1690–1510

In 1996, when the charcoal samples were analysed, archaeologists generally did not attempt to date cremated bone. It was not until the discoveries such as the composite skeleton at Cladh Hallan, South Uist (Parker Pearson *et al* 2005), that multiple dates from single burials were thought to be a sensible investment. The recently obtained dates suggest that the cremation burials at Lairg are broadly contemporary with the charcoal sample beneath the bank. The mixed sample from the filling of the Cordoned Urn, however, provided a later date than either of the samples of cremated bone from the same vessel. The more precise dates from the burials themselves are to be preferred.

Then together these dates suggest that the enclosure bank and the cremation burials date from the mid-second millennium BC. The entrance was possibly still in use in the later first millennium BC.

The monument and the prehistoric landscape at Lairg

RODERICK McCULLAGH

In this section I want to present the case for viewing the henge at Lairg as a monument that had been built within, and used by, a long-established community living in close proximity to the enclosure. Although closely resembling the houses used by this community, when built the henge was unusual and innovative. A long history of use or, at least, respected presence within the built environment of many subsequent generations followed.

The extensive pollen and soils analysis that accompanied the investigation of the physical remains of settlement in the area place the henge and its cremations into a landscape that, by about 2500 BC, could be characterised as fully agricultural. However, the inherent limitations of those same soils permitted continuous farming only by adherence to a strict regime of intense manuring and deep ploughing. These two practices artificially postponed the degradation to poorly drained acid soils that was the natural trajectory for land in this location. The local population can be seen to have engaged in a contract with their environment that would tolerate no slackening of their work and allowed them no illusion that their continued subsistence was not precarious. It was a contract that ran on until probably the early first millennium BC. We did not discover any conclusive evidence to explain the end of this long tradition though it seems to have been associated with a change to extensive land-use, with a transition from an even distribution of settlement to a more irregular pattern, and was possibly linked to the appearance of a few more overtly defensive sites.

In illus 4.29 I have attempted to show that the radiocarbon dates, whether just from the landscape sampling survey in 1989 or from all aspects of the project, cluster within the second half of the second millennium BC. Part of this distribution must be an artefact of the erosion of early features − there is very good evidence for plough truncation and scouring throughout the second millennium BC − and a reduction in erosion in the first millennium BC. Nonetheless the dates from the henge show that it was constructed within a long and deep tradition of land-use and settlement.

Already by the time that the charcoal included in the buried soil was burnt it is likely that every useable area of better drained land had been in cultivation for a long time. When this cycle began is not clear; certainly there is good evidence that the local soils and climatic conditions favoured the formation of podzols and yet, despite some very early dated examples for this process (Carter 1998, 153), in general cultivation, especially after about 2000 BC, retarded this process. There is very clear evidence from some locations at Lairg for a cycle of land-use: at the same location (House 2) we found that the building had been levelled and its site tilled and then the ground reclaimed for building. This sequence probably persisted throughout the second millennium BC. Indeed, for much of the second millennium BC, the only permanent structures were clearance cairns (including some with burials), field boundary cairns and burnt mounds.

Using the evidence from soils, plant macrofossils and pollen studies and excavation we were able to identify a series of impacts on the landscape that, while individually probably adverse and unsustainable, nonetheless combined to allow subsistence agriculture on the naturally poor soils of the locality. Farmers in the area were probably already locked into this regime in the later third millennium BC, and throughout the

second millennium BC they probably could not escape from farming by ever more erosive tillage coupled with continuous manuring. We do not suggest that land-use and landscape were static through this period. Changes in the food produced may have occurred (for example, the plant remains and pollen evidence could be interpreted as signalling a change from cereal production to cereal importation, or from arable tillage to pasture tillage (Tipping & McCullagh 1998, 207). But what seems ever prevalent was that the local society could not afford a radical change in direction. In essence it was obliged to be deeply conservative.

If we look at the artefact record, the story seems to be that these people would have been focused on local self-sufficiency, with few material signs of distant contacts. However, the occasional discovery of small weathered fragments of Beaker pottery in earlier contexts perhaps hints at people who retained an intellectual hold on wider contacts, even if they seldom or never had direct experience of them.

As we failed to recognise this monument for what it was during our first four years of fieldwork, there has to be a possibility that we missed other examples of this kind of monument. I have looked at the survey results again but cannot another see an obvious candidate and so my view is that it is unique within the 3km road corridor.

In the course of our fieldwork we discovered cremated human bone assemblages from seven other

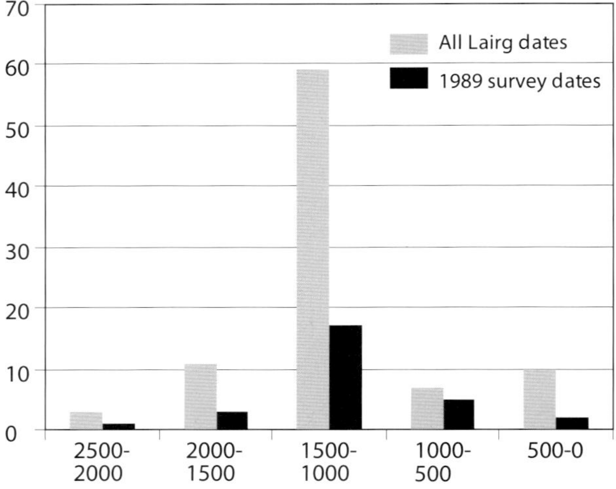

Illustration 4.29
The chronological distribution of radiocarbon dates from the Lairg project

locations. In total, we recovered the remains of ten individuals (Table 4).

Very much smaller quantities of cremated human bone were recovered from sample sieving programme. The contexts of these samples include five separate hut-circles, a clearance cairn, a buried tilled soil and from four other contexts within Burial Cairn 1. It is very likely that cremated human bone was present over a much wider range of excavated contexts and locations, but our techniques did not, and could not, detect this part of the spectrum of disposal. And, of course, cremated human bone must have existed outside the limits of our fieldwork. It is therefore quite ambitious, perhaps misguided, to look for a pattern within the known assemblage, but I feel obliged to try.

My guess is that cremations 1 to 4 represent the remains of a monument that was removed in the first half of the second millennium BC during tillage. Cremations 5 and 6, and also the much smaller assemblages detected by sample processing from this site, were not formal burials; indeed the 'site' classification is probably a misnomer. Instead the site was a small oval arena defined by large quartz boulders within which sediments accumulated and into which highly fragmented human bone was deposited. It is possible that the bone became fragmented by activities within the arena. The cairn element was more of a closing of the monument at the end of a sequence of actions within the arena. Cremation 7 was buried within an accumulating clearance cairn.

Table 4
Finds of cremated human bone from the Lairg Project

Human Bone	Location	Weight (g)	Approx radocarbon date	Comment
1	One of a group of pits truncated by Bronze Age ploughing and close to House 2	1720.7	1600 BC	Older mature adult
2	One of a group of pits truncated by Bronze Age ploughing and close to House 2	1881.2	No radocarbon date but probably contemporary to No 1.	Younger, mature adult, possibly female
3	One of a group of pits truncated by Bronze Age ploughing and close to House 2	117.7	1800 BC	Adult, possibly female, associated with Food Vessel and spatulate bone pin
4	Discrete grouping of burnt bone fragments found within Bronze Age plough soil some 7 m from Nos 1–3	37.5	No radocarbon date but presumed to be broadly contemporary to Nos 1–3	Sub–adult or adult, possibly female
5	A more fragmented assemblage found within Burial Cairn 1	257.3	2000 BC	Mature older adult probably male
6	A more fragmented assemblage found within Burial Cairn 1and revealed by modern disturbance	5.3	No radocarbon date but presumed to be broadly contemporary with No 5	Sub–adult or adult
7	Found within a pit dug into a tilled soil buried by subsequent clearance stone	524.8	2000 BC	Adult
8	Found within Cordoned urn in Pit 2 in the henge	2299.1	1200 BC	Two individuals: a young sub–adult, probably female, and an adult male
9	Found in Pit 3 in the henge	1244.3	No radocarbon date but presumed to be broadly contemporary with No 8	Older adult, probably female

All seven burials probably took place centuries before the three cremations buried within the henge.

It seems therefore that some cremations received burial within a formal location or monument. Certain cremations, such as those used within Burial Cairn 1, acquired some role in performance rather than burial. Others, such as Cremation 7, were buried in a setting that now strikes us as informal, but it is not unreasonable to presume that even tillage entailed some ritual to which use of the dead contributed. On the other hand, some tillage could take place, as it did in the case of Cremations 1 to 4, with no concern for safeguarding the remains of the dead of previous generations. At face value, the burial of the three cremated individuals within the henge could have been an attempt to provide some sanctuary for them over subsequent generations. If that was the case, then it worked. The worn ground surface within the entrance also suggests that the dead within the henge received numerous visits, perhaps of veneration, before the entrance was closed. If we allow ourselves to overlook the limitations of the sample, then the henge by its form and by its survival may be evidence for a society bending to a package of greater orthodoxy around the middle of the second millennium BC.

Chapter 5

THE EXCAVATED SITES IN THEIR REGIONAL CONTEXT

RICHARD BRADLEY

with contributions by Hugo Lamdin-Whymark & Roderick McCullagh

Introduction

The excavations at Pullyhour, Migdale and Lairg were conducted under very different circumstances and each took place for a different reason. A very small area was investigated at Migdale, while work at Lairg was carried out under particularly onerous conditions. Only the fieldwork at Pullyhour was conceived as part of a larger project. Moreover the sites were interpreted in distinctive ways. The television programme considered the earthwork at Migdale in relation to henge monuments in other parts of Britain, while its counterpart at Lairg was initially interpreted as the remains of a round house: one of the series of such structures in a well populated archaeological landscape. Pullyhour, however, was chosen for excavation because it typified a series of earthwork monuments whose distribution extended across northern and north-eastern Scotland. It was a major focus of the research reported here, and the findings of the other excavations make most sense in relation to fieldwork at that monument.

Despite these contrasts, the three excavated sites have a surprising amount in common. It applies not only to their surface appearance; it is also true of their siting, chronology and the structural sequences identified by fieldwork. The first section of this chapter reviews these connections, while the second compares these sites with the surface remains of other earthworks in the same region. It is equally important to emphasise the various ways in which such monuments contrast with larger henges like Broomend of Crichie. For that reason the third section utilises those differences as the basis for a new interpretation of the sites in northern Scotland.

Similarities and differences between the excavated monuments

The excavated earthworks were similar in extent. All were small and inconspicuous: so much so that those at Pullyhour and Migdale can easily be overlooked in the field. The form of the perimeter was not the same in all three cases. Pullyhour was defined by an unusually broad internal ditch, and the same was true at Lairg where there may have been a second ditch outside the bank. The earthwork at Migdale was much narrower. Not surprisingly, the same contrast extends to the enclosure banks. On the other hand, the interior space is of the same order at all three excavated monuments. Where the bank and ditch were unusually wide that effect is very striking, for it creates the illusion that the enclosed area is smaller than is really the case. At all three sites it was less than 10m in diameter, leading to the suggestion in the original project design for work at Migdale that it might have been a 'mini-henge' or a 'hengiform enclosure' (Videotext Communications 2003).

The contrast between the interior and the surrounding earthwork is easy to explain. The enclosure at Migdale was constructed on a low rise in an area of glacial till, and for that reason it was better drained than much of the land around it. The ditch would not have held water. That contrasts with the situation at Lairg where the site flooded during excavation. The same happened at Pullyhour where the fact that a large post survived intact in the entrance shows that there has always been a high water table. In this case there is a further clue, for the earthwork was constructed on sloping ground, yet the base of the ditch was at the same level around the whole of the perimeter. That would have ensured that the entire circuit filled with water. It would create a striking visual effect because the earthwork was so wide.

A feature that Pullyhour shares with the sites at Lairg and Migdale is the presence of a single narrow entrance. This feature is so inconspicuous that it has not always been recognised in the field. One reason is suggested by the results of excavation which show that when these earthworks were decommissioned their entrances may have been closed. In principle the causeways could have been removed entirely, making it extremely difficult to appreciate the original character of those monuments. Similarly, at Lairg the bank may have continued across the entrance.

Another characteristic of the three sites was only apparent with excavation. All had features at their centre. At Pullyhour a small post was set in the ground during the second period of construction, and at Lairg the interior contained two cremation burials, one of them in an inverted urn. The evidence from Migdale is more difficult to understand as this part of the monument had been investigated on a previous occasion, but again there was a substantial stone-packed post-hole in the middle of the monument. Other features may have been peculiar to individual sites. There had been an area of burning at the centre of the enclosure at Migdale. There was also an arc of stakeholes which were roughly concentric with the ditch. At Pullyhour the inside of the monument was capped by a thin layer of yellow-brown soil, introduced for the purpose. During the second phase this was replaced by a cobbled surface made up of white stones.

Distinctive features were identified at the entrances of all three sites, although it seems that a large post-hole in the entrance at Lairg was significantly later in date than the other components of the monument. At Migdale there was a standing stone in the equivalent position, and at Pullyhour there were two post sockets of contrasting dimensions. The larger one cut through the bank.

These comparisons extend to the structure of the banks themselves. The evidence from Pullyhour and Lairg is actually very similar, although it cannot be interpreted in much detail. At Pullyhour the most likely reconstruction is that the inner edge of the earthwork was revetted by a deposit of rubble, conceivably a low wall. At Migdale a comparable deposit followed the outer edge of the bank and may have been confined to the area around the entrance. It is more difficult to offer an explanation for this deposit as there are clearance cairns in the area around the henge. It seems quite possible that these stones were collected when the ground was tilled. That could have happened long after the monument had been abandoned. A similar interpretation is unlikely to apply to Pullyhour where the rubble was associated with the *inner* edge of the enclosure bank. Although clearance cairns can be identified near the site, there was no evidence of a similar deposit against the outer margin of the earthwork.

One reason for emphasising the importance of such deposits is the evidence from the entrance at Pullyhour. Although the structure was left unexcavated, it was clear that both bank terminals had been flanked by a kerb and that when the enclosure finally went out of use the gap between them was blocked by a small

cairn. The surviving remains of the kerb may give some indication of the original form of the bank as it appeared to people inside the monument.

At least two of the sites were rebuilt. At Pullyhour a circular ditched enclosure was recut to an oval outline. The interior was surfaced by a layer of cobbling, delimited by a low clay bank. At Lairg the earthwork could have been supplemented by an external ditch. There is some evidence of a secondary structure at Migdale, although the small scale of the excavation makes the evidence difficult to interpret. Here the perimeter of the monument was built in two separate phases. The first is represented by the earthwork, but for most of the circuit a narrow trench cuts through the top of the infilled ditch. It extends around more than half the circuit. Where it was investigated by excavation at the entrance it terminated at a post-hole. Other post-holes were recorded in longitudinal section and cut through the filling of the earthwork. The ditch could have silted up rapidly, so the timber structure may not have been significantly later in date than the original monument. It is not clear whether the timber phase was associated with the last use of the enclosure, for there is no stratigraphic evidence to relate this feature to the monolith in its entrance.

The decommissioning of the other sites is easier to interpret. The blocking of the entrance at Pullyhour may have been part of the same process as the demolition of the structure supporting the bank, but this cannot be proved. The same may have happened at Lairg. On the other hand, there are other indications that the closure of these monuments was a significant event. Posts or standing stones were erected in or beside the entrances of all three monuments. At Migdale the raising of a standing stone would have impeded access to the interior. At Pullyhour a low pile of stones blocked the entrance passage and could have had a similar significance. There was also a post in the entrance at Lairg, but in this case it has a radiocarbon date at 2σ of 751–241 BC (AA-26222).

If one of the last events at Pullyhour was the levelling of a stone revetment, there is other evidence for the destruction of that monument. Just outside the entrance there had been a large post. It was broken at ground level so that only the bottom remained intact. One of the boulders that had held it in position was smashed, then the fragments were collected and used to cover – or even to conceal – the position of the stump. That process may have been particularly significant as the wood was bog pine and must have been recognised as an antiquity though its actual age was not known.

There is also the question of chronology. The structures at Migdale, Pullyhour and Lairg may have features in common but were they built during the same period? Again the evidence is limited. The earthwork at Migdale is entirely undated. No artefacts were discovered in excavation and the work did not produce suitable samples for radiocarbon dating. It is tempting to draw attention to the site of the nearby hoard which dates from the Early Bronze Age, but there is no way of establishing whether the two features were contemporary with one another. Since the artefacts were associated with a conspicuous rock outcrop, the site may have been remembered for a long time afterwards. Alternatively, the rock itself may have possessed a special importance before the hoard was deposited.

Pullyhour and Lairg each produced three radiocarbon dates. In both cases one of them poses problems. At Pullyhour there is a Late Neolithic date for the piece of bog pine erected towards the outer edge of the enclosure bank. It must have been treated as a relic for it was almost a thousand years old when it was put there. By contrast, the post in the entrance at Lairg is much later than the monument.

A charcoal sample found beneath the bank at Lairg provides *a terminus post quem* for its construction of 1600–1270 BC at 2σ (AA-26223), while all three cremation burials from the centre of the enclosure have provided dates between 1690 and 1450 BC at 2σ (SUERC-29043–29045). These determinations overlap in the sixteenth and fifteenth centuries BC, and this may provide the best estimate of the actual age of the monument. Two of the dated burials were associated with a Cordoned Urn. This style is usually assigned to the period between 1800 and 1500 BC. Excavation at Pullyhour provided two samples for radiocarbon dating, one from each of the buried soils sealed beneath its bank. The first phase of construction has a *terminus post quem* of 1620–1450 BC at 2σ (OxA-3257), and the second a *terminus post quem* of 1369–1126 BC (OxA-18156). The evidence is very limited but it suggests that the histories of the two sites began at about the same time, although the earthwork at Pullyhour was later rebuilt. Both monuments share so many features with Migdale that the enclosure there might be of similar age.

These comparisons can be taken further. How were the three monuments related to the surrounding landscape? In some ways their contexts differ from one another. As McCullagh shows in Chapter 4, the site at Lairg was located in an area with Bronze Age houses, cairns, land boundaries and burnt mounds; indeed, its remains were first identified as those of a dwelling. Not far from the monument were two round houses with dates in the Middle to Late Bronze Ages. There was also a burnt mound of the same period (McCullagh & Tipping 1998, 32–7).

The Migdale henge was in another landscape which contained evidence of clearance cairns, and in the surrounding area there was a house platform as well as the findspot of the Early Bronze Age hoard. Unfortunately, that deposit is the only feature with any dating evidence, and the signs of land clearance may be associated with an Iron Age crannog or even with the remains of a shieling investigated by Time Team in 2003 (Videc Communications 2003). The evidence from Pullyhour is different again. Pollen analysis suggests that the monument was beyond the limits of the settled landscape. There were no indications of arable land before the ditch reached its present form. That episode may be connected with the remains of an abandoned farm near the enclosure and with another series of clearance cairns. On the other hand, a cist of unknown date is recorded from the field to the north of the henge and there had been an isolated standing stone between the earthwork and the river. On the opposite side of the Thurso River are the remains of a cairn which may be of Neolithic origin.

In other respects the excavated sites share more in common. Both Pullyhour and Migdale are situated on sloping ground and their entrances face downhill towards a river or a loch. Their earthworks are comparatively slight. Although both monuments are small and cannot be picked out from a distance, it would certainly be possible to see inside them from farther up the slope. In the same way, the positions of anyone inside these earthworks would have been highlighted from the lower ground. Much the same applies to the earthwork at Lairg. In this case its orientation is less exact, but the entrance faced SSW towards a minor tributary of the River Shin 200m away.

Two of these monuments also had a more specific alignment. The long axis of Pullyhour is orientated on a conspicuous round cairn in a small area of raised ground on the opposite bank of the Thurso River. It is much larger than the cairns associated with Bronze Age burials in Caithness and its dimensions are more like those of passage graves in the same region. Its distinctive siting resembles that of chambered cairns at Loch Calder (Corcoran 1966, 34–48). The orientation of the monument at Pullyhour extends even farther. The massive post erected towards the end of the sequence points towards a conspicuous mountain near the coast, Ben-a-Chielt. The significance of this distant hill is unclear, but the area around this landmark was in the same region as numerous standing stones, cairns and the stone setting at Achavanich. No monuments are recorded from Ben-a-Chielt itself, but a carved stone ball has been found there (NMRS ND13 NE3). The monument at Pullyhour has another alignment too, as the long axis of the earthwork is directed towards the position of the rising full moon at midsummer as it appears on the horizon behind the site of the cairn.

The relationship between the two monuments is intriguing. Whatever its precise date, the cairn is likely to be considerably older than the enclosure and yet the connection between them was carefully contrived. The people who built Pullyhour would have been aware that they had aligned the henge on what was already an ancient monument. In the entrance they erected a piece of bog pine which was a thousand years old. They could not have known its precise age, but they would have recognised it as a natural curiosity and must have realised that it survived from a distant past. The link between these two features can hardly have been accidental.

The Migdale henge has an equally striking orientation, for it faces a conspicuous cleft where the flanks of two mountains meet above the loch. This is the position of the sunrise about a week before the spring equinox and a week after the autumn equinox. Moreover, it is approximately where the full moon rises close to the autumn equinox (I am grateful to Douglas Scott for this information). It cannot be proved that such relationships were intentional, but they could certainly have been observed by people visiting the monuments.

A final issue may be more difficult to resolve. It is not clear why the earthworks at Migdale and Pullyhour survived when there is so much evidence for later agriculture in the areas around them. On the other hand, the continuing significance of the enclosure at Lairg is apparent from the post which was placed in its entrance during the Iron Age. Still more striking

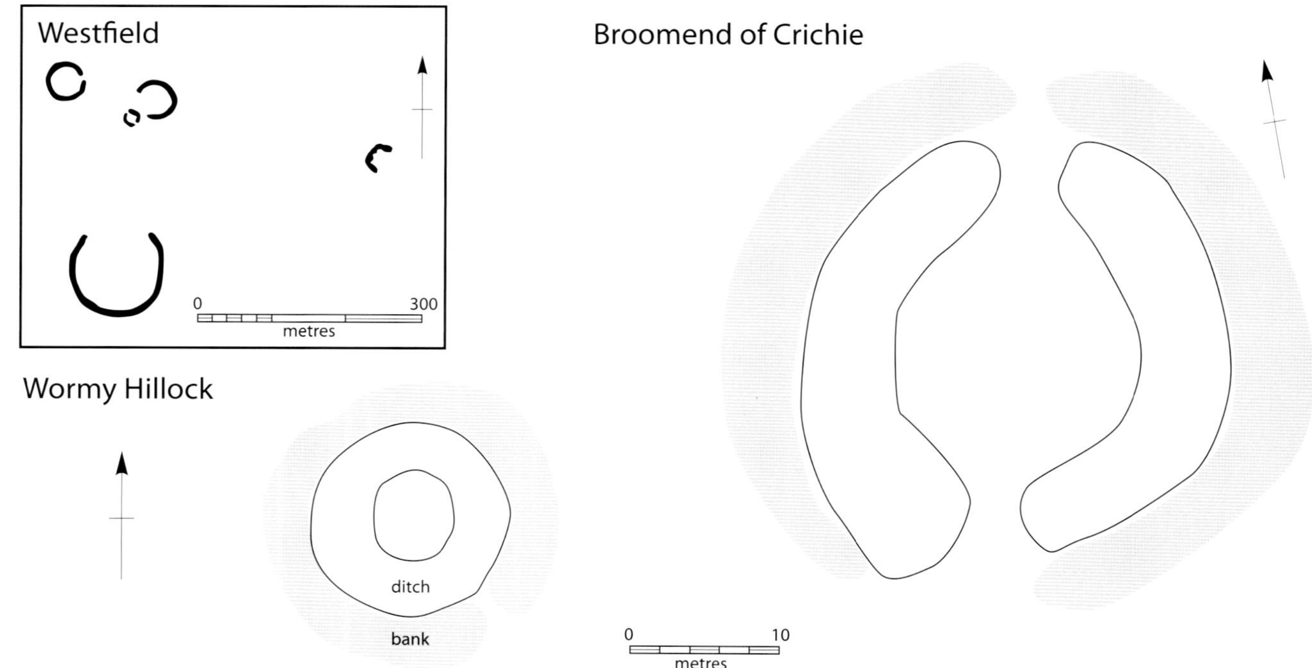

Illustration 5.1

Outline plans of the earthwork enclosures at Broomend of Crichie and Wormy Hillock, compared with those of putative henges in the crop mark complex at Westfield. Information from RCAHMS (2007) and (Barclay 2005)

is the fact that this earthwork was not damaged by later prehistoric cultivation when it happened to the remains of other structures in the vicinity. Perhaps the distinctive character of the enclosure gave it a special significance.

Comparisons with unexcavated monuments

There are two problems in comparing this evidence with that of unexcavated sites. Both set limits on this study. The first is that most of the distinctive features of these three monuments depend on their survival as earthworks. They would not be apparent if they were visible as crop marks. Had they been levelled by the plough, it would be difficult to tell them apart from round barrows, ring-ditch houses or souterrains. It follows that similar structures will be easier to identify where they are outside arable land. That may explain why there are so many examples between Caithness and the Moray Firth and significantly fewer to the south and east. Only parts of their overall distribution may have been identified so far, although some candidates have already been suggested in Moray and Aberdeenshire (Harding & Lee 1987). On the other hand, nearly all the sites classified as henge monuments on the evidence of air photography have narrower ditches than the sites considered here. They also enclose larger areas. That is not to question their credentials, for they could be henges of a different kind.

A second problem is that such small enclosures need not exist in isolation from larger monuments (illus 5.1). The two are sometimes found together, and in such cases it remains to be seen whether any chronological distinction should be made between them. That is apparent at Forteviot, Dunragit and Blackshouse Burn farther to the south, but the same problem arises on the east coast with a group of crop marks at Westfield in Angus (Barclay 2005, fig 8.3). Some may have been like the sites considered here, but it is known that small henge monuments already existed during the Neolithic period. Size alone is not a useful criterion. It is better to consider the other attributes of these earthworks.

In 1953 Anthony Woodham identified a group of henges in northern Scotland where their distribution focused on the Beauly Firth. Like the examples considered already, most are characterised by unusually wide ditches and banks and by a disproportionately small interior (illus 5.2). Their internal diameter is often between 7 and 9m but rises to 15m or more in exceptional cases. The perimeter, on the other hand, can be as much as 11m wide. Apart from a large enclosure at Muir of Ord, all had a single entrance. Similar monuments can now be identified farther to the north and east. A good example is Wormy Hillock in Aberdeenshire which has an internal diameter of 7m and an earthwork perimeter which is no less than 6m wide (RCAHMS 2007, 56–8).

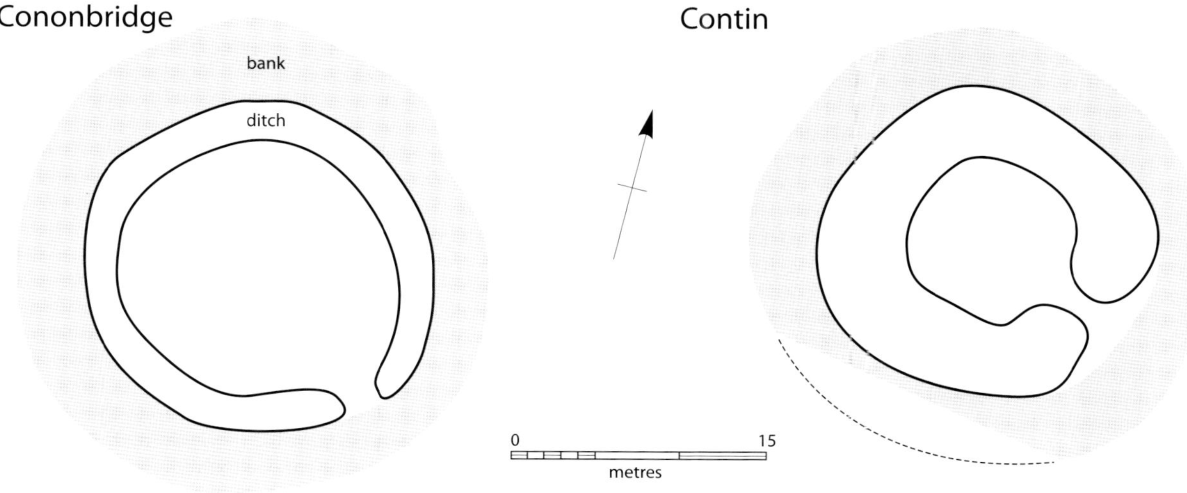

Illustration 5.2
Outline plans of the small henges at Cononbridge and Contin. After Woodham (1953)

These monuments share a number of other characteristics, but they are not represented on every site. There are more enclosures where the ditch could have held water. This certainly applies to an earthwork enclosure at Ascoile and probably to those at Achilty and Wormy Hillock. Their entrances can be distinctive, too. Some are exceptionally narrow and in several cases it seems as if the bank is continuous while the ditch is broken by a causeway. That arrangement is suggested at Lairg and can be recognised from surface evidence at Achilty and Conon Bridge. In other cases the causeway is partly blocked, as it was at Pullyhour. There even seem to be sites where the entrance has been modified, so that a shallow step continues the line of the ditch. This happened at Lagnagreisach Wood and the well preserved site of Wormy Hillock. There could be other monuments where any causeway was removed. It may have happened at the Hill of Tuach at Kintore. Another example in Aberdeenshire might be an enclosure at Nether Towie (RCAHMS 2007, 58).

Certain of the monuments have other features in common, but again it does not happen on every site. Some of the enclosures were built on a slope, and in such cases the entrance often faces downhill. It happened at Migdale and Pullyhour, and unexcavated examples include the small earthwork at Lagnagreisach Wood, as well as a larger monument at Culbokie on the Black Isle. All these monuments can be overlooked from higher ground. That was also the case at Wormy Hillock where the monument was located at the foot of a prominent bluff which resembles an enormous (but entirely natural) long barrow. It would have offered a vantage point from which to view activities inside the monument. The same applies to Ascoile where a small enclosure was built at the base of a conspicuous terrace.

The monument at Culbokie commands an extensive view over the Cromarty Firth. It is not the only henge that seems to be associated with water, and smaller enclosures illustrate the same relationship. It was an obvious characteristic of the excavated sites at Migdale, Pullyhour and possibly Lairg, and is also found at Wormy Hillock where the entrance faces a stream. Small henges at Shiel Bridge and Achilty illustrate the same relationship with water, for both were near to lochs. In the first example the entrance of the monument was directed towards the shoreline, as it was at Migdale; in the other case, it faced in the opposite direction. This association may be more important than it seems, for some of the enclosure ditches may have contained water for all or part of the year. It seems as if the ditch at Pullyhour was designed with that idea in mind.

Few of these sites have any direct associations. The small enclosure on the Hill of Shebster forms part of a wider monument complex which includes a variety of structures of Neolithic and Bronze Age date, although their overall chronology is poorly understood (Harding & Lee 1987, 380). A second example in Caithness was at Pullyhour. Again it was built in a landscape that included other kinds of monuments: a cist, a standing stone and possibly a chambered tomb. The relationship between them is not clear, apart from the obvious point that the henge is aligned on the cairn on the opposite bank of a river.

For the most part the henges found farther to the south lack these associations, although the small earthwork at Lairg was established in a domestic landscape. On the other hand, two of the most distinctive monuments were close to the sites of Early Bronze Age hoards. The evidence from Migdale has been mentioned already (Anderson 1901), but the same issues arise with the enclosure at Wormy Hillock which was only 80m from the findspot of a hoard on the Hill of Finglenny (Stevenson 1948). In neither case is there any evidence that the henge was built during the same phase. It may be that these locations remained significant for a long time.

Although there may have been a standing stone at Migdale, only two sites, both in Aberdeenshire, were associated with a formal setting of monoliths. One was the Hill of Tuach where Dalrymple's excavation revealed a series of cremation burials associated with Cordoned Urns; a vessel in the same style was found at Lairg. The examples from Tuach were probably deposited at about the same time as the first enclosure at Pullyhour was built. Like Pullyhour, the earthwork was on a hillside and seems to have been directed towards an older monument. At Pullyhour it was perhaps a passage grave; in this case it was a long cairn.

Near to the Hill of Tuach a second site, at Fullerton, was supposedly bounded by a ditch, 2m wide. It contained seven monoliths. Little remains today. One reason for drawing attention to this monument is the discovery of a circular crop mark only 250m away. Again it is defined by a broad ditch with a single entrance and encloses an area less than 10m in diameter. Harding and Lee suggest that it might have been another henge (1987, 357).

Lastly, 'a few empty earthen jars' were also found in the well preserved enclosure at Achilty during the nineteenth century. It is not known whether they were associated with cists, standing stones or even with burials (Woodham 1953, 73).

Interpretations and comparisons

There are two ways of addressing the interpretation of these monuments. Both involve comparisons with other structures.

The first set of comparisons is between diminutive monuments like those at Migdale, Lairg and Pullyhour, and large henges such as Broomend of Crichie. They are based on their distinctive earthworks and the features associated with them. At this stage it is not necessary to discuss their chronology. That question is reserved for Chapter 6.

With few exceptions, the small sites are comparatively isolated and only a few examples in Caithness, Sutherland and Aberdeenshire occur with other monuments. Unlike the structures considered in Chapter 3, they rarely form parts of larger complexes. Nor is there much evidence that there were settings of posts or monoliths inside these sites, although two earthworks in north-east Scotland may have enclosed stone circles, and an arc of stakeholes was identified within the enclosure at Migdale. Only the structures at Fullerton and the Hill of Tuach seem to have been associated with cists, but neither of these monuments is entirely typical of the group. Where the henges at Broomend of Crichie, North Mains and Balfarg were accompanied by other features – some of them built on a massive scale – Pullyhour was near an isolated cist and a single standing stone.

At the same time, the perimeter of the smallest monuments was built on a tiny scale. Although the ditches could be disproportionately wide, they were never deep and their banks were low. They would not have concealed the interior from people outside, nor could the surrounding area have been excluded by such an earthwork. In fact the alignments of posts at Pullyhour extend across the top of the bank. The siting of some of these monuments is equally distinctive. The smallest enclosures could be built on slopes so that it would have been easy to see into them from above. Similarly the positions of anyone inside the monuments would be highlighted if their earthworks were viewed from lower ground. They are so inconspicuous that this could only have happened at close quarters.

The small size of these structures means that they could not hold many people. The widths of the entrances support this interpretation, for in most cases

visitors must have entered and left in single file. Unlike a larger enclosure like Broomend of Crichie, the sites usually had one break in the perimeter. Its importance as a threshold would have been especially obvious when the ditch was filled with water. The monuments have another characteristic, too. Several are aligned on streams, rivers or lochs, and in two cases there is persuasive evidence that the individual structures conformed to celestial alignments: in one case they were orientated on the rising sun; in the other, on the full moon. Although these effects could probably be recognised by people standing just behind the earthwork, the ideal position from which to observe them was the centre of the enclosure where space was extremely restricted. The internal face of the bank at Pullyhour was probably defined by a wall or kerb. Again it was best seen by people within the henge.

Inside some of the larger monuments there were inhumations and cremations. Other burials could be found in the surrounding area, a number of them associated with structures built for the purpose. That happened at Balfarg and even more obviously at North Mains where an enormous mound was constructed close to the henge (Mercer 1981; Barclay 1983). By contrast, there is little evidence from the smaller monuments. They have sometimes been compared with ditched round barrows, but there is little to suggest that they were primarily concerned with mortuary ritual. For the same reason it is misleading to classify them as 'enclosed cremation cemeteries'. In fact human remains are not common on the smaller sites. There were represented at Lairg but were not found in the equivalent position at Migdale or Pullyhour. Nothing is known about the finds of pottery vessels at Achilty. There were cists within the stone settings at Fullerton and the Hill of Tuach, but the original forms of both monuments remain in question. If few burials have been found at the smallest henges, the same applies to artefacts. Two flint flakes and two pieces of worked quartz were associated with the Bronze Age phase at Pullyhour, and there were no finds from the recent excavation at Migdale, although chips of quartz were discovered there in 1970. Despite the quantity of material associated with prehistoric houses at Lairg, the only material from the earthwork enclosure was the Cordoned Urn associated with one of the cremations, and eighteen lithic artefacts.

There are at least two different ways in which to interpret the evidence. People may not have been allowed to deposit cultural material at these sites, but another possibility is that such places were used for very

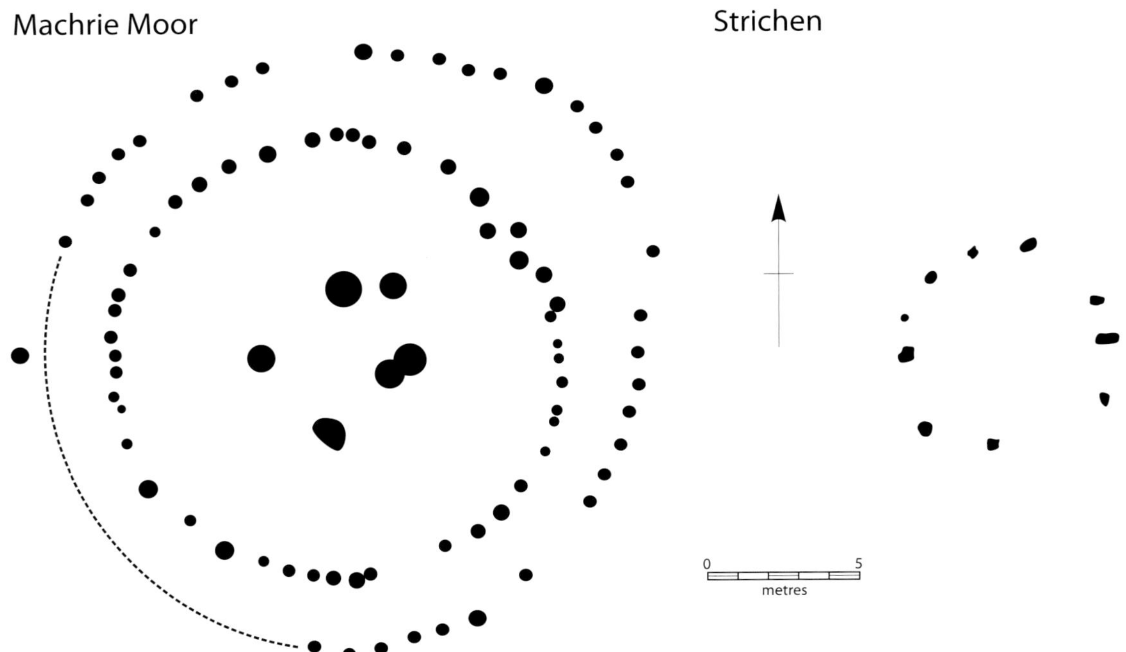

Illustration 5.3

Large and small post circles constructed in the image of a house. The Late Neolithic structure on Machrie Moor was replaced by a stone circle. The structure at Strichen was built inside a recumbent stone circle and replaced by a larger Late Bronze Age/Early Iron Age timber building. Information from Haggarty (1991) and Phillips, Hampshire-Monk and Abramson (2006)

short periods, even if they were later rebuilt. There is important evidence that the excavated sites were decommissioned, and in two cases their earthworks seem to have been destroyed. The entrance at Lairg showed signs of wear, but once these sites had served their purpose they were closed.

So far this discussion has compared larger henges with smaller ones and has discussed the differences between structures like Broomend of Crichie and sites like Pullyhour. More light can be shed on these issues by comparing both kinds of monument with domestic buildings.

Some of the biggest henges were associated with settings of timber or stone (illus 5.3). There is reason to believe that wooden structures were more common on the earlier sites and rings of monoliths at later ones. The most impressive post circles of the Late Neolithic period are so massive that it would have been difficult to roof them, yet they conform to exactly the same organisation of space as small domestic dwellings. For that reason they can be interpreted as the 'great houses' of entire communities (Bradley in press). Some of them were replaced by monoliths, but only at Stonehenge is

there any suggestion that the form of the newly built structure copied that of a timber building (Gibson 2005). On the other hand, a similar argument might account for the striking similarities between the stone structures identified inside the henge at Stenness and the domestic buildings in the neighbouring settlement of Barnhouse (Richards 2004, 222–3).

The small henges considered in this chapter have a different character, for none contains a timber circle and only two poorly dated examples enclose a setting of monoliths. On the other hand, the internal areas of the earthwork enclosures are the same as those of Bronze Age round houses found in the same region. That may be no accident as their remains look strikingly similar on the ground. As McCullagh points out in Chapter 4, it was certainly the case at Lairg where the excavated monument was located within a group of circular buildings. Although those particular structures were not investigated, they are likely to have been used in the later second or earlier first millennium BC.

The resemblance between small henges and abandoned round houses may explain why it took so long for these unusual monuments to be recognised

– and longer still before any of them were excavated. The earthwork enclosure at Pullyhour was recorded at the beginning of the last century, but it did not receive much attention afterwards, perhaps because the Royal Commission described it as a 'mound'. The inventory stated that 'its character … is doubtful' (RCAHMS 1911b, 42). It was easy to misunderstand the distinctive form of its earthwork for it had some of the attributes of a ring-ditch house, of which there are many examples in the north. Although the remains at Pullyhour were in good condition, there appeared to be nothing exceptional about the site.

A similar process occurred at Lairg where excavation identified a series of ring-ditch houses of Bronze Age date. The earthwork considered in this chapter seemed to be no exception, and in this case it was not especially well preserved. For that reason it was not chosen for excavation and its true character only became apparent during a watching brief. The identification of the structure as an enclosure, even at such a late stage, proved to be very revealing. If its surface traces looked like the remains of a round house, was the resemblance between the two types entirely fortuitous?

Croft Moraig

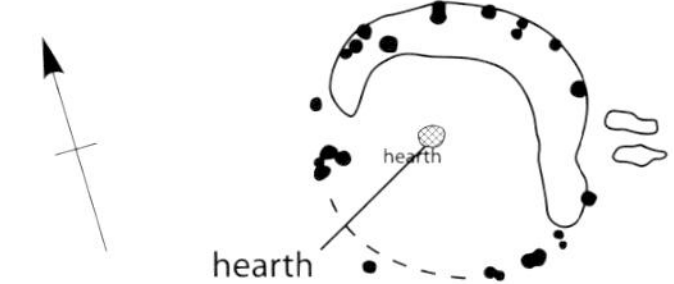

Lairg

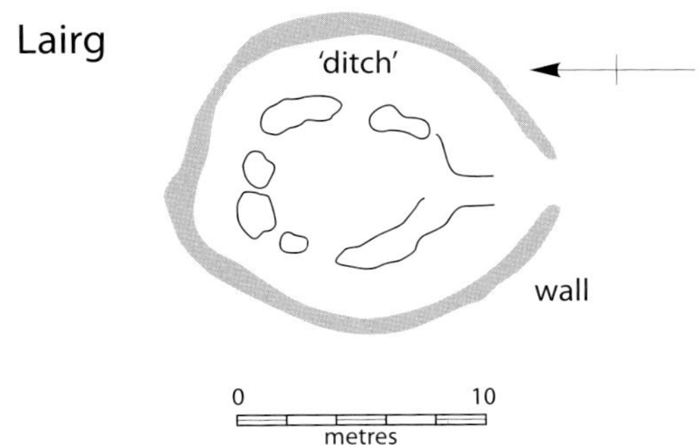

Illustration 5.4
The ring-ditch house at Lairg, compared with a similar structure built inside an earlier stone circle at Croft Moraig. Information from Piggott and Simpson (1971) and McCullagh and Tipping (1998)

There were other reasons why the distinction between these different kinds of structure has been blurred (illus 5.4). The excavation of domestic buildings has often identified a hollowed area around the outer limit of the floor. It is not clear how it formed, but if the remains were subjected to modern cultivation, little would survive but a 'ditch'. That was certainly the case when such a structure was discovered inside the stone circle at Croft Moraig (Piggott & Simpson 1971). The excavation of two neighbouring houses at Lairg, both of them dating from the Bronze Age, raises another possibility (McCullagh & Tipping 1998, fig 30). When the older building went out of use, its position was still respected, and the foundations of its outer wall were treated as an annexe to the dwelling built beside it. Thus even in the prehistoric period an abandoned house could assume a new identity as a circular enclosure.

That may have happened more often than is commonly supposed, for the round houses at this site did not replace one another directly. The spaces left by older buildings could be recognised unless they were levelled by the plough. Those houses were about the same size as the small 'henge' at Lairg, and their entrance porches shared roughly the same orientation as that monument. There are other connections between these two kinds of structure. There were two burials inside the 'henge', but, as McCullagh shows in Chapter 4, excavation showed that other cremated bones were found in domestic contexts. At the same time it seems as if a few abandoned houses in Britain were closed with the same formality as earthwork monuments (Barnatt, Bevan & Edmonds 2002). In the circumstances it is possible that small earthworks like that at Pullyhour were conceived *in the image of a domestic dwelling.*

It would be easy to misunderstand this argument and to suppose that small henges and the sites of ring-ditch houses were *mistaken* for one another in the past. That is not the point. The word 'house' has more than one connotation. It can be a physical structure within which people live, but it also refers to the 'household' as the inhabitants of that building. In one sense the house is a solid structure; in another, it is a social unit.

It is in this second sense that the connections between henges and dwelling places may have been important. Just as the giant timber circles at a site like North Mains might have been conceptualised as the 'great houses' of an entire community (Bradley in press), small earthworks like those at Pullyhour, Migdale and Lairg may have served a limited number of people, and possibly a single household. They might be interpreted as domestic shrines or, to use Thomas Kendrick's useful term, as the 'meeting places' for the occupants of a settlement. If so, it may be why the form of the round house provided such a potent symbol.

The challenge is to work out the character of the rituals associated with these sites. They can hardly have been secret as the interiors of these enclosures were no longer concealed by massive earthworks. Nor can they have involved large numbers of participants as the monuments are tiny and most have only one entrance. If the earthwork at Broomend of Crichie could be described as a screen, the interior of Pullyhour was a stage. It was the place where various rituals could be seen and the point from which other events could be viewed. It may have been used in a variety of different ways, from ceremonies that punctuated the life course of a particular household to the commemoration of its dead, and from rituals that involved observations of the sun and moon to others that reflect the growing importance of water in the cosmology of the Bronze Age. Those rituals seem to have been small-scale and short lived, and, once they were over, the sites themselves were closed. There could not be a greater contrast with the original uses of henge monuments.

Such comparisons may be helpful, but they have their limitations. Important questions remain to be addressed. Were sites like Migdale and Pullyhour the successors of larger monuments such as Broomend of Crichie and, if so, did their chronologies overlap? Were the small henges discussed in this chapter confined to the east coast of Scotland between Aberdeenshire and Caithness, or are there indications of similar structures in other regions? A third question poses an even more important challenge. Were these structures really a self-contained phenomenon? Why were they created at a time when other kinds of monuments were reused? It remains to work out the best ways of characterising the earthwork enclosures. All these topics will be discussed in Chapter 6.

THE EXCAVATED SITES IN THEIR WIDER CONTEXT

RICHARD BRADLEY

Chapter 5 concluded with a series of questions that need to be considered now. All were concerned with the significance of Pullyhour, Lairg and Migdale in a wider chronological and cultural context.

One tradition or two?

The first question was a deceptively simple one. Were these distinctive earthworks directly related to larger and apparently earlier monuments like Broomend of Crichie, or did they represent a completely different phenomenon? Should the earthworks classified together as henges be studied as one unbroken tradition, or were there two traditions with an interval between them? As in Chapter 3, these questions are best addressed by discussing individual sites.

Montcrieffe (illus 6.1)

Some of the places considered in this chapter are associated with radiocarbon dates, but that is not true of an excavated monument at Montcrieffe (Stewart 1985). It had been damaged long before it was investigated, but enough remained to establish an important sequence. At first sight it included a bewildering variety of structures. There was a roughly circular ditched enclosure approximately 9m in internal diameter, broken by an entrance to the north. Inside it was a timber circle defined by a setting of post-holes, but the central area was also occupied by at least two successive cairns. The earlier one may have been accompanied by a rectangular setting of four standing stones, while its successor was a small ring cairn enclosed by a circle of seven monoliths. There may have been another stone towards its centre, while a cremation in an inverted Cordoned Urn was found outside the monument.

The artefacts from the excavation range from Beaker sherds to others which may be of Late Bronze Age date. The latter could have been associated with deposits of cremated bone in the centre of the site. One observation is especially significant. The enclosure ditch contained Beaker pottery and had been filled *before* any of the stone structures were built over it.

The sequence at Montcrieffe provides unambiguous evidence that the earthwork of the henge was earlier than the stone settings. It may have been constructed while Beaker pottery was in use, although the quantity of finds is minimal. The small earthwork enclosure could be as old as the large monument at Broomend of Crichie.

Balneaves (illus 6.2)

A second site is Balneaves, where excavation identified an 'enclosed cremation cemetery' (Russell-White, Lowe & McCullagh 1992, 289–301). Gordon Barclay (2005) has suggested that it is better interpreted as a small henge monument. It consisted of a comparatively slight enclosure, 10m in diameter with a single entrance to the north-east. It included a series of cremation pits and other features that came so close to the ditch edge that the monument might have had an external bank. The ditch itself was associated with three radiocarbon dates. Their ranges overlap between about 1950 and 1750 BC. The burials also provided dates, and in this case the area of overlap is between 1850 and 1550 BC. Like some of those at Broomend of Crichie, they were associated with Collared Urns.

The enclosure also included the socket for a standing stone, the remains of which were buried on the site. In fact it was only one of four subsoil features which could have held monoliths. Taken together, they form a square. Two of them were directly associated with groups of cremation burials, while another cremation was buried in the centre of the enclosure. It seems possible that these deposits were arranged around the base of the stones in the way that happened at Broomend of Crichie but there is a problem, for one of those features was cut by several of the burial pits. If it had held an upright, the stone must have been removed by then.

The form of the putative stone setting at Balneaves recalls a number of sites in the surrounding area (Burl 1988 b). They are usually described as 'four posters'

Montcrieffe

A. Timber circle

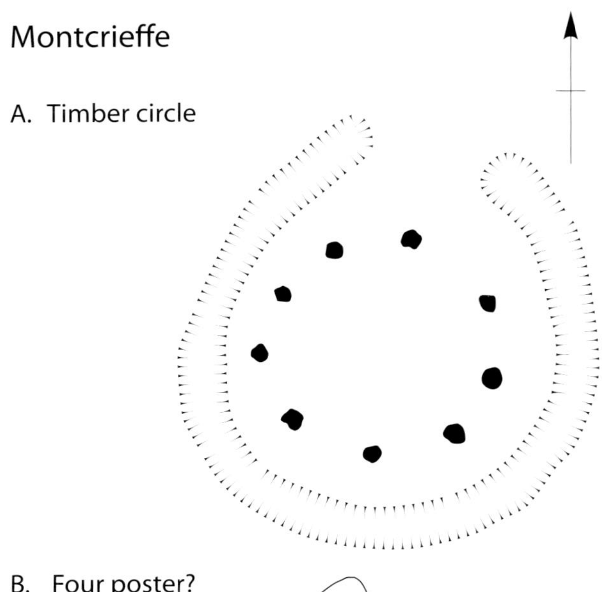

B. Four poster?

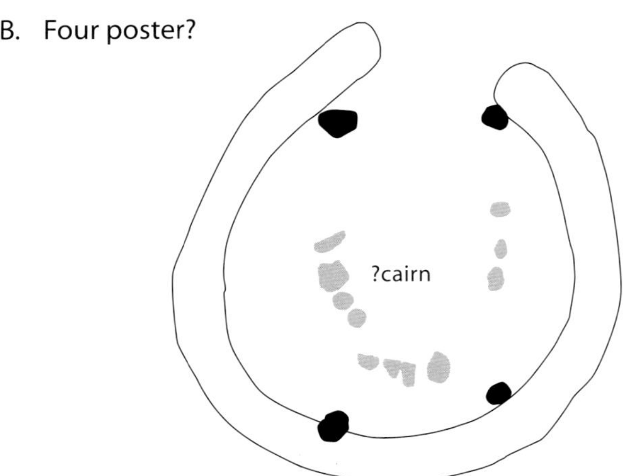

C. Stone circle and ring cairn

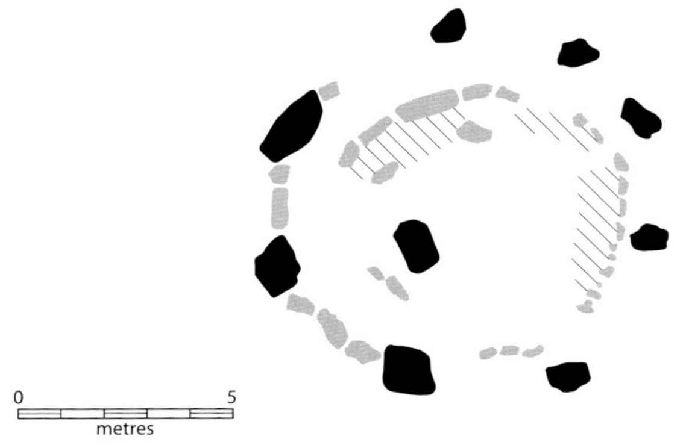

Illustration 6.1
The structural sequence at Montcrieffe. After Stewart (1985) and Bradley (2005)

and are also associated with cremations and Collared Urns. A similar structure can perhaps be identified in the second phase at Montcrieffe (Bradley 2005, 104). There is even a parallel for the 'missing' stone, as excavation at Park of Tongland in Galloway showed that the monoliths there had been erected at different times (Russell-White, Lowe & McCullagh 1992, 312–21). At no stage were all four of them standing simultaneously.

There are sites where a square stone setting was built on a circular platform (eg Burl 1988, 186–7), but the important point is that the earthwork at Balneaves was probably a henge. Again it is significant that the positions of the cremations may have been marked by standing stones. Both features recall the situation at Broomend of Crichie. Not only were they associated with Collared Urns, the burials at that site are dated between about 1950 and 1700 BC and those from Balneaves between about 1850 and 1550 BC. There is a significant overlap.

There is another reason why the chronology of these monuments is significant. The enclosure at Balneaves is of a similar size and construction to earthworks in northern Scotland, although its ditch is not exceptionally wide. The dates from the ditch suggest that it was built *before* the monuments at Lairg and Pullyhour. On the other hand, the first enclosure at Pullyhour could have been used at the same time as burials were deposited at Balneaves. That is also possible at Lairg, although the dates on the cremated bone from the site may suggest a slightly later period.

Broomend of Crichie, Fullerton and the Hill of Tuach

Another area in which to investigate the chronology of henges and stone circles is between Inverurie and Kintore, for here it is possible to compare two, and possibly three, excavated sites: Broomend of Crichie, the Hill of Tuach and (with due caution) Fullerton. There are contrasts between the sizes of these monuments – the monument at Broomend of Crichie is very large, while those at Fullerton and the Hill of Tuach are small. Nonetheless all three were circular ditched enclosures with external banks. At least two of these earthworks contained a setting of monoliths: six at Broomend of Crichie, and another six on the Hill of Tuach (Coles 1901, 192–6). There seem to have been seven monoliths at Fullerton, but the only one that remained intact at the time of Fred Coles's survey was outside the bank (Coles 1901, 218–19). No plan survives of the original monument at Fullerton,

Balneaves

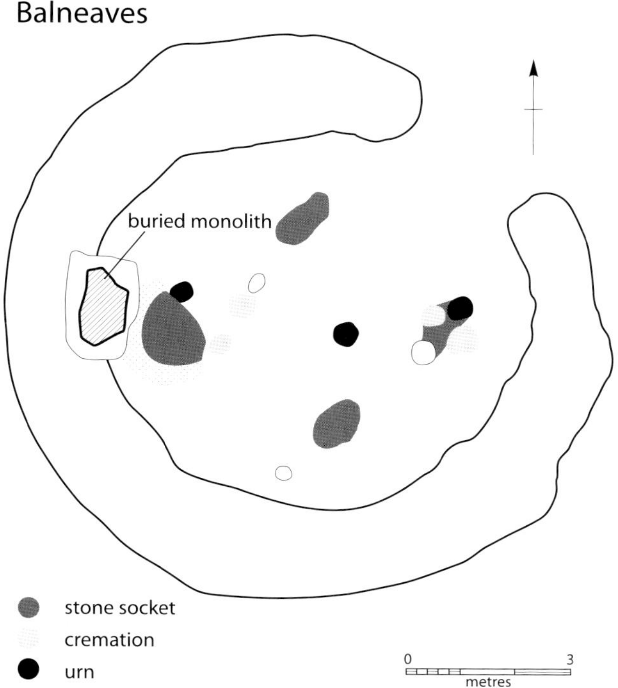

Illustration 6.2
The excavated monument at Balneaves interpreted as a small henge containing a square stone setting and associated cremation burials. Information from Russell-White, Lowe and McCullagh (1992)

but all three contained burials, although the details of the deposits are seldom clear. In each case a ring of cremations surrounded a central grave.

The age of Fullerton is uncertain. Although a sample of cremated bone from the nineteenth-century excavation has a date in the Late Bronze Age, it may not be related to the initial use of the site (Sheridan 2003, 169). The Hill of Tuach, however, was associated with Cordoned Urns. This would indicate the period between about 1800 and 1500 BC. By contrast, the cremation burials at Broomend of Crichie date from 1950–1750 BC. They were accompanied by Vase Urns/ Collared Urns, flint arrowheads and a battle axe: a quite different assemblage from the Hill of Tuach.

The contrast between the artefacts from two of the sites has important implications, for it means that the monument on the Hill of Tuach should have been later than both the earthwork and the burials at Broomend of Crichie: a site which it resembles in other respects. At the same time, the small enclosure on the Hill of Tuach could have been contemporary with the timber circle outside the henge at Broomend of Crichie, with the first earthwork at Pullyhour and perhaps with

that at Lairg. The Aberdeenshire monuments share many different elements. Although they were used at different times, it suggests that they belonged to a single tradition.

Summary

This section has considered a series of monuments whose structures have something in common, yet it has shown that their earthworks were built over a long period of time. The evidence is not as detailed as one might wish, but it is sufficient to answer the question posed at the beginning of this chapter. It seems as if the practice of building henges in Bronze Age Scotland extended down to at least the middle of the second millennium BC. Some of the smallest sites were among the later examples, but this provides no indication of the date of unexcavated monuments. Superficially similar earthworks were contemporary with larger constructions.

The reuse of older monuments

There are other sites whose history is punctuated by intervals in which there is no obvious evidence of activity. The original monuments take many different forms. What is striking is that they were brought back into use at approximately the same time. In most cases their secondary use was associated with the treatment of the dead. Sometimes cremations were buried at these sites, and there are a few cases in which older structures provided the sites for pyres. There is even the possibility that during a secondary phase such monuments were used by bronzesmiths, although this evidence is limited to Loanhead of Daviot (Kilbride-Jones 1935 and 1936), Montcrieffe (Stewart 1985) and Tillicoultry (O'Connor 2007).

The evidence of later activity extends across a series of architectural traditions, but it seems as if the distinctive character of those sites was not especially important. Monuments of different types were reused in very much the same ways. The most convincing evidence is provided by radiocarbon dates, some of them on cremated bone. Among the sites with evidence of secondary activity between about 1200 and 800 BC were the recumbent stone circles at Castle Fraser, Aikey Brae, Tomnaverie and Old Keig, while there is similar evidence from the Clava Cairns at Balnuaran of Clava and Newton of Petty, and possibly Raigmore and Gownie (Sheridan 2004b; Bradley & Sheridan 2005). The same punctuated sequence is probably represented at the larger stone circle at Temple Wood (Scott 1989; Sheridan 2008, 202) and perhaps Balbirnie (Ritchie 1974). Another case may be a four-poster at Fortingall (Sheridan 2008, 203). Further instances are suggested by the pottery from similar sites, particularly the collections from Montcrieffe (Stewart 1985) and the recumbent stone circle at Loanhead of Daviot (Kilbride-Jones 1935).

The larger henges do not conform to this pattern. Either they were completely disused or any later features were excluded from the enclosures themselves. Thus the use of Broomend of Crichie apparently came to an end and the last structure to be built there was *outside* the enclosure. North Mains illustrates a comparable development. Here a series of cremation burials with radiocarbon dates in the Late Bronze Age was excluded from the henge and deposited beyond its earthwork. Similarly, there was no evidence of Late Bronze Age activity within the henge excavated by Roger Mercer (1981) at Balfarg, but cremation burials were found some distance outside it.

There was a different sequence at the smaller monuments. The earthwork enclosures at Montcrieffe and Fullerton seem to have been reused, and there are signs of renewed activity at recumbent stone circles, Clava Cairns, and sites like Croft Moraig and Temple Wood. Perhaps the bigger monuments were no longer considered appropriate. The structures that did see secondary activity during the Late Bronze Age must have catered for a more restricted audience, and the same applies to the last of the earthwork enclosures. Again it would have been possible to observe what was happening inside them. Unlike Broomend of Crichie and similar sites, they were no longer concealed behind an enormous screen.

Two of the reused sites are particularly informative.

Cairnwell (illus 6.3)

The first is Cairnwell where the Bronze Age structures were built in two phases on a site that had already been used during the Neolithic period (Rees 1997). The first saw the construction of a circular fenced enclosure, 5m in diameter with a narrow gap to the SSE. It enclosed a group of cremation burials. Two have dates at 2σ of 1395–1050 BC and 1420–1135 BC respectively (GU-4398 and GU-4376), while the enclosure itself has a *terminus post quem* of 1435–1035 BC (GU-4400). The closest parallel for this structure may be the timber monument that replaced the henge at Migdale. It had a similar ground plan and was only

7m in diameter. That is not much larger than the structure at Cairnwell.

The wooden enclosure at Cairnwell was replaced by a ring cairn, buttressed by a layer of rubble and enclosed by a small stone circle which may have been built soon afterwards. The monoliths followed the outline of the timber structure and emphasised the position of its entrance with a large slab set upright between two standing stones. As the excavator observed, this arrangement recalls the structure of a recumbent stone circle, but it represents it in miniature. There is no evidence that such monuments were still being built in Late Bronze Age Scotland, but their remains were certainly reused. Perhaps they provided a source of inspiration for this structure. The old ground surface sealed by the ring cairn has a radiocarbon date at 2σ of 1515–1180 BC (GU-4397) and another sample provides a *terminus post quem* for the timber enclosure of 1435–1035 BC (GU-4400).

Croft Moraig (illus 6.4)

Croft Moraig is a monument whose chronology has posed many problems, and what is suggested here is a modified version of an interpretation already published by Alison Sheridan and the writer (Bradley & Sheridan 2005; cf Piggott & Simpson 1971). For that reason it is not necessary to present the argument in detail. It depends on two key features: a new consideration of the plans and orientations of the structures; and a fresh analysis of the pottery excavated there in 1965.

The earliest monument was probably a stone circle with its entrance to the east. Outside it were two large stones, each of them apparently marking the position of a grave. There were no other monoliths beyond the perimeter of the circle, but in the light of the evidence from Broomend of Crichie it seems possible that they formed part of a more extended avenue. The association between the portal stones and burials also recalls that monument.

The reuse of the site is associated with 'flat rim ware'. At one time it was assigned to the Neolithic period and compared with Grooved Ware, but radiocarbon dating of cremated bone associated with similar vessels shows that this tradition is essentially Bronze Age and most common between 1200 and 800 BC. The importance of this revision is that the sherds from Croft Moraig were securely stratified. They were associated with the remains of a timber building inside the original monument which was replaced in the same position by a setting of standing stones. That was probably the latest structure on the site. It was concentric with a drystone wall which encloses the entire monument.

The timber building and the later stone setting have parallels on other sites. Following the excavators' account, an earlier interpretation of the sequence separated the ring of post-holes with its porch from the shallow gully just inside it. That no longer seems necessary as excavations at Lairg and Kintore have shown that these can be integral parts of the same buildings. That is why they are described as 'ring–ditch houses' (I am grateful to Derek Alexander for

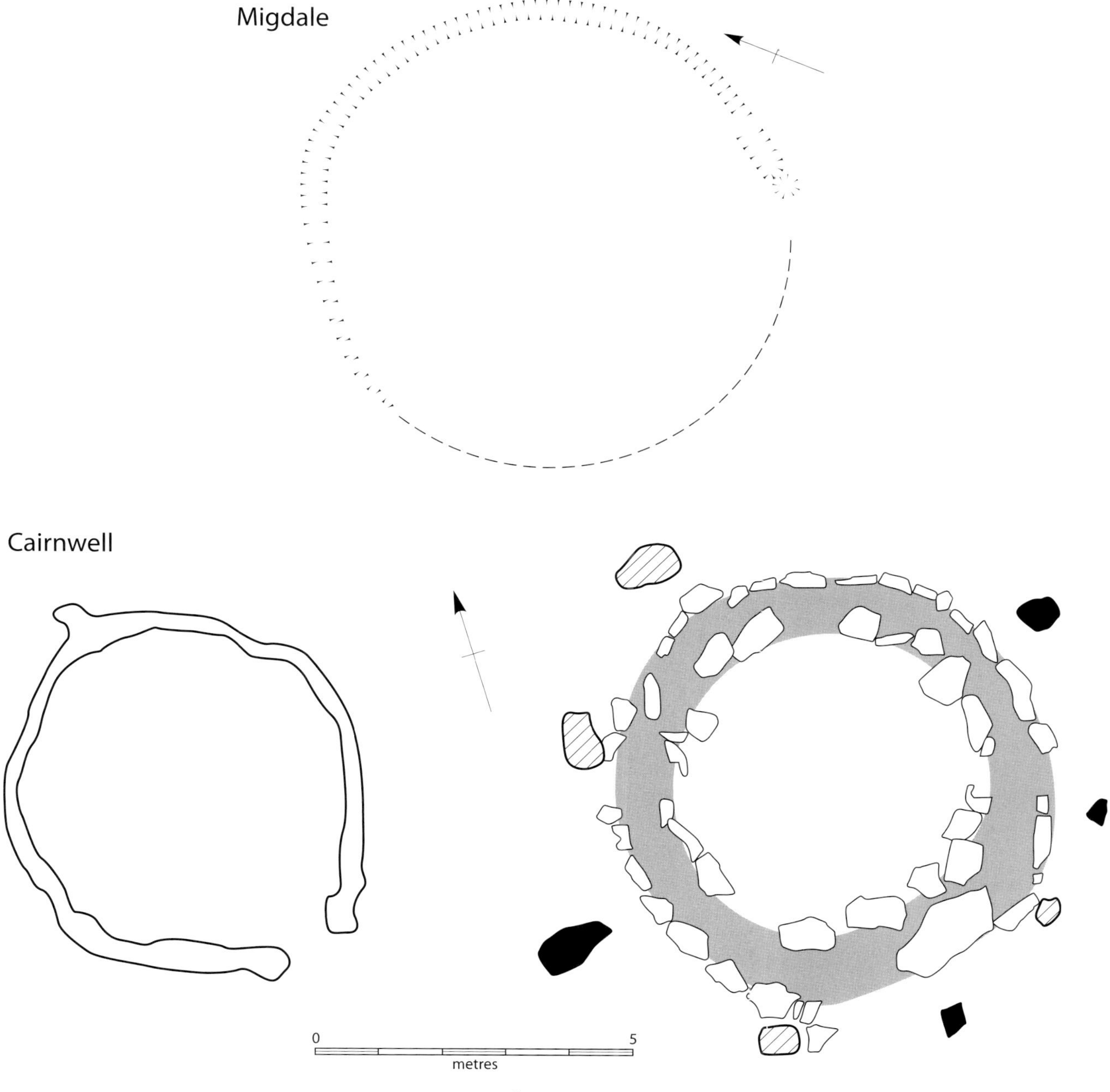

Illustration 6.3
The secondary fenced enclosure at Migdale compared with a similar structure at Cairnwell and the ring cairn that replaced it.
Information from Rees (1997)

171

Croft Moraig

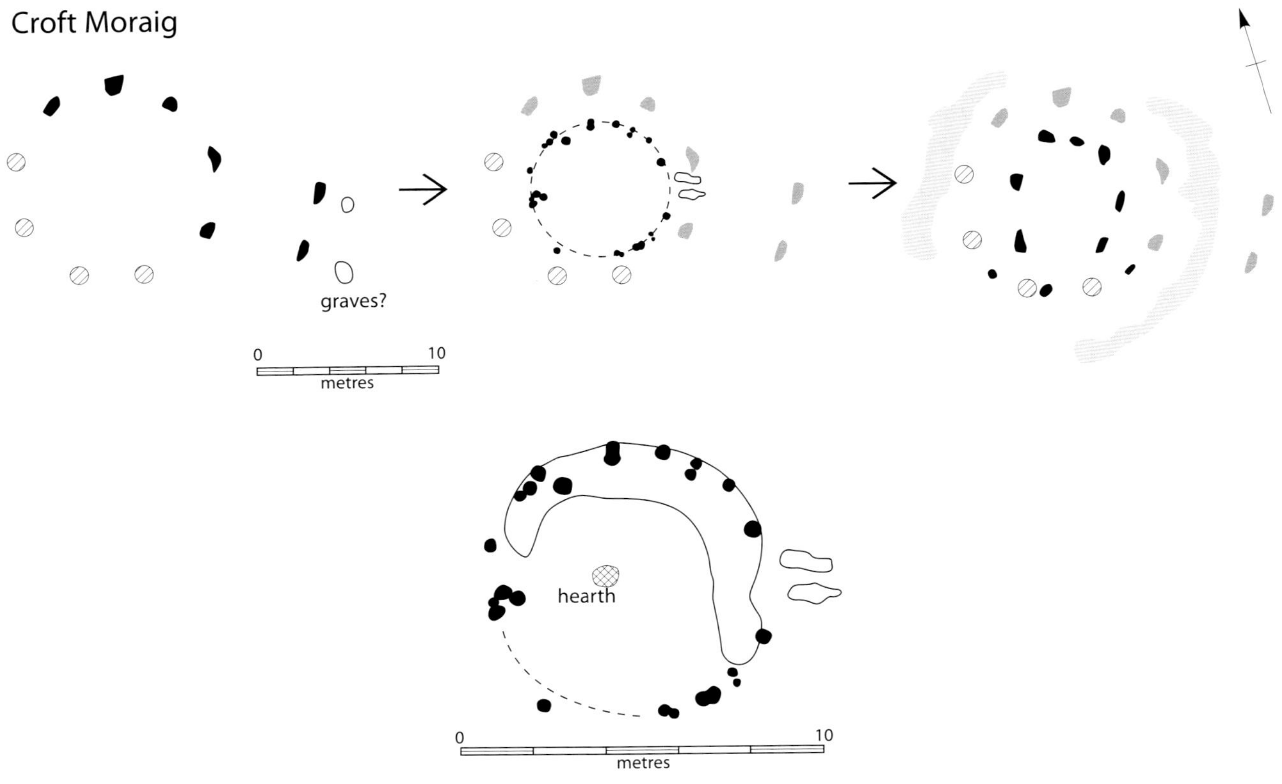

Illustration 6.4

An interpretation of the structural sequence at Croft Moraig. Information from Piggott and Simpson (1971) and Bradley and Sheridan (2005)

suggesting this interpretation of Croft Moraig). Structures of this kind have long been accepted as a feature of Iron Age settlements, but more recent fieldwork shows that they were already present in the Late Bronze Age: the likely age of the pottery from Croft Moraig (McCullagh & Tipping 1998; Cook & Dunbar 2008). If this reasoning is correct, a timber building of a kind associated with occupation sites was established inside an already existing stone circle with parallels in the Early Bronze Age. The interior of the timber building may have been paved and had a central hearth. It retained the axis of the older monument, which was still standing, and its porch was aligned on the entrance to the circle.

It is unusual, though not unique, for a building of this kind to be erected inside an intact stone circle, but what followed is unprecedented. The position of the timber structure was replaced by an oval setting of monoliths which established a new alignment for the site. Now the stones were graded in height towards the south-west and some of their sockets were cut through

the layer containing Late Bronze Age pottery. The excavation records are of such high quality that this chronological relationship is unambiguous. It is more difficult to establish the age of the perimeter wall, but it is exactly symmetrical with the new stone setting and cuts across the entrance to the original monument. For those reasons it should belong to the last phase at Croft Moraig. It is worth comparing this sequence with that at Pullyhour where a circular enclosure was rebuilt to an oval ground plan (illus 6.5). This structure has a *terminus post quem* at 2σ of 1369–1126 BC (OxA-18156).

If the timber structure resembles domestic buildings of the same date at Kintore and Lairg, it is likely that it played a more specialised role. Otherwise it is hard to account for its distinctive siting, or for the curious way in which its position was commemorated in stone. On the other hand, settings of monoliths directed towards the south-west are known on other sites in the same region. One, at Sandy Road, Scone, enclosed a cremation burial with a date at 2σ of 1190–890 BC

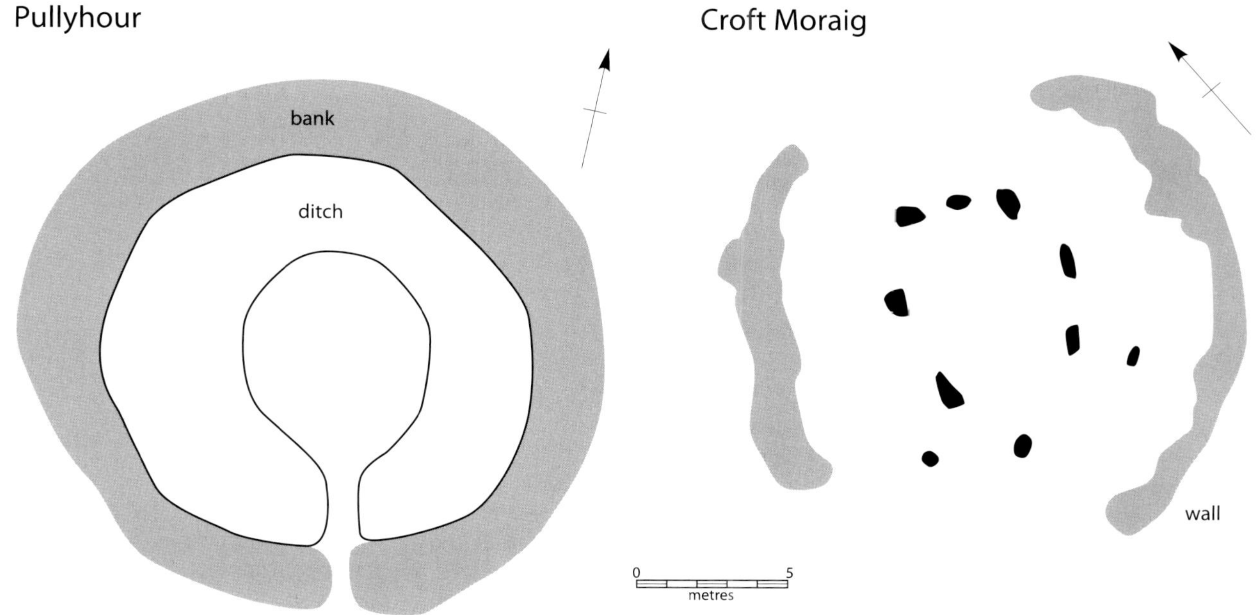

Illustration 6.5

The rebuilt enclosure at Pullyhour compared with the oval stone setting attributed to the final phase at Croft Moraig. The walled enclosure on the latter site seems to belong to the same period. Information from Bradley and Sheridan (2005)

(GrN-23986; Stewart 1966; Sheridan 2003, 168). Like the last stone setting at Croft Moraig, it was slightly oval in plan. Another site with the same characteristics was the stone circle inside the older henge monument at Montcrieffe (Stewart 1985). It included the same number of monoliths as the oval setting at Croft Moraig and was slightly elongated towards the south-west; the stones also rose in height towards the west. The sizes of these structures compare closely with one another. The long axis of the oval monument at Croft Moraig was 9m; at Montcrieffe it was 10m. Another comparison is with the stone monument at Cairnwell discussed earlier in this chapter (Rees 1997). It was perhaps of Late Bronze Age date. Here the small stone circle included an estimated eight monoliths. Again it was 9m in diameter. Perhaps the timber structure it replaced was conceived in the image of a house.

The last structure that needs to be considered is the perimeter wall at Croft Moraig. It seems to have been associated with the latest setting of monoliths. It can be compared with a ring cairn, but it could also be related to the earthwork enclosures that were built at about the same time. It is 17m in diameter and in plan it certainly resembles one of those monuments. It appears to have had an entrance to the south-west.

Summary

This section has considered the evidence that earlier stone-built monuments in the north and north-east of Scotland were reused between about 1200 and 800 BC. It happened at a variety of different sites, but three are of special relevance here. At Montcrieffe a stone circle was built over the position of an older henge. Some of the monoliths were erected in its infilled ditch. In this case they did not replace the earthwork directly, as the site already contained a cairn and some standing stones. On the other hand, its bank could still have been visible.

At Croft Moraig, the earliest structure was a stone circle which may have been approached by an avenue. It was apparently associated with two inhumation burials. During the Late Bronze Age a timber roundhouse was built inside it. A similar building was erected within the recumbent stone circle at Strichen and even utilised a decorated stone associated with the earlier monument (Phillips, Hampshire-Monk & Abramson 2006). It was replaced by a larger timber building, but its counterpart at Croft Moraig was succeeded by a setting of monoliths and enclosed by a wall *similar in layout to a henge*.

The sequence at Cairnwell has points in common with both these monuments. In this case the earliest

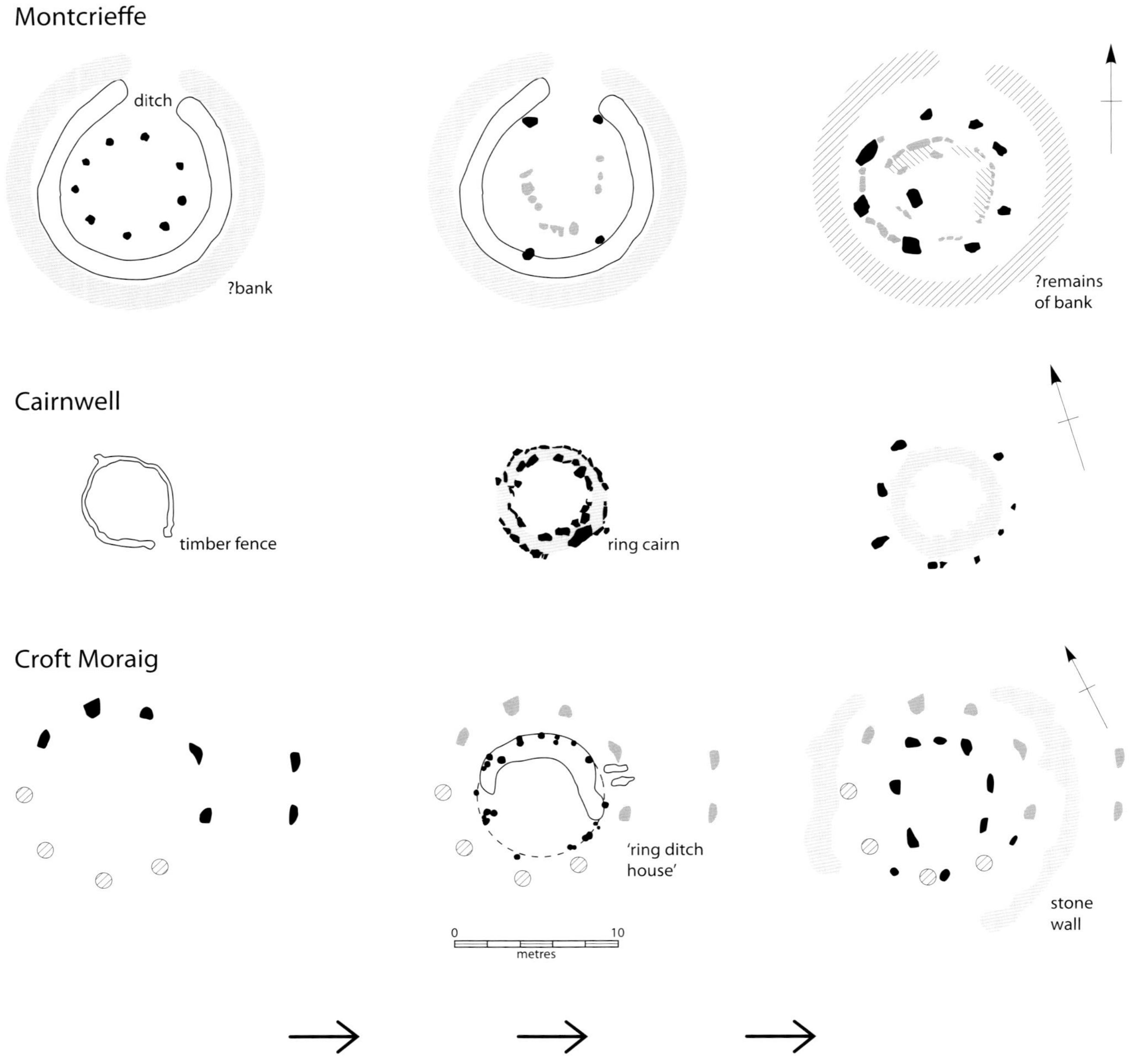

Illustration 6.6
Outline plans showing the structural sequences at Montcrieffe, Cairnwell and Croft Moraig. They began as very different kinds of monuments, but when they were reused all three sites contained small settings of monoliths. Information from Stewart (1985), Bradley (2005), Rees (1997) and Bradley and Sheridan (2005)

structure was neither a henge nor a stone circle: it was a small timber building not unlike the enclosure that was built over the henge at Migdale. At Migdale its construction marked the end of activities on that site, but the enclosure at Cairnwell was replaced by a ring cairn and by a circle of monoliths. What is striking is that these sequences converged, possibly in the Late Bronze Age. The oval stone setting at Croft Moraig shares a number of features with the latest structures at Cairnwell and Montcrieffe. Despite so much diversity, *the use of these monuments appears to have ended at a common point* (illus 6.6).

Northern henges and Irish ring barrows (illus 6.7)

A different question is whether the small earthworks discussed in Part II conformed to a regional tradition or whether their distinctive attributes were widely shared.

The practice of building small circular enclosures with internal ditches is best represented between Caithness and the Moray Firth (Woodham 1953). Although some comparable sites have been identified across a larger area, the concentration of sites cannot be explained entirely in terms of their survival. The links between the earthwork monuments in this area have been considered already. There is only one other region with a similar concentration of monuments of this form. Although

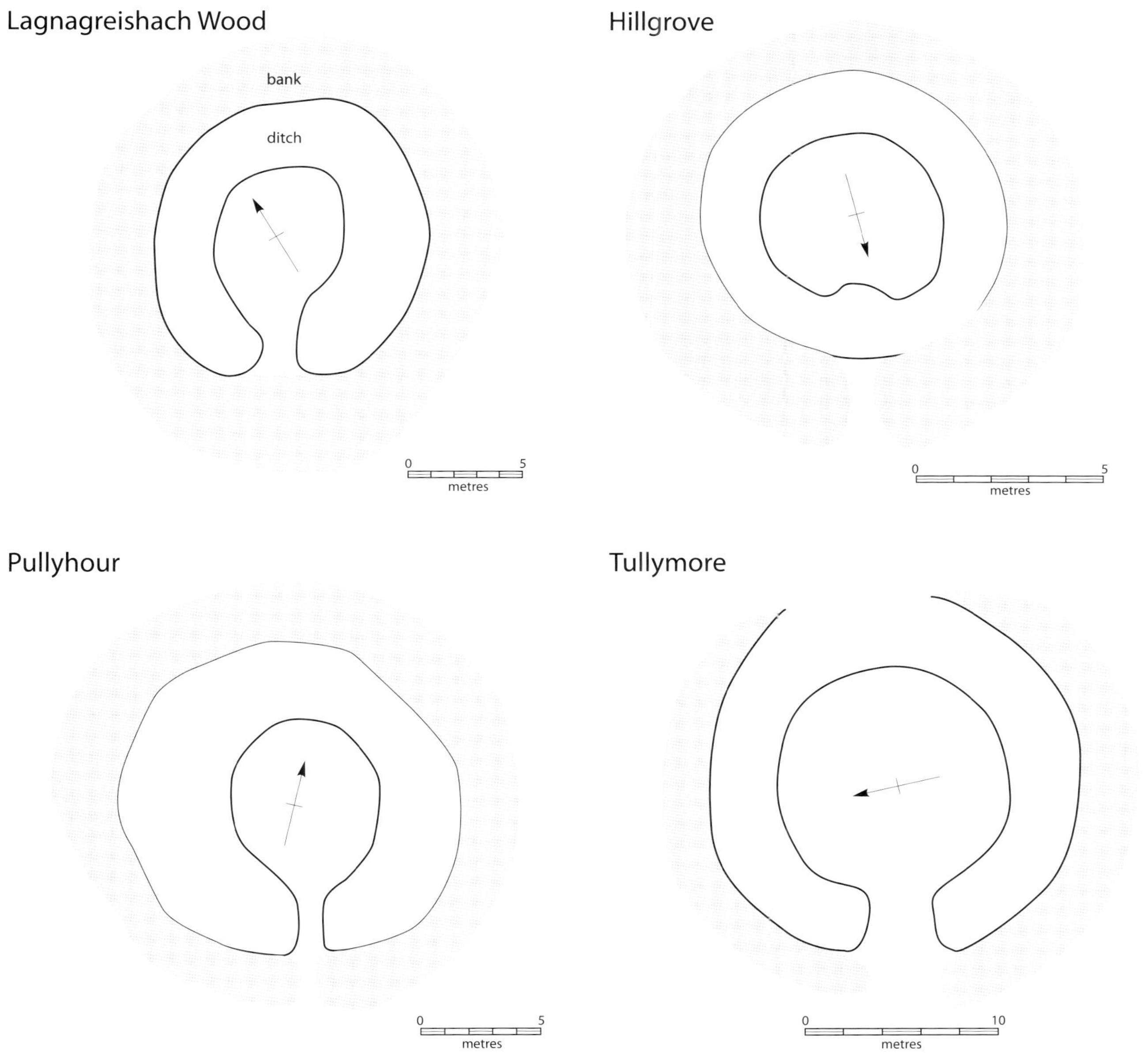

Illustration 6.7
Outline plans of two small 'henges' in northern Scotland (left) and two Irish 'ring barrows' (right). Information from an unpublished survey by Annette Jack and Ronnie Scott and from O'Brien (2004)

the resemblance between these groups is striking, it has seldom been discussed.

On the opposite side of the Irish Sea are the structures that archaeologists call *ring barrows* (Waddell 1998, 365–8). The term may be confusing to British readers who think of a barrow as a mound, for these are earthwork enclosures. They have external banks and internal ditches, interrupted by either one entrance or two. They enclose a small circular area and their earthwork perimeter is disproportionately wide. It is sometimes claimed that they contain low mounds or platforms but this has rarely been substantiated. They are the same size as the Scottish monuments and they share the curious feature that some of their entrances were apparently blocked in antiquity. The causeways were modified and sometimes removed and there are

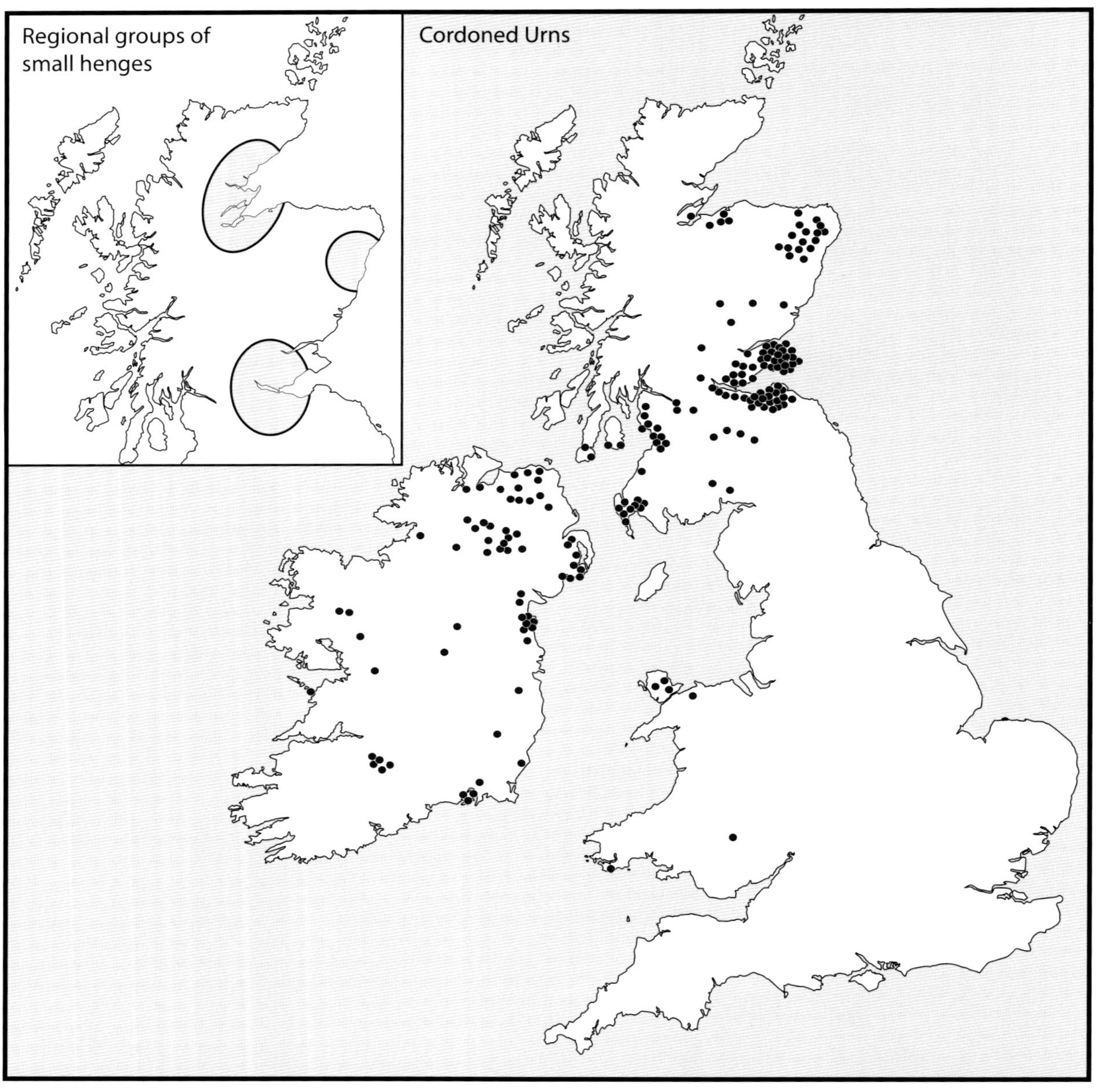

Illustration 6.8
Regional groups of small henges in Scotland (information from Harding and Lee (1987), and the distribution of Cordoned Urns in Britain and Ireland (after Waddell (1995)

also sites where the bank continues without a break across the entrance. Irish ring barrows have never been considered in detail, but published inventories and field surveys suggest that they are found in most parts of the island. They can occur singly, or in groups like that investigated by Séan Ó Ríordáin (1950) at the Curragh. Only in the south-west have ring barrows been studied in much depth, and here William O'Brien (2004) has discussed their distribution and dating.

If the size and appearance of Irish ring barrows recall the features of small henges in northern Scotland, so do their dates and associations. Some of the enclosures in Ireland include cremation burials, although they are seldom found with many artefacts. The first ring barrows were associated with Irish Bowls and Vase Urns, while others enclose cremation burials associated with bronze razors and Cordoned Urns. That may be significant as their chronology runs in parallel with that of small henge monuments in Scotland. The earliest sites in Ireland would have been roughly contemporary with the earthworks at Montcrieffe and Balneaves, while the finds from the Hill of Tuach are similar to those from a ring barrow at Carrowjames in County Mayo (Raftery 1941) and a related monument at Urbalreagh in County Antrim (Waterman 1968). They were of about the same age as the dated monument at Pullyhour.

There is good evidence for contacts across the Irish Sea during the Early Bronze Age, and several styles of pottery – Bowls, Collared Urns, Vase Urns and Condoned Urns – are found on both sides of the water. Vase Urns and Cordoned Urns have the widest distributions, and it may no coincidence that two of the main clusters of Cordoned Urns in Scotland are in areas where groups of small earthwork enclosures are found (Waddell 1995, fig 11.3). One is in Aberdeenshire and another is around the inner Moray Firth. The greatest concentration of Cordoned Urns is around the Firth of Forth where another series of small henges has been identified by field survey and air photography (illus 6.8). Unfortunately, none has been excavated (Harding & Lee 1987, fig 24).

It is likely that the building of these enclosures continued into the later Bronze Age both in Scotland and Ireland, but then the local sequences diverge. The last Irish examples date from the Iron Age and have very few obvious counterparts in Britain. Although the enclosure at Lairg may have been reused in the Iron Age, the Scottish 'henges' appear to date from the Bronze Age.

One reason for this difference is that ring barrows in Ireland assumed new roles during the late first millennium BC. Although small earthworks like those in northern Britain were still used as funerary monuments, larger examples were also built at that time. They are found in distinctive contexts, for the biggest ring barrows of all were associated with Iron Age 'royal centres' (Newman 1997, 163–5). These are major monument complexes and provide evidence for feasting, craft production and the erection of enormous wooden buildings. In the earliest Irish literature such places – Navan Fort, Knockaulin, Rathcroghan and Tara – were where new rulers were inaugurated (Waddell, Fenwick & Barton 2009). There is evidence that Navan Fort was first used in the Late Bronze Age (Waterman 1997), but otherwise such sites show little connection with the archaeological sequence in Scotland. The one anomaly is Pict's Knowe in the south-west of the country which did see Iron Age activity (Thomas 2007).

O'Brien's work in Munster sheds new light on the Bronze Age structures and provides the best basis for comparisons between Britain and Ireland (O'Brien 2004). Two observations are particularly important. The distribution of these distinctive earthworks complements that of the last stone circles, although their features were sometimes combined in what are described as 'circle henges'. At the same time, there is evidence that some of the freestanding earthworks also date from the Late Bronze Age. Like some of the Scottish sites, they contain cremation burials.

Reanascreena (illus 6.9)

Few of these monuments have been thoroughly excavated and published. Perhaps the most informative is at Reanascreena in County Cork (Fahy 1962). It is worth considering it in detail as it has a number of elements that recall the Scottish evidence. The earthwork comprised an external bank and an internal ditch, with a single entrance to the ENE. The enclosure had an internal diameter of just over 10m and a perimeter up to 3.75m wide. Inside the monument there were two pits. One contained a cremation burial while the other, at the centre of the monument, may have held a post. There was also a stone setting inside the enclosure at Reanascreena. It had all the attributes of the local stone circles, with two tall portal stones facing the entrance to the monument. Directly opposite it was the lowest stone on the site. A charcoal sample sealed by the bank at Reanascreena provides a *terminus*

Reanascreena

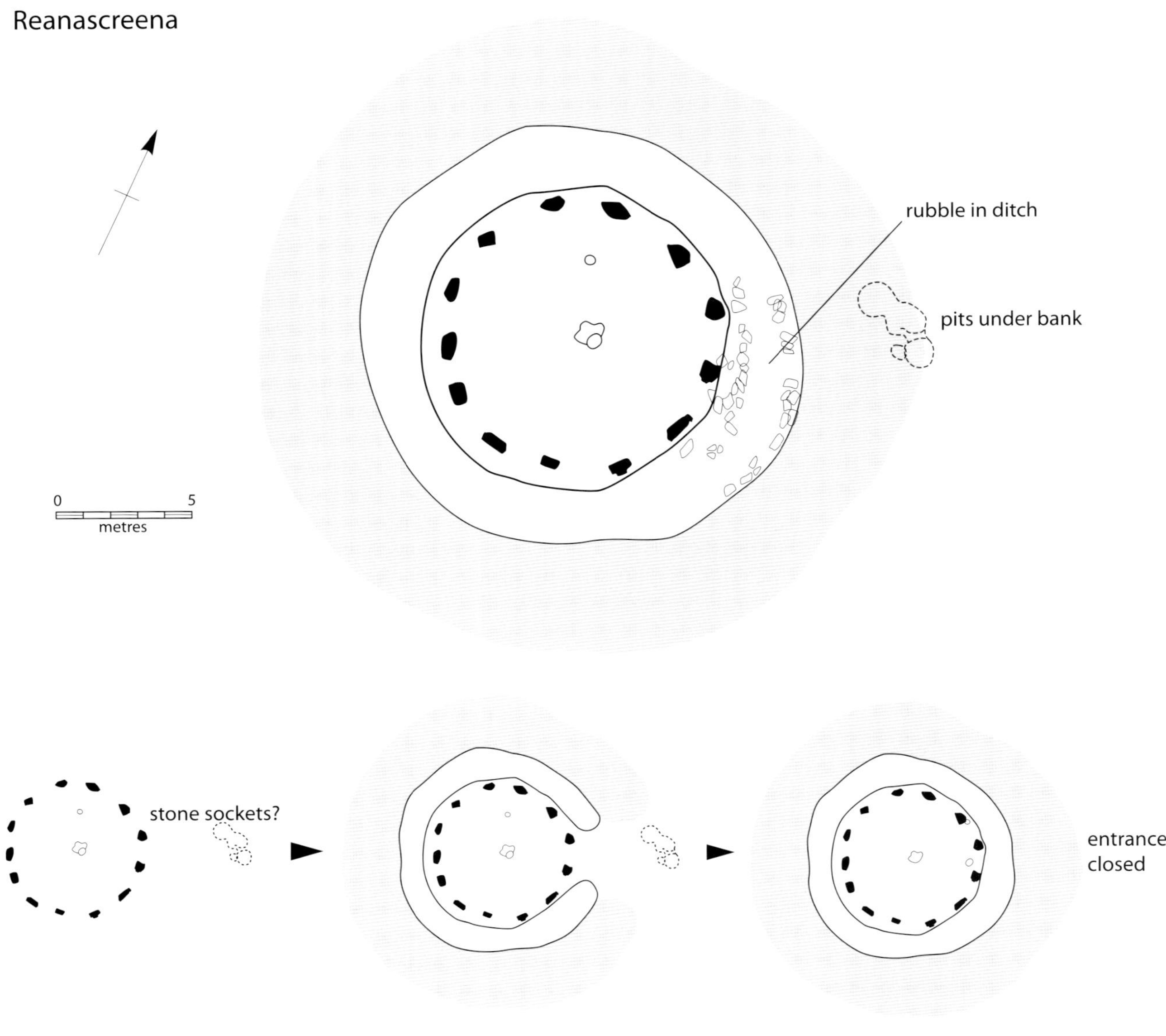

Illustration 6.9
An interpretation of the structural sequence at the ring barrow at Reanascreena, County Cork. Information from Fahy (1962)

post quem at 2σ for the earthwork of 1253–940 BC (GrN-17510), and another from the burial pit is dated to 1001–835 BC (GrN-17509; O'Brien 2004, 326–8). This was probably a Late Bronze Age monument.

There are some indications of the structural sequence at Reanascreena: a sequence that recalls the evidence from northern Scotland. The orientation of the monument extends from the portal stones towards the WSW, yet the bank and ditch follow a continuous course. The only evidence for an entrance is close to those portal stones where a layer of rubble was found in the filling of the ditch. It was thought to prevent erosion as people entered the monument, but it is difficult to understand why no causeway had been provided. Beside this feature but sealed by the enclosure bank was a series of intercutting pits containing broken boulders and chips of rock. How should they be interpreted?

One possibility is that the earthwork and the stone setting were of different dates. As happened at some of the sites considered in Chapter 3, the stone circle and the earthwork are not concentric with one another, and on the eastern side of the monument the edge of the ditch almost undermines the monoliths. The obvious explanation is that the stone setting was built first and the 'henge' was added afterwards. At the same time, it is difficult to account for the pits buried under the bank. From the published description they might have been shallow sockets, in which case they could have been filled by broken packing stones and by the debris that resulted from removing or destroying a monolith. They are located outside the entrance to the stone circle and may have been associated with its initial construction and use. It may be no coincidence that these pits were close to the point where the ditch was filled with rubble.

Taken together, these observations suggest a complex sequence at Reanascreena. The first structure was perhaps a stone circle of a well known local type that is normally attributed to the Late Bronze Age (O'Brien 2004). It had a clearly defined entrance with a standing stone outside it. That monolith could have been replaced on more than one occasion. Some time afterwards the stone setting was enclosed by a circular earthwork with an external bank and a wide, shallow ditch on the inside. It seems possible that it was originally interrupted at the entrance and that an isolated standing stone was incorporated in the new design. In a subsequent phase that stone was destroyed and the ends of the bank could have been extended to form a continuous perimeter. The deposit of rubble in the ditch may not have been intended to consolidate the earthwork in the way that the excavator suggested. Instead it might result from the demolition of a kerb like that at Pullyhour. When that happened, the monument was closed.

Of course this sequence is hypothetical but the purpose of this section is not to insist on a new interpretation of Reanascreena but to draw attention to some of the ways in which its distinctive structure echoes features that have also been recognised in northern Scotland. The Bronze Age was a period in which people travelled long distances by land and sea. It is possible that traditions of earthwork building were closely connected on either side of the water. The problem is that they have been studied separately until now.

General trends

It is only recently that the chronology of Scottish Bronze Age monuments has become clear. That is due to two main developments: AMS dating of short-lived samples and cremated bone; and a fresh appreciation of ceramic chronology. A new understanding of 'flat rim ware' has made a special contribution. As a result it is possible to identify a series of monuments, including small henges, whose chronology had never been established. These developments have also allowed researchers to identify the widespread reuse of older structures during the Late Bronze Age. Some of the sites have been discussed here, but are there any general patterns that cross-cut these detailed studies?

The first is that the latest structures were generally self-contained. Their characteristic forms might echo older styles of architecture, like henges or recumbent stone circles, but the newly built structures were usually created on new sites and may not have formed parts of larger monument complexes. The evidence from Lairg even suggests they could be built within the settled landscape. The earthworks and stone settings were normally much smaller than their predecessors on other sites, and it even seems possible that small monuments were preferred for reuse during later prehistory. Thus the henge at Montcrieffe shows a continuous archaeological sequence, while its larger counterparts at Balfarg and North Mains had Late Bronze Age burials *outside* them. Broomend of Crichie was apparently disused by that time. Towards the end of the Early Bronze Age miniature versions of the same design were created not far away, on the Hill of Tuach and perhaps at Fullerton.

Many of the smaller monuments were of similar dimensions to the houses found in settlements of the same period. Indeed, there are sites where timber buildings of the same form were built in more specialised contexts. In such cases it is only their distinctive contexts that suggest a special role. Thus buildings in the form of a round house were constructed inside the stone circles at Strichen and Croft Moraig and one of them was directly replaced by a setting of standing stones. A similar argument applies to the timber structure outside the south entrance at Broomend of Crichie. Seen in plan, it resembles a circular house with a porch, but analysis of the post-holes suggests that the timbers were graded in height towards the north-east.

The orientation of this particular structure was completely different from that of the henge monument on the same site. It introduced a new alignment towards the nearby river. That may be no coincidence, for the small earthworks classified as henges in northern and north-eastern Scotland illustrate a similar concern. Some, like Pullyhour and Wormy Hillock, are directed towards nearby rivers or streams, while other sites, such as those at Migdale or Shiel Bridge, are aligned on lochs. This connection with water happens sufficiently often to suggest a new emphasis on an environment in which metalwork might be deposited. During the Early Bronze Age it could be associated with prominent outcrops, like that at Migdale (Cowie 2004). In the later Bronze Age its distribution focused on rivers and lakes. A good example is the well known collection from Duddingston Loch (Callender 1922). It seems possible that the siting of newly built monuments reflected something of the same concern. If so, it marks the beginning of a trend that continued long after the use of henges was over.

SUMMING UP

RICHARD BRADLEY

A short history of henges

The geographical limits of this study were laid down from the outset, for the project took place in an area where henges had not been excavated. It also explored a region in which other monuments assigned to the Neolithic had proved to be of later date. The results of this fieldwork emphasise the diversity of the earthwork enclosures. They were built and used for longer than anyone had expected and were subject to significant regional variations. Such findings are surprising and need to be explained.

Chronology and regional patterns

The history of henges is more protracted than earlier writers had supposed. Although Thomas Kendrick was studiedly vague in dating the monuments in this class, he believed that they were used in the Late Neolithic and Early Bronze Age. By the 1990s their origins had been traced back to the Middle Neolithic period (Harding 2003). The present project has found that their history could have extended into the Late Bronze Age. The larger examples were built at different times, and their chronology – like that of stone and timber circles – covers more than a thousand years. The smaller sites had an even longer currency.

During this time there were three periods of increased activity, although the available radiocarbon dates are not precise enough to show whether they represent 'horizons' when different structures were built simultaneously. It is clear that each phase witnessed the construction of some exceptional monuments. The first was around 3000 BC when the first stone circles were erected. Some, like that at Calanais, were not enclosed, while others, like the earliest setting of monoliths at Stonehenge, were bounded by an earthwork perimeter (Ashmore 1999; Parker Pearson *et al* 2009). These sites should not be described as 'henges' as they lack internal ditches. A second group of enclosures was built between about 2700 and 2500 BC. In this case they were defined by enormous palisades. Again they are not henges, although they played similar roles.

Their distribution extends from Scotland to Wessex (Gibson 1998).

The third period of increased activity was between about 2500 and 2300 BC and ran in parallel with the reception of Beaker pottery. In this case there are claims that a whole series of monuments was built at the same time (Parker Pearson *et al* 2007). Although this development is supposedly limited to Wessex, it is documented in both the Thames and Trent valleys (Barclay, A 1995; Buteux & Chapman 2009). In this case the sites are characterised by timber settings, stone circles and usually by enormous earthworks.

Other monuments were built afterwards. One feature that they share with both these groups is that they were in particularly accessible locations: along major rivers or at confluences, on long distance routeways, or in areas that could be reached by sea (Noble 2006, 188–92). It is this feature that unites Scottish sites like North Mains, Blackshouse Burn, Ballymeanoch and the Ring of Brodgar. Some examples share similar architectural devices although they are far apart (Bradley 2007, 116–32). Thus there are sites in northern England which are best paralleled in Ireland. The structural details of large timber circles conform to the same organisation of space from Knowth to Durrington Walls, and the curious structures described as 'coves' are found from Orkney to Dorset (Burl 1988a). Long distance connections were obviously important and pilgrims may have undertaken journeys between these areas.

Scottish henges are distributed differently from their English counterparts and are unevenly spaced across the landscape. The largest monuments do not lend themselves to the kind of territorial analysis employed by Colin Renfrew (1973) in Wessex. Indeed, the presence of an earthwork enclosure may be the exception rather than the rule, as the structures associated with English henges – post circles and stone circles – are commonly found in isolation in the north. That applies to such major monuments as the timber settings at Machrie Moor (Haggarty 1991) and Temple Wood (Scott 1989). It is also true of freestanding stone circles like those at Callanish (Ashmore 1999) and Lochmaben (Crone 1983). Something similar may have happened in other regions where earthworks are unusual. East Anglia is an example.

Some of these contrasts may be due to chronological factors. At present it seems as if the largest henges in southern England (or the structures they enclosed) were constructed during the Late Neolithic period. That was not necessarily the case in the Milfield Basin, and farther to the north few examples are precisely dated. Although henge monuments developed as passage graves went out of use in Scotland, the frequency with which they were built may have been lower than it was in England. Sites like the Stones of Stenness (Ritchie 1976) and Balfarg Riding School (Barclay & Russell-White 1993) are undoubtedly of Neolithic origin, but others were not constructed until later. For example recent excavation at Pict's Knowe suggested a *terminus post quem* for the earthwork of about 2400–2050 BC (Thomas 2007). At North Mains the equivalent figure was 2200–1900 BC (Barclay 1983), and at Broomend of Crichie it was probably 2150–1900 BC.

Henges and mortuary ritual

Some of the later monuments were associated with mortuary rituals. Both North Mains and Broomend of Crichie enclosed Early Bronze Age cemeteries and in each case there were other burials in the vicinity. By contrast, monuments in southern England had different associations. There are indications that some of these places were used at the turning points of the year. They contain large collections of artefacts and animal bones, but human remains are rare. The distinction should not be exaggerated, since Durrington Walls was built at about the same time as the sarsen structure at Stonehenge (Parker Pearson *et al* 2007). Whilst Durrington was employed for large gatherings and seasonal feasts, Stonehenge was apparently associated with the dead.

Just as Stonehenge may have coexisted with Durrington Walls, monuments of different sizes could have been built and used simultaneously. That has always been accepted in southern England where groups of henges can be found together. The monuments in the north were also built on different scales. Here they can occur in the same complex, as they do at Westfield. An important difference is that small enclosures were still constructed long after larger sites went out of use. That is one of the characteristics of the Scottish sequence.

Northern British henges were not the only ones associated with mortuary rituals, but here the connection takes a distinctive form. There are a number of graves within the enclosures. In some cases their positions were indicated by posts or stones, and in several instances the locations of the burials seem to have influenced the organisation of the site. Bodies were sometimes placed inside deep pits or cists, and there is little evidence that these features were reopened. The enclosures may have played a part in funeral ceremonies and the commemoration of the dead.

That is very different from the situation in southern England where a number of henges had gone out of use by the Early Bronze Age. Groups of round barrows could be built nearby, but only those associated with Beaker burials are likely to be of similar age to these monuments (Parker Pearson *et al* 2007). The same may be true in north-east England where round barrows are associated with the excavated monuments at Ferrybridge (Roberts 2005) and West Heslerton (Haughton & Powelsland 1999). A further contrast is that in the south some of the graves were permeable and were frequently reused. New burials were placed alongside older ones and relics may have been taken away. Again that is very different from what happened in Scotland.

The limits of henge building

When and where were the last henges built? The Scottish evidence is limited but consistent. A continuous sequence links an Early Bronze Age structure like Broomend of Crichie with smaller enclosures like those at Pullyhour where the sequence extends as far as the Middle Bronze Age.

The most satisfactory comparisons are with monuments in Ireland. They raise certain problems as the earliest henges there assumed a different form from most of those in Britain. They include embanked enclosures with a hollowed interior, and palisaded enclosures associated with timber circles (Bradley 2007, 114–18). Both types have occasional parallels in Wales and northern England, but at present it seems as if the earliest monuments of a more conventional kind date from the Early Bronze Age. Dun Ruadh was discussed in Chapter 3. At 2σ its construction is bracketed by radiocarbon dates of 2140–1940 BC (UB-3047) and 1880–1700 BC (UB-3048). In this case the henge was associated with cist burials and a ring cairn (Simpson, Weir & Wilkinson 1992). The other site is Tonafortes where the basal filling of the ditch provided a date of 1760–1610 BC (Beta-196291);

(Danagher 2007, chapter 4). The histories of these sites overlapped.

Chapter 6 suggested that there were close links between small henges in northern Scotland and some of the Irish ring barrows. Their earthworks have much in common and both are associated with cremation burials. Such contacts between Ireland and northern parts of Scotland began in the Beaker period and continued into later phases when Vase Urns and Cordoned Urns are found on both sides of the water. In fact they extended into the Late Bronze Age, so it would not be surprising if those regions shared similar mortuary rites. The connection did not end entirely until the following period when the character of Irish ring barrows changed and their Scottish counterparts had already gone out of use. In Scotland the only Iron Age monument that had any of the characteristics of henges was the rebuilt earthwork at Pict's Knowe (Thomas 2007). There were a few enclosures of the same form and date in Cornwall (Jones 2010).

There are few signs of similar connections with other regions of England where even the Middle and Late Bronze Age sites have little in common with the last henge monuments in the north. There are a few small ring ditches but it is uncertain whether they are related to the older tradition of henges. Large enclosures pose the same problem. Only two sites might be related to those monuments. One is a double post circle about 20m in diameter at Abingdon in the Thames Valley (Allen & Kamash 2008, 9–13). Only part of this has been excavated, but at 2σ it has radiocarbon dates of 1690–1510 BC (OxA-12376) and 1520–1310 BC (OxA-12377). The other is a more extensive circular earthwork at Thwing on the Yorkshire Wolds (Manby 2007, 405–11). It had the external bank and internal ditch typical of a henge, but it was soon enclosed by a larger monument with a timbered rampart and a ditch on the outside. The first of those enclosures dates from about 1150–950 BC.

The latest Scottish henges may have been built during a period in which other kinds of monument were reused. They were generally small. New structures, including diminutive stone circles, were built at a few of these sites. This phase of secondary activity is associated with cremation burials and has been identified through a programme of radiocarbon dating which has not extended to other areas. For that reason it is difficult to say whether similar evidence exists there. It seems possible that a number of monuments in Wales, the Cotswolds and the West Midlands were treated in the same ways as those in the north (Barclay, Glass & Parry 1995, 31–7 and 48–9; Lewis & Mullin in prep), but the question requires more research. Similarly, some of the henges in the Milfield Basin saw secondary activity during the later Bronze Age (Gibson 2002), but this was probably an extension of the pattern recognised in Scotland.

In the south the situation was different again. Older barrows were employed as the sites of cremation cemeteries, but other kinds of monument were largely ignored. The remains of ancient earthworks like henges lost much of their significance and a few were levelled by cultivation. Others were incorporated in the land divisions that were being constructed at the time. Where some of the monuments in Scotland evoked the ground plan of a domestic building, in the south it was the dwellings themselves that provided a focus for rituals (Bradley 1998, 147–58; Brück 1999). If the later Bronze Age saw rapid changes in the landscapes of lowland England, in northern and north-eastern Scotland there is more evidence of continuity.

In the long term

There are certain developments that appear to transcend the detailed patterns highlighted in this study. They are worth considering now. None is clearly defined, and they are offered as observations to be investigated in the future.

The first point is that henge monuments remained in use for a longer time in the regions where they had originated. Although the earliest stone circles are widely distributed, the oldest henges were probably in the north, and here their history extended into at least the Middle Bronze Age. That may also apply to small earthwork enclosures in northern Scotland and to ring barrows in Ireland. It seems possible that these monuments were so long-lived because their form was familiar. On the other hand, the histories of henge monuments were briefer where this kind of architecture was adopted from another area. Scottish henges lasted for well over a thousand years. In Wessex, where the largest examples were built, they were a comparatively late development and were used for a shorter time. Only two monuments – Stonehenge (Cleal, Walker & Montague 1995) and Mount Pleasant (Wainwright 1979) – have sequences which extend far into the Early Bronze Age. Other sites may have been employed over a more limited period.

A second observation is that the roles played by henge monuments in different parts of Britain may reflect the contexts in which they first appeared. In the north and probably in Ireland they began as open arenas associated with megalithic tombs (Bradley 1998, chapter 7). It is not clear how far the two kinds of structure were used together, but it is evident that the enclosures assumed a growing importance over time. Maeshowe epitomises this development, for here the passage grave and its covering mound were associated with an external platform bounded by a bank and an internal ditch. Excavation shows that these structures were built together. It suggests that the first henges were associated with the dead (Richards 2004, chapter 9).

Only a few sites in the south contain burials. The larger henges were more often associated with the activities of the living and are accompanied by evidence of feasts. Again there is a local precedent for this activity, for it is also found with causewayed enclosures which occur widely in lowland England and only occasionally farther to the north and west. That is not to suggest that these enclosures were the direct precursors of henges, as Jan Harding (2003) has argued. Rather, both groups of monuments were used in the same ways, but at different times. The practices associated with them may have happened at other locations during the intervening period. Even though a site like Hambledon Hill played a role in mortuary ritual, it also saw the large scale consumption of meat (Mercer & Healy 2008, chapter 8). The people who built henges in the south seem to have maintained that emphasis.

In the north there was a lasting connection between henge monuments and the dead. It could have come about for many reasons, but perhaps the link was reinforced because the interiors of many chambered tombs remained accessible. It is obvious that they were visited and sometimes used as burial places, for they contain Beaker pottery (Bradley 2000, 220–4). The remains of the dead could still be inspected even though these buildings were hundreds of years old. Moreover, new structures were being built which owed something to these monuments as a source of inspiration. Around the Inner Moray Firth there were Clava passage graves, and across the Irish Sea wedge tombs shared their distinctive orientation towards the south-west. Both were built at approximately the same time (Bradley 2000; Brindley & Lanting 1992; Schulting, Sheridan, Clarke & Bronk Ramsey 2008). In southern England, however, chambered tombs were usually closed during the Middle Neolithic period (Darvill 2004, chapter 7).

Lastly, the results of this project suggest that the latest henges in Scotland were small and comparatively isolated. They do not seem to have served large communities and there is nothing to suggest that they were located for easy access from the surrounding area. Their earthworks are inconspicuous and can be difficult to find. They could have been built by small numbers of people and it is unlikely that they were maintained for long periods of time. As the use of the last Scottish henges ended they seem to have been decommissioned and sometimes their entrances were closed. By that time the henges had become just one group of small circular monuments, like ring cairns, the stone settings of the southern Highlands and the round barrows of Orkney. It was only in Ireland that such earthworks were widely distributed, and by the time that the large ring barrows were being built on the Hill of Tara similar structures hardly existed in any part of Britain.

Henge monuments were a northern invention in the past and a southern invention in the development of modern archaeology. The two perspectives have been hard to reconcile. This study has suggested why they are so different and some of the ways in which these extraordinary monuments might be thought about in the future.

REFERENCES

Allen, T & Kamash, Z 2008 *Saved from the Grave: Neolithic to Saxon Discoveries at Spring Road Municipal Cemetery, Abingdon, Oxfordshire*. Oxford: Oxford Archaeology.

Andersen, S Th 1979 'Identification of wild grasses and cereal pollen', *Danmarks Geologiske Undersøgelse Årbog 1978*, 69–92.

Anderson, J 1882 'Notice of urns in the Museum that have been found with articles of use or ornament', *Proceedings of the Society of Antiquaries of Scotland* 17, 446–59.

Anderson, J 1901 'Notice of a hoard of bronze implements and buttons of jet found at Migdale', *Proceedings of the Society of Antiquaries of Scotland* 35, 266–75.

AOC Archaeology Ltd 1996 'Lairg Site 204/5030 (Dornoch parish), enclosed cremation cemetery', *Discovery and Excavation in Scotland* 1996, 62.

Ashmore, P 1999 'Radiocarbon dating: avoiding errors by avoiding mixed samples', *Antiquity* 73, 124–30.

Atkinson, R 1950 'Four new henge monuments in Scotland and Northumberland', *Proceedings of the Society of Antiquaries of Scotland* 84, 57–66.

Aubrey, J 1665–1693 (1980) *Monumenta Britannica Parts 1 and 2*. Milborne Port: Dorset Publishing Company.

Barclay, A 1995 *Excavations at the Devil's Quoits, Stanton Harcourt, Oxfordshire, 1972–3 and 1998*. Oxford: Oxford University Committee for Archaeology.

Barclay, A, Glass, H & Parry, C 1995 'Excavations of Neolithic and Bronze Age ring-ditches, Shorncot, Somerford Keynes, Gloucestershire', *Transactions of the Bristol and Gloucestershire Archaeological Society* 113, 21–60.

Barclay, G 1983 'Sites of the third millennium BC to the first millennium AD at North Mains, Strathallan, Perthshire', *Proceedings of the Society of Antiquaries of Scotland* 113, 122–281.

Barclay, G 1999 'Cairnpapple revisited', *Proceedings of the Prehistoric Society* 65, 17–46.

Barclay, G 2005 'The "henge" and "hengiform" in Scotland', in Cummings, V & Pannett, A (eds), *Set in Stone. New Approaches to Neolithic Monuments in Scotland* 81–96. Oxford: Oxbow.

Barclay, G & Russell-White, C 1993 'Excavations in the ceremonial complex of the fourth to second millennium BC at Balfarg/Balbirnie, Glenrothes, Fife', *Proceedings of the Society of Antiquaries of Scotland* 123, 43–210.

Barnatt, J 1990 *The Henges, Stone Circles and Ring Cairns of the Peak District*. Sheffield: University of Sheffield Department of Archaeology & Prehistory.

Barnatt, J, Bevan, B & Edmonds, M 2002 'Gardom's Edge – a landscape through time', *Antiquity* 76, 51–6.

Bell, M, Fowler, P & Hillson, S (eds), 1996 *The Experimental Earthwork Project 1960–1992*. York: Council for British Archaeology.

Bennett, K D 2002 *Psimpoll v.4.10*. Uppsala: University of Uppsala.

Bradley, R 1998 *The Significance of Monuments*. London: Routledge.

Bradley, R 2000 *The Good Stones: A New Investigation of the Clava Cairns*. Edinburgh: Society of Antiquaries of Scotland.

Bradley, R 2005 *The Moon and the Bonfire: An Investigation of Three Stone Circles in North-east Scotland*. Edinburgh: Society of Antiquaries of Scotland.

Bradley, R 2007 *The Prehistory of Britain and Ireland*. Cambridge: Cambridge University Press.

Bradley, R in press 'Enclosures, mounds and Great Houses', in O'Sullivan, M (ed), *Tara. From the Past to the Future*. Dublin: Wordwell.

Bradley, R & Fraser, E 2011 'Round barrows and the boundary between the living and the dead', in Mullin, D (ed), *Places in Between: The Archaeology of Social, Cultural and Geographical Borders and Borderlands*, 40–7. Oxford: Oxbow.

Bradley, R & Sheridan, A 2005 'Croft Moraig and the chronology of stone circles', *Proceedings of the Prehistoric Society* 71, 269–81.

Brindley, A 2007 *The Dating of Food Vessels and Urns in Ireland*. Galway: National University of Ireland Galway, Department of Archaeology.

Brindley, A & Lanting, J 1992 'Radiocarbon dates from wedge tombs', *Journal of Irish Archaeology* 6, 19–26.

Brück, J 1999 'Houses, life cycles and deposition on Middle Bronze Age settlements in Southern England', *Proceedings of the Prehistoric Society* 65, 145–66.

Brück, J 2009 'Women, death and social change in the British Bronze Age', *Norwegian Archaeological Review* 43, 1–23.

Bullock, P, Fedoroff, N, Jongerius, A, Stoops, G & Tursina, T 1985 *Handbook for Thin Section Description*. Wolverhampton: Waine Research Publication.

Burgess, C B 1986 '"Urnes of no small variety": Collared Urns reviewed', *Proceedings of the Prehistoric Society* 52, 339–51.

Burl, A 1988a 'Coves: structural enigmas of the Neolithic', *Wiltshire Archaeological Magazine* 82, 1–18.

Burl, A 1988b *Four-Posters: Bronze Age Stone Circles of Western Europe*. Oxford: British Archaeological Reports.

Burl, A 2000 *The Stone Circles of Britain, Ireland and Brittany*. New Haven: Yale University Press.

Burl, H A W 1969 'Henges: internal structures and regional groups', *Archaeological Journal* 126, 1–28.

Buteux, S & Chapman, H 2009 *Where Rivers Meet: The Archaeology of Catholme and the Trent-Tame Confluence*. York: Council for British Archaeology.

Callander, J G 1905 'Notice of two cinerary urns and a pendant of slate found at Seggiecrook, in the parish of Kennethmont, Aberdeenshire', *Proceedings of the Society of Antiquaries of Scotland* 39 (1904–5), 184–9.

Callender, J G 1922 'Three hoards recently added to the national collection, with notes on the hoard from Duddingston Loch', *Proceedings of the Society of Antiquaries of Scotland* 56, 351–65.

Campbell, G 2004 'The pyres and biers', in Cool, H (ed), *The Roman Cemetery at Brougham, Cumbria: Excavations 1966–67*, 267–71. London: Britannia Monographs.

Campbell, G 2007 'Cremation deposits and the use of wood in cremation ritual', in Harding, J & Healy, F (eds), *The Raunds Area Project: A Neolithic and Bronze Age Landscape in Northamptonshire*, 30–3. Swindon: English Heritage.

Canti, M 1995 'A mixed approach to geoarchaeological analysis', in Barham, T, Bates, M & Macphail, R I (eds). *Archaeological Sediments and Soils: Analysis, Interpretation and Management*, 183–90. London: Institute of Archaeology.

Canti, M G & Linford, N 2000 'The effects of fire on archaeological soils and sediments: temperature and colour relationships', *Proceedings of the Prehistoric Society* 66, 385–95.

Carter, S 1998 'Palaeopedology', in McCullagh, R & Tipping, R (eds), *The Lairg Project 1988–1996: The Evolution of an Archaeological Landscape in Northern Scotland*. Edinburgh: Scottish Trust for Archaeological Research.

Carter, S P & Davidson, D A 1998 'An evaluation of the contribution of soil micromorphology to the study of ancient arable agriculture', *Geoarchaeology* 13,(6), 535–47.

Carter, S P & Davidson, D A 2000 'A reply to Macphail's comments on "An evaluation of the contribution of soil micromorphology to the study of ancient arable agriculture"', *Geoarchaeology* 15(5), 499–502.

Chalmers, J 1866 'Notice of the discovery of a stone kist at Broomend, near Inverurie, Aberdeenshire', *Proceedings of the Society of Antiquaries of Scotland* 7, 110–14.

Charman, D J 1994 'Late-glacial vegetation history of the Flow Country, Northern Scotland', *New Phytologist* 127, 155–68.

Clark, J D G 1936 'The timber monument at Arminghall and its affinities', *Proceedings of the Prehistoric Society* 2, 1–51.

Clark, R L 1982 'Point count estimation of charcoal in pollen preparations and thin sections of sediment', *Pollen et Spores* 24, 523–35.

Clarke, D L 1970 *The Beaker Pottery of Great Britain and Ireland*. Cambridge: Cambridge University Press.

Clarke, D V 2007 'Reading the multiple lives of Pictish symbol stones'. *Medieval Archaeology* 51, 19–39.

Clarke, D V, Cowie, T G & Foxon, A 1985 *Symbols of Power at the Time of Stonehenge*. Edinburgh: Her Majesty's Stationery Office.

Cleal, R, Walker, K & Montague, R 1995 *Stonehenge in its Landscape: Twentieth Century Excavations*. London: English Heritage.

Coles, F 1901 'Report on the stone circles of the North East of Scotland, Inverurie district', *Proceedings of the Society of Antiquaries of Scotland* 35, 187–248.

Cook, M & Dunbar, L 2008 *Rituals, Roundhouses and Romans: Excavations at Kintore, Aberdeenshire 2000–2006*. Edinburgh: Scottish Trust for Archaeological Research.

Corcoran, J X W P 1967 'The excavation of three chambered cairns at Loch Calder, Caithness', *Proceedings of the Society of Antiquaries of Scotland* 98, 1–75.

Courty, M A, Goldberg, P & Macphail, R I 1989 *Soils and Micromorphology in Archaeology*. Cambridge: Cambridge University Press.

Cowie, T G 1978 *Bronze Age Food Vessel Urns*. Oxford: British Archaeological Reports (British Series 55).

Cowie, T G 2004 'Special places for special axes? Early Bronze Age metalwork from Scotland in its landscape setting', in Shepherd, I & Barclay, G (eds), *Scotland in Ancient Europe*, 247–61. Edinburgh: Society of Antiquaries of Scotland.

Crampton, C B 1914 *The Geology of Caithness: Sheets 110 and 116, with Parts of 109, 115 and 117*. Edinburgh: HMSO.

Craw, J 1931 'Further excavations of cairns at Poltalloch, Argyll', *Proceedings of the Society of Antiquaries of Scotland* 65, 269–80.

Crone, A 1983 'The Clochmabanestane, Gretna', *Transactions of the Dumfriesshire and Galloway Natural History and Antiquarian Society* 58, 16–20.

Cushing, E J 1967 'Evidence for differential pollen preservation in late Quaternary sediments in Minnesota', *Review of Palaeobotany and Palynology* 4, 87–101.

Dalrymple, C E 1884 'Note on the excavation of the stone circle at Crichie, Aberdeenshire', *Proceedings of the Society of Antiquaries of Scotland* 18, 319–25.

Danagher, E 2007 *Monumental Beginnings: The Archaeology of the N4 Sligo Inner Relief Road*. Dublin: National Roads Authority.

Darvill, T 2002 'White on blonde: quartz pebbles and the use of quartz at Neolithic monuments in the Isle of Man and beyond', in Jones A & MacGregor G (eds), *Colouring the past: the significance of colour in archaeological research*, 73–93. Oxford: Berg.

Darvill, T 2004 *Long Barrows of the Cotswolds and Surrounding Areas*. Stroud: Tempus.

Davidson, C 1866 'Notice of further stone kists found at Broomend near the Inverurie Papermill', *Proceedings of the Society of Antiquaries of Scotland* 7, 115–18.

Edwards, B 2007 'A henge too far? Reinterpreting the Neolithic monument complex at Milfield, Northumberland', *Proceedings of the Prehistoric Society* 73, 59–73.

Edwards, K & Ralston, I 2003 *Scotland after the Ice Age: Environment, Archaeology and History 8000 BC–AD 1000*. 2nd edition. Edinburgh: Edinburgh University Press.

Fahy, E 1962 'A recumbent stone circle at Reanascreena South, Co Cork', *Journal of the Cork Historical and Archaeological Society* 67, 59–69.

Fenton, M B 1983 *Scottish Battle-axes and Axe-hammers: Petrology, Typology, Manufacture and Source*. Unpublished PhD thesis, University of Nottingham.

Fenton, M B 1984 'The nature of the source and the manufacture of Scottish battle-axes and axe-hammers', *Proceedings of the Prehistoric Society* 50, 217–44.

Finlayson, B 1998 'Worked flint and quartz', in McCullagh, R & Tipping, R (eds), *The Lairg Project 1988–1996. The Evolution of an Archaeological Landscape in Northern Scotland*, 132–9. Edinburgh: Scottish Trust for Archaeological Research.

French, C & Lewis, H 2005 'New developments on Holocene landscape development in the Southern English chalklands: The Upper Allen Valley, Cranborne Chase, Dorset', *Geoarchaeology* 20 (2), 109–134.

Gale, R 1997 'Charcoal', in Fitzpatrick, A (ed), *Archaeological Excavations on the Route of the A27 Westhampnett Bypass, West Sussex. Volume 2: the Late Iron Age, Romano-British and Anglo-Saxon Cemeteries*, 77–82. Salisbury: Wessex Archaeology.

Gale, R & Cutler, D F 2000 *Plants in Archaeology: Identification Manual of Vegetative Plant Materials Used in Europe and the Mediterranean to c 1500*. Otley: Westbury.

Garwood, P 2007 'Before the hills in order stood: time and history in the interpretation of Bronze Age barrows', in Last, J (ed), *Beyond the Grave: New Perspectives on Barrows*, 30–52. Oxford: Oxbow.

Gebhardt, A 1995 'Soil micromorphology data from traditional and experimental agriculture', in Barham, A J & Macphail, R I (eds), *Archaeological Sediments and Soils: Analysis, Interpretation and Management*. London: Institute of Archaeology, 25–39.

Gibson, A (1993) 'The excavation of two cairns and associated features at Carneddau, Carno, Powys', 1989–90 *Archaeological Journal* 150, 1–45.

Gibson, A 1998 'Hindwell and the Neolithic palisaded sites of Britain and Ireland', in Gibson A & Simpson D (eds), *Prehistoric Ritual and Religion*, 68–79. Stroud: Sutton.

Gibson, A 2002 'A matter of pegs and labels. A review of some prehistoric pottery from the Milfield Basin', *Archaeologia Aeliana* 30, 175–80.

Gibson, A 2004a 'Round in circles. Timber circles, henges and stone circles. Some possible relationships and transformations', in Cleal, R & Pollard, J (eds), *Monuments and Material Culture*, 70–81. East Knoyle: Hobnob Press.

Gibson, A 2004b 'Visibility and invisibility: some thoughts on Neolithic and Bronze Age sites', in Barclay, G & Shepherd, I (eds), *Scotland in Ancient Europe*, 155–69. Edinburgh: Society of Antiquaries of Scotland.

Gibson, A 2005 *Stonehenge and Timber Circles*. Stroud: Tempus.

Gibson, A 2007 'A Beaker veneer? Some evidence from the burial record', in M Larsson & M Parker Pearson (eds), *From Stonehenge to the Baltic*, 47–64. Oxford: British Archaeological Reports.

Gibson, A & Kinnes, I 1997 'On the urns of a dilemma. Radiocarbon and the Peterborough problem', *Oxford Journal of Archaeology* 16, 65–72.

Gillings, M, Pollard, J, Wheatley, D, Peterson, R 2008 *Landscape of the Megaliths: Excavations and Fieldwork on the Avebury Monuments, 1997–2003*. Oxford: Oxbow.

Glentworth, R & Muir, J W 1963 *The Soils of the Country Round Aberdeen, Inverurie and Fraserburgh (Sheets 77, 76 and 87/97)*. Edinburgh: Soil Survey of Great Britain.

Gray, H St G 1903 'On the excavations at Arbor Low', *Archaeologia* 58, 461–98.

Greenwell, W 1877 *British Barrows*. Oxford: Clarendon Press.

Greig, M & Shepherd, I 1993 'Allanshaw (Kintore parish)', *Discovery and Excavation in Scotland 1993*, 34.

GSB Prospection 2003 Loch Migdale, Sutherland. Bradford: GSB Prospection.

Haggarty, A 1991 'Machrie Moor, Arran: Recent excavations of two stone circles', *Proceedings of the Society of Antiquaries of Scotland* 58, 51–94.

Harding, A 1981 'Excavations in the prehistoric ritual complex near Milfield, North Northumberland', *Proceedings of the Prehistoric Society* 47, 87–135.

Harding, A & Lee, G 1987 *Henge Monuments and Related Sites of Great Britain*. Oxford: British Archaeological Reports.

Harding, J 2003 *Henge Monuments of the British Isles*. Stroud: Tempus.

Haughton, C & Powelsland, D 1999 *West Heslerton: The Anglian Cemetery*. Yedingham: The Landscape Research Centre.

Henshall, A 1963 'A Bronze Age cist burial at Masterton, Piteavie, Fife', *Proceedings of the Society of Antiquaries of Scotland* 96, 145–54.

Hunter, J & MacSween, A 1991 'A sequence for the Orcadian Neolithic', *Antiquity* 65, 911–14.

Jacobi, R 1978 'The Mesolithic of Sussex', in Drewett, P (ed), *Archaeology in Sussex to AD 1500*, 15–22. York: Council for British Archaeology.

Jones, A 2010 'Misplaced monuments?: a review of ceremony and monumentality in the first millennium BC Cornwall', *Oxford Journal of Archaeology* 29, 203–28.

Kendrick, T & Hawkes, C 1932 *Archaeology in England and Wales 1914–1931*. London: Methuen.

Kilbride-Jones, H 1935 'An account of the excavation of the stone circle at Loanhead of Daviot, and of the standing stones, Echt', *Proceedings of the Society of Antiquaries of Scotland* 69, 168–223.

Kilbride-Jones, H 1936 'Late Bronze Age cemetery: being an account of the excavations of 1935 at Loanhead of Daviot', *Proceedings of the Society of Antiquaries of Scotland* 70, 278–310.

Kirk, W & McKenzie, J 1955 'Three Bronze Age cist burials in North East Scotland', *Proceedings of the Society of Antiquaries of Scotland* 88, 1–14.

Lancaster, S, Davidson, D & Simpson, I 2005 'Soil micromorphology', in Bradley, R, *The Moon and the Bonfire: An Investigation of three Stone Circles in North-east Scotland*, 42–46 and 68–72. Edinburgh: Society of Antiquaries of Scotland.

Last, J 2007 'Covering old ground: barrows as closures', in Last, J (ed), *Beyond the Grave: New Perspectives on Barrows*, 156–75. Oxford: Oxbow.

Lewis, J & Mullin, D in prep 'Excavations at a crop mark henge near Bredon, Worcestershire'.

Limbrey, S 1975 *Soil Science and Archaeology*. London: Academic Press.

Longworth, I H 1984 *Collared Urns of the Bronze Age in Great Britain and Ireland*. Cambridge: Cambridge University Press.

Macphail, R 1998 'A reply to Carter and Davidson's "An evaluation of the contribution of soil micromorphology to the study of ancient arable agriculture"', *Geoarchaeology* 13(6), 549–64.

Macphail, R & Cruise, J 2001 'The soil micromorphologist as team player: a multi analysis approach to the study of European microstratigraphy', in Goldberg, P, Holliday, V T & Reid-Ferring, C (eds), *Earth Sciences and Archaeology*, 241–67. New York: Kluwer Academic Publishers.

MacSween, A 1995 'Urn 1 and accessory vessel', in Smith, A N 'The excavations of Neolithic, Bronze Age and early historic features near Ratho, Edinburgh'. *Proceedings of the Society of Antiquaries of Scotland* 125, 84–8.

MacSween, A & Dixon, D 1998 'Prehistoric pottery', in McCullagh, R & Tipping, R (eds), *The Lairg Project 1988–1996. The Evolution of an Archaeological Landscape in Northern Scotland* 139–44. Edinburgh: Scottish Trust for Archaeological Research.

Manby, T 1967 'Rudston Barrow LII: Beaker cremation associations', *Yorkshire Archaeological Journal* 42, 254–8.

Manby, T 2007 'Continuity of monumental traditions into the late Bronze Age?' 403–24, in Burgess, C, Topping, P & Lynch, F (eds), *Beyond Stonehenge*, 162–85. Oxford: Oxbow.

McCullagh, R P J & Tipping, R (eds), 1998 *The Lairg Project 1988–1996: The Evolution of an Archaeological Landscape in Northern Scotland*. Edinburgh: Scottish Trust for Archaeological Research.

McKinley, J 1993 'Bone fragment size and weights of bone from modern British cremations and its implications for the interpretation of archaeological cremations', *International Journal of Osteoarchaeology* 3, 283–7.

McKinley, J I 1998 'Burnt and cremated bone', in McCullagh, R & Tipping, R (eds), *The Lairg Project 1988–1996. The Evolution of an Archaeological Landscape in Northern Scotland*, 118–22. Edinburgh: Scottish Trust for Archaeological Research.

McKinley, J I 2000 'The analysis of cremated bone', in Cox, M & Mays, S (eds), *Human Osteology*, 403–21. London: Greenwich Medical Media.

Mays, S 1998 *The Archaeology of Human Bone*. London: Routledge.

Mercer, R 1981 'The excavation of a late Neolithic henge-type enclosure at Balfarg, Markinch, Fife, Scotland', *Proceedings of the Society of Antiquaries of Scotland* 111, 63–171.

Mercer, R & Healy, F 2008 *Hambledon Hill, Dorset. Excavation and Survey of a Neolithic Monument Complex and its Surrounding Landscape*. Swindon: English Heritage.

Miket, R 1985 'Ritual enclosures at Whitton Hill, Northumberland', *Proceedings of the Prehistoric Society* 51, 137–48.

Millican, K 2007 'Turning in circles: a new assessment of the Neolithic timber circles of Scotland', *Proceedings of the Society of Antiquaries of Scotland* 137, 5–34.

Moloney, C, Holbrey, C, Wheelhouse, P & Roberts, I 2003 *Catterick Racecourse, North Yorkshire: The Reuse and Adaptation of a Monument from Prehistoric to Anglian Times*. Morley: West Yorkshire Archaeology Service.

Morrison, A 1968 'Cinerary Urns and Pygmy Vessels in South-West Scotland', *Trans Dumfriesshire and Galloway Natural History and Antiquarian Society* 45, 80–140.

Moore, P D, Webb, J A & Collinson, M E 1991 *Pollen Analysis*. Oxford: Blackwell.

Murray, H & Murray, C 2007 'Broom Lodge, Mill Road, Inverurie', *Discovery and Excavation in Scotland 2007*, 25.

Murray, H & Murray, C 2008 'South east Kintore', *Discovery and Excavation in Scotland 2008*, 24.

Murray, H, Murray, C & Fraser, S 2009 *A Tale of Unknown Unknowns: A Mesolithic Pit Alignment and a Neolithic Timber Hall at Warren Field, Crathes, Aberdeenshire*. Oxford: Oxbow.

Myatt, L 2005 *The Standing Stones of Halkirk Parish*. Privately published.

Needham, S 2004 'Migdale – Marnoch: sunburst of Scottish metallurgy', in Barclay, G & Shepherd I (eds), *Scotland in Ancient Europe*, 217–45. Edinburgh: Society of Antiquaries of Scotland.

Needham, S P 2005 'Transforming Beaker culture in north-west Europe: processes of fusion and fission', *Proceedings of the Prehistoric Society* 71, 171–217.

Needham, S, Parfitt, K & Varndell, G 2006 *The Ringlemere Cup: Precious Cups and the Beginning of the Channel Bronze Age*. London: British Museum.

Newman, C 1997 *Tara: an Archaeological Survey*. Dublin: Royal Irish Academy.

Newman, V 1998 'Reflections on the making of a "royal site" in early Ireland', *World Archaeology* 30, 127–41.

Noble, G 2006 *Neolithic Scotland: Timber, Earth, Stone and Fire*. Edinburgh: Edinburgh University Press.

O'Brien, W 2004 '(Con)fusion of tradition? The circle henge in Ireland', in Gibson, A & Sheridan, A (eds), *From Sickles to Circles*, 323–38. Stroud: Tempus.

O'Connor, B 2007 'Two Late Bronze Age socketed axes from Tillicoultry, Clackmannanshire, and other lost axes from northern Britain', *Tayside and Fife Archaeological Journal* 13, 74–9.

Ó Ríordáin, S 1950 'Excavation of some earthworks on The Curragh, Co Kildare', *Proceedings of the Royal Irish Academy* 53C, 249–77.

Pacitto, A 1972 'Rudston Barrow LXII: the 1968 excavation', *Yorkshire Archaeological Journal* 44, 1–22.

Pannett, A, 2002a 'Caithness Fieldwalking Project', *Discovery and Excavation in Scotland 2002*, 60.

Pannett, A, 2002b *Excavations of a Mesolithic Site at Oliclett, Caithness*, Cardiff: Cardiff University.

Parker Pearson, M 2007 'The Stonehenge Riverside Project: excavations at the east entrance of Durrington Walls', in Larsson, M & Parker Pearson, M (eds), *From Stonehenge to the Baltic*, 125–44. Oxford: British Archaeological Reports.

Parker Pearson, M, Chamberlain, A, Craig, O, Marshall, P, Mulville, J, Smith, H, Chenery, C, Collins, M, Cook, G, Craig, G, Evans, J, Hiller, J, Montgomery, J, Schwenninger, J-L, Taylor, G & Wess, T 2005 'Evidence for mummification in Bronze Age Britain', *Antiquity* 79, 529–46.

Parker Pearson, M, Chamberlain, A, Jay, M, Marshall, P, Pollard, J, Richards, C, Thomas, J, Tilley, C & Welham, K 2009 'Who was buried at Stonehenge?', *Antiquity* 83, 23–39.

Parker Pearson, M & Ramilsonina 1998. 'Stonehenge for the ancestors. The stones pass on the message', *Antiquity* 72, 308–26.

Peglar, S 1979 'Radiocarbon-dated pollen diagram from Loch of Winless, Caithness, north-east Scotland', *New Phytologist* 82, 245–63.

Phillips, T, Hampshire-Monk, I & Abramson, P 2006 'The excavation and reconstruction of the recumbent stone circle at Strichen, Aberdeenshire, 1979–82', *Proceedings of the Society of Antiquaries of Scotland* 136, 111–34.

Piggott, S 1948 'The excavations at Cairnpapple Hill, West Lothian, 1947–1948', *Proceedings of the Society of Antiquaries of Scotland* 82, 68–123.

Piggott, S & Simpson, D 1971 'The excavation of a stone circle at Croft Moraig, Perthshire, Scotland', *Proceedings of the Prehistoric Society* 37(1), 1–15.

Pollard, J 2010 'The materialization of religious structures at the time of Stonehenge', *Material Religion* 5, 332–53.

Raftery, J 1941 'The tumulus cemetery of Carrowjames, Co Mayo', *Journal of the Galway Archaeological and Historical Society* 19, 16–85.

RCAHMS 1911a *Third Report and Inventory of Monuments and Constructions in the County of Caithness*. London: HMSO.

RCAHMS 1911b *Third Report and Inventory of Monuments and Constructions in the County of Sutherland*. Edinburgh: HMSO.

RCAHMS 1999 *Kilmartin Prehistoric and Early Historic Monuments*. Edinburgh: RCAHMS.

RCAHMS 2007 *In the Shadow of Benachie: A Field Archaeology of Donside, Aberdeenshire*. Edinburgh: RCAHMS and Society of Antiquaries of Scotland.

Rees, T 1997 'The excavation of Cairnwell ring-cairn, Porthleven, Aberdeenshire', *Proceedings of the Society of Antiquaries of Scotland* 127, 255–77.

Renfrew, C 1973 'Monuments, mobilisation and social organisation in Neoliothic Wessex', in Renfrew, C (ed), *The Explanation of Culture Change*, 539–58. London: Routledge.

Reynolds, A 2009 *Anglo-Saxon Deviant Burial Customs*. Oxford: Oxford University Press.

Richards, C 2004 *Dwelling Among the Monuments*. Cambridge: McDonald Institute for Archaeological Research.

Ritchie, G 1974 'Excavation of the stone circle and cairn at Balbirnie, Fife', *Archaeological Journal* 131, 1–32.

Ritchie, G 1976 'The Stones of Stenness, Orkney', *Proceedings of the Society of Antiquaries of Scotland* 107, 1–60.

Ritchie, G 1998 'Tyrebagger recumbent stone circle, Aberdeenshire: a note on recording', in Gibson, A & Simpson, D (eds), *Prehistoric Ritual and Religion* 176–82. Stroud: Sutton.

Ritchie, J 1920 'The stone circle at Broomend of Crichie, Aberdeenshire', *Proceedings of the Society of Antiquaries of Scotland* 54, 154–72.

Roberts, I 2005 *Ferrybridge Henge: The Ritual Landscape*. Morley: West Yorkshire Archaeology Service.

Robinson, D E 1987 'Investigations into the Aukhorn peat mounds, Keiss, Caithness: pollen, plant macrofossil and charcoal analysis', *New Phytologist* 106, 185–200.

Rodwell, J S 1991 *British Plant Communities, Volume 2: Mires and Heaths*. Cambridge: Cambridge University Press.

Roe, F E S 1966 'The battle-axe series in Britain', *Proceedings of the Prehistoric Society* 32, 199–245.

Romans, J C C & Robertson, L 1975 'Soils and archaeology in Scotland', in Evans, J, Limbrey, S & Cleere, H (eds), *The Effect of Man on the Landscape: The Highland Zone*, 37–40. London: Council for British Archaeology.

Romans, J C C & Robertson, L 1983 'The general effects of early agriculture on the soil profile', in Maxwell, G (ed), *The Impact of Aerial Reconnaissance on Archaeology*, 136–41. York: Council for British Archaeology.

Russell-White, C, Lowe, C & McCullagh, R 1992 'Excavations at three Early Bronze Age burial monuments in Scotland', *Proceedings of the Prehistoric Society* 88, 285–323.

Scheue, L & Black, S (2000) *Developmental Juvenile Osteology*. London: Academic Press.

Schulting, R, Sheridan, A, Clarke, A & Bronk Ramsey, C 2008 'Largantea and the dating of Irish wedge tombs', *Journal of Irish Archaeology* 17, 1–17.

Scott, J 1989 'The stone circle at Temple Wood, Kilmartin, Argyll', *Glasgow Archaeological Journal* 15, 53–124.

Shepherd, I 1986 *Powerful Pots: Beakers in North-east Prehistory*. Aberdeen: University of Aberdeen.

Sheridan, A 2003 'The NMS dating cremated bone project: results obtained during 2002/3', *Discovery and Excavation in Scotland 2003*, 167–9.

Sheridan, A 2004a 'Scottish Food Vessel chronology revisited', in Gibson, A & Sheridan, A (eds), *From Sickles to Circles* 243–67. Stroud: Tempus.

Sheridan 2004b 'The National Museums of Scotland radiocarbon dating programme: results obtained during 2003/4', *Discovery and Excavation in Scotland 2004*, 174–6.

Sheridan, A 2004c 'Going round in circles. Understanding the Grooved Ware "complex" in its wider context', in Roche, H, Grogan, E, Bradley, J, Coles, J & Raftery, B (eds), *From Megaliths to Metal* 26–37. Oxford: Oxbow.

Sheridan, A 2007a 'Scottish Beaker dates: the good, the bad and the ugly', in Larsson, M & Parker Pearson, M (eds), *From Stonehenge to the Baltic*, 91–123. Oxford: British Archaeological Reports.

Sheridan, A 2007b 'Dating the Scottish Bronze Age: "There is clearly much that the material can still tell us"', in Burgess, C, Topping, P & Lynch, F (eds), *Beyond Stonehenge*, 162–85. Oxford: Oxbow.

Sheridan, A 2008 'Radiocarbon dates arranged through the National Museums of Scotland Archaeology Department during 2007/8', *Discovery and Excavation in Scotland 2008*, 201–5.

Simpson, D D A 1990 'The stone battle axes of Ireland', *Journal of the Royal Society of Antiquaries of Ireland* 120, 5–40.

Simpson, D, Weir, D & Wilkinson, J 1992 'Excavations at Dun Ruadh, Crouck, Co Tyrone', *Ulster Journal of Archaeology* 55, 36–47.

Simpson, I & Davidson, D 2000 'Palaeosols of the Clava Cairns', in Bradley, R, *The Good Stones: A New Investigation of the Clava Cairns*, 89–96. Edinburgh: Society of Antiquaries of Scotland.

Smith, B H 1991 'Standards of human tooth formation and dental age assessment', in Kelley, M A & Larsen, C S (eds), *Advances in Dental Anthropology*, 143–68. New York: Wiley-Liss, Inc.

Speak, S & Burgess, C 1999 'Meldon Bridge: a centre of the third millennium BC in Peeblesshire', *Proceedings of the Society of Antiquaries of Scotland* 129, 1–118.

Stevenson, R 1948 'Notes on some prehistoric objects', *Proceedings of the Society of Antiquaries of Scotland* 82, 292–5.

Stewart, M 1966 'Excavation of a circle of standing stones at Sandy Road, Scone, Perthshire', *Transactions and Proceedings of the Perthshire Society of Natural Science* 11, 7–23.

Stewart, M 1985 'The excavation of a henge, stone circles and metal-working area at Montcrieffe, Perthshire', *Proceedings of the Society of Antiquaries of Scotland* 115, 125–50.

Stuart, E, 1998 'Stemster House Farm (Bower parish): Lithic scatters', *Discovery and Excavation in Scotland 1998*, 48–9.

Stuart, J 1856 *Sculptured Stones of Scotland*. Aberdeen: The Spalding Club.

Terry, J 1997 'Upper Largie', *Discovery and Excavation in Scotland 1997*, 19 and 21.

Thomas, J 2006 'On the origins and development of cursus monuments in Britain', *Proceedings of the Prehistoric Society* 72, 229–41.

Thomas, J 2007 *Place and Memory. Excavations at the Pict's Knowe, Holywood and Holm Farm, Dumfries and Galloway, 1994–8*. Oxford: Oxbow.

Thomas, J 2010 'The return of the Rinyo-Clacton folk? The cultural significance of the Grooved Ware complex in Later Neolithic Britain', *Cambridge Archaeological Journal* 20, 1–15.

Thompson, G B 1999 'The analysis of wood charcoals from selected pits and funerary contexts', in Barclay, A & Halpin, C (eds), *Excavations at Barrow Hills, Radley, Oxfordshire*. Volume 1, 247–54. Oxford: Oxford Archaeology.

Tipping, R 1994 'The form and fate of Scotland's woodland', *Proceedings of the Society of Antiquaries of Scotland* 124, 1–54.

Tipping R & McCullagh R 1998 'A dynamic landscape', in McCullagh, R & Tipping, R (eds), *The Lairg Project 1988–1996: The Evolution of an Archaeological Landscape in Northern Scotland*, 202–14. Edinburgh: Scottish Trust for Archaeological Research.

Turner, V 1969 *The Ritual Process*. London: Routledge & Kegan Paul.

van Gennep, A 1909 *Les Rites de Passage*. Paris: Nourry.

Varley, W 1938 'The Bleasedale Circle', *Antiquaries Journal* 18, 154–71.

Videotext Communications 2003 *Proposed Archaeological Evaluation at Loch Migdale*. London: Videotext Communications.

Vyner, B 1988 'The Street House Wossit: the excavation of Late Neolithic and Early Bronze Age palisaded ritual monument at Street House, Loftus, Cleveland', *Proceedings of the Prehistoric Society* 54, 173–202.

Waddell, J 1995 'The Cordoned Urn tradition', in Kinnes, I & Varndell, G (eds), *Unbaked Urns of Rudely Shape: Essays on British and Irish Pottery for Ian Longworth*, 113–22. Oxford: Oxbow.

Waddell, J 1998 *The Prehistoric Archaeology of Ireland*. Galway: Galway University Press.

Waddell, J, Fenwick J & Barton, K 2009 *Rathcroghan. Archaeological and Geophysical Survey in a Ritual Landscape.* Dublin: Wordwell.

Wainwright, G 1969 'A review of henge monuments in the light of recent research', *Proceedings of the Prehistoric Society* 35, 112–33

Wainwright, G 1979 *Mount Pleasant.* London: Society of Antiquaries of London.

Wainwright, G 1989 *The Henge Monuments.* London: Thames & Hudson.

Walker, I C 1967 'The counties of Nairnshire, Moray and Banffshire in the Bronze Age', *Proceedings of the Society of Antiquaries of Scotland* 98, 76–125.

Warner, R 2000 'Keeping out the Otherworld. The internal ditch at Navan and other Iron Age "hengiform enclosures"', *Emainia* 18, 39–44.

Waterman, D 1968 'Cordoned Urn burials and ring ditch at Urbalreagh, Co Antrim', *Ulster Journal of Archaeology* 31, 25–32.

Waterman, D 1997 *Excavations at Navan Fort 1961–71.* Belfast: The Stationery Office.

Watkins, T 1982 'The excavation of an Early Bronze Age cemetery at Barns Farm, Dalgety, Fife', *Proceedings of the Society of Antiquaries of Scotland* 112, 48–141.

Watt, A 1865 *The Early History of Kintore.* Privately printed.

Wickham-Jones, C 1997 'The flaked stone', in Masters, L, 'The excavation and restoration of the Camster Long chambered cairn, Caithness, Highland, 1967–80', *Proceedings of the Society of Antiquaries of Scotland* 127, 160–71.

Wilson, C 2000 *Processes of Post-burial Change in Archaeologically Buried Soils.* Unpublished PhD thesis, University of Stirling.

Woodham, A 1953 'Four new henge monuments in Easter Ross', *Proceedings of the Society of Antiquaries of Scotland* 87, 72–9.

ADDENDUM

The results of the projects at Dyffryn Lane and Kilmartin referred to briefly in the text were published while this study was in proof. For details of this important work the reader is referred to:

Cook, M, Ellis, C & Sheridan, A 2010 'Excavations at Upper Largie Quarry, Argyll & Bute, Scotland: New light on the prehistoric ritual landscape of the Kilmartin Glen'. *Proceedings of the Prehistoric Society* 76, 165–212.

Gibson, A 2010 'Excavations and surveys at Dyffryn Lane henge complex, Powys, and a reconsideration of the dating of henges'. *Proceedings of the Prehistoric Society* 76, 213–48.

INDEX